NATIONALISM AND THE CRISES OF ETHNIC MINORITIES IN ASIA

Recent Titles in Contributions in Sociology
Series Editor: DON MARTINDALE

NATIONALISM
AND THE CRISES OF
ETHNIC MINORITIES IN ASIA

Edited by Tai S. Kang

Contributions in Sociology, Number 34

GREENWOOD PRESS
Westport, Connecticut • London, England

DS
13
N36

Library of Congress Cataloging in Publication Data
Main entry under title:

Nationalism and the crises of ethnic minorities in Asia.

  (Contributions in sociology ; no. 34 ISSN 0084-9278)
  Bibliography: p.
  Includes index.
  1. Asia—Race relations. 2. Minorities—Asia.
3. Nationalism—Asia. I. Kang, Tai S
DS13.N36   301.45'095   78-19295
ISBN 0-313-20623-6

Library of Congress Catalog Card Number: 78-19295
ISBN: 0-313-20623-6
ISSN: 0084-9278

First published in 1979

Greenwood Press, Inc.
51 Riverside Avenue, Westport, Connecticut 06880

Printed in the United States of America

10 9 8 7 6 5 4 3 2 1

CONTENTS

ACKNOWLEDGMENTS

I wish to express my thanks to the authors, who graciously consented to minor or major revisions of their original drafts for inclusion in this volume.

Sincere appreciation goes also to all those who have contributed to the preparation of this volume: to Kenneth Inada, Gay Kang, Don Martindale, and Jean Wischerath for their continued support that sustained my efforts in this work, and to Doris Gettings for her typing of the manuscript. This project was in part funded by the Council on International Studies at the State University of New York at Buffalo, and in part by the Conversations in the Disciplines Program administered by SUNY Central. For this help I am grateful to Albert Michaels and James S. Smoot.

TAI S. KANG

A THEORETICAL INTRODUCTION

TAI S. KANG

The rise of nationalism and the awakening of ethnic identities in Europe during the nineteenth century have had profound effects worldwide. The inclusion of the principle *self-determination* for ethnic communities in the peace treaties of World War I reflected and inspired the strife for cultural autonomy and the nationalist movements of many ethnic groups around the world. After World War II, a dramatic change of power balance occurred in Asia. With the surge of fervent nationalist movements, colonial powers retreated from their former colonial possessions: India, Burma, Malaysia, China, Korea, Philippines, Dutch East Indies, and French Indochina. Colonial powers in retreat often created political entities that included many ethnic groups with conflicting economic and political interests. National independence and preservation of cultural identity have become sacred words for most of these ethnic groups. In their view, equal opportunities in the life of the larger society and cultural autonomy have come to be regarded as inherent and inalienable rights of man. Frequently, these demands for autonomy and equality by ethnic minority groups pose threats to the solidarity of modern states. The interrelations between subordinate minority groups and the larger society have displayed widely varying patterns. At one end is an extensive range of autonomy granted to ethnic minorities by the dominant society, as in China; at the other end is the forceful and violent suppression or expulsion of ethnic minorities, as in Indonesia or Burma. Between the two extremes are several types of interaction patterns emerging between the majority society and ethnic groups.

In this book ethnic relations are examined mainly through focused analyses of the dynamics of majority-minority relations. An ethnic minority group is a collectivity of individuals who, because of their cultural characteristics and their common ancestry, are singled out from others in society for differential treatment. Therefore, they regard themselves as objects of collective discrimination (Gordon, 1964; Wirth, 1945). This definition is broad enough to include race, national origin, and religion, since each bears a relationship to ancestry. Within this broad framework the subject was approached through a wide range of interdisciplinary orientations: political science, history, anthropology, economics, and sociology. The groups included in the volume are also equally widespread: minority groups in China, Burakumin and Koreans in Japan, ethnic minorities in Malaysia, overseas Chinese in Southeast Asia, Tamils and Singalese in Ceylon, and Jews, Parsis, and untouchables in India.

FORMATION OF ETHNIC COMMUNITY

Coexistent with a minority group exists a majority group that enjoys higher social status and greater economic and/or political privileges. The dominant society has the leverage of advantaged status, acting as gatekeeper of desirable positions. In such a social setting, members of an ethnic minority generally share a common nature of problems centering on differential treatment and discrimination. Together, they work out a set of behaviors for handling those issues. They often establish places for their own religious worship and social clubs for people from the same region of their homeland, form mutual-aid societies and their own local chambers of commerce, and organize their own ethnic schools. Comprehensiveness of these ethnic institutions is largely determined by the traditional value and belief systems of the group as well as power relations between the minority and majority groups (Schermerhorn, 1967). Once these patterned responses are set to work, they are woven into a system where members of the group can manage a more or less complete way of life. At this point an ethnic community emerges (Martindale, 1960).

Careful examination into the dynamics of intergroup relations reveals two sets of forces at work: barriers that the majority community raises against minority groups and inducements they offer for minority groups in certain restricted areas. Members of the dominant group seek to monopolize the socially prized values they have won in forming a community. In recognizing possible competition for these values from minority groups, they become defensive. Barriers are raised against the threats of minority groups to the vested interests. They are excluded from fully participating in the life of the larger society. Ethnic minority members are often denied equal opportunities for employment and are excluded from selected residential areas and from certain places of recreation.

Along with the push-and-pull forces exercised by the dominant group is the tendency toward intra-closure by the minority group.[1] A conscious effort at self-help among the members of the subordinate group is engendered. Members of the ethnic group seek to preserve their distinctive way of life from the attraction of the majority community. These forces for intra-closure of the ethnic community are either reinforced or reduced by the prejudice exercised by the majority community. The degree of intra-closure drive that prevails in the ethnic community is dependent upon: 1) the ability to perpetuate the traditional ethnic memories; 2) the capability to create values superior to those of the majority community; 3) the number and size of the ethnic community; 4) the difference in physical features; 5) the rigidity or flexibility of prejudice on one or both sides; 6) the possession of economic skills and specialties that permit viable economic articulation within the larger community; 7) the aspiration level of the members of the ethnic group within the framework of the majority society; 8) the nature of power relations between the majority and minority groups; and 9) the institutional completeness of the ethnic community.[2]

An ethnic community is subtly balanced by the pulls and pushes of the majority community. In a society where the pushes against minority groups are absolute, the formation of an ethnic community is impossible. Some tolerance of minorities is necessary for the ethnic community to come into its existence in the first place. While members of the majority community may close off access to cherished values, the selective reception of the minorities into the larger society may be sustained by minorities' possession of valued talents, labor power, managerial skills, or specialized knowledge. While it is impossible to create an ethnic community when absolutely impermeable barriers are raised against it, it is also difficult for an ethnic community to form when there is complete receptivity of minority group by the majority community. Complete receptivity may result in rapid assimilation of the minority in the larger society. The combined existence of tolerance and prejudice toward the minority group by the majority community is a prerequisite for the formation of an ethnic minority community.

TYPES OF MAJORITY-MINORITY RELATIONS

The forces of intra-closure in the ethnic community and the pulls and pushes of the majority society may pair off in several different types of combinations. The modes of minority response to the majority society may be classified as follows: Assimilationist, Segregated Pluralist, Accommodated Pluralist, Exotic Pluralist, Secessionist, or Militant orientations. When barriers imposed by the larger society are low or permeable and the intra-closure of the ethnic minority community is moderately low, rapid assimilation of the minority group may result—Assimilationist.

An ethnic minority may remain as part of the larger society and the intergroup relations stay as pluralistic processes. Under this condition can be observed: 1) the combination of high barriers imposed by the majority society and the high intra-closure of the minority produces a segregated ethnic enclave for the minority group—Segregated Pluralist: for example, Semai in Malaysia, Koreans in Japan, Aboriginal tribes in Taiwan, Untouchables in India; 2) when in-group morale is high for the ethnic group and reception by the dominant group is moderately mixed, the minority group is likely to retain its identity while making accommodating adjustments to the prevailing social orders of the larger society—Accommodated

Pluralist: for example, the Chinese in Thailand, Malaysia, Philippines; 3) where both in-group morale for an ethnic group and acceptance for the ethnic group by the dominant society are high, valued traditions of the ethnic group are retained by its members. This situation may result from a strongly felt sense of superiority of their ethnic culture and tradition or their perceived advantages in attaining valued opportunities in the larger society—Exotic Pluralists: for example, Parsis and Jews in India, Chinese in many rural areas of Southeast Asian countries.

Facing impermeable barriers to the valued opportunities in the larger society, the members of an ethnic minority with their strong intra-closure and in-group morale may see two possible alternatives: 1) they can seek establishment of a separate independent community or state of their own—Secessionist: for example, Moslems in Philippines, Papuans in Indonesia; 2) they strive to attain opportunities by militant means with the ultimate goal of dominating others—Militant.

Relative power positions between indigenous and migrant groups during their initial contacts set an important stage for the ensuing mode of interaction between the groups. The combination of superordinate migrant group and subordinate indigenous group generally produces early violent encounters, which result in physical and cultural decimation of the indigenous group. In the face of assault against their existing order, the subordinate indigenous population often refuses to participate in the new economic, political, and social system. The dominant society needs to fill the vacuum created by the restructured order. Therefore, new subordinate ethnic groups are brought in as middlemen to assist and to maintain the new social system (for example, Chinese and Indians in Malaysia, Indonesia, Philippines, and Indians in Burma). These subordinate migrants subsequently establish firm roots in local retail trades and in lower rank positions of the political administration. The indigenous group frequently comes to regard these new subordinate migrants as instruments of the new order forced upon them by the dominant group.

The presence of a common enemy, detribalization with emergence of a lingua franca, and a corresponding rise of in-group morale result in a militant struggle of the indigenous group to rid the dominant migrant group. Examples of this situation are successful attainment of national independence in India, Pakistan, Burma, Malaysia, Indonesia, Philippines, Vietnam, Laos, and Cambodia and the rise of nationalist movements among East-Papuans in Indonesia. When the indigenous group succeeds in achieving its independence and deposes the dominant migrant group, it also frequently turns against the middlemen groups brought in by the former dominant group. Wirth stated, "No imperialism is as ruthless as that of a relatively small upstart nation" (Wirth, 1945)—for example, bloody persecution of Chinese in Indonesia and expulsion of Indians in Burma.

When the immigrant group is subordinate, their relations with the dominant indigenous group are generally without long-term conflict. New migrations are limited in numbers and sources to prevent the indigenous group's loss of political and economic control—for example, Koreans in Japan, Chinese in Thailand, Indonesia, Philippines, and Malaysia.[3]

The theroetical framework described here is a synthesis of several major theories of ethnic relations and a theory of ethnic community. It provides the analytic basis for examining concrete case studies of ethnic relations included in this book.

The articles in this book explore the following:

1. review of existing theories in ethnic group relations with particular emphasis on the application of these theories to Asiatic settings;
2. description of the existing ethnic group relations in Asian countries (that is, exclosure and assimilation, and varying degrees of social, economic, and political discriminations against minorities);
3. description of the life pattern of those ethnic groups;
4. examination of the behavioral and social psychological correlates of discrimination on ethnic minorities and analyses of the political and economic implications of such inter-group conflicts; and
5. comparison of these Asian ethnic relations with Western experience, particularly with the American experience.

The results of such exploration should prove fruitful and contribute singularly to studies in ethnic relations. More specifically, this book:

1. provides the readers with a comprehensive perspective in the study of ethnic relations;
2. enables Asian specialists to develop a broad yet critical understanding of intergroup relations;
3. furnishes a forum where applicability of existing theories in ethnic group relations will be examined in relation to non-Western settings.

The book is divided into four sections: Theoretical Perspectives, Far East, Southeast Asia, and South Asia. Although it deals primarily with the Asian experience, it is hoped that this book will help stimulate a development of global theory in ethnic relations. This study is of interest to a wide range of social scientists and is adaptable for college courses in Ethnic Relations as well as Asian Studies offered in sociology, anthropology, political science, and history departments.

FOOTNOTES

1. Pushes and pulls of the dominant group are equivalent to Martindale's terms *extra-community closure* and *extra-community innovation* (Martindale, 1960:394-398). Rinder (1965) defines the forces exercised by the larger society as *external environment* and those by the minority community as *internal environment*. Study of intergroup

relations within the framework of a dynamic interplay between dominant and subordinate groups has been largely influenced by Lewin (1948). Lewin calls the factors that pull the members of an ethnic minority into its own boundary *centripetal forces* and those that pull them toward the larger society *centrifugal forces*.

2. Brenton (1964) claims that the ability of an ethnic community to attract its members into its boundaries is largely dependent on the degree of institutional completeness of the ethnic community. For other factors that affect the ability of an ethnic community to maintain its identity, see Warner and Srole (1945), Park (1950), Wirth (1945), and Schermerhorn (1967).

3. Further discussion of types of ethnic interrelations are in Park (1950), Wirth (1945), and Rinder (1965). Power balances between ethnic groups during their initial contacts and their influence on the modes of interaction between the groups is discussed in Lieberson (1961).

REFERENCES

Bogardus, Emory S.
1930 "A race relations cycle." American Journal of Sociology 35 (January):612-617.
Breton, Raymond
1964 "Institutional completeness of ethnic communities and the personal relations of immigrants." American Journal of Sociology 70 (September):193-205.
Gordon, Milton M.
1964 Assimilation in American Life. New York: Oxford University Press.
Lewin, Kurt
1948 Resolving Social Conflicts. New York: Harper and Row, pp. 186-200.
Lieberson, Stanley
1961 "A societal theory of race and ethnic relations." American Sociological Review 26 (December):902-910.
Martindale, Don
1960 American Social Structure. New York: Appleton-Century-Croft.
Park, Robert E.
1950 Race and Culture. Glencoe, Illinois: The Free Press.
Rinder, Irwin D.
1965 "Minority orientations: an approach to intergroup relations through social psychology." Phylon 26 (Spring):5-17.
Schermerhorn, Richard A.
1967 "Polarity in the approach to comparative research in ethnic relations." Sociology and Social Research 51 (January): 235-240.
Warner, W. Lloyd, and Leo Srole
1945 The Social Systems of American Ethnic Groups. New Haven, Connecticut: Yale University Press, pp. 284-296.
Wirth, Louis
1945 "The problems of minority groups." Pp. 347-372 in Ralph Linton (ed.), The Science of Man in the World Crisis. New York: Columbia University Press.

I. THEORETICAL PERSPECTIVES

Martindale defines a community as a collectivity of individuals with a more or less complete way of life. This is a set of patterned solutions for the common nature of problems with which the plurality must deal. From this definition of a community, Martindale develops a theory of community formation. He perceives an ethnic group as a type of community. In addition to the general forces which generate the shape of a community, the partial acceptance and exclusion of an ethnic group, by the majority members of the society, gives rise to an ethnic community. Moreover, the boundry negotiation and maintenance of the ethnic community was examined in terms of the contrasting styles of Eastern and Western civilization. Here, Martindale lays out a general framework for analyzing ethnic relations in widely different social settings — Chinese in Southeast Asian countries, Koreans in Japan, Tamuli in Cylon, Indians in Southeast Asia and in Burma, and Parsis in India, etc.

Walker Connor provides a broad survey of ethnic relations in Asian countries. Its geographic scope extends from Japan to Afghanistan, inclusive of Southeast Asian and South Asian countries. Connor criticizes the popular use of the term 'a nation-state' and distinguishes a nation from a state; a nation is defined as a self-conscious and self-differentiating ethnic group, whereas a state is a territorial-political unit. He lists six major variables that determine the influence relations among groups in a state: number of groups in the state; relative balance of political forces, form of government; representations in strategic occupations; historical factors; and demographic distribution—who populates the strategic territory. Utilizing these variables he examines the intergroup dynamics which prevail in Asian states. Furthermore, particular attention was given to the ethnic discord that exists along those borders of states where political and ethnic borders fail to concide. Since the current trend appears to be the acceptance of the principle of self-determination as a self-evident truth, Connor foresees continued expansion of ethnic group conflicts throughout the area.

In this section, Martindale furnishes a general theoretical framework which could be fruitfully utilized in examining minority-majority relations. Connor identifies a set of key variables in probing ethnic relations and delineates a general over-all picture of intergroup relations in Asian states. These two articles, lay the groundwork for further detailed studies of ethnic relations in concrete settings.

1
THE GUEST COMMUNITY: Asian Style

DON MARTINDALE
University of Minnesota

ABSTRACT

A community is defined to be a more or less complete way of life managed by a plurality of people. Within this framework, a theory of community formation was suggested in terms of the following main dynamic processes: patterning of solutions for common problems of the collectivity; adjustment of patterned solutions for mutual accommodations and consistency; and stabilization and completion of consistent solutions. Extending this approach, a theory of guest community formation was proposed. Inter-play between selective receptivity (exclusion and reception) of guest members by the host and the forces of inner enclosure for the guest members was examined in explaining the boundry negotiation and maintenance of the guest community. Furthermore, contrasting style components of Eastern and Western civilization were compared and their influence on the guest community was investigated.

In the present context, the term "community" is taken to refer to a more or less complete way of life practiced by a human plurality, that is a community is an actual on-going system of behavior; the term "culture" is taken to refer to the system of learned or invented forms practiced by the members of a community considered in abstraction from their behavior. "Societies" are community formations of a comprehensive sort; "civilizations" are comprehensive systems of culture.

It is conventional in the present world to distinguish at least two great civilizations: the Eastern and Western. It is also conventional in both East and West to distinguish various types of communities in which the respective cultures are manifest; tribes, villages, cities and nations are among the more important types of communities found in both East and West.

COMMUNITY AND CULTURE

It is essential to distinguish clearly between "community" and "culture" if one is to understand how guest communities (in the category of which ethnic communities are included) may form and how they may be shaped by civilizational forces.

Communities are systems of interactive behavior; cultures are systems of norms which guide interactive behavior. A community is *what* people do together; their culture is *how* they do it. A human community without a culture would represent formless behavior; a culture without communities in which it is realized would be a set of empty forms. At the same time community as what people do and culture as how they attempt to do it, are always analytically distinguishable and there is no contradiction in the fact that the same culture may be shared by numerous distinct communities or that in any given community cultural innovations may be made that place it somewhat in tension with the culture shared with other communities.

Once he accepted the conclusions of the biological sciences, that man is the terminal creature in a series that was once social by instinct, but gradually lost their instincts in a manner which cast them on their resources for learning and inventing, the social scientist was forced to see the human community and culture as arising together, but inevitably coming into partial conflict. Lacking instinctive precommitment of behavior, humans must learn from others or invent solutions to their problems. One could expect numerous variations to arise if for no other reason as accidents of the learning process. Furthermore a creature clever enough to learn or invent all the forms necessary for survival could also be expected continuously to invent new forms or to seek short cuts around old arrangements. Thus the very processes involved in the rise of a system of culture in the first place enriches it and creates conflicts with it.

In the course of transmitting their culture, dealing with intended or inadvertent conflicts arising within it and defending it against alternatives and challenges from the outside humans inevitably become to some extent selfconscious of their culture. The very success of a community and its culture, sets in motion the tendency for a type of socio-cultural formation to diffuse to the entire area where it is superior to alternative formations. A distinctive culture, thus, comes to be distributed among numerous communities. Each of these communities is subject to its own special forces for cultural innovations from within or for adoption of successful innovations that may arise in nearby communities. One must expect streams and currents of cultural diffusion throughout any given cultural area.

Whenever a more or less homogeneous culture is diffused across numerous communities, the possibility is present for the formation of new and more complex communities, within which the common culture may be further refined and elaborated and so, for example, in a world of villages, cities and nations may arise. Moreover, highly elaborate systems of culture, which are conventionally called civilization, may persist in an ever-changing, but still more or less identifiable form, for a millenium. Not the least properties of a civilization are the orientations it contains toward the community: it may, for example, involve a preference for one over other types; it may give all or some communities high or low relief.

CIVILIZATIONS OF THE EAST AND WEST

An enormous volume of literature has developed in the attempt to characterize and account for the differences between Eastern and Western civilization. Among relatively recent attempts to sum up the differences between East and West is that of Northrop (1946:294). Western knowledge and with it the Western outlook is characterized by Northrop as possessing an utopian, theoretic property.

> Confronted with himself and nature, Western man arrives by observation and scientific hypothesis at a theoretical conception of the character of these two factors. This theoretical conception, even when determined by empirically and experimentally controlled scientific methods, always affirms more, as Democritus and Plato were the first to see, than bare facts by themselves provide. In short, scientific theory always asserts more than observation gives, and is not verified directly, as Aristotle and the Humean and modern Positivists supposed, by mere observation; instead, it is a hypothesis proposed *a priori*, verified in part

at least indirectly through its experimentally checked deductive consequences.

In all forms of Western thought, social experience and art, this pursuit of a theoretic (utopian) factor beneath the palpable surface of events gives Western culture its restless dynamism.

By contrast Northrop (1946:375) finds the essence of Oriental civilization in the full immersion and acceptance of the palpably given.

> The meaning of Oriental civilization—that characteristic which sets it off from the West—may be stated very briefly. The Oriental portion of the world has concentrated its attention upon the nature of all things in their emotional and aesthetic, purely empirical and positivistic immediacy. It has tended to take as the sum total of the nature of things that totality of immediately apprehended fact which in this text has been termed the differentiated aesthetic continuum.

The West, in Northrop's view (1946:375), originally began with the palpable world and still periodically returns to aspects of it "to confirm its syntactically formulated, postulationally prescribed theories of structures and objects." But in the end the properties of the immediately apprehended world are in the West "mere correlates or signs" of its theories and this world is rarely enjoyed, as in the Orient, in and for itself.

It is conventional to trace the different orientations of East and West to their respective philosophical and religious traditions. In *The Taming of the Nations* Northrop (1952:186) argued that there is a system of

> values which Australia, Canada, Ibero-America, New Zealand and the United States have in common with the other nations of the West. . .
> The classical and spiritual values of the West are two in number: (1) Greco-Roman science and philosophy with their unique concept of law, and (2) the Hebrew-Christian religion.

In the Orient all students have observed, no single religion or philosophy became dominant over the entire cultural area, rather religious tolerance to a degree generally unknown in the West and a diversity of subforms of religion were typical. Northrop (1946:312-313), like many other students of civilization, argues the diversity of the Orient did not prevent the emergence of a single civilization.

> Nevertheless, to specify. . . fact which distinguish one country or culture from the other is at the same time to indicate the equally evident interconnections and identities which tie them all together to constitute a single civilization of the East. Confucianism and Taoism are religions of Korea and of Japan as well as of China. Buddhism is as influential in China, Korea and Japan as are Confucianism and Taoism. Buddhism and Hinduism occur in India, Ceylon, the Malay Peninsula, and the Southwest Pacific Islands. . . It is the unity provided by these essential relations and identities which merges the cultures of the Oriental countries into one traditional culture of the Far East.

The habit of students of civilization of looking at people's religions and philosophies for clues to their distinctive values, is justified by the theory that it is in these institutions that people seek orientation to the ultimate implications of their lives: to the nature of life and death, to the world of nature, to the values and limitations of their particular systems of social life. They see the world religions as stylizing value orientations over extensive areas and through long time periods. When religions lose adherents, this is taken as evidence that a unified orientation toward the world is decaying or being supplanted.

While some central characterization of the civilizational value system is usually sought by students as Northrop does in characterizing western civilization as involving a theoretical orientation toward immediate experience in its totality, such epitomization is usually employed as a hook for more extensive comparisons and contrasts. The following, in tabular form, are some of the more frequent characterizations of contrasting style components of Eastern and Western civilization.

Style Components of Eastern and Western Civilization

Trait	Western Civilization	Eastern Civilization
Orientation toward immediate experience	Theoretic, Analytical	Aesthetic, Synthetic
Concept of Time	Linear	Cyclical
Approach to man and nature	Segmental	Holistic
Orientation to social change	Progressive, Revolutionary, Dynamic	Traditional, Passive
Style of intellectual	Active	Contemplative
Forms of prophecy	Emmisary	Exemplary
Orientation to society	Utopian	Ideological

It is hardly necessary to point out that such characterizations of contrasting styles are ideal types, summing up differences in grouping of traits and emphasis rather than absolute contrasts.

CIVILIZATIONAL STYLES IN COMMUNITY FORMATION

While the same general types of communities appear in both East and West, it is an interesting question whether their respective civilizations result in different styles of community formation, even though the general principles of community formation are universal.

Empirical Principles of Community Formation

If we take community to refer to a more or less complete way of life that tends to rise for a human plurality at least three empirical regularities seem to account for community formation. Any human collectivity tends to stabilize its collective solutions to problems; the nature of the human organism and the environment presents the collectivity with a variety of problems, and the solutions to any one inevitably must be more or less consistent with the solutions to another; the problems that must be solved belong to the daily, yearly and life cycle. Hence a set of problem solutions gradually tends to lock together into a set sufficient to these basic cycles. The empirical principles of community formation, thus, are stabilization, consistency and completeness. Whether the plurality is in the Occident or Orient the same general processes are at work.

Depending upon which institutions form the core of the system, and such properties as the degree of integration and scope of the institutional system, communities may differ: the core of the agricultural village is formed, for example, by the basic cultivating institutions (with considerable frequency the patriarchal family); the city centers on market, administrative or military institutions or some combination of both; the nation centers on the state with its monopoly of administrative and military power.

All of this is roughly common to both East and West.

Civilizational Stylization of Community Formation

However, though the same types of institutions are common to East and West and the same general kinds of communities appear, the distinctive mentalities have influence on their eventual form.

The Western mind tends to be theoretic and analytic, hence it tends to fasten on differences and contrasts; the Eastern mind is intuitive, aesthetic and synthetic, hence it tends to emphasize similarities and continuities. This difference of emphasis is manifest in orientation toward communities. In the West, the tendency is to sharpen the boundaries of communities within the wider world and to emphasize the contrast between community types; in the East the continuities of community with community is insisted upon and all tend to merge into the great society as a whole. Throughout the East there is a tendency to reason directly from the family, or clan or caste to the village, the city or the nation, as if they were only general forms of such primary groups. The West sees all larger social forms as contrasts with primary groups.

Also the relation between individual and society tends to vary between East and West. In the East the individual tends to be merged with the primary group and seen as inseparable from it; in the West the individual is seen in confrontation with society at large, responding to a system of trans-community natural laws. F.L.K. Hsu (1963: 226-227) had some of these notions in mind when he attempted to epitomize the contrasts between the Hindu, Chinese and American ways of life in terms of the respective place of caste, clan and club in each.

> The American family orientation . . . glorifies self-reliance. In neither the Hindu nor the Chinese situation does the individual stand or fall alone. If the Hindu advances, the gods have been good to him. If the Chinese does well, his ancestors must have been virtuous . . . the Chinese . . . has little doubt about his permanent place in the great continuum and about the intentions of the dead and the yet-unborn. The American's uncertainty is far greater than the Hindu's . . . Success is his own triumph and defeat his own burden . . . In the face of such self-reliance, and the ideal of freedom of the individual, the American solution to the problem of social needs is the formation of groupings, among peers who enter into relationships with each other predominantly as equal, contractual partners . . . The constant process of emergence, division, merging, and multiplication of these clubs for achieving the most diverse objectives known to mankind is the secret of the dynamism of the American World.[1]

Essential to the Western individual's freely self-chosen relation to social formations of all sorts, was the employment of law for the settling of disputes and for confirming social arrangements of all sort. Western law had roots in Hebrew as well as the Greco-Roman traditions. Though the starting point for the relation of individual to society was the patriarchal

family in both East and West, there is a marked difference between relations within the patriarchal family of the Ancient Jews and the Chinese and Indians according to Northrop (1946:187).

> In the latter . . . the use of law as a method for settling disputes is regarded as something to be avoided. Individuals are not measured against determinate rules, but are instead encouraged to cover up their transitory, relativistic rights and differences and to cultivate, through mediation, the all-embracing formlessness common to all things—human and inorganic objects alike.

By contrast with this Asian practice, Northrop urges, already in the Old Testament men, even while retaining the patriarchal family form, had begun to measure themselves against univeral rules. Henry Sumner Maine had long since expressed the same argument in general form insisting that all relations we consider to be modern in the Western world, follow the curve of the emancipation of Western man from status in the patriarchal family to that of an individual free to enter contractual relations on terms of equality under law with his socio-political peers apart from all other considerations.

During the same period that Western man was learning how to release the individual from his original groups, freeing him to employ legal institutions to frame social formations of a most diverse kind, he was also learning how to give incisive manipulable form to new complex types of communities. Central to Ancient Judaism which arose as the religion of a tribal military confederation was the conception of a covenant between God and the individual confederates, which made the social history of the people conditional upon the observance by the chosen people of the terms of their contractual relations to the War God. The unity provided by their religion permitted an unprobably confederation of tribal associates to carry out the conquest of the hold land and to establish a new type of complex community. Ancient Isreal was the first nation of a contemporary type to appear—a thousand years before the formation of the modern nations. At the same time period in Greece and on the Islands of Ionia off the Asistic coast, revolutions of feudal aristocrats against the Homeric-type castled kings, were establishing a new type of polis community composed of sworn associates who bound themselves together in oath bound confererations. Within these new types of urban communities, politics and warfare were shared by the warrior confederates. Within their circles domocratising movements soon got underway.

The counterpart of the emancipation of the individual from his original organic groups and freeing him for new social arrangements under a rule of law, thus, was the formation of new complex communities—the city and the world's first nation—in which individuals had membership as contractual associates and the community as a whole was visualized as a delimited association bound by the terms of a covenant (in the case of Israel) or of a constitution (in the case of the Greek city states).

In these new types of complex communities, men in the West came in time to employ the legal device of the corporation to create all sorts of new groups with the properties of individuals before the law. Moreover, they came also to give the community the properties of a corporation making it incisively definable and manipulable in a new way.

While the same types of communities occur in East and West, in the East the old organic groups have tended to retain a power they have long since lost in the West. Moreover, all communities even the village, tend to be less sharply incised in the East than in the West. In the West the village is viewed as a primary group. In his study of Taitou, Shantung Province, Martin Yang (1947:X) treats it as a secondary group.

> The village is a secondary group. Between the family and the village, there are various transitional groupings—clans, neighborhoods, the association of families on the basis of similar social or economic status or school affiliations, and religious groups.

Early students of the village in India tended to apply Western conceptions to it and to emphasize its unity and autonomy. However, when students came to view it first hand, much of its apparent definiteness seemed to vanish and the power of the castes or jatis leaped forth as a dominant fact, leading Mandelbaum (1970:327) to argue

> A jati cannot stand alone. Its people necessarily cooperate with some people of other jatis; commonly they compete with still others. The main locale of this cooperation and competition is the village . . . to the student and observer it is a principle unit for the understanding of the society. Yet some observers have doubted the signifiance of the village either as a corporate group or as a useful unit for analysis.

Weber (1958:337-338) was convinced, that the power of the old organic groups was a major factor in the failure of the full city and its attendant behavioral orientation in the Occidental sense to appear in the Orient.

> In the Occident the establishment of a national, inner-worldly ethic was bound up with the appearance of thinkers and prophets who developed a social structure on the basis of political problems which were foreign to Asiatic culture; these were the political problems of civic status groups of the city without which neither Judaism nor Christianity nor the development of Hellenic thought is conceivable. The establishment of the "city", in the occidental sense, was restricted in Asia, partly through sib power which continued unbroken, partly through caste alienation.

The same types of factors have been a component in the slowness of the contemporary nation-state complex to emerge in the Orient.

THE GUEST COMMUNITY

Among the specialized types of communities that tend to appear within the framework of complex societies are ethnic communities which enjoy a guest-like status.

A guest community is a minority community tolerated within the framework of the wider society of the majority. In origin a guest community could consist of the original inhabitants of an area engulfed by outsiders and turned into a guest in what was originally the homeland of its sustaining population: such were the Jews in Ancient Isreal after the Babylonian conquest; the American Indians after the conquest by the Europeans; the Ainu of Japan. On the other hand, the guest community can arise by the immigration of outsiders who are permitted to settle and pursue their special socio-economic ways as a tolerated guest by the majority. Such were the gypsies, the Jews in Diaspora, the Indians in Africa, the Koreans in Japan, and the many hundreds of ethnic communities in the United States and elsewhere.

The Formation of the Guest Community

There are a number of relatively obvious factors in the formation of ethnic communities. They are a phenomenon primarily of complex communities, for they have the properties of communities in a guest-host relation. More interesting, however, is the complex pattern of interlocking ambivalence that tie host and guest together.

Members of the host community typically experience a combination of prejudice and tolerance toward the guest people. They may experience a combination of suspicion, disgust or even fear of the alien ways of the guest people together with some pity, sympathy and even some admiration. The guest people may be expected to perform a variety of lowly paid, rough, unskilled or disreputable services. On the other hand, the guest people may all be ambivalent, being both grateful to the host for permission to live and work in the wider society, but experiencing considerable resentment of the social and economic restrictions placed on them. Whatever gratitude they may feel moreover, is often tempered by the perception of the fact they they are expected to do the "dirty work" of the majority community. The prejudice-tolerance ratio of the host and the gratitude-resentment ratio of the guest occur in endless variations with important consequences for the distinctiveness and duration of guest community formation.

The prejudice-tolerance ratio of the host toward a guest people seems to vary with: qualitative characteristics of the guest culture; the amount and kind of services performed by the guest people; the degree to which the guest people are seen as threatening. In the mildest case the guest people is looked at as comical and not the least threatening and as performing a variety of menial or disreputable services cheaply. Moreover the host people is often far from unified in its outlook, and where fear of cultural contamination or of economic damage from a guest people is intense, this often is among the lower ranking members of the host community, strata that would otherwise perform the services it sees the guest people preempting. When prejudice on the part of some or all of the host takes the form of active persecution, this may itself be a component in reactive community formation on the part of the guest.

The extent of difference between the guest and host culture (particularly when there are language barriers) and relative lack of preparation for life in the host country, may be important factors in the formation of a guest community even without the pressure of prejudice and persecution. It can be depressing to find one's self alone in a foreign land where one does not understand the language and customs. Persons under such circumstances often cling together like shipwrecks on alien shores, with common problems and common miseries. Under such circumstances information about job opportunities or places to live, news from back home, and angles for coping with the wider society are shared. At the same time the banding of cultural aliens together for mutual protection, may make them visible and be a factor in the intensification of prejudice. Hence a set of reciprocal forces may enhance the tendency of cultural aliens to band together and form an array of institutions to perform for themselves services that the wider community does not furnish at all adequately.

Once a group of countrymen finding themselves in an alien environment make common cause and undertake collective action for one purpose, there is an inclination to organize for others. A process of crystalization thus gets underway which may result in extensive organization throughout the subcommunity.

Types of Guest Communities

The model for the formation of the guest community that

has been outlined was developed specifically for the formation of the ethnic community in the United States and addressed primarily to the formation of guest communities of other Western nationals. However, if one takes account of the possible role of civilizational style in ethnic community formation and if one considers only Eastern and Western civilizations at least four types of guest community formation are possible:

Guest Community Formation by Civilizational Type

Source	Type of Guest Community	
	Eastern	Western
Intra Cultural Guests	Other Eastern Guests	Other Western Guests
Extra Cultural Guests	Western Guests	Eastern Guests

Guests may be of intra or extra cultural origin whether in the Eastern or Western civilization area. It is plausible to assume that the guest-host relation could take a somewhat different form depending on the cultural origins of both. While the potential for value conflict would appear to be greater when guest and host are of different civilizations, it is also possible that in some situations the coincidence of the basic values of guest and host could institute sharper conflicts. However, it is also possible that the cultural variations within any given civilization are greater than the between-culture variations. Hence the full potential for conflict in the given case can only be determined empirically.

Civilizational Style and Guest Community Formation

At least four properties seem to differentiate the Eastern and Western styles of community formation.

1. In Eastern communities generally some form of the kin group (family, extended family, clan or caste) plays a far more extensive role than in Western communities.
2. In the resolution of community problems Eastern communities tend to place far greater stress on primary socialization (reeducation) than is the rule in Western communities. In other words, the scope of socialization extends far into what the West conceives as the proper sphere of social control. What the East sees as routine reeducation is interpreted as brain washing in the West.
3. In Western communities individuals are far more fully emancipated from their status situations in the primary groups than in the East. The behavior so freed in the West is reordered under the rule of law.
4. In the West communities tend to be more sharply incised against their social backgrounds than in the East. With far greater frequency than in the East, communities are given the status of organized corporations and subject to various sorts of conscious manipulation. In the East the community is far more frequently seen as a natural organic growth inseparable from its setting.

The Eastern and Western styles of community formation seem also to be manifest in guest community formation in which the basis of specialized communalization is a system of cultural differences between guest and host. In the West guest communities tend to form easily, they tend to be sharply drawn against the surrounding world, they tend to acquire formal legal status and to be subject to conscious manipulation, but the relation of members to the community is in the form of a freely chosen arrangement. Hence, often by the time of the third generation more members of an ethnic

community are making their way in the world outside than inside. In fact in the West, often by the time of the third generation the community as a whole is well on the way to dissolution.

In the East guest communities tend to arise slowly and retain the properties of organic growth, the pressures to form them both from within and without seem more gentle but more enduring. They are far less inclined to come into overt formal conflict with the surrounding world than is true in the West. Within them, primary structures are stronger and individuals are held more by their status in the primary groups than by bonds of rational self-interest.

However, there are variations in the manner in which Eastern civilization has handled the guest community: in China the long range pressure is toward absorption of the guest through resocialization into the wider socity; in India, the traditional pressure was toward enclosing the guest community in an endogamously, occupationally and ritualistically closed caste, assigning the community as a whole a general rank within the organically relativized society.

Such evidence as we have of Western guest communities in the Orient suggest that in China they have tended to float on the surface of society only eventually to disappear; in India guest communities of Western origin have tended gradually to yield to the pressures toward caste.

Chinese and Indian ethnic communities in the Western world tend to retain the power of primary group ties long after they have eroded in ethnic communities of Western origin. But again the subdivisions of the Eastern civilizational style is manifest. The Chinese guest community responds flexibly to the surrounding Western World, but somehow in the end usually remains unassimilated. The property that Arthur H. Smith (1894:80) described as flexible inflexibility seems to characterize Chinese guest communities outside China.

> Few comparisons . . . hit the mark more exactly than that which likens the Chinese to the bamboo. It is graceful, it is everywhere useful, it is supple, and it is hollow. When the east wind blows it bends to the west. When the west wind blows it bends to the east. When no wind blows it does not bend at all. The bamboo plant is a grass. It is easy to tie knots in grasses. It is difficult, despite its suppleness, to tie knots in the bamboo plant.

On the other hand, Indian guest communities in the Western world tend to respond to the west not only with internally strong family and kin ties, but with a set of ritualistical proscription against the surrounding world. They confront the surrounding Western world with many of the features of a withdrawn sect; hence, they often have caste-like properties in a caste-free world. They are not, however, as whole communities assigned some approximate standing in an organically relativized social world.

It is hardly necessary to observe in conclusion that the various propositions outlined in the present paper are theoretically derived from the theory of community, the theory of civilization and the theory of guest community. Such evidence as has been available to check these notions is fragmentary. Moreover, one of the properties of our times has been the accelerated diffusion of various features of Western civilization to the entire world. In the long run the two styles of community formation should grow more alike. Nevertheless, these propositions are intriguing enough to suggest the potential value of systematic research into the formation of the guest community in a framework of comparative civilization.

FOOTNOTES

1. F.L.K. Hsu, *Clan, Caste, and Club* (Princeton, New Jersey: D. Van Nostrand, 1963), pp. 226,227. Professor Hsu takes issue with many students who treat India and China as representing a single mode of civilization. He urges that the Hindu is "supernatural-centered" the Chinese is "situation centered." Max Weber and others whom Hsu opposes were aware of these differences, however, treating them as polarities of the Eastern mind.

REFERENCES

HSU, F.L.K.
1963   Clan, Caste and Club. Princeton, N.J.: D. Van Nostrand

MANDELBAUM, D.
1970   Society in India, Vol. II. Berkeley: University of California Press
NORTHROP, F.S.C.
1946   The Meetings of East and West. New York: MacMillan
1952   The Taming of the Nations. New York: MacMillan
SMITH, A.H.
1894   Chinese Characteristics. New York: Fleming H. Revell
WEBER, M.
1958   The Religion of India, Trans. Hans H. Gerth and Don Martindale. Glenco, Ill.: Free Press
YANG, M.C.
1947   A Chinese Village. London: Kegan, Paul, Trench, Trubner

2

AN OVERVIEW OF THE ETHNIC COMPOSITION
AND PROBLEMS OF NON-ARAB ASIA

WALKER CONNOR

State University of New York at Brockport

ABSTRACT

A survey of non-Arab Asia illustrates the instability inherent in situations where political and ethnic borders fail to coincide. All of the multiethnic states have experienced some measure of violent ethnic discord, and an increase in the frequency and scope of such discord can be anticipated as the national consciousness of groups progresses. No particular classification of states appears to be immune to ethnic discord: afflicted states include both industrialized and non-industrialized, communist and non-communist, democratic and authoritarian, federative and unitary, large and small, literate and illiterate, rich and poor. Many of the ethnic problems are not purely domestic; most land borders divide ethnic groups, causing ethnic issues to be major factors in the relations among the region's states. A number of ethnic problems have been exacerbated by governmental efforts to manipulate the ethnic aspirations of groups within neighboring states.

I

Analyses covering huge segments of the globe are quite legitimately suspect. Broad-brush treatment of a large region usually leads to facile but fallacious generalizations, and to the obscuring of significant differences within the region. The phenomenon termed ethnic nationalism, however, constitutes at least a partial exception to this warning concerning the perils of undertaking a too geographically large or a too multicultured approach.

The growing tendency of peoples to perceive human relations from the vantage point of the ethnic group and to demand that political institutions and borders be made to conform with the interests of that ethnic group, is truly a global phenomenon, exemplifying a remarkable disdain for geography, for level of economic development, for form of government, and for political philosophy, Europe, for example, has *inter alia*, its Basque, Breton, Croatian, Flemish, Lithuanian, Scottish, Slovak, Ukrainian, and Welsh nationalist movements; Africa, its Ganda, Huto, Ibo, Luo, and Zulu nationalisms; and the Americas their Franco-Canadian, Black nationalist, East Indian and Amerindian movements. While the detailed knowledge and particular insight of the one-culture or single area specialist are essential if analysis is to proceed beyond the superficial, it is equally essential that the analyst not perceive a single illustration of ethnic unrest as an isolated phenomenon that is totally unique to a particular environment. Familiarity with the global dimensions of ethnic nationalism and with the specifics of ethnic nationalism as it has developed in a number of other environments affords the specialist some guides for identifying symptons, for differentiating trivia from essence, and for determining what in fact is unique to the particular ethnic problem that he is studying. While this paper therefore attempts to survey the political implications inherent in the ethnology of a huge segment of the globe, it should nevertheless be viewed as only a partial treatment of the ethnic nationalist phenomenon.[1]

It is beyond the purpose of this paper to probe the essence of ethnic nationalism, but a few words concerning its relation to the state are necessary. Elsewhere, this author (1971, 1972) has noted the serious consequences arising from the common practice of interutilizing the words *nation* and *state*. This practice is surprising because the two concepts are so vitally different. The nation can be succinctly defined as a *self*-conscious, *self*-differentiating ethnic group, so its essential quality is subjective in nature. The state, by contrast, is a fully tangible concept, a territorial-political segment of the globe.

It is probable that the tendency to interutilize the two words is an outgrowth of their being joined together to form the term *nation-state*, a hyphenate originally intended to designate a situation in which the borders of a state and a nation essentially coincided. All of this confusion would be only of semantic interest, were it not for the resulting tendency of scholars and statesmen to equate nationalism with loyalty to the state (or, more commonly, to the term nation, when improperly employed as a verbal substitute for the state), rather than with loyalty to the nation as properly understood. In cases of nation-states, such as Japan, this terminological confusion has not had significant ramifications, because the people have viewed the state as the political expression of the nation. Much the same could be said of peoples like the Han Chinese, who, being dominant in a state, view it as the state of their particular nation. In all such cases, references to the state and references to the nation trigger the same ethnonational response from the masses. But if the state is not viewed as the political manifestation of one's nation, then distinctive identities (namely, citizenship in the state as contrasted with membership in the nation) come into play. In such an instance, national identity does not reinforce identity with the state, and is very likely to compete with the latter. Thus, the leaders of the People's Republic of China, including Mao, often intersperse their public utterances with references to "Mother China" or to the state of the "New China". But while such references unquestionably trigger a positive psychological response among the Han Chinese masses, they are likely to evoke a quite different psychological response from the Hui, Mongol, Tibetan, Uighur and other non-Han inhabitants of the Chinese state.

As noted, a true nation-state is not seriously troubled by such considerations. But only a handful of states are sufficiently homogeneous to deserve the "nation-state" appellation. Thus, only two of the twenty-six states surveyed in this paper would qualify. Most state governments are therefore either already under pressure or, consonant with growing ethnic conciousness on the part of their minorities, will increasingly be under pressure to find answers to this serious threat to continued state unity. Attempted answers have been quite varied. Within China, for example, the ultimate strategy is to amalgamate the minorities into the pre-existing, dominant, Han nation. Within other states, the ultimate goal is to mold the diverse ethnic elements into a single, new nation termed Indonesian, Filipino, Indian, Pakistani, Iranian, etc.

Are such programs likely to succeed? It is axiomatic that nationalism is still one of the most vigorous motivational forces affecting group behavior, and since nationalism has been erroneously identified with loyalty to the state, much of the literature on political development reflects a presumption that the state will prove victorious in matters of competing allegiance. Such a prognostication hardly appears justified.

The post-World War II record of widespread and accelerating instances of ethnic discord illustrates (1) that the aspiration of state unity is likely to be viewed by ethnic minorities as conflicting with, if not mutually exclusive of, their own group aspirations and (2), that in matters of conflict, the psychological ties that bind a person to his state are not likely to prove the emotional equals of the ties that bind him to his nation. Does one die for the Tibetan nation or China; the Bengali nation or Pakistan; the Naga, Mizo, Kashmiri nation or India; the Kurdish nation or the states of Iran, Iraq, or Turkey; the Karen, Kachin, Shan nation or Burma; the Meo nation or for Laos or Thailand? Even if restricted to Asia, this listing of peoples who have indicated that the concept of the state is no match in their value system for the emotional attachment to nation could be greatly enlarged.

II

The states of non-Arab Asia are characterized by extreme ethnic heterogeneity. As indicated in Table I, only Japan and Korea are sufficiently homogeneous to qualify as nation-states. (Korea and Vietnam are each treated as single entities despite their present political division.) Three other states, each containing a single group accounting for more than 90 percent of the total population, also contain at least one politically significant minority. In nearly one third of the states (8), the major group accounts for between 75 and 89 percent of the population, and in a like number, the major group only accounts for between one-half and three-fourths of the population. In five states, there is no ethnic group accounting for a majority. It is also worth noting that over half of the states contain at least six significant ethnic groups.

Table II shows the ethnolinguistic composition of the twenty-six states in greater detail. A number of warnings are in order, however:

(1) Ethnological knowledge of Asia is much less satisfactory than the use of numbers and percentages would suggest. In many instances, the basic population data on which the statistics rest are subject to a margin of error so substantial as to render them almost useless. Most states of Asia either have no valid basis for making an estimate of their population or, for strategic reasons, purposefully distort their publicized estimates. For example, officials of the People's Republic of China (PRC) are still prone to use a 700 million population figure, although a United States Department of State publication, using high and low projections from the Chinese 1953 census, estimated that China's population, as far back as January 1966, was somewhere between 760 and 895 million.[2] Afghanistan has never undertaken a census, and estimates of its population range from 10 to 17 million (Area Handbook for Afghanistan: 58). If the overall population statistics of states are subject to error, it follows that subcategories, such as ethnicity, are still more so. Moreover, governments tend to be more sensitive concerning ethnic statistics than general population figures, and are therefore more prone to distort the former.[3]

(2) Even if reasonably accurate figures are available, statistical approaches to ethnopolitical analysis are dangerous in that they imply that relative statistical weight of groups can be translated into relative influence. In some cases, such as that of the Han Chinese within the PRC, statistical domination (94 percent of the total population) may well legitimize an inference of sociopolitical pre-eminence within the state. But relative numbers become less accurate indicators of political influence in the absence of such an evident numerical advantage of a single group. Indeed, as indicated by the position of the Bengalis prior to their secession from Pakistan, a numerical majority may even be a political minority. The relative influence of a group depends upon a host of variables that can, in turn, develop in a number of different patterns. Some of the variables are historical and psychological, peculiar to a given society. But some of the more common and obvious factors affecting a group's influence include (a) the number of groups within a state, (b) the relative balance of political

Table I. ETHNOLINGUISTIC COMPOSITION OF NON-ARAB ASIAN STATES BY MAJOR CATEGORIES

ETHNIC DESCRIPTION	STATES	TOTAL NUMBER
ESSENTIALLY HOMOGENEOUS	JAPAN, KOREA	2
LARGEST GROUP ACCOUNTS FOR MORE THAN 90%	BANGLA DESH, PRC, TURKEY	3
LARGEST GROUP ACCOUNTS FOR 75-89%	BHUTAN, BURMA, CAMBODIA, CYPRUS, MONGOLIA, SINGAPORE, TAIWAN, VIETNAM	8
LARGEST GROUP ACCOUNTS FOR 50-74%	AFGHANISTAN, CEYLON, IRAN, LAOS, MALDIVE, MAURITIUS, PAKISTAN, THAILAND	8
LARGEST GROUP ACCOUNTS FOR LESS THAN 50%	INDIA, INDONESIA, MALAYSIA, NEPAL, PHILIPPINES	5

Table II. ETHNOLINGUISTIC COMPOSITION OF NON-ARAB ASIAN STATES

STATE (estimated population in parentheses	Ethnolinguistic Groups by Percentage of Population		STATE	Ethnolinguistic Groups by Percentage of Population	
Afghanistan (17 million)	Pushtun	60	India (cont.) (547 million)	Assamese	1
	Tajik	30		Kashmiri	1
	Uzbek	5	Indonesia (121 million)	Javanese	45
	Hazara	3		Sundanese	14
	Turkomen	1		Madurese	8
Bangla Desh (75 million)	Bengali	98		Coastal Malay	8
				Makasarese-Buginese	4
Bhutan (800 thousand)	Bhote	75		Minangkabau	3
	Nepali	20		Chinese	2
Burma (28 million)	Burman	75		Balinese	2
	Karen	12		Batak	2
	Shan	6		Atjehnese	1
	Indian-Pakistani	*3	Iran (29 million)	Persian	70
	Chinese	1		Azarbaijani	12
	Kachin	1		Kurd	6
	Chin	1		Baluchi	5
Cambodia (7 million)	Khmer	90		Lur and Bakhtiari	2
	Chinese	6		Arab	1
	Cham	1	Japan (104 million)	Japanese	99
	Mon-Khmer Tribes	1		Korean	1
Ceylon (13 million)	Sinhalese	70	Korea, North (14 million)	Korean	99
	Ceylon Tamil	11			
	Indian Tamil	11	Korea, South (32 million)	Korean	99
	Moors	7			
Chinese People's Republic (800 million)	Han	94	Laos (3 million)	Lao	67
	Chuang	1		Mon-Khmer Tribes	19
Cyprus (700 thousand)	Greeks	79		Tai-other than Lao	5
	Turk	18		Meo	4
India (547 million)	Hindi -- including			Chinese	3
	Hindustani	33	Malaysia (11 million)	Malay	44
	Telegu	9		Chinese	36
	Bengali	8		Indian-Pakistani*	10
	Marathi	8		Iban (Sea Dyak)	3
	Tamil	7		Kadazan (Dusun)	2
	Gujarati	5		Land Dyak	1
	Kannada	4		Senoi	1
	Malayan	4		Bajan	1
	Oriya	4			
	Rajasthani	3			
	Punjabi	2			

Table II. (continued)

STATE (estimated population in parentheses)	Ethnolinguistic Groups by Percentage of Population		STATE	Ethnolinguistic Groups by Percentage of Population	
Maldive (110 thousand)	**		Thailand (36 million)	Thai	60
				Lao	25
				Chinese	10
Mauritius (800 thousand)	Indo-Maritian	67		Malay	3
	Creole	27		Khmer	1
	Chinese	4			
			Turkey (35 million)	Turk	92
Mongolia (1 million)	Khalka Mongol	76		Kurd	6
	Other Mongol	13		Arab	1
	Kaskh	5			
	Other Turkic	2	Vietnam, North (21 million)	Vietnamese	85
	Chinese	1		Tho	3
	Russian	1		Muong	2
				Tai	2
Nepal (11 million)	Pahari-Nepali	49		Nung	2
	Tarai	24		Chinese	1
	Tamang	6		Meo	1
	Newar	5		Yao	1
	Thary	4			
	Magar	3	Vietnam, South (18 million)	Vietnamese	87
	Rai	3		Chinese	5
	Curung	2		Khmer	3
	Limbu	2		Mountain Chain Tribes	3
	Bhote	1		Mon-Khmer Tribes	1
Pakistan (50 million)	Punjabi	66			
	Sindhi	13			
	Pushtun	8			
	Urdu	8			
	Baluchi	2			
	Brahui	1			
Phillipines (38 million)	Cebuano	24			
	Tagalog	21			
	Ilocano	12			
	Hiligaynon	10			
	Bicol	8			
	Samar-Leyte	6			
	Pampangan	3			
	Pangasinan	3			
Singapore (1 million)	Chinese	75			
	Malay	14			
	Indian-Pakistani*	8			
Taiwan (15 million)	Taiwanese	79			
	Han	19			
	Aborigines	2			

* Otherwise undifferentiated.
** Statistics not available, Diverse Arab, Dravidian, and Sinhalese strains.

forces within a state (e.g., a small ethnic group may be wooed assiduously by all sides involved in a competitive situation), (c) the form of government (in general, the more democratic, the more responsive to group pressure), (d) disproportionate representation in strategic or highly visible occupations and positions (the "overseas Chinese" are a case in point), and (e) the demographic distribution of the ethnic group. The last factor is often of key importance, and underlines the need to employ ethnic statistics or an ethnic map only in conjunction with one another. Their co-use lessens the chance of serious distortion.

Ethnic minorities often inhabit disproportionately large territories. Thus, though minorities constitute less than 6 percent of the PRC's population, their historic homelands account for more than half of that country's territory; similarly, though the Vietnamese account for more than 85 percent of the population in both North and South Vietnam, in each case they account for less than 30 percent of the total territory. Moreover, the significance of an ethnic group is often enhanced by the strategic value of their territory. Within Malaysia, for example, the concentration of Chinese in the economically and politically important urban areas reflects a disproportionate influence relative to that of the rural-dwelling Malays. Who controls the capital and its environs can be particularly significant; thus, Tamils and other southern people of India tend to view New Delhi as the captive of northern elements. Perhaps even more important in terms of strategic location is that, with very few exceptions, it is not the dominant groups who populate the border regions of Asia's mainland states. Afghanistan, Bangla Desh, Bhutan, Burma, Cambodia, China, Iran, Laos, Nepal, Pakistan, Thailand, Turkey, and Vietnam are all largely or totally afflicted by this phenomenon. Moreover, no matter what group populates the borderlands, the political border seldom corresponds with an ethnic border. Along the many thousands of miles of land borders that divide Asian states, it is unusual to encounter even a few-mile stretch in which the border does not bisect an ethnic group.

The possible ramifications that this conflict between ethnic and state borders holds for Asian politics would be difficult to exaggerate.[4] Nationally (i.e., ethnically) conscious peoples are not likely to view a political division of their group as legitimate; Kurdish disdain for the borders that divide their nation into Iraqi, Irani, Syrian, Soviet, and Turkish components is illustrative. It is nevertheless difficult to generalize concerning either the manner in which demands for the rectification of this discrepancy in borders are likely to manifest themselves or the depth of the commitment underlying such demands. Governmental campaigns for uniting a politically divided people are often only a ploy in a game for much larger stakes. Thus, appeals made by the governments of the PRC and the Soviet Union to the ethnic sensibilities of the other's minorities constitute but a single stratagem in the rivalry of these titanic states. Similarly, Afghanistan's support for self-determination of Pakistan's Pushtuns and Iran's support for Iraqi Kurds can only be understood as part of a larger strategy. On the other hand, a government, with or without enthusiasm, may be acting primarily in response to irredentist pressure emanating from that part of the politically divided group dwelling within its own jurisdiction. Thus, while official Cambodian support for the Khmers living within Thailand and Vietnam is a domestically popular course of action, there is no reason to suspect the genuineness of the ardor with which Sihanouk and his successors have pursued this policy. By contrast, there is evidence that New Delhi was

only reluctantly forced by events and by growing pressure from her own Bengali people to commit herself to a separate state of Bangla Desh. It is also possible that demands for dissolving a border that violates an ethnic homeland may operate quite independently of the policies, as well as the wishes, of all governments. Thus, Kurdish demands for a single state of Kurdistan run counter to the wishes of Iraq, Iran, Syria, Turkey, and the Soviet Union.[5]

(3) The fact that the borders of so many states bisect ethnic groups points up still another serious inadequacy of the statistical approach set forth in Table II. The state-by-state treatment ignores the fact that many of the most volatile ethnic situations involve two or more states. Moreover, the state-by-state approach implies an equality of significance among states and tends to obscure mammoth differences in this regard. The resulting distortions can be quite pronounced. Thus, Table II quite arbitrarily employs one percent of each state's population as the minimal figure for statistical significance. Following this guideline, the Nagas and Mizos, both of whom have posed real problems for the Indian Government, do not appear in the Table. Meanwhile, groups such as the Meo and Mon-Khmer appear as important segments of the population of Laos. However, these states are so disparate in size of population that one percent of India's population is greater than the total population of Laos.

III

With the preceding qualifications in mind, we turn to an ethnopolitical survey of non-Arab Asian states. The grouping of states into three regional categories (Eastern Asia, Southeast Asia, and South and Southwest Asia) is purely arbitrary.

Eastern Asia:

The seven states treated under this heading are Japan, the two Koreas, Mongolia, China, Taiwan, and the Philippines. There are no generalities that can be made concerning their ethnic composition, for they range from essentially homogeneous to complex.

Japan is the world's most populous state that deserves to be called homogeneous. Excluding aliens, the only non-Japanese element consists of a small and diminishing number of aborigines who are characterized by Aryan features and are called the Ainu. Both of the Koreas are also essentially homogeneous. The salient ethnopolitical fact concerning the Koreans is therefore their political bisection which has created an irredentist situation. The government of North Korea is uncompromisingly committed to union, and it illustrated in 1950 its willingness to use force to this end. More recently, following the 1971 announcement that the American President would visit Peking, North Korean officials indicated a desire to promote union by more peaceful means. The Chinese-North Korean border also bisects Koreans, and the resulting irredenta within China may well someday become a factor influencing Chinese-Korean relations.

China contains what is easily the world's largest ethnic group, the Han. In speculating upon those elements that most contributed to the successful incorporation of so large a number into a single ethnic group, three factors appear particularly noteworthy. The first factor was the availability of adequate time as a result of political unification under a number of dynasties stretching back over thousands of years. The second factor was the development and adoption of a pictographic, rather than a phonetic alphabet. This type of alphabet permitted a common means of written communication among the people of widely separated regions at a time when communications and transportation technology were not sufficiently developed to permit interregional contracts of such an intensity as to give rise to a single oral language.[6] A common cultural and, ultimately, a national consciousness was thereby made possible. A third element, only speciously contradicting the second, is that from the beginning the Chinese Empire had an effective communication system because the Empire developed along river systems which were interconnected toward their mouths by canals and at their mouths by costal waters. As shown by the earliest civilizations along the Nile, Tigris-Euphrates, and Indus Rivers, as well as by later coastal empires such as the Athenian and early Roman, navigable rivers and coastal waters have for millennia constituted channels of continuous and pervasive contacts between widely separated people. By contrast, the ethnic map of China (see Figure 1) illustrates the relative lack of influence that Han culture exerted upon the hinterland of

Figure 1. Ethnologuistic Composition of the People's Republic of China

National Autonomous Regions

Inner Mongolian Autonomous Region: Mongols
Kwangsi Autonomous Region: Chuang
Ninghsia Autonomous Region: Mohammedans (Hul)
Sinkiang Uighur Autonomous Region: I-li (Kazakh), K'e-tzu-le-su (Khalka), Ch'ang-chi (Hui)
Tibetan Autonomous Region: Tibetans

Larger Provincial Minority Autonomous Districts (Chou)

Hainan
South: Li and Miao
Hunan
West: Tuchia and Miao
Kirin
East: (Yen-pien border): Korean
Kweichow
Southeast: Miao, Tung
South: Puyi, Miao
Szechuan
West (Kan-tzu, A-pa areas): Tibetan
South (Liang-shan): Yi

Tsinghai
West (Kuo-lo, Yu-shu): Tibetan
Northwest (Hai-hsi): Mongol, Kazakh, Tibetan
East: (Hai-pei, Hai-nan, Huang-nan): Tibetan
Yunnan (Shan)
South: Thai, Chingpo, Hani, Yi
Northwest: Lisu, Tibetan
West: Pai, Thai, Chingpo, Chu-ang, Miao
Central: Yi

the Empire. The Han Chinese have until very recently been restricted to the eastern third of the country. The ethnic map of China also illustrates a factor touched upon earlier; despite the fact that the minorities account for only 6 percent of China's population, they possess a disproportionate strategic significance because their homelands represent more than 50 percent of the total area, including practically all of the borderlands. The ethnic map, however, can no longer be assumed to indicate accurately the dominant group in each area, for as a matter of government policy, literally millions of Hans have been relocated in minority areas since 1950. This practice, plus a traditional hostility on the part of the minorities toward the Chinese because of the latter's penchant for treating non-Chinese as cultural inferiors, plus the desire of the minorities not to lose their national identities, plus irredentist propaganda broadcast from the Soviet Union and Mongolia, have combined to keep China's minority situation restive.

Mongolia has important ethnic and linguistic minorities of both Mongolian and non-Mongolian heritage, but, as in the case of the Koreans, the most salient aspect of ethnic distribution is the division of Mongols by state borders. There are substantial numbers of Mongols living on either side of the Chinese-Mongolian border. Unlike the case of the North and South Koreas, however, the bifurcated people are dominant in just one of the adjoining states, forming only a small minority in the other. But despite the fact that the Mongols within China represent only an approximate 0.2 percent of China's population, they nevertheless slightly outnumber the entire population of Mongolia. In the absence of allies, it would clearly be unwise for Mongolia to provoke China by advancing irredentist claims, but the close alliance between Mongolia and the Soviet Union has caused the political allegiance of the Mongol people to be a factor in the rivalry of the two Marxist-Leninist giants. Appeals to Mongol unity, including references to past Mongol greatness under Ghenghis Khan and, more pointedly, under Kublai Khan -- the conqueror of China -- have been beamed into China's Inner Mongolia. Though China veils internal discord, symptoms of unrest among its Mongol population have occasionally surfaced.[7]

There are also Mongols living immediately across a sector of Mongolia's northern border shared with the Soviet Union, primarily within the Buryat-Mongol Autonomous Soviet Socialist Republic. We shall later note that the fact that minority peoples of Turkey, Iran, and Afghanistan extend across the Soviet border increases the vulnerability of these states to political pressures emanating from Moscow. The case of Mongolia is distinguished, however, by the fact that Mongols are clearly the dominant element within that state. Those within its confines have thus realized national self-determination. Therefore, if one could ignore power realities (or if, which appears most unlikely, Mongolia should become more closely allied with China at the expense of its Soviet ties), it is the Soviet Union rather than Mongolia which would be at the greatest disadvantage in regard to the political distribution of Mongol people. From all that has been said, it is evident that the triangular relations of the Soviet Union, China, and Mongolia will be heavily affected by the level of ethnic nationalism among the Mongols. But despite a history of empire and the existence of a separate Mongol state since 1921, ethnic awareness *per se* has been relatively slight, in large part due to the traditional nomadic lifeways of the Mongol which cause any grouping beyond the nomadic unit to be viewed as remote. However, as a result of the introduction of industrialization and of intentional governmental policy, the people are being diverted into sedentary occupations, and an increasing identification with the Mongol nation may grow apace.

Taiwan's major ethnic group is an offshoot nation. Although the ancestors of the Taiwanese were Han and came from Mainland China, the island fell under Japanese control from 1895 to 1945. There are little available hard data on public attitudes, but it is widely held that the Taiwanese increasingly came to consider themselves a separate nation during this period when they were largely isolated from the mainland by their Japanese overlords (Bessac, 1967). The decision of the victorious powers to return the island to Chinese control after World War II was made without regard for Taiwanese attitudes. The situation was further inflamed by a massive influx of mainlanders as a result of the evacuation of the mainland by the Nationalists under Chiang Kai-shek. The mainlanders, who represent approximately 20 percent of the island's population, have subsequently dominated the island's government while keeping the more violent manifestations of Taiwanese indignation suppressed by expelling or incarcerating potential Taiwanese nationalistic leaders. The present governments of both Taiwan and mainland China describe Taiwan as merely one of the more than twenty provinces comprising greater China, a designation hardly consonant with a Taiwanese desire for independence. The result is a unique situation in which two governments -- in part on ethnic grounds -- lay claim to the allegiance of a people who consider themselves ethnically distinct from both.

Despite hundreds of years of nominal political unity under Spanish, then American, and now independent rule, the Philippine archipelago has never been culturally integrated. Ethnic descriptions of the Philippines are apt to be particularly misleading because governmental statistics, though purporting to show majority-minority ratios, limit themselves to racial distinctions. Thus, the only reported minorities consist of a handful of Chinese, Negritoes, Europeans, and people tracing their ancestry to India. *In toto*, these disparate peoples account for less than one percent of the population. Lumped under the general heading of Filipino, however, are a variety of ethnic groups, speaking more than eighty different languages and dialects (see Figure 2). The absence of intensive historic contact between the groups is pointed up by the fact that the four major indigenous tongues (Cebuano, Tagalog, Iloko, and Hiligaynon which are the primary tongues of respectively 25, 21, 14, and 12 percent of the population) are mutually unintelligible. And unlike the case of China, this barrier to a

single group-identity has not been offset by a single written language or other common system of communication. The government is intent upon developing a common tongue, but, as of 1970, only some 40 percent of the population could converse in English and an overlapping group of approximately the same number could understand Tagalog. In the absence of a single cultural tradition that is coextensive with the Republic, primary identities closely parallel linguistic patterns, and gulfs between the various groups are wide and deep. One of the principal reasons for the failure of the guerrilla Hukbalahap movement that sprang up in central Luzon following World War II was that the Huks came to be identified with a single ethnolinguistic group and were greeted as an alien force when they attempted to penetrate into other cultural areas (Liberman, 1966: 26,27). Ethnocultural divisions have also underlay the periodic outbursts of violence occasioned by the resistance of the indigenous peoples of the southern Philippines to settlement by the Christian "outsiders" from more northerly parts of the country. A Moslem organization (MIM) openly proclaims secession from the Republic as its goal.

Southeast Asia:

Under this heading we include that tier of states stretching from Burma and Malaysia eastward to the Vietnams and Indonesia. All of these states are ethnically complex, containing several distinct ethnic groups.

Figure 2. Major Ethnolinguistic Groups of the Philippines

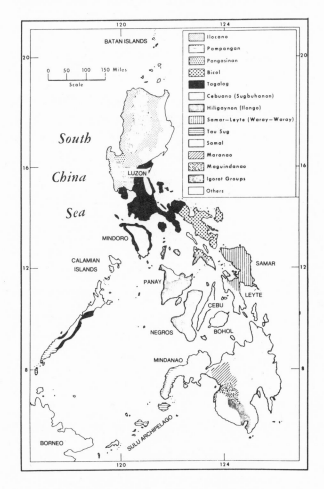

A comprehensive investigation of the ethnic composition of Indonesia has never occurred. The number of distinct ethnic groups is known to substantially exceed sixty, and it has been estimated that more than four hundred languages are spoken throughout the archipelago. This picture of ethnic and linguistic complexity is alleviated somewhat by the fact that the dominant Javanese account for 45 percent of the total population, and by a government-instituted program to impose a single state language, Bahase Indonesian. However, the ethnic consciousness of the individual groups has not shown evidence of giving way to the concept of membership in a single Javanese nationhood. Popular references to the dominant Javanese as "Javanese colonialists" or "brown Dutchmen" indicate the level of dissatisfaction with the present ethnopolitical structure (Hanna, 1967: 70). In its short history of independence, the government has had to suppress a number of anti-Javanese separatist movements. Self-determination movements in the South Moluccas and in the southern Celebes have proven to be particularly resilient. Violent resistance to Jakarta's control of West Irian (western New Guinea) also appears unlikely to abate; and the eastern half of the island, once it achieves its scheduled independence from Australia, is likely to provide sanctuary for an irredentist-liberation movement. Another source of severe ethnic tension within Indonesia has been the immigrant Chinese, who here as elsewhere throughout Southeast Asia conjure up a popular impression

of a presence out of all proportion to their actual numbers and who have periodically paid for that image of pre-eminence by being the targets of appallingly savage pogroms.

The mainland sector of the region which we have termed Southeast Asia is composed of six states and part of another, Malaysia. As the ethnic map of this region makes evident (see Figure 3), the ethnic pattern is incredibly intricate. The map also illustrates a number of principles to which we earlier alluded.

First, the map indicates the wisdom of employing ethnic statistics only in conjunction with a knowledge of ethnic distributions and vice versa, for with few exceptions the minorities of the region are more strategically significant than their numbers would indicate. For example, although there is a dominant group comprising a majority within Burma and Laos, in each instance more than half of the state's territory is populated by minorities. As noted, North and South Vietnam offer similar patterns. The map also illustrates that it is the minorities and not the dominant group who tend to populate the border regions. Consequently, without exception, every interstate landborder in the region could be cited as justification for irredentist claims by one or both states.

Still another consideration made evident by the map is the crazy-quilt quality of the distribution of a number of groups. Rather than inhabiting a single, contiguous area, some groups are separated into a number of widely spread, tiny enclaves. Such a distribution lengthens ethnic borders and increases interethnic contacts, thereby increasing the potentiality for ethnic tensions. It also raises the question of whether non-contiguous segments of an ethnic group can share a common nationhood. In the past, poor communications within the region have isolated various ethnic islands from each other, but an awareness of the existence of ethnically akin, yet geographically and politically separated counterparts, is almost certain to grow very rapidly, furnishing data against which to test such speculations.

Finally, the ethnic map, when contrasted with the physical map, vividly illustrates the immense impact that topography has often exerted upon ethnicity. Nowhere is this relationship more clear than in the case of mainland South East Asia. Within most of the states, the most numerous and dominant group (the group which has given its name to the state) is a lowland people, strung out along river valleys and coasts and surrounded by other ethnic groups living in highlands. Thus, in the case of Burma, a coexamination of the linguistic and relief maps illustrates that the Burmese-speaking people are limited essentially to the valleys of the Irrawaddy and Sittang Rivers, their deltas, and a stretch of coastal plain. The surrounding highlands are populated by a number of non-Burmese peoples, including the Mons, Karens, Shans, Kachins, and Chins.

The case of Thailand is very similar. The dominant, Siamese-speaking Thais populate the valley of the Chao Praya River, its delta, and the coastal areas. Surrounding the Thais are Malays, Karens, Khmers (Cambodians), Lao, and, in the northern reaches, hill-tribesmen of varied ethnic background. By far the largest minority is the Lao-speaking people of the northeast. Were it not for the intervening mountains that form the watershed between the Chao Praya and the Mekong River systems, it is very probable that the Lao and Thais would comprise a single ethnic group. Both are lowland dwellers and probably have an interrelated

Figure 3. Ethnolinguistic Groups of Mainland Southeast Asia

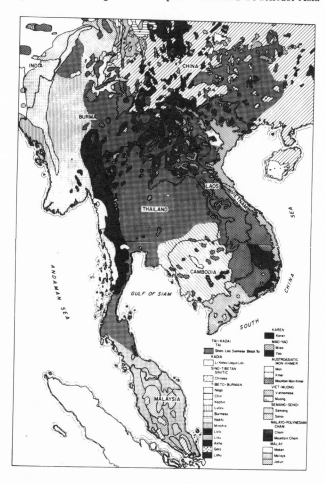

ancestry, as indicated by the fact that the two languages are from the same family. However, the topography severely limited communication between the two river systems, and two highly differentiable dialects resulted. With contacts minimized, there was also the growth of a feeling of uniqueness that developed sufficiently to cause the Lao to perceive the Siamese in terms of an "us-them" syndrome (Keyes, 1966).

The Lao are today a politically bisected people because the Mekong River forms the interstate border between Thailand and Laos. A river has often been viewed by a far distant peace conference as an attractive means of demarcating a border due to the river's geographic definiteness. Unfortunately, however, seldom do rivers make good ethnic borders, because a river valley usually constitutes a single network of intensive contacts which have been maintained for centuries. As a result, both sides of a navigable river are most likely to be populated by a single people. In the case at hand, the resulting division of the Lao people is similar in one important respect to that which we noted in the case of the Mongol people. Those Lao living within Thailand, although a minority, are nevertheless approximately four times more numerous than those Lao who represent a clear majority within the state bearing the Lao name. Laos also contains important minorities, and their distribution again conforms to the highland-lowland, dominant-minority pattern. The vast mountain regions are inhabited by a number of non-Lao peoples.

This same pattern is evident in the cases of North and South Vietnam, for the dominant Vietnamese are clearly a lowland-dwelling people. In a pattern vaguely reminiscent of the outline of an hourglass, they occupy the Red River Valley and its delta in the north of the country; the lower Mekong River Valley and the neighboring, canal-infested, Cochin China plain in the south; and an interconnecting coastal plain in between. Except in the far south, the Vietnamese have been effectively cut off from pervasive contacts with the rest of mainland South East Asia by a mountain chain which is populated by remote hill-tribesmen of diverse ethnic strains.

Immediately to the west of South Vietnam lies Cambodia, the state with the most homogeneous territory in South East Asia. There are important Chinese pockets, but they are concentrated in small areas.[8] With the important exception of the northeast, a large area sparsely populated by diverse hill people, the Khmers (popularly known as Cambodians) are spread throughout the country and spill across into neighboring Vietnam and Thailand as well. Finally, in the case of mainland Malaysia, the Malays predominate in the coastal areas, almost encircling numerically important aborigines in the mountainous interior. Malaysia's two most important minorities, the Chinese and Tamils, tend to concentrate in urban areas.

Clearly, then, if one disregards the case of migrations which have occurred to or within the area during the past three hundred years (the "overseas" Chinese, people from India, etc.), it is apparent that topography, because of its impact upon communication patterns, has played a key role in the composition of ethnic groups. It is also evident that many of the major problems of contemporary South East Asia are the *in tandem* consequence of the attempt to integrate within single states what have hitherto been effectively separated highland and riverine-coastal culture groups.

Ethnopolitical awareness varies greatly among the region's peoples. In some instances, the meaningful world is still coterminous with the village and ethnic consciousness therefore lies in the future. In general, however, the major minorities have evidenced a high degree of ethnocultural awareness and an aversion to being ruled by their state's dominant group. Moreover, though ethnic nationalism is a matter of group self-consciousness, this need not rule out the possibility of an outside force acting as a catalyst. Hanoi and/or Peking have sponsored a national liberation front for each of the non-communist states of mainland South East Asia. The programs of these organizations contain promises that the minorities shall enjoy at least cultural autonomy, if not total political independence. Propaganda, conveyed by individuals, by radio, and by written word, has been aimed at driving wedges between the minorities and the dominant group of their respective state by stressing the thematic question: "Why should you be ruled by those _____ (fill in Burmese, Khmer, Lao, Malay, or Thai) foreigners?" As in the case of the minorities of China, the chance of this propaganda being successful is greatly enhanced by the historical tendency of the lowlander to treat the minority highlander contemptuously as an inferior. The propaganda is also buttressed by military and economic assistance (Connor, 1969).

It is difficult, if not impossible, to measure the contribution that these external stimulants have made to the growth of ethnic consciousness and political unrest throughout the era. Unquestionably, the impact varies greatly from group to group. In some instances, for example within Burma, open warfare between the minorities and the dominant element antedated the assumption of power by the Marxist-Leninist governments of either Peking (1949) or Hanoi (1954), and there is little reason to suspect that these struggles would by now have ended had Peking and Hanoi not become involved. In other situations, such as that within Laos, Chinese and Vietnamese agitprop activities were probably the key factor in crystallizing ethnic consciousness among the hill-tribes and in focusing it against the ruling ethnic group. But in any event, as best illustrated by continued unrest among the minorities within China and North Vietnam, the cause is less important than the fact of ethnic consciousness, for once created, ethnic consciousness does not respond slavishly to calls for its demise (for evidence of minority unrest within China and North Vietnam, see Connor, 1969:75,76). And ethnic consciousness is today a vital force challenging the unity of each of the region's states. Thus, Rangoon's rule is essentially limited to the area populated by the ethnically Burmese, and Bangkok's effective rule is limited to the Siamese-speaking areas of Thailand. Prince Norodom Sihanouk, who, prior to his overthrow in 1970, was almost revered by his Khmer subjects, was unable to effect his will among the non-Khmer minorities in the northeastern sector of his state. In Laos, the Peking- and Hanoi-supported insurrectionist group called the Pathet Lao was composed almost entirely of non-Lao prior to its assumption of power in 1975. And in South Vietnam, the diverse, highland peoples (montagnards) were united only in their conviction that they did not wish to be dominated by Vietnamese, whether from North or South.

It is Malaysia, however, even though geographically far removed from China and North Vietnam, which offers the most intriguing case study of ethnic conflict. The creation and subsequent history of Malaysia as an independent state are inextricably interwound with ethnic distributions and tensions. Malays and the more recently arrived Chinese have long been uneasy neighbors in this former British colony. How to design a political structure that would allay ethnic fears and jealousies was therefore a major preoccupation of the British as independence loomed. The British first comtemplated a single, unitary, peninsular state in which rights would not be associated with ethnicity. But under Malay pressure, this plan was scrapped in favor of a federal system in which the Malays and their culture (including the Malay language and the Islamic religion) were guaranteed privileged status. In this revised form, the Federation of Malaysia achieved independence in 1957. As created, Malays comprised approximately one-half of the population, and the Chinese slightly over one-third. This ratio was radically altered in 1963, when political and economic considerations partially outweighed ethnic considerations in the deliberations of the Malayan authorities, and Singapore, along with two former British dependencies on Borneo (Sarawak and Sabah), were permitted to join with the Federation to create the new state of Malaysia.[9] People of Chinese background clearly predominated within Singapore, and the result of the merger was a state in which the Chinese now slightly outnumbered the Malays, 41.2 percent to 30.2 percent respectively. The Malay leaders believed that a combination of factors would render the change in ethnic composition harmless. Included were (1) the physical separation of the Chinese among Singapore, Borneo, and the Malay Peninsula; (2) an informal understanding that the Chinese political leadership in Singapore would make no attempt to appeal to the Chinese in other areas; and (3) the continuation of constitututionally guaranteed privileges for the Malays. Contrary to these anticipations, the merger hardened positions along ethnic lines, as political leaders blatantly appealed to ethnic loyalties and fears on a state-wide basis. Ethnic riots in Singapore in July of 1964 heralded the death of the new state, and formal separation of Singapore from Malaysia took place the following summer. The union had lasted less than two years. There have subsequently been sporadic reports that many of the indigenous, non-Malay peoples of Sarawak and Sabah also harbor a desire for political separation. And on the peninsula, several bloody struggles between the Chinese and Malays have erupted, casting serious doubt upon the continued viability of even the original federation.

Malaysia has also been troubled for decades by a communist, guerrilla movement, and the fortunes of this movement have also been closely linked to ethnicity. This linkage once again underlines the close relationship between ethnic identity and political loyalty. The movement, which surfaced in the immediate post-World War II period, drew both its membership and its support almost exclusively from the Chinese element. The movement was therefore popularly viewed as an alien, Chinese one by the rural Malays. Cut off from the sympathetic support of the villagers, who regularly reported on the whereabouts of guerrilla units to the British and Malay authorities, the movement was unable to marshal a major threat. By 1970, it was reportedly limited to a few hundred guerrillas operating on either side of the Malaysia-Thailand border. Both sides of this border are populated by Malays, but there has been an important difference of attitude toward the guerrillas on either side. On the Malaysian side, the guerrillas have been unable to elicit the sympathy of the local Malay people who perceive the guerrilla's proclaimed enemy, the Malay-dominated government in Kuala Lumpur, as their rightful government. The guerrillas therefore remain an alien force. However, the same guerrillas have been much more effective with the Malays on the Thai side of the border. Here the revolutionaries have been able to ally themselves with local

ethnic resentment of being ruled by the far distant, and linguistically and religiously dissimilar Thais. A warning note may be appropriate, however. That this type of situation need not always result in this combination of alliances is shown by events in the Borneo sector of Malaysia. There, too, a predominantly Chinese insurrectionsist movement has been operating. But it has been encountering severe hostility on the part of the indigenous peoples, particularly the Dyaks, who have apparently been able to simultaneously resent Malay rule and a Chinese presence. Since ethnic groups vary in the type and level of emotions they feel toward different peoples, generalities are hazardous.

South and Southwest Asia:
Under this heading we include the non-Arab, mainland states from Turkey to the western border of Burma, as well as the island states of Cyprus, Ceylon, the Maldive Islands, and Mauritius. All of the states are multiethnic, although the degree of heterogeneity and the magnitude of minority problems vary greatly.

Location and size of population are not accurate indices to these variations, however. Consider, for example, the Himalayan kingdoms of Nepal and Bhutan. They are extremely heterogeneous, and ethnic rivalry and jealousy plague the unity of both of them. In the case of Nepal, the precise number of ethnic groups is now known, but more than thirty distinct languages and a much larger number of dialects are spoken. The problems arising from this diversity are still manageable because most people are unaware of their membership in the state. Meaningful awareness of the government is confined essentially to the Katmandu Valley.[10] However, as the government has attempted in recent years to extend its control over other sections of the country, ethnic frictions have arisen and separatist sentiments have been voiced by peoples along the southern, lowland border with India, as well as by people living in the eastern hills. Nepal is a relatively populous state by global standards, but the relatively small population of neighboring Bhutan is also characterized by ethnic diversity and by little transethnic, state-wide sentiment.

The development and perserverence of so many tongues and distinct ethnic groups within the Himalayan area testifies to the historic, negative impact that the huge mountain range has exerted upon pervasive, intergroup communications. Yet, paradoxically, the very ease of accessibility helps to account for the ethnic heterogeneity of the small island states of Maldive and Mauritius. Secessionist sentiments in the southern Maldives have corresponded with an ethnic cleavage, and ethnic rioting marred the independence of Mauritius in 1968. But while all states of the area are therefore susceptible to the forces of ethnic factionalism, India, Ceylon, and Pakistan appear to be the most vulnerable.

India approximates, as nearly as any state, an ideal laboratory for the student of ethnic nationalism. Indeed, anyone who has seriously reflected on the plausibility of achieving and maintaining world government might do well to investigate carefully the case of India. Is world government practical? A reasonable case could be made that it is currently being tried in India on a scale too large to be called microcosmic. Here, in a single political unit, are contained well over a half-billion people of the most diverse strains. The great multiethnic empires of history (including the Macedonian, Roman, Islamic, Mongol, Moghul, and Holy Roman) shrink into insignificance in comparison, for the present population of India is greater than was the entire population of the world as recently as the mid-17th Century. And, although less populous than China, there is, unlike the situation in China, no single ethnic group that accounts for most of this number. The diversity is awesome (see Figure 4). All major racial types are represented. At least 1600

Figure 4. Ethnolinguistic Composition of Bangla Desh, Ceylon, India, and Pakistan

different tongues are spoken, and thirteen of these are each the primary tongue of more than five million people, a figure in turn greater than the total population of many independent states.

Given this ethnic mosaic, and a host of other divisive issues[11], the fact that India has survived for more than a quarter of a century is in itself eminently significant. But at the same time, it must be noted that New Delhi has been faced by a number of secessionist movements and that India's history as an independent state has been marked by a clear trend toward ever greater decentralization along ethnic lines. A series of concessions to the various major ethnic groups has been the price of preserving Indian unity. Demands for the retention of their own particular languages, for the drawing of provincial borders to accord with ethnolinguistic distributions, and for other concessions to cultural autonomy have in the typical situation resulted in governmental capitulation. But although such concessions have thus far preserved unity, Kashmiri agitation in the northwest and armed independence movements by the Mizo and Nagas in the northeast offer ominous evidence of the intensity of ethnic convictions and the warning that cultural autonomy is likely to prove only a temporary palliative. It is clear, in any event, that for many the unifying idea of being Indian has not yet replaced in their value system the concept of being Tamil, Bengali, Sikh or any one of the numerous other nations within India.

Ethnicity has also played a key role in India's relations with her neighbors. Admittedly, it would be a gross exaggeration to blame Indian-Pakistani hostility simply upon the Kashmiri question: more to blame are religion and history, particularly the tragic history of mass murder and large-scale suffering that accompanied partition in 1947. Yet, India's insistence on retaining the most valuable segments of Jammu and Kashmir with total disregard for the desires of the Kashmiri people, perpetuates, if not exacerbates, Pakistani hostility. Why has India been so intransigent in this matter? Why has she steadfastly taken precautions to insure that the sentiments of the Kashmiri people not be definitively ascertained? Beginning with Nehru, Indian leaders have refused to permit a plebiscite despite earlier promises to have effect and despite a series of UN resolutions for a plebiscite dating back as far as 1948. Meanwhile, Kashmir has remained essentially an occupied territory, with both its population and leadership subjected to rigorous police control.[12] India's policy on Kashmir therefore obstructs substantial improvement in relations with Pakistan and also renders India vulnerable to charges of reneging on promises, of snubbing UN resolutions, of violating a number of basic, democratic concepts, and of denying the principle of self-determination of nations. Part of her intransigence is unquestionably due to the economic and strategic potentiality of the area in question. A second factor is that the Kashmiri issue was almost immediately elevated to a highly emotional plateau within India, as within Pakistan, and any political party which surrenders Kashmir would certainly be pilloried by the political opposition and would probably be ousted from office. Still another major factor is the fear of precedent. The multinational state, just as the multinational empire, can recognize the internal legitimacy of self-determination of nations only at the peril of further disintegration.

India's relations with Ceylon have also been heavily influenced by ethnic considerations. Ceylon's dominant element, the Sinhalese, account for approximately 70 percent of the island's population. Tamils form the largest minority (more than 20 percent of the total population), but they are divided nearly equally into Ceylon Tamils (those whose ancestry arrived in Ceylon during the Middle Ages) and Indian Tamils (those whose ancestors arrived since the mid-19th Century). In addition to this historic distinction, the settlement pattern of the two Tamil groups has caused them to be geographically distinct. The Sinhalese have followed a divide-and-rule strategy designed to enhance their domination relative to all Tamils by stressing and appealing to this cleavage. Indian Tamils are denied the same legal, political, and social rights enjoyed by the Ceylonese Tamils.

Ethnic relations have been far from harmonious. The Sinhalese have pressed for special privileges and have made their language (Sinhala) the sole official tongue. They have also succeeded in denying citizenship to most Indian Tamils, while insisting on their deportation. Dissension on the part of the minorities has been endemic, manifesting itself in sporadic violence and in the expression of separatist sentiments.

The Ceylon situation cannot be separated from India's internal politics. Tamizhgam (home of the Tamils) is located in southeastern India, immediately across the narrow straits from Ceylon. The Tamils within India constitute about 7 percent of that country's population and therefore represent a significant force in Indian politics. The program of the dominant party in Tamizhgam (the DMK) calls for a single political union embracing all Tamils, including those in

Ceylon, where the movement has some adherents. Because the Tamils are a potent force in Indian politics, because of the interest of the Tamils within India in the fortunes of their ethnic kin abroad, and because Tamil ethnic nationalism within India has proven to be a volatile force requiring very little provoation to break out in denunciations of New Delhi or in pro-separatist activities, the Indian Government has often felt compelled to act as the guardian of the rights of Tamils within Ceylon. The level of restiveness among Ceylon's Tamil minority is therefore one barometer of Indian-Ceylonese relations. An indication of the pressure that this bi-state ethnic distribution exerts upon New Delhi can be seen in an agreement between the two states signed in 1964. Under its terms, badly overpopulated India agreed to the repatriation of more than a half-million Indian Tamils over a fifteen year period. And a reflection of Sinhalese prejudice against this minority can be seen in the reaction to an attempt by the Ceylonese government four years later to implement, at least in token fashion, their part of the agreement. Even a proposal to grant citizenship to a tiny fraction of the 300,000 members of the Indian Tamil community who were promised citizenship under the treaty was attacked by the opposition as a means of buying votes in the coming election.[13]

The Indian Government's policies involving Kashmiri and Tamil nationalism help to explain its policies during the 1950s and 1960s toward what was then East Pakistan. Avid and growing resentment on the part of the Bengalis of East Pakistan toward West Pakistani control was a poorly concealed fact. Given the poor relations between India and Pakistan, the seemingly logical course of action for New Delhi would have been to encourage Bengali separatist sentiments, thus depriving her primary enemy of more than 50 percent of its population and eradicating the risk of a two-front war. India's hesitancy to ride Pakistan's major trojan horse again reflected her own ethnic problems. Possible reactions among her own restive minorities to governmental support for Bengali self-determination must have been a major consideration. The inconsistency of espousing Bengali separatism while forcibly denying the same right to Nagas, Mizos, and others would certainly be pointed out. Then there was the matter of India's own 45 million Bengalis. So long as East Pakistan was viewed as part of the theocratic Islamic Republic, its appeal to India's predominantly Hindu Bengalis would be tempered. But the attractiveness of a secular Bengali state would be much greater. India's reluctance to support a radical change in the *status quo* is therefore understandable. Separatist sentiments within East Pakistan grew stronger even in the absence of New Delhi's support, however, and the outbreak of a secessionist, guerrilla war forced the Indian authorities to re-evaluate their position. Though the stream of Bengali refugees into India was given as the official reason for the latter's decision to intervene militarily on the side of the Bengalis, it is more probable that the key elements were the realization that events had proceeded too far to be reversed and that the activities of her own Bengali people made clear that they would not much longer countenance New Delhi inaction in the face of reports of massive Pakistani atrocities being committed against their Bengali kin.

The creation of Bangla Desh is significant for a number of reasons. Authorities on the South Asian region had long maintained that religion, rather than ethnicity, determined basic identity in the area. Pakistan and India had divided essentially on religious grounds, and Pakistan had subsequently attempted to maintain her multiethnic state by stressing the common Moslem faith of her inhabitants. Although India ostensibly became a secular state, the spectre of a threatening, encircling Islamic enemy was an important element in the mystique of an India trying to hold disparate ethnic elements together. Bangla Desh exploded this myth of primary identity being determined by religion rather than by ethnicity. Desperate, last-chance attempts by the authorities to save the Pakistani union by identifying Hindu Bengalis as the sole source of separatist sentiment and by exhorting the Moslem Bengalis to wreak their vengenance upon the Hindu minority failed miserably. Only the non-Bengali Moslems (Biharis) did so. And as already noted, India's own predomininatly Hindu Bengali community evidenced a strong feeling of solidarity with their Bengali kin across the border.

The secession of the Bengalis will also serve as a symbol to ethnic groups everywhere that self-determination movements can succeed in a post-colonial situation and, as such, should steel the resolve of similar movements presently underway, while acting as a catalyst for still others. Its impact as a symbol should be greatest, however, upon South Asia, particularly upon India and former West Pakistan, and most particularly upon the Indian Bengalis. That such prognostications are more than idle theorizing is shown by the new propaganda campaign on the part of India's Tamilnad movement (DMK), which has stressed a number of embarrassing parallels between West Pakistan's former domination of East Pakistan and New Delhi's present control of Tamizhgam. Moreover, the creation of Bangla Desh set off increased demands for greater independence within what was formerly called West Pakistan.

The surviving segment of Pakistan is itself divided into a number of self-differentiating ethnic groups. An attempt was made in the early 1950s to erode these distinctions by merging West Pakistan's several provinces into a single unit. The eliminated provinces had corresponded to the major ethnic divisions within the country, and it was feared that the perpetuation of the provinces would therefore act as a continuous reminder (symbol) and reinforcer of the tendency to identify with one's ethnic group at the expense of a Pakistani identity. This attempt at ethnic fusion through institutional centralization failed, and pressures for greater ethnic autonomy led to the recreation of the provinces in 1970. The secession of Bangla Desh signalled an outburst of separatist activities among the Baluchis in the southwest and the Pushtuns in the northwest, and a demand for linguistic autonomy on the part of the Sindhi in the south. Pakistan has thus paralleled India in a trend toward decentralization and ethnic particularism.

Pakistan is also one of those many states whose outer borders bisect ethnic groups. This factor has thus far significantly influenced relations only with Afghanistan, but future problems with Iran and India over the allegiance of divided peoples are a strong possibility.[14] Pakistan's dispute with Afghanistan involves the Pushtun people. No accurate census of these people exists, but it is likely that there are between 10 and 20 million Pushtu-speaking people, divided fairly equally between the two states. However, while constituting only a minority within West Pakistan, the Pushtuns represent a numerical majority and the politically dominant element within Afghanistan.

As a matter of policy, Afghan governments for generations have intrigued among the Pushtun people immediately across their southern border. But while the strategy of intrigue has been a constant element of Afghan foreign policy, the purposes behind the strategy have fluctuated. In the days when a powerful Britain was

Afghanistan's southern neighbor, Kabul desired a restive, unruly population in the border region as a means of keeping the British too preoccupied with pacifying their own territory to permit further involvement in Afghan affairs. The ultimate goal of the policy in those days was therefore defensive. But as British withdrawal from the subcontinent became probable, Kabul envisioned a means of breaking out of its landlocked status by annexing all British-held territory west of the Indus River.[15] The British refused this request and the territory in question became part of the new state of Pakistan. Kabul has subsequently muted talk of annexation, but in its stead has championed the creation of a new state of Pushtunistan, which would consist of precisely the same territory previously requested by Kabul. The ultimate purpose behind the support of Pushtunistan by the Afghan ruling house remains obscure. Perhaps the Afghans view the creation of such a state as leading to annexation. It is certainly not inconceivable that the leaders of the proposed state, being Pushtun, would soon seek union with a neighboring state whose rulers were also Pushtun. Or perhaps the Afghans feel that they could more readily overpower and infiltrate the smaller and weaker state of Pushtunistan. On the other hand, it may well be that the Afghan leaders no longer anticipate union, but simply feel that their influence -- predicated upon ethnic kinship -- would be certain to be greater in a Pushtun state. Minimally, it is safe to conclude that Kabul would prefer a southern neighbor that is weaker rather than stronger than itself.

Whatever Kabul's anticipations, the inconsistencies in its position on Pushtunistan are glaring. Pushtunistan -- literally "land of the Pushtuns" -- would incorporate a large number of non-Pushtun people; indeed, without its proposed inclusion of the great, though sparsely populated territory of the Baluchi people of West Pakistan, Pushtunistan, as Afghanistan, would be landlocked. Secondly, there is no suggestion that the newly created state of the Pushtuns will include the Pushtuns presently within Afghanistan. Thirdly, while the Afghan Government supports the proposition that the ethnicity of the Pushtuns within Pakistan constitutes a legitimate basis for their secession and the subsequent creation of their own state, Afghanistan is itself a complex ethnic hodge-podge.

Afghan inconsistencies in this matter have lent an added flavor to the Soviet Union's position on Pushtunistan. On the occasion of a head-of-state visit in 1955, Premier Khrushev pledged Soviet support for the creation of Pushtunistan. There were many who felt at the time that the Afghan Government's quite evident pleasure concerning this official support should have been dampened by the realization that the principle that ethnicity constitutes the legitimate basis for statehood could at any time be employed by the Soviet Union to challenge Kabul's right to rule over northern Afghanistan. Although southeastern Afghanistan, which includes the capital area, is essentially homogeneous, the country's overall population is characterized by extreme ethnic diversity. Despite the fact that Pushtu-speakers represent approximately 60 percent of the population, more than a score of languages and dialects are spoken by the remaining 40 percent. Afghanistan would appear particularly vulnerable to Soviet machinations in the north, where the Tadzhik, Turkmen, and Uzbeks dwell immediately across the border from the Tadzhik, Uzbek, and Turkmen Soviet Socialist Republics of the Soviet Union.

Despite these fears, the Soviets have thus far courted Kabul, and have not tried to drive wedges between it and its minorities. Moreover, the minorities have not experienced any self-generated surge of interest in greater independence from their Pushtun rulers. Ethnic consciousness remains at a very low level throughout all of Afghanistan, in large part because of ineffective transportation and communication systems. Basic identity is still largely in terms of the village, clan, or tribe, and only a small percentage of the population is aware of the presence of the national government (Area Handbook for Afghanistan, 1969:2-4). Ethnic consciousness can be expected to increase as the communication and transportation facilities improve and as the Kabul government makes its presence increasingly felt throughout the state. Meanwhile, both Afghanistan and the Soviet Union must be fully aware that Moscow can try to stir up nationalistic proclivities whenever Kabul's policies significantly diverge from Soviet interests. From the viewpoint of effectiveness as a technique of foreign policy, appealing to the ethnic aspirations of minorities in another state has much in common with the technique of violence: the threat of its employment may be at least as effective as its actual employment.

As Afghanistan's immediate neighbor to the west is well aware, the Soviet Union has not always been so reticent to manipulate the ethnic aspirations of minorities within neighboring states to its south. During World War II, Soviet occupation forces in Iran supported separatist movements on the part of the Azerbaijani and the Kurds (see Figure 5). Although both movements subsequently succumbed to the Iranian armed forces, one might have expected that the Azerbaijani movement would have proven the more deeply and firmly rooted, in light of the fact that an Azerbaijani Soviet Socialist Republic had long existed immediately across the Soviet border. In point of fact, however, most Kurds resisted the re-establishment of Iranian rule, while the Iranian victory over the Azerbaijani separatists was greeted as

Figure 5. Ethnolinguistic Composition of Iran and Turkey

a-TURKEY

b-IRAN

c-IRAQ

an act of emancipation by the bulk of the Azerbaijani people (Cottam, 1964:particularly 73).

The explanation apparently again lies in the level of ethnic consciousness. The situation that we noted in the case of Afghanistan holds generally true for most groups within Iran and Turkey as well. Outside of the urban area, the meaningful world is still apt to end at the village, the clan, or perhaps the tribe. Consciousness of the ethnic group as a distinct, closely interrelated entity is not yet widespread, and the ethnic groups therefore remain merely ethnic groups, not yet nations.

The Kurds represent a marked exception to these generalities, however, for Kurdish struggles for independence span more than half-a-century. Kurdish representatives appeared at the Peace Conference following World War I to request their own state. Despite their publicly proclaimed commitment to the principle of self-determination, the leaders of the victorious powers were recalcitrant in extending this principle to the Kurds, and the result has been sporadic warfare ever since.[16] Iran was forced to deal with several Kurdish uprisings in the interwar period, and the creation, with Soviet assistance, of an independent Kurdish state within Iran during World War II has already been mentioned. Since the forcible dismemberment of that short-lived Kurdish experiment with independence in 1946, Iran has not been seriously challenged by Kurdish separatism. At least part of the explanation is that the primary target of Kurdish nationalism switched from the Iranian to the Iraqi government. The disdain of the Kurds for political borders that divide the Kurdish homeland (a contiguous territory divided into Iranian, Iraqi, Syrian, Turkish, and Soviet components) is shown by the fact that the principal Kurdish military forces in the struggle against the Iranian Army in 1946 were composed of Barzani, a Kurdish tribe located in Iraq. Throughout the 1950s, 60s, and early 70s this same tribe spearheaded the struggle for autonomy within Iraq. Kurdish strategy, it is clear, has been to concentrate upon one enemy at a time, using the transborder sectors of the Kurdish homeland as sanctuaries and as sources of needed supplies.

Prior to 1975, this strategy was aided by the extremely poor relations between Iran and Iraq. In a multi-faceted dispute with Iran, covering, *inter alia*, spheres of influence in the Persian Gulf area, oil, shipping rights, anti-Israeli attitudes, ideology, and form of government, Iraq and a number of other Arab states stressed the theme that the dominant group within Iran, unlike most of the people in the area of the Persian Gulf, were Persian and not Arab. The potential consequences of this theme were underscored in the late 1960s, when Arab communication media began referring to the Persian Gulf as the Arabian Gulf. Teheran responded by drawing attention to the dominant role played by Iran in the Persian Gulf region for centuries prior to the coming of the British. It did this by resurrecting the term *Persia* as a valid substitute for Iran in official parlance, thereby reintroducing a practice which had been outlawed since 1935. The government must have deemed the matter rather important, for use of the term Persia runs the risk of drawing the attention of Iran's minorities to the unique ethnic background of the dominant group, in much the same way that a reference to Great Britain or to the United Kingdom as England would be apt to disturb a Scot or Welshman.

A more direct and simultaneous threat to Iran was the initiation of a propaganda campaign directed by Arab states to the Arabs living in southwestern Iran. This region,

officially known as Khuzistan, contains Iran's most valuable oil deposits and is therefore of great strategic value. Arab governments now resurrected an earlier title, referring to it as Arabistan -- "land of the Arabs." They also began openly appealing to sepratist sentiments on the part of Khuzistan's inhabitants. Teheran countered by offering its support to the Kurds in the anti-Iraqi campaign. It also attempted to exacerbate tensions among the Iraqi Arabs by appealing to a religious division: the majority of the Arabs in southern Iraq are, like the Persians, Shi'ite Moslems, while the majority of the Iraqi Arabs, overall, are Sunni. Thus, the Shi'ite Persians were simultaneously courting Iraqi Arab Shi'ites and supporting the Sunni Kurds in the latter's struggle with the Sunni Arab dominated Iraqi government. Overall, the situation ably illustrates the inconsistencies and complexities that can characterize ethno-cultural alliances.

There are not sufficient data to evaluate the relative efficacy of these appeals to religious and ethnic diversity. It is probably safe to venture that religious appeals proved less effective than those addressed to ethnicity. As early as World War I, the Ottoman Caliph's cry for a jihad (holy war) that would unite all Moslems against the infidels failed to overcome anti-Turkish sentiments on the part of Arabs and a number of other Moslem peoples, causing an authority on the region to remark that "in a crisis nationalism was a stronger force than was religion" (Lenczowski, 1962:52). On the other hand, we have noted that the Kurds are the only minority within Iran which has thus far given evidence of a strongly developed national consciousness. In the past, the low level of national consciousness among its other minorities, has permitted Teheran to concentrate successfully upon the Kurdish threat. But as national consciousness permeates the other minorities, the government's problems will be multiplied. Iran's ethnic pattern is very alike that which we found so common in southeast Asia. The Persians, although representing approximately 70 percent of the total population, are essentially surrounded by minorities. Should resentment at Persian rule arise among these surrounding peoples, the predicament of the Persians would resemble that of the Burmese.[17]

In any case, Kurdish fortunes took a calamitous turn in early 1975, when Iran and Iraq at least temporarily resolved their differences. A major condition of the settlement was Teheran's promise to cease all assistance to the Kurdish guerrillas, thus highlighting the role of pawns which the Kurds had occupied in the perceptions of the two governments. Whether this new accord will prove enduring and, if so, whether it will prevent Kurdish guerrilla's activities against either or both governments is a matter of speculation. But the passion for independence which the Kurds have demonstrated for more than a half-century in a series of bloody uprisings within Iran, Iraq, and Turkey, suggest that it would be dangerously premature to write their movement's obituary.

At least by Asian standards, Turkey is an ethnically homogeneous state. More than 90 percent of the population are Turks. This relatively homogeneous situation is the result of a purposeful policy stretching back to the beginning of the century. The closing years of the Ottoman Empire witnessed several enforced transfers and massacres conducted by the authorities against non-Turkic people living in Asia Minor. The founder of modern Turkey, Kemal Attaturk, furthered this trend toward homogeneity, driving foreign forces from Turkish soil by engineering repatriation programs (particularly that involving the exchange of ethnic nationals with Greece), and by winning back territory in which Turks predominated. Had Attaturk been willing to accept the concept of an independent Kurdish state (as set forth in the Treaty of Sevres), Turkey would today be one of the world's most homogeneous states. If it were possible to exclude the Kurds, who presently account for approximately 6 percent of Turkey's population, Turks would then represent almost 98 percent of all inhabitants. The only other numerically significant group consists of Arabs.

Both the Kurds and the Arabs have stoutly resisted Turkish attempts to further homogeneity through assimilation. The Kurds, however, have constituted the more serious problem. Despite Turkish attempts to suppress news of minority unrest and even to camouflage the ethnic identity of the Kurds by referring to them as "Mountain Turks," the magnitude of Kurdish dissatisfaction has precluded its masking. Kurdish revolts were put down in 1925, 1929, and 1930. Continuing unrest required the imposition of martial law throughout the Kurdish area in 1936 and the forcible transfer of some Kurdish families to the western portion of the state. Civilian rule was re-inaugurated following World War II, but it soon became evident that the Kurds had not become reconciled to Turkish rule. In 1960, the President of Turkey felt compelled to issue a threat to destroy Kurdish towns if nationalistic activities continued, and forty-six Kurdish nationalists were tried and imprisoned shortly thereafter. Matters further deteriorated during the late 1960s, leading to further arrests and a governmental ban on Kurdish political activities and on the importation of publications in the Kurdish language. This pattern of action and reaction escalated, and in the Spring of 1971, the Turkish authorities again instituted martial law. The interstate nature of Kurdish nationalism was again underscored by the Government's announcement that weapons for an armed revolt were being stockpiled with the complicity of Mustafa Barzani, the Kurdish leader within Iraq. And following the agreement between Iran and Iraq in early 1975, the Turkish Government still once again felt compelled to institute martial law in its eastern provinces as a means of quelling sympathetic support among the Kurds for their kin across the border.

The Arab minority is substantially fewer in number than the Kurds and has not posed so serious a problem. Nevertheless, most Arabs jealously retain their separate identity, and in this determination are aided by the porous border shared with Arab Syria. Transborder migrations and smuggling are commonplace, and help to insure that the cultural lifelines to Arabdom are kept open. Moreover, periodic attempts of the Turkish authorities to assimilate them have been regularly followed by large-scale exoduses into Syria, and the likelihood of this response has probably deterred more determined Turkish efforts. Those Arabs concentrated near the Syrian border constitute a classic irredenta, and Ankara charged Syria in 1971 with conducting annexationist activities.

The Turkish Government has also been embroiled in an ethnic struggle on nearby Cyprus. Since long before its inception as an independent state, this island has been the setting of a bloody ethnic struggle between its Greek and Turkic components. The only noteworthy interlude to ethnic warfare coincided with an ill-fated attempt at transethnic government in this period 1960-1963. Greeks outnumber Turks in the island by more than four to one, and the matter would have long ago been settled by force in favor of the Greeks had it not been for the threat of direct intervention by forces from Turkey. Just such an eventuality

occured in 1974 when a series of events appeared to portend a Greek attempt to alter the precarious balance of power and privileges between the two communities. The Turkish intervention led to the massive relocation of peoples and to the unilateral proclamation in early 1975 that the northern sector of Cyprus would henceforth be known as the Turkish Cypriot Federated State. This territory, in which Turks were now clearly to predominate, was at some indefinite future time to be federated with southern Cyprus, a territory which Greeks were to dominate. The precedent for coercive transferring of minorities was already firmly established in Greco-Turkish relations: Grecian children are well versed in the story of how, at Attaturk's insistence, some one-and-one-half million Greeks were expelled from Asia Minor following World War I. In addition to the role of Turkey and of emotion-evoking history, the Cyprus problem is further complicated by the relationship of the Greek majority to Greece and vice versa. Sentiment for union with Greece ("enosis") rather than for independence has often had outspoken support among Grecian elites of both Cyprus and Greece. Estimating the actual support for union has been made more difficult by the tendency of Greek Cypriot leaders to sometimes carry its banner and at other times to repudiate it.[18]

IV

Even a superficial and admittedly incomplete survey of ethnic problems within non-Arab Asia illustrates the instability inherent in situations where political and ethnic borders fail to coincide. The principle of self-determination of nations, which today is broadly accepted as a self-evident truth, makes ethnicity the ultimate standard of political legitimacy, thereby challenging the validity of the multi-ethnic state, as well as of borders that bifurcate ethnic groups. The spirit with which groups pursue the grail of self-determination is dependent upon their level of national consciousness, and this level, as we have noted, varies greatly. The seriousness of the challenge which ethnic diversity has thus far posed to Asian states has therefore also varied markedly from unit to unit. But all of the multiethnic states have experienced some measure of violent ethnic discord, and an increase in the frequency and scope of ethnic warfare (particularly of the guerrilla variety) can be anticipated.

The ubiquity of ethnic discord also illustrates its remarkable disregard for a number of variables. Among the states afflicted are some that are urbanized-industrialized (Singapore) and preindustrial-rural (Laos); communist (PRC, North Vietnam) and non-communist; relatively democratic (India, Singapore) and dynastic (Afghanistan); federative (India, Malaysia) and unitary (Iran, Turkey); the world's most populous (India, PRC) and among the least populous (Bhutan, Maldive); highly literate (Taiwan) and highly illiterate (Iran); characterized by a relatively high and rapidly improving standard of living (Singapore) and by a tragically low and almost stagnant one (Afghanistan). The seeming imperviousness of ethnic discord to changes in such variables, caused Singapore's Prime Minister Lee Kuan Yew to note despondently that "I used to believe that when Singaporeans became more sophisticated, with higher standards of education, these problems would diminish. But watching Belfast, Brussels, and Montreal rioting over religion and language, I wonder whether such phenomena can ever disappear." (New York Times, 6/10/71).

Our survey also makes clear that ethnic diversity is not merely an internal problem, but one that is a most significant factor in interstate relations. It also points up the glaring inconsistencies that often characterize the position of governments with regard to the right of self-determination for groups, depending upon whether the groups reside within or without the state. Thus, the PRC periodically proclaims support for the right of self-determination of the Kashmiri, while denying it to the Tibetans; Iran supports the Kurds of Iraq and suppresses their movement at home; Thailand gives sympathetic support to the Shans in their struggle against the Burmese (Fareastern Economic Review, 4/8/72: 12, 13), while quelling similar movements among their own Lao, Malay, and Meo people; Cambodia and South Vietnam have each demanded the right of cultural autonomy for members of their ethnic group residing within the other state, while condoning or ignoring repressive treatment of members of the other state's major ethnic group who reside under their jurisdiction; Hanoi promises autonomy to the minorities of South Vietnam, while denying it to their own minorities despite similar promises made prior to their assumption of power (Connor, 1969). But perhaps the most flagrant illustrations of such inconsistency revolve about the creation of Bangla Desh. For some years Pakistan, a state denying the right of self-determination to its own groups, had been using East Pakistani territory to train and supply Mizos and other separatist groups operating within eastern India. The desire to stamp out these self-determination movements by denying them sanctuarial bases and logistical centers within East Pakistan was probably a subsidiary factor in India's decision to support (Eastern) Bengali self-determination. Following its independence, Bangla Desh has in fact permitted elements of the Indian Army to use its territory to stamp out these nearby anti-Indian separatist movements. Thus, Bangla Desh, the most recent successful illustration of self-determination of nations, becomes the instrument for denying this same right to others. While consistency is seldom considered a virtue in statecraft, self-determination appears to engender an exceptional proneness to opportunism. But ethnic aspirations ignited among one group have a tendency to spread to others without regard to state borders. Today's opportunism may prove distressingly myopic.

FOOTNOTES

1. The exclusion of Arab Asia (i.e., those states of Asia in which Arabs predominate) is due to the fact that the political implications of their ethnology must be viewed in the broader context of Arab nationalism. The inclusion of Arab Asia would therefore necessitate the inclusion of several Arab states within Africa. Israel has also been excluded because of the inextricable relationship between its ethnic problems and Arab nationalism.

2. An atlas recently published within the PRC put the 1970 population at ·697 million; the UN had estimated the 1970 population at 759 million, and the U.S. Census Bureau had estimated it at 870 million. (New York Times, 8/6/72).

3. The motives behind governmental distortion of ethnic statistics can range from narrowly defined self-interest to a desire to avoid bloodshed. The political elite, being members of the dominant ethnic group, may undervalue the population of a competing group within a state, so as to avoid augmenting the latter's political "clout". Or it may wish to hide figures that indicate a proportionately rapid growth of a group, in order not to instill fear and provoke hostility from other groups.

4. The dismal record of governmental attempts to suppress a guerrilla struggle in its borderlands in areas where the ethnicity of the local people on either side of the border is identical underlines the potential strategic significance of conflicting ethnic and political borders.

5. Iranian assistance covertly given to Kurdish guerrilla activities within Iraq might seem to repudiate the validity of this example, but Teheran has long violently suppressed any manifestation of Kurdish separatism within its own borders.

6. By way of illustration, a tree is visually a tree to everyone, regardless of language. But it is impossible to convey in English the concept of tree -- either orally or in writing -- to a group of unilinguists who know tree only as arbe, Baum. Note: This is the Russian word for tree. In the cyrillic alphabet, this is DépeBo, or arbol. By contrast, those within the Chinese Empire who were orally limited to the mutually unintelligible vernaculars of Cantonese, Fukienese, or Mandarin could all understand the same written messages.

7. See, for example, the New York Times of 6/21/70 for a report that the PRC was redrawing Inner Mongolia's administrative borders as a means of better controlling the Mongolian minority.

8. A significant number (approximately 400,000) of Vietnamese also resided within Cambodia prior to 1972. However, as a means of solidifying their control, the group who overthrew Sihanouk unleashed an anti-Vietnamese hate campaign. As a result, a combination of genocide and forcible expulsion had all but eradicated the community by late 1972, a tragic testament to the depth of interethnic animosity that characterizes the relations between many ethnic groups in Southeast Asia.

9. A third British dependency on Borneo (Brunei) elected to remain outside of Malaysia.

10. The inhabitants of the Katmandu Valley have also tended to perceive their political world as coterminous with the valley rather than wtih Nepal's actual borders. In 1958, the King formally decreed that people must desist from using the term Nepal in reference to the valley only.

11. Included are religious diversity, strong caste divisions, and extensive poverty.

12. Kashmir's single most important leader, Sheik Mohammed Abdullah ("the Lion of Kashmir"), spent 13 of the 14 years between 1954 and 1968 in prison. When not interred, Kashmiri nationalist leaders are often debarred from Kashmir.

13. Keesings Contemporary Archives, 1969:2313; and 1970; 24049. For a report on how Sinhalese Buddhist monks campaigned against the DMK during the election, see the article by A.B. Mendis in the Christian Science Monitor of 4/5/69.

14. Independence-motivated activities among the border-straddling Baluchis in 1973 threatened to harm relations between Pakistan and Iran. We have noted that the Kashmiri people have long been a major factor in Indian-Pakistani relations. But though a cease-fire line divides the Kashmiri between Indian and Pakistani military control, Pakistan does not technically claim sovereignty over the sector it occupies.

15. All of the territory in question was once under the

suzerainty of Kabul. The duration of Afghan control varied among sections of the area from 50 to 150 years.

16. The 1920 Treaty of Sevres, imposed upon Turkey by the victorious powers, required Turkey to acknowledge the right of the Kurds to self-determination if the Council of the League of Nations should make such a recommendation within a year from the date of the Treaty. However, the successful revolution of Kemal Attaturk made the Treaty unenforcible from the outset, and the subsequent Treaty of Lausanne (1923) made no mention of either Kurdish autonomy or Kurdish independence. Even had the Kurds been granted independence in 1920, the grant would not have extended to the Kurds of Iran.

17. For a note on rising national consciousness among the Baluchis of Iran's extreme southeast, see footnote 14.

18. Archbishop Makarios, who was once the acknowledged leader of the enosis movement, has more recently championed independent statehood.

REFERENCES

Area Handbook for Afghanistan
1969   Department of the Army Pamphlet Number 550-565. Washington: United States Government Printing Office.

Bessac, Frank
1968   "Cultunit and Ethnic Unit -- Processes and Symbolism." Pp. 58-71 in Essays on the Problem of Tribe. Proceedings of the 1967 Annual Spring Meeting of the American Ethnological Society.

Seattle: University of Washington Press.

Connor, Walker
1969   "Ethnology and the Peace of South Asia." World Politics, XXII (October): pp. 51-86.

1971   "Nationalism Reconsidered." Paper presented at the 1971 Annual Meeting of the Northeast Political Science Association.

1972   "Nation-Building or Nation-Destroying?" World Politics, XXIV (April): pp. 319-355.

Cottam, Richard
1964   Nationalism in Iran. Pittsburgh: University of Pittsburgh Press.

Hanna, Willard
1967   "Nationalist Revolution and Revolutionary Nationalism." Pp. 129-177 in K.H. Silvert (editor), Expectant Peoples. New York: Vintage Books.

Keyes, Charles
1966   "Ethnic Identity and Loyalty of Villagers in Northeastern Thailand." Asian Survey VI: pp. 362-369.

Lenczowski, George
1962   The Middle East in World Affairs. Third Edition. Ithaca: Cornell University Press.

Lieberman, Victor
1966   "Why the Hukbalahap Movement Failed." Solidarity I (October-December): pp. 22-30.

II. EAST ASIA

The first two papers deal with minority policy in Chinese government. Deal examined the policies of central governments in handling Southwest minority groups during the period of 1927 to 1965. He finds a difference in the official policies of minority group affairs advocated by the Nationalists and the Communists - the former for assimilation of minorities to Han culture and the latter for the cultural pluralism. However, Deal claims, they both in fact carried out a policy of assimilation. The minorities were expected to draw nearer to a Chinese norm.

While measured against the Nationalist policy of assimilating minorities, the Mao regime enjoyed considerable success. Yet, Deal concludes, that local nationalism did not easily die out.

Hirata analyzes the leadership composition of local government under the Maoist regime in minority nationalities autonomous regions. She observes a strong national policy of eradicating nationality issues. The central government emphasizes the class-interest over ethnic-interests and denounces both the Han chauvinism and local nationalism. More specifically, greater concessions were made for minority groups under the Communists in the forms of deferment of more drastic reforms and higher minority representation in government and party leadership positions in early years of the regime and somewhat reduced but proportionate representation in leadership compositions in the '60s.

The next two papers examine two of the dominant minority group problems in Japan. Wagatsuma studies "Japanese Untouchable Group (Burakumin - the Untouchable of Japan)". He traces the historical background of Burakumin and investigates the social psychological consequences of the wide range of discriminations which Burakumin suffer. They are given a selective reception into a handful of categories of socially despised occupations and totally excluded from majority society in other areas of participation. Wagastuma discusses the problems of passing into majority society and the behavioral correlates of a negative self-image imposed on Burakumin.

The history of forced immigration of Koreans into Japan is briefly reviewed and deep-seated Japanese prejudices and discriminations against Koreans are examined by Kim. Discriminations against Korean are pervasive in all phases of life--social, educational, economic and political.

They are excluded from schools, employment into work other than socially despised areas, and political participation. A rigid selective reception and total exclusion from desirable participation into majority society is the typical treatment of Koreans by Japanese.

Social psychological effects of prejudice and discrimination appear in the form of a high rate of suicide, a high crime rate, and a high rate of mental illness. Kim is pessimistic about the Korean minority. Citing the absence or organized public concern, Kim predicts no improvement of Korean life in Japan for a long time to come.

McBeath's study of Chinese elites in the Philippines reveals certain common features of overseas Chinese communities in emerging Asian nations. Chinese in the Philippines are predominantly urban and have a high degree of success in business. However, Filipino pressure for the assimilation of Chinese has been consistantly increasing, and the government at all levels has imposed various measures for reducing Chinese influence in business. There are some signs of assimilation by Philippine-educated Chinese elites but, reservations for complete assimilation still remains.

3
POLICY TOWARD ETHNIC MINORITIES
IN SOUTHWEST CHINA, 1927-1965

DAVID M. DEAL

Whitman College

ABSTRACT

The focus of this paper is on minority policy as implemented in southwest China between 1927 and 1965. The theoretical roots of minority policy as formulated by the Nationalists lay in traditional Chinese concepts of race and border, an imported idea of self-determination, and a belief in assimilation. The implementation of policy by the Nationalists in three areas--administration, economic development, and education--was largely unsuccessful. The problem of political administration over the southwestern minorities was never satisfactorily solved, the limited economic development of this region which did take place had little positive effect on the minorites, and education was inadequate.

The theoretical bases for the minority policy of the Chinese Communists lay in Marxist-Leninist doctrine, in the Soviet Union as a model of a multinational state, and in the experience of the CCP before achieving power. The implementation of minority policy by the Communists in three areas--administration, agrarian reform, and education--was a qualified success in southwest China. The minorities of this frontier region were better integrated into the Chinese state than in the past; they were, however, less eager to become new socialist men than Mao had anticipated.

The objective of this study is to describe and analyze Nationalist and Communist policies towards southwestern minorities from 1927 to 1965. It is an attempt to show that although, in theory, the Nationalists advocated assimilation and the Communists advocated cultural pluralism, they both in fact carried out a policy of assimilation; i.e., the minorities were expected to draw nearer to a Chinese norm. It will be seen that although the Chinese Communists had many revolutionary ideas, much of their program was anticipated by the Nationalists. Given a common problem (national integration), there evolved a significant continuity in the approaches of the two governments. I shall discuss certain theoretical considerations underlying the minority policies of both the Nationalists and the Communists, and outline implementation of policy under both governments.

Traditional Chinese concepts of race and border, an imported Western idea of self-determination, and a profound belief in assimilation helped form Chinese minority policy in Nationalist China. The ethnocentrism of Mencius, revealed in his statement, "I have heard of man using the doctrines of our great land to change barbarians, but I have never yet heard of any being changed by barbarians," (Legge, 1960: II, 253) was echoed by a Kwangsi magistrate who expressed a desire in the 1940's to ". . . do something practical to civilize these aboriginal people, and make them good citizens of China." (Young, 1943: 14). In the eyes of Mencius and Nationalist officials, the non-Chinese tribes may have been rude and barbarous, but they could be civilized and reformed by the power of Chinese culture. They were not condemned to eternal inferiority by virtue of their birth. Those Chinese who displayed a measure of racism, men such as Fang Hsiao-ju (1357-1402), Wang Fu-Chih (1619-1692), Tsou Jung (1885-1905), or Hu Han-min (1879-1936), were rather exceptional. The minorities were generally deemed inferior not because of physical differences but because they were thought to lack culture or to possess a lower culture (Chang Wen-t'ung, 1947: 8).

Related to this traditional Chinese concept of race is the Chinese concept of border. During the Nationalist era, the usual term for ethnic minorities within China was "border nationalities" *(pien-chiang min-tsu)*, defined as those nationalities in the border provinces with "a comparatively low level of civilization." (Chou, 1962a: 2). The "border area" was viewed as comprising 60% of China's total area; it was not simply the land along China's political boundaries (Chou, 1967: 417). The border, therefore, was seen not as a line but as a vast zone, embracing different ethnic groups, different political systems, different forms of livelihood, and different cultures. The southwestern frontier in particular was a "dynamic, fluid, and constantly receding" (Schafer, 1967: 14) one as the Chinese continually moved south in a search for arable land (Schafer, 1967: 14; Wiens, 1954: xiii). This view of the border lands deeply colored minority policy, as frontier areas were seen as areas to exploit and develop for the benefit of the dominant nationality.

A third idea--that of self-determination--also helped shape the minority policy of the Nationalists. Sun Yat-sen was deeply influenced by the idea of national self-determination as formulated in Woodrow Wilson's Fourteen Points and in the Declaration of the Rights of the Peoples of Russia (Chin, et. al., 1956: 127; Tseng, 1930: 92; Ruey, 1954: 4). In 1924, Sun Yat-sen advocated that the government should help the "weak and small nationalities" within China gain self-determination and self-government (Sun, 1953: 10; Ruey, 1954: 7), and that same year the First National Congress of the Kuomintang affirmed the principle of self-determination for all peoples within China (Ruey, 1954: 7; Tseng, 1930: 93). It is apparent that the term self-determination did not contain the same meaning for Woodrow Wilson and for Sun Yat-sen. Woodrow Wilson sought to use the concept of self-determination to strengthen the position of the smaller nations in Europe; it is doubtful that he intended this concept to apply either to national minorities within China or to China as a nation threatened by outside domination. By national self-determination Sun Yat-sen meant primarily the right of China, and secondarily the right of minorities within China, to be free from foreign domination. In 1921 Sun Yat-sen had stated that Manchuria had fallen into the Japanese sphere of influence, Mongolia was under the sway of Russia, and Tibet was becoming a dependency of England. He though it evident that the minority groups in China could not protect themselves from outside domination without the help of the Chinese (Chou, 1962b: 45; Chang, 1957: 22, 53-54). Thus, to Sun Yat-sen, self-determination for the "weak and small nationalities" within China meant the right of these minorities to escape from foreign, not from Chinese control. That this link between the need for self-determination and the threat of foreign imperialism was an enduring one in the minds of many Chinese is revealed by an article written in 1948 which stated that "now the Powers use the name of self-determination of nationalities to promote the fact of imperialist aggression" (Ma, 1948: 22).

Fourth, the idea of assimilation was a dominant theme throughout the Nationalist era. The Chinese wished to rule areas in which ". . . the steady stream of Chinese culture has flowed into the dry pool of aboriginal drought" (Young, 1943: 19). They preferred a world in which there was no distinction between Chinese and the minorities; a world in which minorities became Chinese. The desire for assimilation was totally consistent with the ancient Chinese ideal of uniformity as expressed in the *Chung Yung:* "Now over the Kingdom, carriages have all wheels of the same size; all writing is with the same characters; and for conduct there are the same rules" (Legge, 1960: I, 424). The Nationalists, in their policy of assimilation, pursued this elusive ideal. Ethnic minority place-names were replaced with Chinese place-names (Li, 1940: 44-51), minorities adopted Chinese surnames (P'ing-pa hsien-chih, she-hui, 1932: 27; Wen, 1957: 563), and Chinese officials in minority areas advocated the adoption of the Chinese language, wearing of Chinese dress, and intermarriage as a means of assimilation ("Transcript," Academia Sinica). In 1928, the Ministry of Interior sent a letter to the provincial governments of the southwestern provinces asking them to report on the efficacy of various methods used to "civilize" (*k'ai-hua*) the tribes. Implicit in this concept of civilizing the aborigines is the idea that they must draw nearer to the Chinese norm *(Nei-cheng kung-pao,* 1928: 13-14). There was, in sum, stress on the unity of China's nationalities under the Nationalists, and a desire to make the minorities aware that the best course for them to follow was to become part of a great Chinese nationality, rather than to cultivate a sense of ethnic loyalty (Chang, 1939: 2).

The above four ideas--race, border, self-determination, and assimilation--were important theoretical considerations during the Nationalist era. How did these ideas relate to practice? To answer this question I propose to examine briefly three areas--administration, economic development, and education--in which theory was translated into practice.

The Nationalists failed to solve the problem of political administration over the tribes in southwest China. The central government failed to exert effective control on the local level in minority areas, and it failed to integrate politically the more militant minorities. One sign of administrative failure was the *de facto* continuation of the *t'u-ssu* system.[1] Although both Chinese administrators and scholars harshly criticized this system, accusing the *t'u-ssu* of possessing powerful private armies, of ruthlessly exploiting their subjects, of "eating in idleness" and serving no useful function, and of owning ". . . fields of a thousand *mou,* while the poor do not have a place on which to put the tip of an awl" (Chen, 1940: 58-59, 172-173; Chao, 1953: 85-86; Li, 1947: 12-13; "Transcript," Academia Sinica; Chou, 1962a: 226), no practical alternative to the *t'u-ssu* system was implemented. In theory no new *t'u-ssu* were appointed after 1931; in fact, most county magistrates in border areas did not succeed in becoming more than puppets of the local *t'u-ssu* (Hsu, 1936: 90). In areas where Chinese authority was minimal, the lack of a *t'u-ssu* meant lack of administrative order, and in some remote areas, a period of over ten troubled years elapsed with no *t'u-ssu* and no local

magistrate (Ling, 1943: 2). When one governor of Kweichow visited an area inhabited by many Yi, local inhabitants informed him that they had never before seen even a local magistrate, much less a provincial governor ("Transcript," Academia Sinica).

The Nationalists generally administered the minorities of southwest China poorly, or not at all. Given the pressure of other problems, however, perhaps no more could be expected. It was a peripheral area and the minorities did not constitute a major threat. Neglect of the minorities of southwest China was perceived by the Nationalists as far less dangerous than the neglect of a host of other problems--the Communists, the Japanese, and the economy, to name but a few. The Nationalist administration of the minorities in southwest China was in fact, though not in theory, largely a holdover from dynastic China. Centralization did not replace indirect rule, *t'u-ssu* often continued to hold power, and local self-governement whereby local people would participate in local administration did not thrive.

How could the need for economic development of the border area be reconciled with the economic and cultural needs of the minorities? This problem, along with that of administration, was also never adequately solved by the Nationalists. In 1940, for example, a writer complained bitterly that the minorities of Sikang were hindering development by disrupting peace and order and discouraging Chinese migration (Sun, 1942: 22-23). That the minorities may have had valid reasons for disliking Chinese migration into their homeland apparently did not enter his mind; concern for the welfare of minorities was outweighed by concern for economic development (for an American example of this phenomenon see Walker, 1964: 227).

The southwest in general benefited economically during World War II as the Nationalists sought to build a base from which to oppose Japanese aggression. In 1935, the provinces of Szechuan, Hunan, Kwangsi, Shansi, Kansu, Yunnan, and Kweichow together had but 6.03% of China's factories; by 1940, however, Szechuan alone had 45% of the factories in regions controlled by the Nationalists (Afanas'yeskiy, 1962: 94-95). Unfortunately this boom in the growth of industry in Szechuan did not benefit the minorities, as 60% of the industrial production was concentrated in Chungking (Afans'yeskiy, 1962: 94-95). As Yunnan, Kweichow, and Kwangsi became "opened and civilized" during and after World War II, the tribes were generally forced back into poorer lands and their economic well-being was not promoted.

In spite of great hopes for the economic development of China, the Nationalists did not have the capacity or the will to implement sufficient social changes for the economic modernization of China to take place. This fact is true of China in general and is no less true of minority areas of southwest China. In the realm of economic development in minority areas, the Nationalists lacked a realistic plan which they could successfully implement.

Minority education was handled in a variety of ways in Nationalist China, depending upon the locality and time under consideration. Schools for minorities were established by local authorities, such as the *t'u-ssu*, by provincial authorities, and by the central government. Some provinces provided for minority education even before the 1920's (Ling, 1947: 17), and in the province of Kwangsi, nominally under Nationalist rule but in actuality controlled by the warlord, Pai Ch'ung-hsi, the provincial bureau of education began, in 1929, to establish schools in Miao and Yao villages in order to make these minorities "...regular Chinese citizens in the coming Republic of China" ("Reforming the Aborigines of Kwangsi," 1929: 48). In 1936 and in 1942, Kweichow provincial authorities established institutions for Miao teacher training and, by 1948, twenty-one *hsien* with heavy concentrations of minorities had schools enrolling a total of 692 students. Elsewhere in the southwest, Yunnan province enrolled 237 in border middle schools, 116 in normal schools, and 3,208 in primary schools. Hunan had one hundred short-term primary schools for the Miao in Hsiang-hsi and Kwangsi had 541 elementary schools (*Chung-kuo chiao-yu nien-chien*, 1948: 1250; *Chung-hua nien-chien*, 1948: 1707).

It is difficult to determine the exact proportion of minority students enrolled in the various border schools throughout the southwest. In Szechuan, however, figures are available for twelve of the fourteen border primary schools in 1947. These twelve schools enrolled a total of 471 students, and 351 of these, or nearly seventy-five percent, were minority students (*Chung-kuo chiao-yu nien-chien*, 1948: 1246-1247). If this percentage holds true for the rest of southwest China (that is, if seventy-five percent of those students enrolled in the border schools were minority students) then, in 1946, school-age minority children enrolled in border primary schools in the southwest were approximately 1-1/3% of those eligible to attend.

After 1930, with the establishment of a border education section within the Ministry of Education, the central government also became involved in minority education. In 1935, it appropriated 500,000 *yuan* for border education. Little, however, was accomplished until the war with Japan forced the central government to move to Chungking. Then, between 1939 and 1947, the following border education institutions were established by the central government:

34 National border primary schools
13 normal schools
 8 vocational schools
 2 middle schools
 3 specialist schools
60 Total (*Chung-hua nien-chien*, 1948: 1707)

From 1935 to 1947, a total of 837,867,088 *yuan* was allocated by the Ministry of Education for border education; only 16 percent of this total, however, was reserved for the southwest (*Chung-hua nien-chien*, 1948: 1722). In view of the numbers of minorities in the southwest, this percentage is surprisingly low.

In 1944, the Ministry of Education stipulated that border students were to receive subsidies and to be given special considerations in entrance requirements. In 1947, food subsidies were 20,000 *yuan* per student per month, book subsidies 600 *yuan* per student per month, and clothing subsidies 50,000 *yuan* for each new student (*Chung-hua nien-chien*, 1948: 1724). In addition to these efforts to encourage minority education, the central government also published the *Central Border Paper (Chung-yang pien-pao)* in Mongolian and Tibetan, and primary school books translated into a few minority languages (*Chung-hua nien-chien*, 1948: 1718). Research teams to investigate minority education were sent into southwest China as early as 1938, and by 1947 fifteen border research societies were in existence, due in part to encouragement from the Ministry of Education, which also subsidized border research in eight universities (*Chung-hua nien-chien*, 1948: 1719; Ling, 1947: 17).

The Ministry of Education attempted to adapt education to fit border conditions. One educator, realizing that many of the primary school students in border areas were not small children but rather young people in their teens, advocated that textbooks be modified accordingly. Health, language, social, vocational, and scientific education were all necessary in the border areas because of the prevalence of disease, the lack of knowledge of characters, the backwardness of production techniques, and the reliance on superstition. In addition, in an effort to assimilate the tribes and prevent the influence of Western powers from becoming pervasive, special stress was put on teaching Chinese culture, Chinese history, and Chinese morality (Chang Yu-ts'ai, 1947: 9). Confucian virtues, such as *li* and *i* were stressed in the educational system in order to promote Sinicization and to neutralize the "wildness" of the tribes. Once the leaders of the tribes knew *li*, so the argument ran, they would be friends, not enemies, of the Chinese (Yu, 1948: 1213).

In general, there were six kinds of border education open to minority students: (1) primary school education in which students were trained in citizenship, production techniques, and national defense, (2) middle school education for teacher training and advanced production techniques, (3) higher education for those students wishing to pursue specialized studies, (4) social education for elementary medicine, music, and audio-visual training, (5) remedial education for those students wishing to enter middle school but who had inadequate preparation, and (6) special education for party cadre training (*Chung-kuo chiao-yu nien-chien*, 1948: 1212). The goals of all six types were basically the same--to spread the ideals of the Three People's Principles and to promote national solidarity (*Chung-kuo chiao-yu nien-chien*, 1948: 1211; *Chung-hua nien-chien*, 1948: 1729).

The Nationalists made a rather poor beginning in minority education in southwest China. Many mistakes were made, many difficulties were never satisfactorily overcome, and many prospective students were never reached. And yet, however harshly one might judge the Nationalists for their shortcomings, the Chinese Communists at least inherited from them a precedent for minority education utilizing minority teachers and, occasionally, minority languages. As we shall see, Chinese Communist minority education policy represents an amplification, not a reversal of tendencies in pre-1949 China. Minority education was expanded on the fragile base inherited from the Nationalists.

In summary, although the Nationalists anticipated much of the later program of the Communists in regard to the southwestern minorities, the effectiveness of the Nationalists' program was minimal. Beginnings were made in administration, economic development, and education; these beginnings, however, did not constitute a well integrated approach to the solving of minority problems.

The theoretical bases for the minority policy of the Chinese Communists lay in Marxist-Leninist doctrine, in the Soviet Union as a model of a multi-national state, and in the experience of the CCP before achieving power. Before World War I the term "self-determination" meant, for Lenin, the right of a nationality to secede from a state and form its own government. There was, however, only one alternative to secession and that alternative was to remain within the state. Lenin did not look with favor upon either federalism or cultural autonomy (Shaheen, 1956: 101; Pipes, 1957: 44; Inkeles, 1960: 28; Pipes, 1953: 23).

Although critics of Lenin's theory of self-determination argued that this right would lead to the breakup of the state, Lenin thought otherwise. He argued that because there were economic advantages to a large state, people would "resort to secession only when national oppression and national friction made joint life absolutely intolerable and hindered all and any economic intercourse" (Lenin, 1921: I, 349; Shaheen, 1956: 103). By extending certain rights and freedoms to the minority nationalities, those nationalities would develop even firmer ties with Russia. He wrote, for example, that if the Ukrainians in Russia had more liberty than the Ukrainians in Austria-Hungary, Ukrainians in general would be more closely tied with Russia (Lenin, 1921: I, 348: Shaheen, 1956: 103).

At the same time, Lenin qualified the right of self-determination by stating that to advocate the right of self-determination was not the same as advocating actual separation, and in cases of conflicting interests involving national minorities and the proletariat, the interests of the proletariat must come first (Shaheen, 1956: 104; Pipes, 1957: 1945). "The recognition . . . of the *right* of nations to secede in no way precludes *agitation* against secession by Marxists of a particular *oppressed* nation, just as the recognition of the right to divorce does not preclude agitation against divorce in a particular case" (Lenin, 1921: I, 383; Shaheen, 1956: 106). Lenin clearly stated elsewhere that he neither desired nor foresaw self-determination of nationalities being exercised as secession (Pipes, 1957: 45; Shaheen, 1956: 109). He desired, on the contrary, that the proletariat would fight all forms of nationalism, including Great Russian nationalism, and that eventually there would be amalgamation involving all workers of all nationalities (Shaheen, 1956: 109). In this final stage, linguistic assimilation would also take place, as the advantages of those members of a national minority who could read, write, and speak Russian would be obvious (Shaheen, 1956: 110; Pipes, 1957: 46).

In summary, Lenin's pre-revolutionary minority policy, in general and his doctrine of self-determination in particular were dictated by tactical considerations. According to Richard Pipes, "Lenin looked upon national problems as something to exploit, and not as something to solve. But as a psychological weapon in the struggle for power, . . . the slogan of self-determination . . . was to prove enormously successful" (Pipes, 1957: 49). Lenin, in his desire to create a new order, needed the minorities to help him to destroy the old one (Shaheen, 1956: 148).

Similarly, Chinese Communist national minority policy before 1949 was formulated primarily to gain the support of the minorities in the continuing struggle for power. Regional autonomy within a "Chinese Federated Republic" for national minorities was advocated as early as 1922 at the Second Party Congress of the CCP (Brandt, et. al., 1952: 64; Ma Ta-chun, 1958: 5), and the 1931 Kiangsi Soviet Constitution explicitly stated that the minorities within China had both the right of self-determination and the right of secession (Mao, 1934: 78; Brandt, et. al., 1952: 220-221; Yakhontoff, 1934: 220-221). Mao Tse-tung reaffirmed these rights in his report to the Second National Soviet Congress in 1934, although by that time it was evident that Mao, like Lenin in 1916, neither desired nor expected self-determination to be expressed by secession in a Communist China. Mao expected rather a "free union of nationalities" (Yakhontoff, 1934: 276-277). As the Kiangsi Soviet came under increasing pressure from KMT forces, the CCP sought, more desperately than before, to enlist the support of the national minorities in their struggle against the Nationalists. Mao flatly stated in 1934 that the Kiangsi Soviet minority policy was designed to gain the support of the national minorities surrounding the Soviet in the struggle against the Imperialists and the Kuomintang (Mao, 1934: 77).

Precisely what happened during the Long March as the Red Army passed through tribal areas of southwest China is a matter of some debate (Wiens, 1954: 146; Dreyer, 1968: 97; Wales, 1952: 65, 70-71; A-erh-mu-hsia, 1958: 51-59; Hsieh, 1958: 162-164; K'ang, 1958: 165-167). There was apparently some opposition to the CCP forces, some cooperation with them, and the establishment of a few Soviets and autonomous governments in minority areas (Dye, 1940: 196; Graham, 1939: 137-138; Wales, 1939: 145; Snow, 1961: 202-203: Hsieh, 1960: 26; Liu, 1953: 99). In a 1938 report to the Central Committee of the CCP, Mao outlined the basis for subsequent policy towards national minorities (Heaton, 1964: 34, 39). Rather than granting the "right to complete separation from China," as did the Kiangsi Soviet Constitution, this statement granted the right to "unite with the Hans in building a unified country" (Mao, 1950: 7). Similarly, in 1945, Mao reiterated the theme of a "free and unified Chinese Republic" without mentioning the possibility of secession (Mao, 1954-1956: IV, 301).

It is probable that in the early years of the CCP, Mao advocated self-determination, including the right to secede, in order to obtain the confidence and support of the national minorities. As a Chinese, Mao was aware of the assimilative power of Chinese culture; as a Marxist-Leninist, Mao was aware that advocating the right of secession was not the same as advocating actual secession. A later writer suggested ". . . there are two ways of understanding national self-determination--either as freedom to separate or as freedom to unite" (Chang, 1956: 69). It was in the latter sense that Mao spoke of self-determination on the eve of victory (Pasternak, 1962: 42).

The above provides a brief description of the evolution of Chinese Communist minority policy and its theoretical roots. I shall now discuss three areas--administration, agrarian reform, and education--in order to illustrate the way in which policy was implemented in southwest China.

During the early years of power, the central government put regional autonomy into effect, establishing some 130 national minority autonomous districts with a total minority population of 4,500,000 by June 1952 (Thomas, 1953: 95). As early as 1957, over 90% of the national minorities were in some form of autonomous unit (Tung, 1957: 9; Chou, 1957: 143). Regional autonomy did not mean that each national minority could separate from China or pursue a goal other than the establishment of socialism; regional autonomy did mean that each national minority had a degree of control over its own internal affairs, and might take more time than the Chinese in achieving socialism (Fei, 1956: 2; Wiens, 1954: 257). In keeping with Stalin's formula of "national in form, socialist in content," the peoples of the various autonomous areas were granted some latitude in choice of administrative personnel, management of local finances, organization of local security forces, use of their own language, and preservation of customs (Chen, 1967: 88; Chang, 1956: 529-530). The intent, however, of this form of administration was not to liberate the minorities from central control, but rather to integrate them more fully into the Chinese state. In spite of propaganda to the contrary (see, for example, Mao, 1955: 253), the minorities were less "masters of their own houses" under the program of regional autonomy than they had been under the *t'u-ssu* system. The power of the CCP, PLA, and minority cadres flowed into tribal areas which had been relatively free from Chinese influence before 1949.

In spite of this power, some of the national minorities proved restive after less than a decade of Communist rule. In 1957, local nationalism was said to have replaced Han chauvinism as the greatest obstacle to the unity of China's nationalities. Local nationalism was branded as "anti-Marxist-Leninist" and "anti-CCP" as some groups demanded separation from China, expressing such sentiments as "all Hui under Heaven are one family." Other minorities refused to study Chinese, refused to accept criticism offered by Chinese cadres, over-zealously censured Chinese cadres, opposed new Chinese settlers, preserved "backward" customs, sought to enlarge the scope of regional autonomy, or even attempted to hinder the development of socialism (Hsieh, 1957: 5; Wang, 1957: 1; Ma Ta-chun, 1958: 2-16; Cheboksarov, 1959: 108; Holubnychy, 1960: 111). In sum, administration of minority areas after 1949 was, although not without its problems, a qualified success. The economic power of the *t'u-ssu* was ended by land reform and their political power undermined by a new group--the cadres. The minorities of the southwest were generally more fully integrated into the Chinese state than ever before.

The second area of policy implementation--that of agrarian reform--presented some unique problems to the CCP. By June 1957, ninety-seven percent of peasant households were members of agricultural producers' cooperatives (APC's) (*Chugoku nenkan*, 1958: 229), and by November, 1958, ninety-eight percent of the rural population were commune members (*Ten Great Years*, 1960: 43). In Liang-shan Yi Autonomous *Chou*, however, the percentage enrolled in APC's did not reach ninety percent until 1962, four years after the introduction of communes in most of China (Wa-cha-mu-chi, 1962: 52; Chu, 1962: 2), and as late as 1967 private ownership and serfdom existed in abundance in certain minority areas of western Yunnan (*China News Analysis*, 1968: 6).

Land reform, co-operativization, and the communes presented special problems in minority areas of southwest China. Not all minorities in Kweichow, for example, had been oppressed tenants under the Nationalists. Some Miao and Chung-chia had been landlords, and, as landlords, they were dealt with harshly by the Chinese Communists (Beauclair, 1956: 279). Certain small minority groups in southern Yunnan lived in a state of primitive communism before 1949 (Ma Yao, 1958: 15). When mutual aid teams were introduced in their homeland in 1956, these minorities found the concept of extra pay for extra labor completely alien; they were accustomed to sharing all produce equally. Chinese cadres argued, to the bewilderment of the Yulo,[2] that the introduction of mutual aid teams was "... a step forward, because the equalitarianism of primitive communal society is no stimulus for production" (Huang, 1957: 29-30; Wiens, 1962: 66-67). The Chinese Communists were somewhat surprised to find that in certain areas they had to combat primitive communism in order to introduce cooperatives.

In working with the Ching-p'o,[3] for example, the Chinese Communists first thought that their primitive Communism would provide a convenient stepping stone in setting up agricultural producers' co-operatives; the reverse was true. Animals given the Ching-p'o by the government to improve production were often slaughtered for communal sacrifices, and the Ching-p'o were particularly hesitant to set up cooperatives. In 1957 there were still only 216 cooperatives, enrolling 12.2% of the population, serving the Ching-p'o and in 1958, as the Commune movement was being launched in

the rest of China, government plans called for a total of 400 cooperatives embracing but 25% of the Ching-p'o population (Winnington, 1962: 246).

Cadres viewed the extreme poverty of southwestern Yunnan as the greatest obstacle they must overcome, and discovered that in this region there were no rigid lines between rich and poor as there were no large landowners. The first step the communist leaders introduced in some areas, therefore, was neither land reform nor an end to exploitation; it was, rather, an attempt to increase production (Ma Yao, 1958: 16). In minority areas on the Yunnan border, landlords were given plots of land the same as former tenants, and they were allowed to retain their tools, homes, grain, and the rights of citizenship. Land reform was conducted in this fashion in certain minority areas because of the desire to increase production and to avoid alienation of the upper classes of the minorities ("On Peaceful Reforms in Minority Areas," 1959: 38-41). In some instances, however, minority landlords were stripped of all possessions and suffered imprisonment or death ("Democratic and Socialist Transformation in the Chinese Nationalities Areas," 1958: 26).

In the field of minority education the Nationalists made a poor beginning up to 1949. The Chinese Communists inherited this frail educational network and strengthened it greatly in the years through 1965. By late 1958, there were eight Nationalities Institutes, four of them in the southwest, designed primarily to provide national minority cadres with political training and Chinese cadres assigned to minority areas with training in national minority languages. The idea of special institutes for national minority higher education was a novel one. Although the Nationalists had established some special primary schools for minority students, those minorities who wanted to pursue higher education did so by enrolling in ordinary colleges and universities (*Chung-kuo chiao-yu nien-chien*, 1948: 1212). In several ways, the establishment of special nationalities institutes was a more effective means of minority education. Political training could be directly slanted to the needs of the minorities, research could be conducted into national minority customs and languages, and the minority students need not travel great distances to attend one of the institutes scattered throughout China. The principal drawback, from the viewpoint of the minority student, was that one obtained a great deal of political training and very little higher education.

As the base of the educational structure an impressive number of primary schools were established for the national minorities (Schwarz, 1963: 327). The enrollment increased considerably throughout the 1950's as indicated by the following figures.

National Minority Students

Year	Nat'l Minor. Prim. School Students	Nat'l Minor. Middle School Students
1951	1,210,000	44,300 (Kuo, 1959: 89)
1953	2,540,000	163,000 (Wang, 1955: 51)
1955	2,460,000	193,000 (Jen-min shou-ts'e, 1957: 629)
1957	3,150,000	267,000 (Feng, 1964: 7-8)
1958	4,240,000	390,000 (Kuo, 1959: 89)

Although these figures for national minority education are impressive, they alone do not give the full story. Chou En-lai made it quite clear that in the early 1950's the primary goals of national minority education were to train minority peoples in patriotism, to train cadres from minority groups, and to overcome local nationalism (*Policies Toward Nationalities in the People's Republic of China*, 1953: 24-25). Education, therefore, is used -- as it was used under the Nationalists -- as a means to promote assimilation and political integration of the national minorities.

The minority policy of the Chinese Communists, as implemented in southwest China, was a qualified success through 1965. The national minorities did not break away from China; there were disturbances but no major rebellions in the area; and a sensitive frontier region was better integrated into the Chinese state than in the past. On the other hand, the minorities were less eager to become new socialist men than Mao had anticipated, and local nationalism did not easily die. Thus, when measured against the attempts of the Kuomintang to assimilate the minorities, the Communists enjoyed considerable success; when measured against the Maoist vision, the implementation of minority policy was successful in part only.

FOOTNOTES

1. Under the *t'u-ssu* system a local tribe was governed either through a Chinese appointee of the imperial court or through a local chieftain upon whom an hereditary title was conferred.

2. The Yulo are a small ethnic group of about 5,100 persons living in southern Yunnan. Their economy is characterized by slash and burn agriculture with some hunting and fishing.

3. The Ching-p'o are a Tibeto-Burmese peoples numbering about 80,000 in Yunnan.

REFERENCES

A-erh-mu-hsia (Wang Hai-min).
1958   "Hung chun, hung chun, Yi-min ti ch'in-jen." Hung ch'i p'iao-p'iao 3 (August):51-59.

Afanas'yeskiy, Ye. A.
1962   Szechuan. Moscow: Publishing House of Oriental Literature. Joint Publications Research Service No. 15, 308, September 17, 1962:1-392.

Beauclair, Inez de.
1956   "Ethnic Groups." in Hellmut Wilhelm (ed.), A General Handbook of China. Seattle: Far Eastern and Russian Institute, University of Washington

Brandt, Conrad, Benjamin Schwartz, and
  John K. Fairbank (eds.).
1952   A Documentary History of Chinese Communism. Cambridge, Mass.: Harvard University Press.

Chang, Chih-i.
1956   Chung-kuo ko-ming ti min-tsu wen-t'i ho min-tsu cheng-ts'e chiang-hua (t'i-kang). Peking: Chung-kuo ch'ing-nien ch'u-pan she.

Chang, Hsia-min.
1957   Pien-chiang wen-t'i yu pien-chiang chien-she. Taipei: Chung-hua wen-hua ch'u-pan shih-yeh wei-yuan-hui.

Chang, Jen-hsiu.
1939   "Ts'ai lun I-Han t'ung-yuan." Hsi-nan pien-chiang 6(May):1-9.

Chang, Wen-t'ung.
1947   "Ch'ou pien so chien." Pien to yueh-k'an 10&11 (January):7-10.

Chang, Yu-nan.
1956   "The Chinese Communist State System Under the Constitution of 1954." The Journal of Politics 18(August):520-547.

Chang, Yu-ts'ai.
1947   "Hsi-nan pien-ti shih-yung hsiao-hsueh kuo-yu ch'ang-shih ko-pen pien-chi i-chien." Chiao-yu t'ung hsun 2(January):8-11.

Chao, Shun-hsiao.
1953   Pai-i pien-min yen-chiu. Hong Kong: Tzu-yu ch'u-pan she.

Cheboksarov, N.E.
1959   "Basic Stages in the Development of Ethnography in China." Sovetskaya Etnografiya 6. Joint Publications Research Service No. 16,431, May 30, 1962: 57-75.

Chen, Sheng.
1940   "K'eng-ma t'u-ssu ti kai-k'uang." Hsi-nan pien-chiang 11(September):52-66.

Chen, Theodore H.E. (ed.).
1967   The Chinese Communist Regime: Documents and Commentary. New York: Praeger.

Chin, P'ing-ou, et.al. (eds.).
1956   San-min chu-i tz'u-tien. Taipei: Chung-hua ts'ung-shu wei-yuan-hui.

China News Analysis No. 720.
1968   Hong Kong: Cathay Press.

Chou, Fang.
1957   Wo kuo kuo-chia chi-kou. Peking: Chung-kuo ch'ing-nien chu'u-pan she.

Chou, K'un-t'ien.
1962a   Chung-kuo pien-chiang min-tsu chien shih. Taipei: T'ai-wan shu-tien.

1962b   Pien-chiang cheng-ts'e yen-chiu. Taipei: T'ai-wan shu-tien.

1967   "Chung-kuo pien-chiang cheng-chih chih-tu chih yen-ke." Hua-kang hsueh-pao 4(December):417-433.

Chugoku nenkan.
1958   Tokyo: Ishizaki shoten.

Chung-hua nien-chien.
1948   Nanking: Chung-hua nien-chien she.

Chung-kuo chiao-yu nien-chien.
1948   Shanghai: Commercial Press.

"Democratic and Socialist Transformation in the Chinese Nationalities Areas"
1958   Chiao-hsueh yu yen-chiu 6(June). Joint Publications Research Service No. 1112-D, January 14, 1960:25-35.

Dreyer, June.
1968   China's Minority Nationalities in the Cultural Revolution. China Quarterly 35(July-September):96-109.

Dye, Daniel S.
1940   "The Challenge of the Far Western Border." Pp. 191-199 in Wu Yi-fang and Frank Price (eds.), China Rediscovers Her West. New York: Friendship Press.

Fei, Hsiao-t'ung (ed.).
1956   Shem-ma shih min-tsu ch'u-yu tzu-chih. Hong Kong: Hsin min-chu ch'u-pan she.

Feng, Wen.
1964   "Peiping's Policy towards China's Ethnic Minorities." Analysis of Current Chinese Communist Problems. Taipei: Institute of International Relations.

Graham, David C.
1939   "Some Recent Events in the Sikang Region." Journal of the West China Border Research Society 11:136-138.

Heaton, H. Grant.
1964   "The Chinese Communist Policy Toward the National Minority Groups: 1949-1954." Seattle: Unpublished M.A. Thesis, University of Washington.

Holubnychy, Lydia.
1960   "Chinese Treatment of the Nationality Problem in Sinkiang." The East Turkic Review 46:81-116.

Hsieh, Fu-min.
1958   "Miao shan i yeh." Hung ch'i p'iao-p'iao 3(August):162-164.

Hsieh, Ho-ch'ou.
1957   "Chuang-tsu chung-ti min-tsu chu-i piao-hsien tsai liang-ke fang-mien." Min-tsu t'uan-chieh 3(December):5.

1960   "The Grand Autonomous Policy for the Minority Nationalities." Min-tsu t'uan-chieh 1(January). Joint Publications Research Service No. 2699, May 23, 1960:26-38.

Hsu, I-t'ang.
1936   "Fei-ch'ang shih-ch'i chih Yun-nan pien-chiang." Chung-kuo hsin lun 2(April):87-93.

Huang, Chang-lu.
1957   "New Days on Yulo Mountain." China Reconstructs 9(September):28-30.

Inkeles, Alex.
1960   "Soviet Nationality Theory in Perspective." Problems of Communism 9(May-June):25-34.

Jen-min shou-ts'e.
1957   Shanghai: Ta-kung pao.

K'ang, Cheng-te.
1958   "Hsin lien hsin." Hung ch'i p'iao-p'iao 3(August): 1965-67.

Kuo, Lin.
1959   "Middle and Elementary Education After Ten Years." Fu-tao-yuan 10(October). Joint Publications Research Service No. 3206, May 2, 1960:89.

Legge, James.
1960   The Chinese Classics. 2nd Ed.; Hong Kong: Hong Kong University Press.

Lenin, V.I.
1921   Selected Works. New York: International Publishers.

Li, Hsi-pi.
1940   "T'eng-ch'ung so-chi." Hsi-nan pien-chiang 11(September):43-51.

Li, Hsiang-chin.
1947   "Lun Kuei-chou ti Hsin-chiang." Pien to yueh-k'an 12(February):10-13.

Ling, Kuang-tien.
1943   "Yueh-sui t'ien-pa t'u-ssu she-hui chien-she kung-tso kai-k'uang." Pien-chiang yen-chiu t'ung-hsun 2(June):2-4.

Ling, Shun-sheng.
1947   "Pien-chiang chiao-yu." Chiao-yu t'ung-hsun 2(January):16-18.

Liu, Ko-p'ing
1953   "Liang nien lai ti min-tsu kung-tso." Min-tsu cheng-ts'e wen-hsien hui-pien. Peking: Jen-min ch'u-pan she.

Ma, Ch'ang-shou.
1948   "Shao-shu min-tsu wen-t'i." Min-tsu-hsueh yen-chiu chi-k'an 6(August):8-23.

Ma, Ta-chun.
1958   "Oppose Local Nationalism, Correctly Settle Nationality Relations." Chiao-hsueh yu yen-chiu 6(June). Joint Publications Research Service No. 1112-D, January 14, 1960: 1-16.

Ma, Yao.
1958   "Jumping Over Centuries." China Reconstructs 7(July):14-16.

Mao, Tse-tung.
1934   Chih yu su-wei-ai neng-kuo chiu chung-kno.
1950   "The New Stage." People's China 1(April):7.
1954-   Selected Works. New York: International Publishers.
1956

Nei-cheng kung-pao.
1928   Nanking: Nei-cheng pu.

"On Peaceful Reforms in Minority Areas"
1959   Min-tsu yen-chiu 7 (July). Joint Publications Research Service No. 998-D, November 4, 1959:38-41.

Pasternak, Burton.
1962   "Continuity and Discontinuity in Chinese Policy Toward the Southwestern Tribes Since 1911." New York: Unpublished M.A. Thesis, Columbia University.

P'ing-pa hsien-chih.
1932   Kwei-yang: 6 chuan.

Pipes, Richard.
1953   "Bolshevik National Theory Before 1917." Problems of Communism 2(May):22-27.
1957   The Formation of the Soviet Union: Communism and Nationalism, 1917-1923. Cambridge, Mass.: Harvard University Press.

Policies Toward Nationalities in the People's Republic of China
1953   Peking: Foreign Language Press.

"Reforming the Aborigines of Kwangsi."
1929   The South China Monthly Review 2(March):46-48.

Ruey, Yih-fu (Jui I-fu).
1954 "So-wei shao-shu min-tsu wen-t'i." Taipei: Unpublished manuscript.

Schafer, Edward.
1967 The Vermilion Bird: T'ang Images of the South. Berkeley: University of California Press.

Schwarz, Henry G.
1963 "Policy and Administration of Minority Areas in Northwest China and Inner Mongolia, 1949-1959." Madison: Unpublished Ph.D. dissertation, University of Wisconsin.

Shaheen, Samad.
1956 The Communist (Bolshevik) Theory of National Self-Determination. The Hague: 's-Gravenhage.

Snow, Edgar.
1961 Red Star Over China. New York: Grove Press.

Sun, Ming-ching.
1942 "K'ai-fa Hsi-k'ang chih i-i chi chi t'u-ching." Hsi-nan pien-chiang 14(January):17-23.

Sun, Yat-sen.
1953 "Kuo-min cheng-fu chien-kuo ta-kang." Fundamentals of National Reconstruction. Taipei: China Cultural Service.

Ten Great Years.
1960 Peking: Foreign Language Press.

Thomas, S. B.
1953 Government and Administration in Communist China. New York: Institute of Pacific Relations.

"Transcript," Academia Sinica.
     I was allowed to use material from one of the oral history projects of Academia Sinica with the understanding that specific reference to it would not be made during the lifetime of the interviewee. Therefore, all footnotes which refer to this material read simply "Transcript," Academia Sinica.

Tseng, Yu-hao.
1930 Modern Chinese Political and Legal Philosophy. Shanghai: Commercial Press.

Tung, Ying.
1957 "Pu-tuan fa-chan wokuo ke min-tsu chien ti t'uan-chieh ho yu-i." Min-tsu t'uan-chieh 2(November):8-11.

Wales, Nym.
1939 Inside Red China. New York: Doubleday Doran and Company
1952 Red Dust: Autobiographies of Chinese Communists. Stanford: Stanford University Press.

Walker, Francis A.
1964 "Annual Report of the Commission of Indian Affairs, November 1, 1872." In William Miller (ed.), Readings in American Values. Englewood Cliffs: Prentice-Hall.

Wang, Feng.
1957 "Chia-ch'iang min-tsu chien ti tuan-chieh t'ung-i." Min-tsu t'uan-chieh 3(December):1.

Wang, Shu-tang.
1955 China: Land of Many Nationalities. Peking: Foreign Language Press.

Wen, Chi (ed.).
1957 T'ai-wan fan cheng-chih. Taipei: T'ai-wan sheng wen-hsien wei-yuan-hui.

Wiens, Herold J.
1954 China's March Toward the Tropics. Hamden, Conn.: The Shoestring Press.
1962 "Some of China's Thirty-five Million Non-Chinese." Journal of the Hong Kong Branch of the Royal Asiatic Society 2:54-74.

Winnington, Alan.
1962 The Slaves of Cool Mountain. Berlin: Seven Seas Publishers.

Yakhontoff, Victor A.
1934 The Chinese Soviets. New York: Coward-McCann.

Young, Ching-chi (Yang Ch'eng-chih).
1943 "Among the Aboriginal Tribes of Kwangsi." Min-su 2(December):3-19.

Yu, Wen-ch'eng.
1948 "Ch'uan k'ang pien-ch'u I-tsu ti hsin ku-chi." Pien-chiang t'ung-hsun 5(July):10-13.

LEADERSHIP IN CHINA'S MINORITY NATIONALITIES, AUTONOMOUS REGIONS—CONTINUITY AND CHANGE

LUCIE CHENG HIRATA

Department of Sociology
University of California, Los Angeles

Abstract

The leadership composition in local government and Party organizations of five minority nationalities autonomous regions in China from the date of their establishment to the conclusion of the Great Proletarian Cultural Revolution was analyzed. We found that (1) there was a decrease in minority representation in local government leadership structure through time, and that this decrease was related to a change in emphasis on the nationalities question. (2) The fluctuation in percentage of minority representation was higher in the government than in the Party, indicating that changes in specific policies toward minorities have little effect on the Party leadership composition. (3) The proportion of leaders holding joint positions in both organizations was rather low. However, a higher percentage of minority than Han leaders held interlocking positions. (4) Leadership composition in both the government and the Party was highly static before the Cultural Revolution, probably one of the contribution factors for the Revolution. The rate of change before and after the Revolution was higher among the Han leaders than the minorities. (5) There was no relationship between overlapping membership before the Cultural Revolution and individual's survival rate as leaders through the Revolution.

It is widely recognized that the Chinese Revolution of 1949 has not only transformed Chinese society, but also brought into being an alternative socialist model of development for countries around the world. China, being a multi-national state, has her share of minority problems, and thus China's policy toward her minority nationalities is of major interest to other states and their minorities.

The minority nationalities question has always been considered a significant question by the Communist Party of China (CPC). Mao Tse-tung, in his widely quoted speech on the correct handling of contradictions, identified "Han chauvinism" and "local nationalism" as representing "a specific contradiction among the people which should be overcome" (1971: 460). Administratively, China has tried to resolve this contradiction by pursuing a policy of regional autonomy for her 54 minority nationalities with 43 million people or 6% of the total Chinese population. Areas with a concentration of one minority nationality or a combination of several minority nationalities are incorporated as autonomous regions (ch'u), districts (chou), or counties (hsien), depending on their sizes. There are now a total of 5 autonomous regions, 29 autonomous districts and 69 autonomous counties (China Reconstructs, Dec. 1972). Approximately 90% of the minorities live in these autonomous areas; the rest are scattered throughout China.

This paper is concerned with the leadership question in China's five autonomous regions: Inner Mongolia, which was established in 1947; Sinkiang Uighur, established in 1955; Kwangsi Chuang and Ninghsia Hui, both established in 1958; and Tibet, which was established in 1965.

Franz Schurmann states (1968: 8-9) that ethos, status group, and modal personality are core elements of a social system, and their functional equivalents in today's China are ideology, organizational leadership and cadre. Two organizations are considered crucial in Schurmann's framework, the government and the party. Leadership in these two organizations has been studied by several scholars. Political Scientists in particular have made considerable efforts to trace the rise and fall of national leaders, and have followed closely through time the composition of the top leadership organizations such as the CPC Central Committee and the Politburo (cf. Tang and Maloney, 1967; Klein and Hager,

1971; and Scalapino, 1972). However, leadership at lower levels, particularly in autonomous areas, has generally been neglected. The few studies that are available tend to concentrate on a handful of well-known figures in specific individual regions. So far, no systematic aggregate analysis of leadership in all autonomous regions has been published. While biographical studies of prominent leaders in minority areas are important in their own right, aggregate analysis will reveal more clearly the evolution of China's policies toward nationalities throughout the years.

Specifically, this paper seeks to answer the following questions regarding leadership in the autonomous regions. (1) What is the degree of continuity and change in regional government and Party leadership structure from the date of their establishment until the organization of the Revolutionary Committees and the new Party committees after the Great Proletarian Cultural Revolution? (2) Does the transition rate vary between Han leaders and leaders of minority nationalities? (3) How does the transition rate for the regional governments compare with that for the CPC organizations at the regional level? (4) What is the degree of overlap or interlock between the government and the Party? Finally, (5) What is the relationship between overlapping membership and continuity?

DATA

A list of top officials, chairman and vice-chairmen of each of the five regional governments was compiled, beginning with the years when they were established and continuing on through subsequent election years 1959 and 1964 until the constitution of Revolutionary Committees during the Cultural Revolution in 1967-68.[1] Since not all the five regional governments were established at the same time, some regions have fewer points in time than others. For example, the Sinkiang Uighur Autonomous Region was established in 1955, local elections were held in 1959, 1964, and the Revolutionary Committee was constituted in 1968, therefore, yielding four

*I should like to acknowledge the helpful comments of Sam Surace, Philip Huang, Tsuen-jen Lei and Lowell Chun-Hoon.

points in time. On the other hand, the Tibet Autonomous Region was established in 1965, and its Revolutionary Committee was constituted in 1968, yielding therefore only two points in time.

Another list was compiled which includes persons who served as Party secretaries in the CPC regional committees before the Cultural Revolution in the same time periods and those who were elected to the regional Party Committees at the local Party congresses held since the Cultural Revolution.

These two lists of names were checked against a number of sources to determine the national identity of the leaders.[2] Throughout this procedure, in cases of doubt or conflicting information, publications issued from China were always relied upon as primary references.

In addition to the general limitations of the sources stated by Klein in his bibliographic essay (Scalapino, 1972: 609-656), several remarks concerning the reliability of the present data have to be registered. First, since information was not available for every single year, it was not possible to follow the leadership composition on an uninterrupted continuous time basis. By using particular points in time as a basic dimension in our analysis, we ignored those individuals who might have dropped in-and-out of the leadership group between two time points. In other words, our analysis does not reflect the extent to which leaders may be purged-and-reinstated between two time points, but only those changes that can be detected at particular points. For example, if "X" appeared as a leader in 1959 and in 1964, we would count him as serving continuously in the leadership position between these two time points, although he might have been purged in 1960 and reinstated sometime before 1964. We realize that the extent of purge-and-reinstatement between time points may be itself an important index of leadership stability, but the limitations of available data do not allow us to explore this possibility at present.

Second, for the period since the Cultural Revolution, we have taken 1967-68, the years when most regional Revolutionary Committees were formed, as a point in time. However, regional Party congresses were not convened until 1971, so there was a lapse of three years. If we examine government and Party leadership composition separately, this lapse does not present any serious problem. But, when examining the degree of overlap between Party and government for the period since the Cultural Revolution, the lapse poses a possibility of considerable bias. For example, Liu Hsing, who was not a leader in the Sinkiang Uighur Autonomous Region's Revolutionary Committee in 1968, became one in 1971. In the same year he was elected as one of the local Party secretaries. Even though in 1971 he had overlapping membership in both the government and the Party leadership structure, he was not included in our tabulation as one who held joint positions. Fortunately, as far as we could determine, this was a rare case.

REGIONAL GOVERNMENT LEADERSHIP COMPOSITION

In 1947, the Inner Mongolia Autonomous Region, first of its kind in China, was established. Subsequently, four others came into being, including Sinkiang Uighur, Kwangsi Chuang, Ninghsia Hui and Tibet. Table I shows the number and percent of leaders who have been identified as minorities in these regional governments for different points in time, together with estimated minority population in each respective region. The table includes only chairmen and vice-chairmen of the People's Committees and the Revolutionary Committees in their respective autonomous regions.

At first glance, one is struck by the decrease in the percentage of minority leaders in all regions through time. For

TABLE I. MINORITY LEADERS IN REGIONAL GOVERNMENTS
AND MINORITY POPULATION IN RESPECTIVE REGIONS,
1947-1968

Region	1947 Leader	1947 Pop.(in 1000's)	1954 Leader	1954 Pop.(in 1000's)	1959 Leader	1959 Pop.(in 1000's)	1964 Leader	1964 Pop.(in 1000's)	1968 Leader	1968 Pop.(in 1000's)
Inner Mongolia	100% (2)	---- ----	63% (5)	16%[a] (1,000)	62% (8)	13%[c] (1,130)	55% (6)	13%[g] (1,200)	25% (1)	5-10%[i] (----)
Sinkiang	NA	NA	75% (3)	75%[b] (3,650)	71% (5)	72%[d] (----)	63% (5)	69%[g] (3,900)	20% (2)	60-70% (----)
Kwangsi	NA	NA	NA	NA	43% (3)	37%[e] (7,174)	33% (3)	36%[g] (7,250)	15% (2)	30-40% (----)
Ninghsia	NA	NA	NA	NA	63% (5)	33%[f] (601)	57% (4)	33%[g] (600)	20% (1)	30-40% (----)
Tibet	NA	NA	NA	NA	NA	NA	75% (6)	75%[h] (1,322)	36% (5)	50-60%[j] (----)

[a] Jen-min shou-tsĕ, 1955.

[b] People's China, Vol. 3, No. 10 (May 16, 1951).

[c] Min-tsu t"uan-chieh, Nov. 1959.

[d] Average between 1954 and 1964.

[e] Peking Review, Vol. 1, No. 3 (March 18, 1958).

[f] Peking Review, Vol. 1, No. 36 (Nov. 4, 1958).

[g] Computed from Nichols, 1968, and Jen-min shou-tsĕ, 1965.

[h] Tibet's Population Increases, New China News Agency release, Aug. 20, 1965, Lhasa, in Union Research Institute, 1968.

[i] Estimated in Orleans, 1972, pp. 110-111.

[j] Tung-feng, 1972, p. 63.

example, the percentage of minority leaders in Inner Mongolia in 1947 was 100%, but in 1968 it was down to 25%. Similarly, the percentage of minority leaders in Ninghsia decreased from 63% in 1959 to 20% in 1968. However, when we juxtapose this set of statistics with the percentages of minority population in the same regions for the same period of time, we find that despite the decrease minorities were over-represented in relation to their population in Inner Mongolia at every time point. For the rest of the Regions, minorities were either over or equally represented until after 1964. In general, during the first years of the establishment of an autonomous region, there was a higher over-representation of minority nationalities in the local government's leadership structure. Gradually, minority leadership tended to level off proportionate to minority population until the Cultural Revolution.

Given the observed decrease in minority representation through time, one apparent interpretation might be that minorities are gradually losing influence in their local governments, particularly since the Cultural Revolution. This loss of formal political power might then indicate the rise of Han racism. However, this apparent interpretation does not seem to be supported by other indications.

First of all, Chinese policy statements have consistently emphasized that neither Han chauvinism nor local nationalism is a correct way of solving the national minorities question (Mao, 1971: 459-460; Liu, 1964). Han cadres working in minority areas are often reminded that they should not retain notions of Han superiority or mechanically apply their work experience from Han areas. Minority nationalities, on the other hand, are asked to be mindful of the importance of centralized and unified leadership in achieving socialist transformation in their own areas as well as in all of China (Chang, 1956). was established. Subsequently, four others came into being, including Sinkiang Uighur, the minorities. For example, the use of Chinese characters made up with the "dog radical" to represent the names of the minorities was a traditional practice. Shortly after its establishment, the Chinese government issued a directive changing all names that were prejudicial and derogatory (Min-tsu cheng-ts'e wen-hsien hui-pien, 1953: 11-12).

Third, recognizing the existence of cultural differences between the minorities and the Han, the Chinese government has given special consideration to their needs. For example, Moslems are exempted from paying the regular slaughter tax for cattle and sheep slain for their own use during their three big religious festivals (Min-tsu cheng-ts'e wen-hsien hui-pien, 1953: 5). In 1963, more than forty types of commercial products were listed as needed especially by the minorities, worthy of special consideration in production, distribution and pricing (Yang, 1963).

Fourth, throughout the history of the People's Republic, there have been rigorous campaigns to recruit minority cadres and Party members. Up until 1968, somewhere between a half million and a million persons of the minority nationalities have participated in the Chinese political structure as cadres and Party members. "Considering total numbers of cadres and total numbers of Party members, the non-Hans seem to have a share of each roughly in proportion to their share of the population in the minority areas" (Nichols, 1968: 296). The latest indication of China's continuous effort to recruit minority cadres is found in the October 7, 1972 issue of the Kuang-ming jih-pao, which praised the accomplishment of minority cadre development program in an autonomous county.

Fifth, Chinese and Westerners have reported on the amazing advancements in health, education and economic conditions in the minority areas. The most dramatic achievement is perhaps the virtual elimination and control of syphilis. Before 1949, the syphilis rate was so high that there was a progressive depopulation in minority areas resulting from lowered fertility, a high miscarriage rate and the large number of babies born dead. For example, the Hulunbu League in Inner Mongolia, which numbered 10,386 in 1933, had fallen to 7,670 by the time of the Revolution and an investigation of 2,334 nomadic families at that time revealed that 58% were childless. Following the anti-syphilis campaign, this depopulation trend was reversed. In 1960, 390 herdsmen's families in Hulunbu League registered increases of 21.6%. In the Wulatechien Banner of Inner Mongolia, where syphilis rate had been nearly 50% in 1952, not a single case of infectious syphilis was found among 3,158 persons examined at random in 1962 (Horn, 1969: 86-87).

In terms of education, Tibet is a good example. Before 1951, there was not a single regular modern school in Tibet, and 95% of the population were reported to be illiterate. By 1965, there were 55,000 students in Tibet's 1,500 primary and secondary schools. In addition, there were many night schools for adults (Union Research Institute, 1968: 449-458). In Kwangsi, 3,000,000 people who were illiterate in 1949 became literate by 1959. Among these 3 million people, 700,000 were Chuang minorities (Min-tsu t'uan-chieh, Oct., 1959).

As far as economic condition is concerned, Tibet, which had no modern industry before 1951, had since then built nearly 70 industrial enterprises including electric power stations, coal mining, flour milling, farm machinery and tool-making plants (Union Research Institute: 1968: 721). The number of livestock in some Mongolian areas in 1971 was 11 times more than in the early 1950s (Peking Review: 1971).

While a systematic study is needed to assess the consequences of China's policy toward the nationalities, these fragmented figures illustrate the general improvement in social conditions in minority areas.

To summarize, although ethnic antagonism, which has its historical roots, may still exist, no theoretical basis for discrimination can be found in Chinese policies since 1949. According to available information, integration based on ethnic equality and pluralism, rather than assimilation based on Han Chauvinism, has been China's preference and aim. We are, therefore, led to conclude that perhaps the most apparent interpretation of our data may not be the most plausible one.

As we have pointed out earlier, the establishment of autonomous regions was a resolution of the perceived contradiction between the Han people and a particular minority or group of minorities. Since ethnic antagonism was considered the major obstacle to democratic reform and socialist construction in the early years of an autonomous region, class differences were largely de-emphasized. The policy pursued at this stage of the development was that of the "United Front."

"The United Front consisted of two alliances: the alliance between the Chinese working class and the laboring people of each national minority; and the alliance between the laboring people of all of China's nationalities." (Moseley, 1966: 130). This policy explains both Han participation in the political structure of the autonomous regions and the appearance of many influential upper strata minorities in leading government positions.[3] Since the Han people have always considered themselves to be the superior people in the past, there exists a tendency toward Great Hanism or Han chauvinism toward the minorities. On the other hand, the minorities, long under the oppression of the Han, have a tendency toward local nationalism. The dominating aspect of this contradiction between nationalities shifted from time to time and from area to area. Sometimes Han chauvinism was considered to be a greater evil than local nationalism; sometimes the situation was reversed. In general, during the early years (up until 1958), Han chauvinism was emphasized over local nationalism as the more damaging attitude to be overcome. Afterwards, local nationalism received equal or more attention.[4]

Local nationalism has its roots in both historical ethnic antagonism and the resistance of the upper strata minorities against socialism. To combat local nationalism, China emphasized the Marxist-Leninist position that "the national question is in essence the class question." The basic cause of the nationalities problem at this stage is that "classes, class contradictions and class struggle, and the struggle between the two paths of socialism and capitalism still exist in the various nationalities" (Liu, 1966: 28). It was the upper strata minorities, having retained their power under the United Front, who tried to capitalize on ethnic sentiments in order to serve their own self-interest rather than the interest of the laboring people in minorities areas (Liu, 1966). Therefore, within each national minority, class struggle was waged. Those minority leaders who belonged to the upper strata or who had served the interest of that class were severely criticized. As a result of this shift in emphasis on the conception of the nationalities question and of the change in practical conditions, the visibility of minorities as leaders in the top government positions was no longer a primary concern. Class background and class interest, rather than ethnicity, became a more important criterion for leadership. It was reflected in the governmental structure as the decrease in ethnic representation and the replacement of traditional minority leaders with new minority leaders of slave and poor herdsman origins.[5]

REGIONAL PARTY COMMITTEES

Since, in China, the CPC is the policy-making body that guides the work of the government, it is important to see whether the pattern that we have observed for the regional governments is also reflected in the local Party committees. Table II shows the percentages of regional Party secretaries who have been identified as minorities at three time periods, 1959-60, 1964-65, and 1971.

TABLE II. MINORITY PARTY SECRETARIES IN
AUTONOMOUS REGIONS, 1959-1971

	1959-1960	1964-1965	1971
Inner Mongolia	57% (4)	56% (5)	20% (1)
Sinkiang	17% (1)	11% (1)	20% (1)
Kwangsi	33% (2)	29% (2)	25% (1)
Ninghsia	33% (1)	50% (3)	33% (2)
Tibet	NA	10% (1)	43% (3)
TOTAL	35% (8)	27% (12)	30% (8)

We can see that while Inner Mongolia, Kwangsi and Ninghsia show a decrease in the percentages of minority Party secretaries, Sinkiang and Tibet show an increase. Since the total number of secretaries in Party committees was smaller than the total of chairmen and vice-chairmen in regional

governments, the statistics given by region are very difficult to interpret. We can only point out that minority representation exists not only in the administrative organ of the state, but also in the Party structure. If we look at the percentage of minority Party secretaries for all five regions, we find that there is not much fluctuation from 1959 to 1971.

A comparison between Table I and Table II shows that the United Front did not boost minority representation in the local Party leadership as it did in the government. This is not surprising, since Party secretaries are drawn from Party members and the number of minority Party members has been very small in the early years. As recruitment efforts continue, we may expect an increase in minority in the local Party leadership structure.

INTERLOCKING RELATIONSHIP BETWEEN PARTY AND GOVERNMENT

Having examined the leadership composition of the regional governments and Party committees, we now turn to the question of interlock or overlap between these two organizations. In general, we expect individuals who hold interlocking positions to have more influence than those who hold positions in a single organization. For those who hold single positions, it may be said that those who are Party secretaries have higher status than those who are chairmen of the local governments. Table III shows the pattern of interlocking relationship in the five autonomous regions.

TABLE III. INTERLOCK BETWEEN PARTY AND GOVERNMENT LEADERSHIP
IN AUTONOMOUS REGIONS, 1959-1971

	1959-1960		1964-1965		1968-1971	
	Han	Minority	Han	Minority	Han	Minority
Government only	44% (11)	62% (13)	25% (11)	57% (16)	60% (30)	39% (5)
Party only	44% (11)	0 (0)	57% (25)	14% (4)	30% (15)	15% (2)
Both	12% (3)	38% (8)	18% (8)	29% (8)	10% (5)	46% (6)
TOTAL (100%)=	(25)	(21)	(44)	(28)	(50)	(13)

The overall percentages of interlock for the three periods are 11 out of 46, or 24%; 16 out of 72, or 22% and 11 out of 63 or 18%, respectively. As we can see, there is a tendency for the regional government and the regional Party committee to have different leaders at the regional level, an effort to avoid the development of local regionalism (cf. Tang, 1967). Certainly, the increasing supply of cadres and Party members would make it possible to diffuse political power among individuals. In comparison to the interlocking relationship observed for the top national leadership (Tang, 1967: 214-219), the degree of overlap at the regional level has been rather small.

How does the interlocking relationship among the Han leaders compare with that among the minorities? From Table III we find that there are proportionately more minorities than Han who have held leadership positions in both organizations. It indicates that although the number of minority leaders is relatively small in comparison to the number of Han leaders, a greater proportion of them occupy the most influential roles. However, when we consider those who were leaders in one or the other organization, we find that a higher proportion of Han occupied Party positions.

CONTINUITY AND CHANGE

The summer of 1966 is generally considered as the beginning of the Great Proletarian Cultural Revolution which was aimed at correcting bureaucratic tendencies within the leadership organization. As a result, China experienced the greatest leadership turnover since her establishment. No quantitative study of the continuity and change at the regional level has yet been attempted. We would like to demonstrate,

through a conditional probability model, that before the Cultural Revolution, regional leadership organization was highly static, and that the Revolution was truly a revolution which resulted in the rise of new regional leadership. We will first look at continuity and change for the government and the Party separately, then we will control for nationality and compare the degree of continuity between the Han and the minority leaders.

FIGURE I. CONTINUITY AND CHANGE IN
REGIONAL GOVERNMENT LEADERSHIP, 1954 - 1968.*

*Circled numbers represent total numbers of government leaders at respective time points.

Based on the information presented in Figures I and II, we computed a series of percentages. These are given in Table IV. It is very obvious that, at the regional level of government, there is a high probability for individual leaders to survive as leaders in that organization from 1954 to 1959 (.92) and from 1959 to 1964 (.74) but a very low probability for them to survive from 1964 to 1968 (.07). The conditional probability for a leader to survive from 1954 to 1959 *and* from 1959 to 1964 is 0.67, but for that person to last through 1968, the probability is only 0.08. A similar pattern is observed for the party leadership. While the survival rate for party secretaries from 1959 to 1964 was 0.82, that from 1964 to 1971 was only 0.09.

We may ask, what is the relationship between organization leadership and survival? Tables IV and V show that the probability for a Party leader to continue in his position is slightly higher than that for a government leader. In other words, a Party position is relatively more secure than a government one. This pattern is particularly true for the minorities.

TABLE IV. DEGREE OF CONTINUITY IN LEADERSHIP, 1954-1971

	1954-1959	1959-1964	1964-1971
Government	92%	74%	7%
N(100%) =	(12)	(35)	(43)
Party	NA	82%	9%
N(100%) =		(22)	(45)

FIGURE II. CONTINUITY AND CHANGE
IN REGIONAL PARTY COMMITTEES, 1959 - 1971.*

*Circled numbers represent total numbers of party leaders at respective time points.

Following the same procedure, the degrees of continuity for Han and minority leadership in government and Party organizations were computed. As indicated in Table V, an abrupt fall of the survival rate occurred from 1964 to 1971 for both groups in both organizations. However, the decline was more dramatic for the Han leadership than for the minorities. In the regional government, the probabilities for a Han leader to survive are 0.75, 0.71 and 0.00 for the three transition periods respectively. In the same organization, the probabilities for a minority leader to survive are 1.00, 0.76 and 0.13 respectively. Again, a similar pattern holds for the Party leadership.

Does overlapping position have an effect on survival in the leadership group during the Cultural Revolution? We examined the 16 individuals who held leadership positions in both the Party and the government in 1964, and found that only 2 of them or 13% remained as leaders. Correspondingly, of the 56 individuals who held leadership positions in either the government or the Party but not in both organizations in 1964, 6 or 11% survived as leaders after the Cultural Revolution. The occupation of an interlock position did not increase the survival probability by an appreciable amount.

SUMMARY AND CONCLUSIONS

The leadership composition in local government and Party organizations of five minority nationalities autonomous regions in China, from the date of their establishment to the conclusion of the Great Proletarian Cultural Revolution, was analyzed. We found that (1) Although the percentages of minority representation in local governments showed a decrease through time, it was a decrease from a high degree of over-representation to proportionate or somewhat under-representation in most areas. (2) Comparing the government with the Party, the fluctuation in percentage of minority representation was higher in the former than in the latter, indicating that changes in specific policies toward minorities have little effect on the Party leadership composition. (3) The proportion of leaders holding joint positions in both organizations was rather low. However, a higher percentage of minority than Han leaders held interlocking positions. (4) In terms of continuity and change, leadership composition in both the government and the Party was highly static before the Cultural Revolution (probably one of the contributing factors for the Revolution). The Revolution deprived about 90% of the leaders of their power, and brought in a new leadership group.[6] However, the rate of change was higher among the Han leaders than the minorities. Finally, (5) we found that overlapping membership in both government and Party organizations before the Cultural Revolution had no effect on the leaders' survival rate as leaders in the two organizations through the Revolution.

TABLE V. DEGREE OF CONTINUITY FOR HAN AND
MINORITY LEADERSHIP, 1954-1971

	1954-1959		1959-1964		1964-1971	
	Han	Minority	Han	Minority	Han	Minority
Government	75%	100%	71%	75%	0%	13%
N(100%) =	(4)	(8)	(14)	(21)	(19)	(24)
Party	NA	NA	79%	88%	3%	25%
N(100%) =			(14)	(8)	(33)	(12)

Although China's specific policies toward the minorities varied from time to time and from area to area according to practical conditions, the overriding principle is clear. China's aim is to build a Socialist nation, composed of all nationalities within her territory. Due to historical factors, many minority areas lagged behind the Han area in economic and social development, and China has exerted a great deal of efforts to improve these conditions. At the same time, China has made important concessions to the minorities in the form of the United Front and the deferment of more drastic reforms. China firmly believes that, once Socialist construction is complete, the nationalities question will cease to be a major contradiction among the people of China.

Admittedly, our analysis is both brief and incomplete. We hope that what we have presented here will prompt other sociologists to confront the "nationalities question" in China seriously.

NOTES

1. Sources consulted include: Jen-min shou-tse, Directory of Chinese Communist Officials, Chung-kung jen-shih pien-tung, Who's Who in Communist China, Fei-ch'ing yen-chiu, Fei-ch'ing nien-pao, Peking Review, Chung-kung jen-ming lu, Min-tsu t'uan-chieh, Klein and Clark, 1971, etc.
2. See Klein's essay (in Scalapino, 1972) for a discussion of the sources consulted.
3. For example, Ngapo Ngawang Jigme, chairman of the Tibet People's Committee, was formerly a slave-owner.
4. Chang (1956) and Mao (1971) both stated explicitly that Han chauvinism was the key element in the nationalities problem in the early period. From the late 50's until the mid-60's, there was no specific statement identifying either Han chauvinism or local nationalism as the greater evil. However, during the Cultural Revolution, local radio broadcasts emphasized the evil of narrow nationalism. (cf. Schwarz, 1971)
5. For example, Tzu-ya, formerly a poor herdsman; and Pa-sang, who was a female slave.
6. The figure may be somewhat higher than is actually the case, since leaders who died between the two time points were also included in the transition rate.

REFERENCES

Chang, Chi-i
1956 Chung-kuo ko-ming ti min-tsu wen-t-i ho min-tsu cheng-ts'e Chiang-hua. Peking.

China Reconstructs
1972 (Monthly) Peking.
Chung-kung jen-ming lu pien-hsiu wei-yuan-hui (ed.)
1967 Chung-kung jen-ming lu. Taipei.

DeFrancis, John
1951 "National and minority policies," Annals of the American Academy of Politics and Social Sciences 277 (Sept.), 146-155.

Dreyer, June
1968 "China's minority nationalities in the Cultural Revolution," China Quarterly 35 (July-Sept.): 96-109.

Fei-ch'ing yen-chiu tsa-chih-she
1967 Fei-ch'ing nien-pao. Taipei.
1971 Chung-kung nien-pao. Taipei.

Gaimusho ajiakyoku Kasumigasekikai (ed.)
1962 Gendai Chugoku jimmei jiten. Tokyo.

Gjessing, Gutorn
1957 "Chinese anthropology and New China's policy toeards her minorities," Acta Sociologica 2 (1957): 45-68.

Great Changes in Tibet
1972 Peking.

Horn, Joshua
1971 Away with All Pests. New York.

Jen-min ch'u-pan she, Peking (ed.)
1953 Min-tsu cheng-ts'e wen-hsien hui-pien. Peking.
1958 Min-tsu cheng-ts'e wen-chien hui-pien. Peking.

K'ai-feng shih-fan hsueh-yuan and
Chung-kuo k'o-hsueh-yuan
1959 Chung-kuo min-tsu ti-li tzu-liao hsuan-chi. Peking.

Kao, Ch'ung-yen
1970 Chung-kung jen-shih pien-tung. Hong Kong.

Klein, Donald
1962 "The 'next-generation' of Chinese Communist Leaders," China Quarterly (Oct. - Dec.) 57-74.

Klein, Donald W. and
Anne B. Clark (ed.)
1971 Biographic Dictionary of Chinese Communism, 1921-1965. 2 vols. Cambridge.

Liu, Chun
1966 The National Question and Class Struggle. Peking.

Mao, Tse-tung
1971   Selected Readings From the Works of Mao Tse-tung. Peking.

Min-tsu ch'u-pan-she (ed.)
1959-   Shih-nien min-tsu kung-tso ch'eng-chiu. 2 vols. Peking.
1960

Min-tsu t'uan-chieh
1959-   (Monthly) Peking.
1966

Moseley, George
1966   The Party and the National Question in China. Cambridge.

Nichols, James Lloyd
1968   Minority nationality cadres in Communist China. (Unpublished doctoral dissertation, Stanford University)

Orleans, Leo A.
1972   Every Fifth Child. Stanford.

People's China
1950-   (weekly) Peking.
1958

Peking Review
1958-   (Weekly) Peking.
1972

Scalapino, Robert A. (ed.)
1972   Elites in the People's Republic of China. Seattle.

Schurmann, Franz
1968   Ideology and Organization in Communist China. Berkeley.

Schwarz, Henry G.
1964   Leadership Patterns in China's Frontier Regions. Washington, D.C.
1971   Chinese Policies Towards Minorities. Bellingham, Washington.

Ta-kung-pao (ed.)
1950-   Jen-min shou-tse'e (Yearbook). Shanghai.
1965

Tang, Peter S.H. and Joan M. Maloney
1967   Communist China: The Domestic Scene, 1949-1967. South Orange, N.J.

Union Research Institute (ed.)
1968   Tibet, 1950-1967. Hong Kong.
1969   Who's Who in Communist China. 2nd ed. 2 vols. Hong Kong.

U.S.
1963   Directory of Chinese Communist Officials. Washington, D.C.
1966   Directory of Chinese Communist Officials. Washington, D.C.
1969   Directory of Chinese Communist Officials. Washington, D.C.

Yang, Te-Yin
1963   Shao-shu min-tsu t'e-hsu shang-p'in. Peking.

Yin-ta kuo-shi yen-chiu she
1972   "Hsi-tsang tzu-chih ch'u yen-chiu pao-kao." Tung-feng, vol. 2. Champaign, Ill.

5

BURAKUMIN IN PRESENT-DAY JAPAN:
Problems of Ex-Untouchability and Self-Identity

HIROSHI WAGATSUMA

*University of California
at Los Angeles*

ABSTRACT

There are an estimated one to three million people in present-day Japan who are believed to be the descendants of members of an "untouchable" caste of the feudal period. This paper briefly describes the historical background, the modern liberation movements and the present-day general conditions of these people. It also discusses the processes through which the negative image of these people, held originally by the prejudiced and discriminating majority society, become internalized by them, forming negative, distorted self-identity, and also discusses some of the social-psychological consequences of such negative self-identity.

In Japan there are approximately one to three million people, residing in over six thousand communities, rural and urban, who are referred to with a left-wing connotation as *Mikaihō Burakumin* (people of unliberated communities), or (paradoxically) *Dōwa-chiku-no-hito* (people of integrated districts). There are pejorative forms, seldom heard now, such as *Eta* (filth-abundant) or *Yotsu* (four-legged). Another term *Tokushu Burakumin* (people of special community), occasionally used, is also pejorative. The neutral descriptive abbreviation, acceptable to all, is *Burakumin*. These Burakumin are the descendants of members of an "untouchable" caste who are still socially and economically discriminated against as the result of prejudice by members of the majority society. Not racially different in any way from the majority Japanese, they can be identified with certainty only by the registry of place of birth and residence. Nevertheless, many Japanese believe that they are in some way or other visibly identifiable.[2] The Burakumin are considered mentally inferior, incapable of high moral behavior, aggressive, impulsive, and lacking any notion of sanitation or manners. Very often they are "the last hired and the first fired." Marriage between a Buraku individual and a member of the majority society, if not impossible, is frequently the cause of tragedy and ostracism.[3]

A BRIEF HISTORICAL BACKGROUND[4]

By the fifteenth century, there appeared in Japan various groups of people collectively designated as *Senmin* (lowly people). Very roughly, they were classified into two large groups; (1) artisans, mainly engaged in leather or bamboo work, and/or dyeing, and (2) itinerant entertainers, prostitutes and quasi-religious itinerants. The leather-workers were engaged in the slaughtering and skinning of animals, the tanning of leather and the making of leather goods, such as foot-gear, saddles, armour, etc. Because of the Shinto tradition of disdaining whatever was considered "polluting," such as the handling of carcases, as well as the proscription in Buddhism against the killing of animals, these leather-workers had been shunned by ordinary folk. The avoided, though certainly needed, artisans often lived in settlements on dry river beds *(kawara)* or on tax-free barren lands *(san-jo)*, away from the communities of "decent" common people. The second group of Senmin, the itinerant entertainers, were engaged in singing, dancing, drama, puppet shows, or in fortune-telling and other magico-religious practices and/or prostitution.[5] and were objects of suspicion, fear, condemnation and avoidance by

the general public.[6] The Senmin also included beggars, fleeing criminals and the crippled. They also often engaged in cleaning roads and gardens, carrying baggage for travellers, escorting and executing criminals, disposing of their corpses, or in some cases, building gardens and houses.

With the establishment of the Tokugawa government in the early seventeenth century, Japanese society was further organized into a rigidly hierarchial structure. At the top was a warrior-administrator ruling class *(shi)*, with numerous strata of sub-ranks. The ruled consisted of peasants *(nō)*, artisans *(kō)* and the merchant *(shō)* classes. Beneath this structure of accepted citizens was the Senmin class, into which all the lowly people of previous times were integrated. Two major groups of the outcaste were designated as *Hinin* (non-human) and *Eta*. During the Tokugawa period, being Eta was inescapably hereditary; one was born, lived and died as an Eta. That was also the case, generally, with Hinin, but also commoners were forced into Hinin status as punishment for certain crimes, such as adultery, escaping the death penalty, or having attempted double suicide. Such individuals could, at least in principle, regain the status of commoners by securing a respectable sponsor and paying a certain fee.[7] Due to this slight mobility that was possible between "non-human" and "human" status, Hinin was considered to be a higher status than Eta. Eta and Hinin maintained separate endogamous groups. They were made to live in particular parts of the cities, and were forced to look different from ordinary citizens, by walking barefooted, using straw to tie their hair, a rope for a sash, and, in many instances, wearing a patch of leather on their clothes. Their main occupations continued to be handling leather--skinning the dead animal, tanning the hides and making leather goods, and working for police--attending, escorting and executing criminals and disposing of their corpses. Depending upon the locale, they were also engaged in dyeing cloth, making bamboo brushes (for the tea ceremony), magico-religious practices and various forms of entertainment, and very often also begging.

BURAKU MOVEMENT IN MODERN JAPAN[8]

In August 1871, an edict of the Meiji Government officially abolished outcaste status and described the people of this caste as "new commoners" *(Shin-heimin)*. According to the governmental document, there were about 280,000 Eta, 23,500 Hinin, and 80,000 miscellaneous outcaste individuals at the time of the emancipation. However, simple legislation was hardly sufficient to change social attitudes of discrimination built up over the centuries. In fact, Shin-heimin lost, without compensation, the special privileges the feudal society had accorded them--for example, economic monopolies in butchering and leather work. At the time of the "emancipation," people classified as Hinin, having mostly had itinerant occupations, could probably more readily melt into the majority population, becoming, for example, rag and metal pickers on streets, constituting the lowest bottom of the modern Japanese society. However, most Eta were tied to their local communities because their income was drawn from the network of social and financial relationships that traditionally supported these communities.

By the Emancipation Edict, members of the former outcaste were confirmed in their right to own the inferior farming areas to which they had earlier been relegated, or they remained tenants farming land owned by landlords. Over half the people of the former outcaste were engaged to some extent in agriculture. Others, in or near the cities, continued to butcher meat and tan hides, and some began to take over jobs generally considered undesirable or not rewarding. Not only did they lose their former monopolies, but they were required to pay taxes and enter military service.

Because of the changes brought about after the Meiji Restoration, severe financial difficulties afflicted many of the ordinary people. Many were suspicious of the new government and came to hate its policies of change. Tensions and hostilities were often directed toward members of the former outcaste, who became scapegoats and butts of aggression for neighboring communities. In some instances, "Eta-hunts" *(eta-gari)* developed. During the ten years following the Restoration, over two hundred separate riots were recorded and government office buildings, new schools and police stations were attacked and burned, and numerous government officials and policemen were killed or injured. Often, the Shin-heimin served as the most readily available victims for the rioters.

A political movement against prejudice and injustice started as the "reconciliation movement" *(yūwa undō)*, joined by both paternalistic Buraku leaders of wealth and the sympathetic elite of the majority society. The core of the movement was the Greater Japan Fraternal Conciliation Society, established in 1903. The reconciliation movement worked for "self-betterment" and "self-improvement" of Shin-heimin, such as the improvement of their morals, customs, manners and sanitation. However, discrimination continued. For instance, when recruited into the Imperial Army, a "new commoner" was usually assigned to the transportation corps or maintenance corps responsible for making and repairing shoes and other leather goods. When assigned to the infantry, he had no hope of moving up, even to a rank of noncommissioned officer.

Following a series of "rice riots" by impoverished peasants at the time of the inflation after World War I, a militant liberation movement was organized; in March, 1922, the National *Suiheisha* (Levellers' Association) was inaugurated, and it adopted as its flag "a crown of thorns in the color of blood against a black background of darkness." An early objective of the Levellers was an "eye for an eye" counterattack against discrimination, which caused frequent bloodshed. From 1924 to 1930, the movement suffered from factionalism and conflicts among anarchists, Communists and non-revolutionists. Then, in 1930, it clearly took a left-wing orientation and established close ties with the laborers' and farmers' unions. The fight against discrimination was incorporated into the broader context of the class struggle and

the fight for the proletarian revolution. The Communists' red flags and flags of the crown of thorns often flew side by side, for nearly ten years. But as the militarists took power and Japan moved into war, such movements, together with other left-wing activities, were either rendered "harmless", forced underground, or broken through the action of special police. At their last national meeting in August, 1940, the Levellers vowed loyalty to the Emperor.

After World War II, in February, 1946, the National Committee on Buraku Liberation was formed, which "inherited the revolutionary spirit of the Levellers". The Committee later changed its name to the Buraku Liberation League, known as the *Kaihō Dōmei*, and still continues its active attempts to end discrimination toward Burakumin.

GENERAL CONDITIONS OF PRESENT-DAY BURAKU[9]

Buraku communities are concentrated in the lands surrounding the Inland Sea, the ancient heartland of early Japanese culture. Heavy secondary concentrations are found at the base of the Noto Peninsula on the coast of the Japan Sea and in a few prefectures in Central Honshu. (see Hall, 1962)[10] They seem, generally, to be located on the outskirts of the ordinary communities that they served in the past. They were allotted the more undesirable sites--river banks, swamp areas, and the northern slopes of hills and mountains. Most rural, farming Buraku still maintain generally unfavorable land.[11]

Since emancipation in 1871, there has been a radical decrease in the number of Burakumin performing the occupational roles that defined their status in the feudal Tokugawa period. Although in certain urban areas many Burakumin are engaged in butchering, shoe-making, and collecting garbage and night-soil, a large number of Burakumin communities do not now include a single member who practices a distinctively outcaste trade.

The economic position of the Burakumin is poor when compared with the nation at large (Inoue, 1960). There are significant differences between the Buraku and the nation in the proportions of those engaged in manufacturing and governmental service. The low proportion of those engaged in service or government is related to the low level of education in the Buraku. Though the most significant occupational trend among Burakumin in modern Japan has been toward agriculture, most of the Buraku located in rural areas and in agricultural settings cannot really be called farming villages (see Tojo, 1960a). While only a little more than ten percent of the farmers in the nation own less than approximately one acre, over sixty percent of the Buraku farmers own less than an acre, and their land is usually located farther away from their residence, a great part of it in the hilly areas. The exclusion of the Burakumin from the occupations of their neighbors is not limited to agriculture. For example, many Burakumin located among fishing villages find the fishing territory closed to them.

Burakumin rely heavily on government-supplied employment, consisting of various forms of unskilled labor on public works projects (Mahara, 1960b, 1960c). Also, the proportion of social welfare financial aid given to Burakumin is far higher than the national average (Mahara, 1960d).

SELF-IDENTITY AS BURAKUMIN[12]

As Kardiner and Ovesey (1951) and Grier and Cobbs (1969) dramatically illustrated in their studies of Black Americans, one of the psychological consequences of the socialization process in the face of discrimination and prejudice is the formation of negative self-identity in the discriminated individuals. This takes place because the members of a discriminated minority group often internalize the negative image of themselves, originally created and held by the discriminating majority society.

Perhaps our most poignant material on the self-identity of the Burakumin deals with early experience of children in discovering themselves and their families to be members of a disparaged group. An incident told to us by a university student with Buraku background well illustrates the experience of the discovery of a Buraku child's identity. It also illustrates the problem of having to internalize an image of oneself as a feared object, and of having to deal with fear of others and of oneself.

One day, our informant, when four or five years old, wandered out of his community to a neighboring hill in search of butterflies. This particular hill separated the Buraku from a residential district of ordinary folk. Then he encountered two children of approximately his age, who stood for a while looking at him, then suddenly screamed and started to run away. These two children must have been told by their parents not to go beyond the hill, not to go into the district where the frightful, untouchable people lived. They must have been extremely frightened when they suddenly realized they had met a boy from the prohibited area. When they started to run, the children cried out the word "Yotsu" meaning "four-legged," a harsh tabooed word designating the outcaste group. Our informant recalled that a shudder went through his body and he felt a mixture of fear, sorrow and anger. He ran after the two children, caught up with them, hit them, choked them, and shouted meaningless words at them in an excited voice. The children did not try to defend themselves but remained passive, pale with fear. At a later date, our informant was again visiting the little hill, and on returning, he met a boy coming from the direction of his own community. Without exactly comprehending what he was doing, he cried out "Yotsu" and ran away from the boy. Somehow, he was attempting to understand the overwhelming sense of fear that he had witnessed in the other two children.

Another informant, from a family that had successfully "passed", told us a number of episodes from his childhood, well illustrating feelings of secrecy and shame relating to self-discovery.

At about the time this informant was ready to go to grade school, his father decided to move out of the Buraku. The first step was to open up a small shoestore in a neutral neighborhood. In addition to selling new shoes, his father continued his previous occupation of repairing shoes and sandals. Since they lived a considerable distance away from the community, the boy went to a grade school with children of the outside society. At school he was not known as a Burakumin. He was "passing" at school, although in his immediate neighborhood his father's occupation made it evident that the family was of Buraku background. When he was in the second or third grade, meeting an assignment of his art teacher, he innocently drew a picture of his father at work. After showing the picture at school, he took it home to show to his parents, expecting praise. However, as he showed the picture to his parents, he noticed that they suddenly became pale and upset. They told him never again to draw a picture of his family at work, or any pictures of their shoestore, but they gave him no reason. From the serious reaction and tone of their voices, he sensed that he had done something terribly wrong and that there was something about his father's job, something secret about his family, that should be hidden from the eyes of ordinary people.

Another incident took place when he was in the fifth grade at school. One day, he was told by his father to deliver a pair of shoes the father had finished repairing. When he delivered the shoes to a customer's house, the man brought out a bamboo stick from the house and tied the money to one end of the stick, which he then stretched out and offered the child, thus avoiding the child's coming close to him. This was not an unusual way of giving money to the untouchable Burakumin. He did not respond with anger to this behavior. Instead, he felt somehow very lonely and helpless.

Internalized disparagement is often turned towards members of one's own group in times of stress or hostility. Our informant recalled some incidents that well illustrate this phenomenon. Not far from his family's store was another small shoestore. From the occupation, it was evident that the owner of this store and his family were Buraku people making an attempt to "pass". The wife of the shoestore owner, for some reason, chose our informant as a target for her aggression. Every time she encountered him, she would cry out "Eta, eta!" or "Yotsu, yotsu!" repeatedly in a loud voice. He felt sad and angry at the same time, so he told his mother of this woman's behavior. The mother became incensed and told him to tell her immediately the next time it occurred. When the woman again shouted at him, he quickly ran home and told his mother. His mother dropped what she was doing and ran to the woman, grabbed her by the hair, and pulled her down on to the street, repeatedly hitting her and shouting wildly. The boy had never seen his mother act in this way before and felt like hiding with fright and shame. He was particularly frightened by her violent behavior; he had usually seen her as a calm, gentle woman, submissive to her husband. He could still recall the wild expression on his mother's face and still remembered the unspeakable fear and threat he felt while watching her hitting another woman on the street. He recalled vaguely that in the community from which he and his family had moved, he had seen other such wild scenes, expressions of physical aggression between women. He thought that he had attempted somehow in his own mind to separate his mother from any connection with what he had perceived to be the wild and rude women of the community from which he came. This incident somehow destroyed the image of his mother as a gentle, calm and refined person.

This story reveals that this young man had in some way psychologically sought to separate himself from the community at a fairly early age. His ego identity was no longer with the Buraku but with the outside society. Nevertheless, his mother's impulsive, passionate behavior destroyed a previous defensive idealization and caused him to feel consciously that he could not completely escape his past.

THE BURAKUMIN'S NEGATIVE SELF-IMAGE

As stated before, minority status requires an individual to cope continually with a negative self-image which is often automatically internalized, as the individual becomes socialized in a disparaging society. A self-image is not always conscious. Sometimes, under stress, one comes face to face with attitudes toward oneself that have been consciously repressed.

Some revealing material has been gathered by Japanese social scientists on the Burakumin's conscious self-concepts. In research in Osaka City, Koyama (1953) asked the Burakumin what they thought was the best way to abolish discrimination against Buraku. Nearly half of the individuals revealed a general attitude of passive resignation, helplessness and avoidance toward the problem of discrimination. About one-third of them gave answers reflecting some passive helplessness and a great deal of self-punishing thinking, such as that they should behave better and give up their slovenly behavior; that they should seek more education and change their occupations to more respectable ones, etc. Most of the remaining answers showed more extra-punitive, emotional and militant attitudes, blaming the majority society for the discrimination. Only very few were objective or realistic answers, pointing out the necessity of enlightenment on the part of the outside society and actual improvement in the Burakumin's life situation.

The research by Yamamoto (1959, 1966) on the Burakumin's image of himself and his image of the outside society shows some interesting results which suggest that a conservative or traditionalist tendency in one way of ensuring self- and group-acceptance. The Buraku people think that, compared with majority society members, they are more filial, more respectful to ancestors, and more stringent in the observation of arranged marriage, more deferential toward persons of higher status. They also believe that outside people are better reared and more educated, more hygienic, better dressed, and have higher and better sexual morals and better speech habits. It is apparent that Burakumin balance their traditionalist attitudes as a counterpoise to a self-disparaging image. According to our informants, there seems to be a certain pride in being more traditional. Older and intellectual members of the community like to refer to a general deterioration of ethical standards among post-war youth. They like to point out the importance of the traditional, conservative Japanese values of conduct. In this respect, the Burakumin in general, by implication, put less emphasis on individualism or innovation and more emphasis on the maintenance of traditionally sanctioned social roles. These community attitudes, fostering a conservative, traditionalist self-image, serve to prevent anomie or deviant tendencies becoming unduly disruptive in stabilized communities.

Turning now to negative self-images on less conscious levels of awareness, we shall use the following examples to illustrate the presence of such images in individuals who are attempting to change their self-identity by "passing".

In the first example, the informant is "passing" as a city official in the municipal government of Osaka, although he is still living with members of his own community in Kyoto. Everyday he commutes to the bureau where he works. By taking a one-hour trip on a train, he changes his identity. At his bureau, he is treated as an ordinary person, both by his supervisors and by those whom he supervises; at home, he remains a member of the Burakumin community. He is looked up to in his community as a success and serves as a symbol of achievement, because, while he has become a fairly high city official, he has not deserted his own people. When we asked this informant whether he thinks the Buraku people are visibly discernible, his answer was affirmative, that--at least for other Buraku persons--they are identifiable. When he meets somebody with a Buraku background who is successfully "passing," he can tell that person's background. When asked how he could tell, he was unable to give us any precise explanation but after some thought he finally told us that living conditions within the Buraku are terrible; torn-down houses, unsanitary conditions, distasteful occupations, dirty food, bad language, violence, fighting, laziness--everything that is bad and distasteful is found in Buraku districts.[13] These conditions produce "something vicious, something dirty, something unnameable, but something which can be felt, like a strong odor . . . . This something horrible permeates or gets into the people who are born and raised and live in this area. It is something like a bad body odor . . . . Even when an individual leaves the community, wherever he may go, this something horrible or discernible always accompanies him." He said that this "something" may be an impression which one gives to another as the result of his way of speech and mannerisms and way of facial expression, gesture and all those personal expressions usually not perceived consciously. He believed that a Buraku person gives one an impression different from that received from a non-Buraku person. Here, a man of considerable learning, who is successfully "passing," inadvertently told that he himself has an image of his people as somehow unclean.

The following incident was told by a young unmarried informant, who is now successfully "passing" as a teacher. His father was very much interested in his children's education and stern to the point of harshness. Our informant, as a young boy, was severely instructed to study hard. Although the father was extremely careful about spending money, he was very generous as far as his children's education was concerned. He sent his two sons to good private schools where they studied hard and always remained at the top of their classes. Later they both graduated from the university.

When he was a child, our informant went through some very painful experiences of being discriminated against, laughed at, or being pointed out as a four-footed animal *(yotsu)*. Every time the boy mentioned the harsh treatment or cold and hateful attitudes of others, his father never failed to tell his sons that the only way to be freed from such painful experiences was to achieve, to get ahead, to "pass" as a successful member of the majority society. Since early childhood, our informant was repeatedly told by his father that the only possible way to free himself from his fate as a member of the outcaste was to be successful in school and to go into a respectable occupation. To him achievement and "passing" were identical words. "Unless you are successful in your achievement, you cannot be successful in your passing." However, the informant told us that his father's attitude toward "passing" had been contradictory, because when the young boy was mistreated by outside people and told such experiences to his father, the father also told him, especially when he was in a bad or irritated mood, not to run away but to go back to the other children and beat them up. We think the father was telling his son two things--to hide his identity and be a successful "passer"; and also to strike back as a member of the outcaste rather than hide his background. This explains, in part, why our informant remained basically ambivalent toward his own successful "passing".

After going to the university near his own community, he transferred to an institution in Tokyo, where he faced keen classroom competition with a more highly selected group of students. He found life in the big city, away from friends and family, somewhat difficult. He began to feel inferior to others in his class. One day he could not respond very well to questions given him by his instructor. He became very depressed, and while on a train, he suddenly noticed that one lady was looking at his face. He suddenly became panicky. He felt that everybody on the train was gazing at him. Suddenly he felt as if his face was starting to become distorted in a strange way. He felt that he was becoming very ugly and that everybody on the train was noticing the change and distortion that were taking place in his face. In his panic, he mutely prayed for people on the train not to look at him saying to himself that he was a harmless person. At the same time, he felt a strong surge of anger at the people who were gazing at him, but also he felt very weak. He was perspiring all over. He got off the train as quickly as possible and took a long rest in the station. Afterwards, this painful delusion of being stared at would come back occasionally. To avoid it, every time he boarded a train he would stand facing away from the other passengers close to the doorway, looking outside, or if this was not possible he hid his face with a weekly magazine.

When he related his experience to us, he obtained considerable cathartic relief. Some forgotten incidents came to mind. In the second grade at school he had failed to become the top student, and when told by his teacher that he was second rather than at the top, he urinated in his pants. Another free association to the face-changing was a memory of a long-forgotten fearful experience when he was in high school. He saw a film called Vampire Dracula, in which the victim of a vampire became a vampire himself or herself, and the face of the man or woman gradually changed into the ugly, fearsome visage of a vampire. This change of face was shown in close-up on the screen. He was so horrified that he could no longer stay in the theatre. That night he had a long nightmare and for about a month he could not free himself from the horror and panic produced by this particular film. He had completely forgotten this incident until he told us the story of his fear of his face suddenly starting to change.

The ugly face symbolized for our informant one of his self-images of being a person of outcaste. The image of the outcaste individual that he had within him is very similar to the image held by the "passing" municipal officer mentioned before. The man who "passes" may maintain the common prejudices of the majority society toward his own people, seeing them as dirty, ugly, full of vice and violence. As he is "passing", he consciously thinks that he himself is free of these characteristics. Unconsciously, however, he has internalized these attributes as part of a disavowed self-image. When under stress, when success of achievement became threatened, our informant's security about successful "passing" also tended to become shaky and anxiety over failure was experienced symbolically in the fear that his face would reveal his ugly identity. Our informant was so horrified by the film of the vampire because it suggested that one's hidden or ugly impulses might disclose themselves. Unconsciously, he must have identified with the fearsome, hideous creature, the vampire, who preyed on ordinary good folk. When he saw the vampire's face changing, he must have felt that the same thing could happen to him, that his Buraku face might suddenly appear, revealing his hatred of others.

There is a further possible reason for his experiencing a Jekyll and Hyde potentiality within himself. He had witnessed the radical change of behavior of individuals within the Buraku and the outside. His family was living in a house outside his community when he was going to grade school. His grandfather, however, was living in the house which had long been owned by his family in the community. As a child, he visited his grandfather and other relatives, all still living in the Buraku. He remembered very well that his mother had showed a drastic change in speech and manner and way of dressing when she was at home in their house outside the community and when she was visiting the Burakumin community. In her own house outside the community she was very careful in speech and manner, identifying herself with ordinary middle-class persons with whom she associated. She was proficient in adopting the behavioral and speech patterns of middle-class non-Buraku ladies and was genuinely spontaneous in her behavior. Yet when she returned to her own people, she spontaneously reverted to the ruder forms of speech and behavior. Our informant told us that the change was so drastic that sometimes as a young boy he wondered if his mother was a single integrated person. He felt as if he had two different

mothers, one within the Buraku, and another outside.

Our last example is a poem written by a Buraku poet. There was once in certain locales the belief that the Burakumin bore upon their persons an inherited physical stigma--a bluish birthmark (aza) under each arm. The poem, originally written in Japanese, depicts well a tormenting part of his negative self-image, a sense of being deeply branded with an inescapable stigma or--worse--carrying deeply within himself a sense of his own despoiled nature.

LET COME THE DAY TO SAY "ONCE IT WAS SO"

I heard whispering like wind from mouth to mouth
That under each armpit I am marked, the size of an open hand.
Was it inherited from an ancient time?
My parents, I've heard, also are thus bruised by nature's brand.
Yet no memory of them affords me sight or feel of such a spot.

But in childhood I learned,
Through cruel heavy winks, instinctively to hide.
What was it I so naively wrapped with rags,
And dragged, hidden, through dark months and years?

In these concealing rags, I hid my heart.
When found, it was so bruised,
Sore, red and shrunken from the stigma I tried to lose.

Without some exposure, my songs would all be lies;
Bruises tightly bound daily increase the inner pain.

Who marked my sides? For what cause?
Why this brand upon my soul?

Even today, my ebbing thoughts,
So pale and cold, transparent as glass,
Hold me awake.

BURAKUMIN RESPONSE TO DISCRIMINATION[14]

One basic means of expressing discontent with discrimination which is available to Buraku individuals has been through concerted political action, as mentioned earlier. Many Burakumin do find outlets for simmering discontent through left-wing political organizations. Such political movements seek to change social attitudes by creating a different pattern of political-legal sanctions within the society. Political movements of the far left, while at times questionable from the standpoint of their unrealistic assessment of possible influence, and in some cases characterized by the over-emotional approaches taken by the reformers, are socially integrative, at least in so far as they seek means of effecting change without the denial of self-identity or a resort to deviant mechanisms of expressing hostility toward authority through illegal or unsanctioned behavior. In addition to such activities, however, Burakumin, like certain minority groups in other societies, show higher indices of various forms of socially deviant behavior than the majority population.

First, we find a high incidence of apathy and non-reachableness in regard to education. Studies by the Japanese (Mahara, 1960a) show that Buraku children come out relatively poorly in school compared with majority-group children. Their truancy rate is often high. (Mahara, 1961; Nishimoto, 1960; Matsuda, et al., 1963; Tojo, 1960b, 1960c) These results reflect early damage to self-identity and self-respect vis-a-vis cultural expectations.

Second, the evidence shows that Burakumin have developed some deviousness and dependent opportunism towards welfare programs initiated by the majority culture. The Burakumin alleviate their feelings of dependence on the majority society by finding ways of being devious in "how one takes."

Deviousness is a balm to the ego and allows the Buraku individual to maintain his self-respect, because his dependent needs no longer make him feel completely helpless. For instance, a woman doctor who lived in Buraku for many years tells of incidents which well illustrate the "expediency-dependent" attitudes of the Buraku toward welfare programs (Kobayashi, 1962).[15]

Third, ecological studies by the Japanese reveal a relatively high frequency of delinquency in Buraku districts, as compared with that among the majority population (Kyoto-fu Seishōnen Mondai Kyogi Kai & Kyoto Daigaku Kyoiku Shakai Gakubu, 1960). Our own research was conducted in a family court, situated in one of the major cities in Japan with a population of over one million. By careful study of case files, we found that youth of Korean background show the highest delinquency rate--over six times that of the majority area--and those identified as boys living in Buraku districts showed a rate of over three times that of the non-Buraku areas. Recidivism was highest among those living in Buraku areas and was also higher among the Koreans than among those living in majority areas. One characteristic of those residing in Buraku areas was that they showed a very high rate of threat, intimidation and extortion. This, however, needs some qualification. In a number of these cases of threat and extortion, one is surprised to find that the age of the delinquent boy involved is often much lower than that of the individuals threatened. It is not unusual to find a 15-year-old boy threatening a group of two or three older boys without the use of any weapon. In some cases the boy would simply state to the other children that he is from a feared Buraku. By so doing, he evokes fear in the minds of the outside children and can obtain from them either money or goods on the basis of simple intimidation.

The foregoing material gives evidence of the social-psychological problems faced by the Burakumin in present-day Japanese culture. It is not that all urban Burakumin are manifestly suffering from some form of social or psychological problem, or, on the other hand, that all Japanese are prejudiced towards members of the former outcaste. There have been many Burakumin who have sustained themselves through the difficulty of their position to make noted contributions to their society and to live felicitous lives.

Nevertheless, the proportionate number of individuals who in one way or another are made to suffer because of their status is certainly as great in the Buraku minority as it is in discriminated minority groups in other cultures.

FOOTNOTES

1. This article, in a little different form and content, first appeared under the title "the pariah caste in Japan: history and present self-image" in A.V.S. deReuck & Julie Knight (eds) *Ciba Foundation Symposium on Caste and Race: Comparative Approaches*, London: J. & A. Churchill Ltd., 1967, pp. 118-140. For a fuller account of the history and present problems of the Burakumin, see DeVos & Wagatsuma (1966).
2. The commonest comment in this regard is that "they have blood-shot eyes"--the statement not without reality basis because the trachoma was once a prevalent disease in Buraku.
3. For the evidence of a high degree of endogamy among Burakumin, see Donoghue (1957), Chapter 7 of DeVos & Wagatsuma (1966); Mahara (1960a); Ohashi (1962) and Suzuki (1953). The evidence seems to indicate, however, that despite the general force of prejudice, an increasing trend is toward mixed marriages. See Chapter 5 of DeVos & Wagatsuma (1966); Mahara (1960a); Suzuki (1953).

4. For a detailed study of the history of the Burakumin, see Chapter 1 of DeVos & Wagatsuma (1966); Ninomiya (1933); Hayashiya et al., (1962) and Inoue (1960).
5. We find an interesting parallel in Korea, where the principal outcaste were the *Paekchōng*, the slaughterers, butchers and tanners; and the *Chiain*, the petty criminals, prostitutes, diviners, beggars and itinerant peddlars. See Passin (1955).
6. The Japanese word, *iyashii*, or "lowly", derives from *ayashii*, meaning "mysterious and suspicious".
7. The practice was called *ashi arai*, or "foot-washing".
8. For the fuller account of the history of Buraku movements, see Chapters 2, 3 and 4 in DeVos & Wagatsuma (1966); Buraku Mondai Kenkyujo (ed) (1955) and Inoue (1959).
9. For a more detailed account of the distribution of Buraku, occupational changes and poverty within Buraku, see Chapter 5 in DeVos & Wagatsuma (1966).
10. According to the 1967 statistics, the Buraku population was the greatest in Hyogo Prefecture (162,845), then Osaka Prefecture (131,516), Fukuoka (121,996), Nara (59,775). It was the smallest in Yamanashi Prefecture (700). See Suzuki (1969, 54-55).
11. For the ethnographic study of a rural Buraku that remained specialized around the traditional occupations of the Buraku, see Donoghue (1957). For the study of another type of rural Buraku, one that has become a relatively progressive farming community and that does not bear the stigma of ritually or aesthetically despised occupation, see Chapters 7 and 8 of DeVos & Wagatsuma (1966) and Cornell (1967a, 1967b).
12. For a detailed discussion on socialization, self-perception and ego-identity of the Burakumin and also on the psychological problems related to "passing", see Chapters 11 and 12 in DeVos & Wagatsuma (1966).
13. The psychological process through which the early experiences of one's environment become part of one's self-identity, as exemplified by the statement of this city official, is also reflected in the following poem written by a Buraku woman. A harsh tabooed word used by the majority society to designate Buraku people is "yotsu" meaning "four". The use of "four" derives from a reference to the fact that the Burakumin were traditionally considered to be nonhuman or an animal species. "Four" refers to the fact that they should be classified with four-footed animals. The use of the word "four" also is associated with an unrealistic fantasy that these "sub-human" people have only four fingers on their hands. In Japan, when two persons, often children, promise something to each other, they interlock their little fingers. It is called *yubi-kiri*. The magical connotation of this practice is that if a person does not keep the promise, his or her little finger will be cut off or lost. Attention should be paid, therefore, when the woman says in the poem that although it was not she but he who broke the promise, it is she who is told that she has only four fingers (as a Burakumin). One may also add that sitting face-to-face in *kotatsu* (a foot warmer with a quilt over it) is associated with a feeling of warmth, security and intimacy.

MY FIFTH FINGER

When for the first time I fell in love,
I was twenty-one; it was autumn.
My love to him was boundless and to me
He was kind and tender, so I thought.
When winter came, in his room
We sat in *kotatsu*, warm and cozy.

We talked of the day when I would be his bride--
The night was quiet, with falling snow.

"When spring comes, we will marry."
Our little fingers were interlocked for the symbol of promise.
My small finger was sweet, he said, and since then,
It became dear to me, as a symbol of our promise.

When was it that he started saying I had only four fingers?
Since the day I met his mother, our spring would never come.

Though I cannot see, he surely told me
There are four fingers on my hand.

Was it my little finger that was lost?
It was not I who did not keep our promise,
And yet he said I was a girl with four fingers,
A girl, born to be different and unhappy.

I cried and I thought
   Of the low-eaved house where I was born,
   Of our *buraku*, crowded houses on a small patch of land,
   Of the abnormal, born from inbred marriage,
   Of desperate and hopeless youth,
   Of women, driven from their husbands' homes,
   Of children whom their fathers have never known.

I thought I would die
   And my wound, so cured,
   And my body, complete.

I would die, crying for my fifth finger,
My fifth finger, suddenly cut off in my mind.

The wound will never heal.
It will be open, wide and deep,
Bleeding with pain and anger
And protest against those
Who took our little fingers away.
The wound will be open, with pain and anger.

14. For the fuller treatment of this subject, see Chapter 13 in DeVos & Wagatsuma (1966).
15. Inoue, a well-known historian and active protagonist of Buraku liberation movements, also points out the frequency of "dependent-expediential" attitudes in older members of the Buraku: ". . . in their campaigns aimed at the prefectural or central governments demanding further administrative measures for Buraku improvement, some of the older members of organized movements express the feeling that they have the right to demand things in compensation for a long period of discrimination, since they have not retaliated in any way against the majority society . . . that they have a special right to ask for governmental help for improvement because they are Burakumin . . . but this is wrong . . ." In this criticism of the Burakumin, Inoue virtually ignores the fact that this demanding attitude is a consequence of social discrimination extending through many generations. Such underlying antagonism to legitimate authority is particularly disturbing to majority Japanese, since within the culture it is traditional to conform to authority. (Inoue, 1961).

REFERENCES

Buraku Mondai Kenkyujo (Research Institute for Buraku Problems) (ed.).
1955   Buraku no Rekishi to Kaihō Undō (Buraku History and Emancipation Movements). Kyoto: Buraku Mondai Kenkyujo.

Cornell, J.
1967a   "Outcaste relations in a Japanese village", American Anthropologist 63, 2, 282-296.
1967b   "Individual mobility and group membership: the case of the Burakumin", in R.P. Dore (ed.), Aspects of Social Change in Modern Japan. Princeton: Princeton University Press.

DeVos, G. & Wagatsuma, H.
1966   Japan's Invisible Race: Caste in Culture and Personality. Berkeley: University of California Press.

Donaghue, J.
1957   "An Eta community in Japan: the social persistence of outcaste groups", American Anthropologist 59, 6, 1000-1017.

Grier, W. & Cobbs, P.M.
1969   Black Rage. New York: Bantam Book.

Hall, R.B., Sr.
1962   "A map of Buraku settlements in Japan", Papers of the Michigan Academy of Science, Arts and Letters, 47.

Hayashiya, T. et al. (eds.)
1962   Burakushi ni kansuru Sōgōteki Kenkyū (An Integrated Study of Buraku History). Kyoto: Buraku Mondai Kenkyujo.

Inoue, K.
1959   Buraku Mondai no Kenkyū - Sono Rekishi to Kaihō Riron (A Study of Buraku Problems - History and Emancipation Theories). Kyoto: Buraku Mondai Kenkyujo.
1960   Buraku Mondai no Kenkyū (A Study of Buraku Problems). Kyoto: Buraku Mondai Kenkyujo.
1961   "Kaihō undō no rekishi ni manabu" (Lessons we receive from the history of liberation movements), Buraku 9, 4-17.

Kardiner, A. & Ovesey, L.
1951   The Mark of Oppression. New York: Norton.

Kobayashi, A.
1962   Buraku no Joi (A Woman Doctor in Buraku). Tokyo: Iwanami.

Koyama, T.
1953   "Buraku ni okeru shakai kinchō no kenkyū" (A study of some characteristics of social tensions in buraku), in Nihon Jinbun Kagaku Kai (Japan Association for Humanities) (ed.), Shakai-teki Kinchō no Kenkyū (Studies on Social Tensions). Tokyo: Yuhikaku.

Kyoto Seishōnen Mondai Kyōgikai & Kyoto Daigaku Kyōiku Shakai Gakubu (Kyoto Prefecture Council on Youth Problems and Department of Educational Sociology of the University of Kyoto).
1960   Shōnen Hikō no Shakaigaku-teki Chōsa Hōkoku: Kyotoshi ni okeru Hikō no Shakai Bunka-teki Haikei no Bunseki (A Report of the Sociological Study of Juvenile Delinquency: Analysis of Sociocultural Background of Delinquency).

Mahara, T.
1960a   "Buraku no shakai" (Buraku society), in Buraku Mondai Kenkyujo (Research Institute for Buraku Problems) (ed.), Buraku no Genjō (Present Situations in Buraku). Tokyo & Kyoto: San-itsu Shobo.
1960b   "Buraku no sangyō to shigoto" (Industry and work in buraku), op. cit.
1960c   "Buraku no shakai" (Buraku society), op. cit.
1960d   "Buraku no kurashi" (Life in buraku), op. cit.
1961   "Buraku no kodomo to shinro shidō" (Buraku children and their guidance), Buraku 9, 55-59.

Matsuda, K. et al.
1963   Buraku Mondai to Kirisuto Kyō (Buraku Problems and Christianity). Tokyo: Nihon Kirisuto Kyōdan Senkyō Kenkyujo (United Church of Christ of Japan, Research Institute for Missionary Work).

Ninomiya, S.
1933 "An inquiry concerning the origin, development and present situation of the Eta in relation to the history of social classes in Japan", Transactions of the Asiatic Society of Japan 10, 47-154.

Nishimoto, S.
1960 Buraku Mondai to Dōwa Kyōiku (Buraku Problems and Assimilation Education). Tokyo: Sobunsha.

Nomura, N.
1956 "Tsukimono no shinri" (Psychology of fox possession), in I. Oguchi (ed.), Shūkyō to Shinkō no Shinrigaku (Psychology of Religion and Beliefs). Tokyo: Kawade Shobo.

Ohashi, K.
1962 Toshi no Kasō Shakai (Urban Lower Society). Tokyo: Seishin Shobo.

Passin, H.
1955 "Untouchability in the Far East", Monumenta Nipponica 11, 3, 27-47.

Suzuki, J.
1953 "Burakumin no chiikisei, shokugyō, kekkon" (Regional characteristics occupation and marriage of buraku people), in Nihon Jinbun Kagaku Kai (ed.), *op. cit.*

Suzuki, J. (ed.)
1969 Gendai no Sabetsu to Henken; Mondai no Honshitusu to Genjō (Discrimination and Prejudice in Modern Japan - Essence and Present Situations of the Problems). Tokyo: Shinsensha.

Tojo, T.
1960a "Mura ni aru buraku" (Buraku in rural areas), in Buraku Mondai Kenkyu Jo (ed.), Buraku no Genjō (Present Situations in Buraku), *op. cit.*
1960b "Sengo no dōwa Kyōiku" (Postwar education for assimilation), in Buraku Mondai Kenkyujo (ed.), Dōwa Kyōiku (Assimilation Education). Kyoto: Buraku Mondai Kenkyujo.
1960c Dōwa Kyōiku Ron (Theories on Assimilation Education). Tokyo & Kyoto: San-itsu Shobo.

Yamamoto, N.
1959 "Sabetsu ishiki to shinriteki kinchō: mikaihō burakumin no ishiki ni kansuru kenkyū" (Discrimination-consciousness and psychological tensions: a study of attitudes among people of unliberated communities), Jinbun Kenkyū (Studies in Humanistic Science) 1, 12, 35-59.
1966 Buraku Sabetsu no Shakaigakuteki Kenkyū (Sociological Studies of Buraku Discrimination). Kyoto: Buraku Mondai Kenkyujo.

6

THE KOREAN MINORITY IN JAPAN AND THEIR DILEMMA OF CULTURAL IDENTITY

YONG MOK KIM

California State University
Los Angeles

ABSTRACT

Korean residents in Japan form the largest ethnic minority in Japan. Political and eoncomic discrimination against Koreans is important and rather well-known. Its social and cultural implications for Koreans are relatively unknown but crucial for the future of Koreans in Japan.

Particularly when 70% of Korean residents were born in Japan and more and more are seeking assimilation, they confront the difficult problem of their cultural identity. However, the highly integrative and homogeneous nature of Japanese society leaves little room for tolerance of different cultures. Koreans seeking assimilation are thus in a dilemma, because their total submission to Japanese society and culture is the price of their assimilation. The untold agony of their dilemma is hopeless and pathetic.

Before undertaking a discussion of the problems which affect Korean residents in Japan, several basic factors, intrinsically related to the structure of discrimination and prejudice in Japan, should be delineated.

Perhaps of primary importance is the fact that the Korean residents in Japan, who number 697,000 (Sandei Mainichi, 1970), are not legally Japanese citizens although about 70% of them were born in Japan. Though naturalization is legally provided for, the Japanese government has adopted the principle of citizenship by birth rather than by place.

Consequently, the implications of the legal status of Korean residents are far-reaching and serious. Since they are legally disfranchised, Koreans are totally excluded from the political process in Japan. They are generally outside the purview of various governmental welfare and social agencies, and they do not enjoy access to such benefits as health insurance, public housing, and government monopoly franchises, e.g., salt and rice (Matsuyama, 1967: 88). They are disqualified from service in government positions, which include tenured positions in government-financed educational institutions. Their political participation and activities are closely controlled and curbed. Recently, a bill was proposed to ban almost completely the political activities, even those Koreans holding a permanent residence status.

The political disfranchisement of Korean residents naturally puts them at an enormous disadvantage to the Japanese both socially and economically. In addition to being excluded from government franchises, they are also disqualified from becoming lawyers, tax accountants, and other government-licensed professions. They are further excluded from consideration for public financial loans and bank loans (Suzuki, 1967: 260).

Quite naturally, the legal status of Koreans has a profound impact on attitude-formation among the Japanese and on their relations with Korean residents. First of all, the generally known legal aspect of the Koreans is, at best, confusing and puzzling to the Japanese themselves. Some Japanese, particularly "progressive" intellectuals (cf. Ubukata, 1962:93), blandly articulate their attitude by maintaining that legal freedom and independence of action should be granted to Korean residents as nationals of an independent nation, and that little or no interference by the Japanese government and people should be allowed to stand in the way of the unique social and cultural life of the Koreans in Japan. However, this attitude totally disregards the historical development which has led to the situation in which Korean residents in Japan

presently find themselves. Furthermore, it is tantamount to avoiding this complex problem altogether. The peculiar legal status of Koreans in Japan leads to yet another extreme view, supported by some Japanese who do not understand why the Koreans are in Japan, and who believe that all Koreans should be repatriated to Korea where they "belong". Not infrequently, this position is inextricably mixed with a strong anti-Korean prejudice (Yamamura, 1971:204).

For the majority of the Japanese, however, the legal status of the Koreans in Japan is beyond their comprehension. That is to say, many Japanese are unable to determine whether Korean residents should be given equal rights, such as the Japanese themselves enjoy, or whether they should be treated as fellow Japanese. This bewilderment on the part of some Japanese concerning the status of Koreans in Japan led to the coining of a peculiar Japanese term--"nationals of a third country (dai sankoku-jin)"--referring to Korean residents in Japan (Hatada, 1968:69).

Among the Koreans themselves, there are some who, primarily in sympathy with the North Korean regime, advocate a strong program from the position that Korean residents are, indeed, aliens. Therefore, they should enjoy autonomy and complete freedom and equal rights, particularly in education. For the majority, however, equal rights and freedom such as Japanese nationals enjoy are the desired goals, even though they are excluded from the political process itself (Izumi, 1963:89).

A second important factor which has been of significant influence in determining the condition of Korean residents in Japan is the fact that both the presence of Koreans in Japan and their present status are largely a result of Japan's program for the colonization of Korea which began in 1910 (Suzuki, 1967:254). This historical fact has given considerable weight to the view that Koreans are intrinsically inferior to Japanese, and that Korean culture possesses nothing of unique value; therefore, discrimination and prejudice against Korean residents in Japan is justified (Hatada, 1968:69).

Thus the historical factor, in which the Japanese themselves played a large role, serves not only to justify the discrimination and prejudice of the Japanese people against Korean residents in Japan, but underlies the structure of the Japanese prejudice against Koreans. On the other hand, this same historical factor arouses a quasi-guilt complex among some "progressive" intellectuals, who suggest that Japanese should compensate the Koreans for past injustices, and for the prejudice to which Koreans in Japan have been subjected

(Suzuki, 1967:253-254; Adachi, 1965:144; Minobe, 1972:46). Nevertheless, regardless of their legal status, and in spite of Japan's colonization and subjugation of Korea and the Koreans, the fact remains that the majority of the Koreans in Japan are basically labor immigrants who intend to reside permanently in Japan. It is true that large-scale wartime conscription of Korean laborers was common during the period, 1941-1945 (Wagner, 1951:25-40). It is also true that the vast majority of such conscript laborers were repatriated to Korea following the end of the war. However, after the massive repatriation of temporary male bachelor laborers to Korea, the remaining Korean immigrants, who originally came as labor immigrants, remained, determined to seek their place in Japan (Chon, 1970:247).

Therefore, the Koreans in Japan are not an ethnic minority in the same sense as the Blacks are in the United States. Nor are they temporary sojourners, who find themselves in Japan by a historical accident, as some maintain. Thus, the position of Korean residents in Japan is unique, and a clear picture of their character is pivotal in understanding their problems. The determinative factors briefly described above compose the foundation upon which stands a superstructure of Japanese discrimination and prejudice against the Koreans within Japanese society itself.

Japanese society presents a tightly-knit homogeneity--the results of an enduring tradition of geographical isolation and historical seclusion. The Japanese people, as a whole, lack experience in inter-racial living. This fact contributes to the uneasiness and suspicion which the Japanese people feel in the presence of different ethnic groups and cultures. Moreover, in a tightly-knit, group-orientated society, little or no room is provided for the integration of an ethnic group or for the integration of individuals with different cultural values. The Japanese people view themselves as the product of a long, uninterrupted history whose ultimate denouement is the formation of a uniquely Japanese character and spirit which cannot be shared or understood by outsiders (Wagatsuma and Yoneyama, 1967:142-146).

Even in those instances where the Japanese people have been exposed to different cultures, exogenous cultural values have been strongly modified and integrated into the traditional Japanese culture. Consequently, unintegrated cultural values of other ethnic groups have seldom been tolerated in Japanese society.

As if to reinforce the highly integrative character of the traditionally monistic Japanese society, the Koreans in Japan formed conspicuous Korean ghettos, mainly concentrated in Osaka, Tokyo, and Nagoya (Suzuki, 1967:253; Naga, 1972:103).

Several forces appear to reinforce the exclusivity practices against Koreans in Japan. The conspicuous Korean ghettos, where the difference in cultural values is obvious, projects an image of the Koreans in Japan as an inferior ethnic group with an inferior, ghetto culture (Naga, 1972:103-104).

It is precisely the unfavorable physical environment of Koreans in Japan, as well as their seemingly inferior culture, which has been crucial to the formation of the structure of Japanese discrimination and prejudice. But there are other sources which have also contributed to the formation of an unfavorable Japanese stereotyped image of the Korean: for example, (1) the direct experience of Japanese during their occupation of Korea, (2) the Japanese image of South Korea, (3) the Japanese image of North Korea and finally, their contact and observation of resident Koreans in Japan (Yi, 1971). Obviously, the last source is more available, more direct, more immediate. It is no wonder, then, that the status

and the culture of Koreans in Japan confined, for the most part, to metropolitan ghettos, has strongly influenced the Japanese image (Wagatsuma and Yoneyama, 1967:127; Suzuki, 1967:254). A number of surveys give considerable credence to this fact. In one survey, conducted by Wagatsuma and Yoneyama (1967), concerned with the formation of the Japanese stereotyped image of the Korean, 32% of the respondents answered by saying that Koreans are dirty; 28.5% stated that they are obsequious (hikutsu); 66% described them as bad-mannered, and 23% characterized the Koreans as being easily swayed by mob psychology. (In this survey, 32 pairs of contrasting adjectives were listed from which the respondents were to choose. The group sampled included a total of 270 people, 145 males and 124 females, of all age groups.) Typically, the English were imagined as calm and intelligent, the French as cheerful, the Americans as friendly, action-oriented, and progressive. Of 13 nations and 2 ethnic groups (Japanese-Caucasian and Japanese-Negro), only the Koreans received all negative responses, which is significant indication of the depth of Japanese prejudice against Koreans.

In another survey, conducted by Izumi (1963), it was demonstrated that the Japanese respondents placed importance on their direct observations and contacts with Korean residents as the source for image-formation. Of a total of 344, 251 respondents had seen Koreans, 90 had personal contacts with them, and only 4 had had no opportunity to observe or meet Koreans. Nevertheless, from their pooled experience, there emerged strikingly similar descriptions of the Korean image. Only 1 respondent was impressed with the outward appearance of Koreans; 11 thought that the Koreans appeared neat and clean, while 3 thought that Korean culture ranked among the advanced. In contrast, 188 regarded the Koreans as cunning, 68 described them as wicked (haraguroi), and 105 thought that the Koreans were contemptuous of Japan. This particular survey canvassed Japanese attitudes toward Koreans, Chinese, Filipinos, Indians, Americans, English, French, Australians, Germans, Russians, and Negroes. Concerning the overall attitude of the Japanese toward Koreans, as surveyed by Izumi, only 2% of the respondents expressed a liking for Koreans, while 44% indicated a marked aversion toward them. Of the 16 races and ethnic groups considered, the Koreans scored 15th on the scale, only just above Negroes. In the survey conducted by Wagatsuma and Yoneyama, referred to above, the Koreans ranked 12th in preference--again the second last position.

There are several general determinants in the racial attitudes of the Japanese toward outsiders which appear to be common to both of these surveys. In the first place, there appeared to be no significant difference among the respondents due to differences of sex, occupation, and age. Second, Europeans and Americans were most favorably projected, while Asian neighbors ranked low on the Japanese scale of affability and esteem. Moreover, among those groups considered, the Koreans (with the exception of the Negroes) scored lowest, revealing the entrenched Japanese prejudice against Koreans to be much stronger than expected.

Of more personal relevance to the problems of Koreans in Japan is the degree to which they are acceptable in Japanese society and to the Japanese people. Here, we are confronted by the problem of social distance held toward Koreans in Japan by the Japanese. 24.8% of the respondents indicated that they would not befriend a Korean, while 26.3% said they would befriend one. 27.8% disapproved of accepting Koreans as family friends; 24.4% would approve it. 33.3% disliked the idea of having a Korean for a travelling companion; 15.9% were not opposed to it. 31.1% were opposed to Koreans living in Japan; only 19.2% favored it. 28.5% would find it obnoxious to attend the same school with Koreans; 17.8% would approve it. 34.4% would resist having Koreans as their neighbors; 1.44% would welcome them. 31.5% would not like the idea of bathing with Koreans at a public bath-house; only 15.2% would approve it. 45.2% would reject lodging together with Koreans at the same hotel, while 12.6% would be willing. A strong 62.6% expressed their resistance to interracial marriage with Koreans, while only 4.4% would allow it. Though 31.9% would support the naturalization of Koreans, 18.5% would oppose it (Wagatsuma and Yoneyama, 1967:122-135).

Some conclusions inferred from above are as follows:

(1) Koreans scored lowest in the various areas of acceptance by the Japanese, again indicating the depth of prejudice.

(2) In all categories, Koreans received the strongest disapproval.

(3) One significant exception was revealed when the Japanese approval of naturalization of Koreans was actually higher than for that of Indonesians, Filipinos, and Negroes. Here, it is the homogeneity of Japanese society, which may accept only those who totally Japanize themselves even if they be Koreans, which reveals itself to be an overriding consideration (Wagatsuma and Yoneyama, 1967:127). This factor is crucial for the future of Koreans in Japan.

The structure of the Japanese prejudice toward Koreans in Japan is closely related to the indoctrination of the children. According to Hatada (1968), a survey of 200 elementary school children, ranging from the third grade to the sixth grade, revealed that prejudice was intensified with age through the indoctrination they received at home, whereby Koreans were cast in the image of undesirable characters. The children were given the idea that Koreans were bad-mannered, uncivilized, and unclean. Simply through the process of experience in their homes, Japanese children, by the time they were advanced to the sixth grade, viewed Koreans as crowding an already crowded Japan, as untrustworthy, and as contemptible. This stereotyped image of the Koreans implies that, to the Japanese, they are a people without a unique culture worthy of recognition.

Thus, the Koreans are sometimes dubiously referred to as the "nationals of a third country".

Given the general deprecatory attitude of the Japanese toward Koreans, and the strongly entrenched and reinforcing structure of Japanese discrimination and prejudice, one may ask what are the pertinent conditions which determine the responses of the Koreans to Japanese and Japanese society.

The majority of the first-generation Korean immigrants were of low socio-economic status. Transposed to Japanese society, they crowded into ghettos far below the socio-economic level of most Japanese. Consequently, their social and economic potentials were, from the beginning, rather low and circumscribed. According to Matsuyama (1967), as of 1965 only 24.4% of the total Korean population in Japan were gainfully employed, compared to 47.5% among the Japanese. Of those gainfully employed, 50% were semi-skilled or unskilled laborers, while the remainder comprised small manufacturers and the self-employed, including restaurant owners and scrap and junk dealers. Employment of semi-skilled and unskilled Korean laborers were characterized as unstable. Approximately 58,000 Koreans were on the welfare roll. Needless to say, the crime rate in Korean ghettos was much higher than in any other area of Japanese society (Suzuki, 1967:263).

Because of strong discrimination in employment practices, even well-educated and qualified Korean youths are quite often excluded from the job market in Japan.

Compared to other aliens, e.g., the Chinese, the Koreans in Japan seem to lack the joint effort and cooperation necessary to successfully overcome their economic disadvantages (Sandei Mainichi, 1970).

The well-known political division of Korean residents in Japan does little to mitigate the already unfavorable image of Koreans in Japanese society. Roughly 52% of the Koreans identify themselves with the Republic of Korea, while the remaining 48% are influenced by the North Korean-sponsored General Federation of Korean Residents in Japan (Soren) (Sandei Mainichi, 1970).

Culturally, the overwhelming majority of Koreans born in Japan, comprising about 73% of the total Korean population, attend Japanese schools. Despite concerted efforts on the part of the North Koreans, only 35,000 Korean youths are enrolled in North Korean-sponsored schools, and only a few thousand more are enrolled in South Korean and neutral schools (Suzuki, 1968:281). It would appear, then, that those Koreans born in Japan--certainly the second, third, and fourth generations-attended Japanese schools and received typical Japanese education. Exposed to Japanese culture, and imbued with the Japanese system of values, Korean youths are thus confronted with the dilemma of their cultural identity.

Given the limitations on their political and economic mobility, and the strongly entrenched structure of discrimination and prejudice inherent in Japanese society, the importance of maintaining a Korean cultural identity among the Korean youth in Japan looms large if they are to maintain their human dignity and their sense of self-respect. However, this very problem of cutural identity presents many dilemmas to the younger Korean generation.

The first problem is presented in terms of generation. The cultural views of the first generation Koreans are a carry-over from Korea. Their cultural views are strongly anti-Japanese. Nevertheless, they appear to have little influence over their second or third generation offspring. Furthermore, the low socio-economic status of the first generation testifies to the inferiority of their own culture to the Japanese-born Koreans. Since the first generation is not familiar with their own cultural heritage, and since their cultural beliefs are rather shaky, their attitudes are not strong enough to bear upon the formation of the unique cultural identity for their offspring.

The cultural discontinuity between the first generation Korean immigrants and the Japanese-born Koreans is further reinforced by the fact that Korea is both a divided nation and an underdeveloped country; as such, Korea presents an image of backwardness and instability to the ordinary Japanese mind. To Japanese-born Koreans, this is to imply another proof that Korean culture deserves less respect, and it is said to prompt many of them to seek assimilation in Japanese society. Otherwise, the identity of Japanese-born Koreans with their cultural heritage is tenuous, leaving them in a cultural limbo.

Japanese-born Koreans are continuously subjected to Japanese cultural indoctrination at school and in their social life. From the Japanese viewpoint, Korea is held, at best, in low esteem. The unique cultural worth of Korea is denied or dismissed by the majority of the Japanese. The Japanese-born Korean suffers both from his lack of identity with and knowledge of Korean culture, and from his inhospitable indoctrination in Japan against Korean culture.

The lack of opportunity and stimulation on the part of Japanese-born Koreans to learn their own history, language, and culture further alienates them from it. Many Koreans confess that, while they have no alternative but to write and express their feeling in the Japanese language, they are painfully aware of its impact as the representative of Japanese history and society (Nakamura, 1971:318).

Although younger Koreans must agonizingly discover that Korean culture is held in low esteem by Japanese society, and in spite of the cultural animosity of the first-generation Koreans toward Japanese culture, Korean youth, by and large, live in the Japanese cultural milieu. One evidence of this is the increasing number of Korean residents who seek naturalization in order to resolve this dilemma. Estimations are that about 60,000 to 70,000 Koreans have already become naturalized, and every year over 3,000 Koreans apply for naturalization (Chon, 1970:246). Whether they like it or not, younger Koreans apparently feel that the only alternative left is to assimilate into Japanese culture; after all, it is the only culture with which they are familiar. They seek naturalization for the betterment of their legal, social, and economic opportunities, and also for those of their posterity.

For many of these younger Koreans, the very decision to assimilate, and the process involved, are fraught with problems for both their personal and cultural identities. Given the all-pervasive nature of Japanese society, its intolerance of difference, and its refusal to recognize an unassimilable culture, successful assimilation, in the cultural sense, requires a total submission on the part of younger Koreans to Japanese culture only after completely severing their Korean cultural identity. The process of denying and severing their tenuous Korean cultural ties and fully embracing and inhospitable Japanese culture must inevitably be a traumatic and agonizing experience for these young people. For, in fact, they must deny themselves.

The tragic death of a young naturalized Korean illustrates this point (Yamamura, 1971). Torn between his Korean national origin and his assimilation into a hostile Japanese society and culture, Yamamura deeply felt the agonies--a personal and cultural dichotomy of being in his late teens and early twenties. One of the major causes leading to his tragic death by self-immolation in October, 1970, was his breakup with a Japanese girl-friend, which was itself due solely to his ethnic origin. What is appalling is this young man's self-imposed sense of inferiority for being of Korean-blood. Because of his ethnic origin, he was gripped with a hopeless sense that his relationship with his girl-friend was doomed, even though he was deeply in love with her. His pessimism proved correct. While he was critical of his parents' naturalization--which seemed to him to be a disgraceful act of submission, particularly in view of past Japanese aggression against Korea, he was, nevertheless, unable to find enough confidence and pride in himself as a decent human being, in his own self-worth, regardless of his ethnic origin, to enter into a normal relationship with a Japanese girl. Hiding his ethnic identity resulted in a guilt complex. Indeed, being of Korean-blood was equated with criminality in his mind.

However, as assimilation is accelerated and more Koreans seek naturalization, they must confront the dilemma of their cultural identity, and many will undergo the same agonizing, but inexorable, process of self-imposed guilt resulting from the pressure of a closed and hostile society at large.

A significant dimension of the overall problem of cultural identity for Koreans in Japan is directly related to interracial marriage. As a general trend, more and more Koreans, particularly males, are marrying Japanese. To begin with, the prospect of an interracial marriage between a Korean and a Japanese irks the Korean parents, who see their son as selling out to the hateful Japanese. On the other hand, when the Japanese parents discover that their daughter is in love with a Korean, they may do everything but disown her. The Japanese parents reluctantly and grudgingly acquiesce in their daughter's marriage on the condition that she will exclude herself from the normal social life with her own relations, that her prospective Korean husband will naturalize, and that no ordinary family relationship with her husband or his family will be carried on (Naga,1972:105). Even if the couple pass all the hurdles before they are marked, their married life, in spite of their determined, personal effort, will fail. Since both Koreans and Japanese will not fully accept the interracial marriage, the couple find the hostile pressure from both sides and society at large too strong to bear. They resolve this dilemma by dissolving their marriage.

The naturalization of Koreans results in similar pressure being brought to bear on those Koreans who become naturalized. Here again, naturalized Koreans must bear the hostile attitude of fellow-Koreans, who regard them as "half-Japanese" (pan chokppari), a term with a distinctively derisive and pejorative connotation (Naga, 1972:105-106). Unfortunately, it is the individual Korean who must confront the overwhelming demand for total submission to Japanese society and culture.

The prospect for ameliorating the intense and pervasive difficulties associated with cultural identity, especially for the younger Koreans in Japan, is very pessimistic indeed. Their personal agony is not likely to be given sympathetic understanding by Japanese society. Nor is there a genuine concern in North or South Korea for their mental anguish. The small minority of younger Koreans in Japan is too fragmented and disorganized to voice their anxiety loudly. Finally, Japanese society is too strongly entrenched in its prejudice against Koreans to become a sympathetic audience for the passionate plea for human equality by Koreans born and raised in Japan.

REFERENCES

Adachi, Kenichi
1965 "Zainichi chosenjin no hyojo." Chuo Koron (December):146-148.

Chon, Chun
1969 "Chosen Soren, Sono futatsu no kao." Jiyu (December):246-252.

Hatada, Takashi
1968 "Nihonjin no chosenjin kan." Sekai (September):64-72.

Izumi, Seiichi
1963 "Nihonjin no jinshu-teki henken, chosen mondai to kanren shite." Sekai (March):82-89.

Matsuyama, Tadashi
1967 "Kikan kyotei no uchikiri to zainichi chosenjin." Sekai (December):87-89.

Minobe, Ryokichi
1972 "Kim Il-song shusho kaiken-ki." Sekai (February):45-74.

Naga, Tomoo
1972 "Ikaino ga nande sonnani." Asahi Janaru (January 14):102-106.

Nakamura, Yujiro
1971 "Seido to shiteno nihongo." Chuo Koron (August):318-322.

O, Im-jun
1971a Chosenjin no nakano nihonjin. Tokyo: Sanseido.
1971b Chosenjin to shiteno nihonjin. Tokyo: Godo Shuppan.

Sandei Mainicho
1970 "Zainichi chosenjin." Sandei Mainichi (October 18):160-168.

Suzuki, Jiro
1967 Gendai no sabetsu to henken. Tokyo: Shinsen-sha

Ubukata, Naokichi
1962 "Hitotsu no chosen." Sekai (December):93-94.

Wagatsuma, Hiroshi and
  Yoneyma, Toshinao
1967 Henken no kozo, nihonjin no jinshu-kan. Tokyo: Nihon Hoso Shuppan Kyokai.

Wagner, Edward W.
1951 The Korean Minority in Japan, 1904-1950. Vancouver: University of British Columbia.

Yamamura, Masaaki
1971 Inochi moetsukiru tomo. Tokyo Shobo.

Yi, Hoe-song
1971 "Chosenjin-kan." Sandei Mainichi (November 14):45.

7

SOCIAL AND POLITICAL ASSIMILATION
OF THE PHILIPPINE CHINESE ELITE

GERALD A. McBEATH

John Jay College of Criminal Justice
City University of New York

ABSTRACT

This article analyzes changes in the socio-economic composition and political attitudes of the Philippine Chinese elite. Eighty members of this elite were interviewed in 1969; on the basis of these interviews and supplementary research, a profile of the elite was drawn, elaborating the length of Philippine residence of the elite, its high rate of educational achievement and considerable support for the Chinese school system, and the wealth and economic power of this group--which have increased dramatically since the Second World War.

Most of the Chinese leaders were fully proficient in Philippine national languages, had adopted the outward forms of Filipino religiosity, and almost half used Filipinized names. Chinese leaders maintained close relationships with Filipinos: all business leaders had Congressional allies, and 70 members of the elite had Filipino compadres. From these data, four analytical types were constructed. Most leaders (30) were fully adapted to Filipino society; leaders of the second largest group (25) had accommodated and were "virtual second generation" Chinese. The two remaining groups represented those leaders who were maladapted (15)--unable to function in Filipino society--and those second and third generation Chinese who were partially assimilated (10) to their environment.

The power structure of the community was examined through the major factions of the Federation of Filipino-Chinese Chambers of Commerce, and then the leaders were ranked politically. Most were politically conservative, aligning themselves with the Chinese Nationalist Party (even though only 33 could be called party loyalists). This political affiliation has prevented greater elite and community change in the direction of either assimilation or integration.

Since the appearance, in 1958, of Skinner's *Leadership and Power in the Chinese Community of Thailand*, little systematic work has been published on the elites of Chinese communities in Southeast Asia. Numerous dissertations and monographs have focused on Southeast Asian Chinese communities since that time (see Nevadomsky and Li, 1970). But no studies replicating Skinner's methods, and few original works on different elites have appeared, thus making it difficult to understand Chinese minority leadership in general.

This article presents preliminary data on another leadership group, the Philippine Chinese elite. It draws a profile of this elite and then suggests the relationship of elite Chinese to Filipino society through a set of assimilation stages. (See Weightman and Amyot, 1960, for comments on Philippine Chinese assimilation in general.) Finally, this study analyzes the political attitudes and leadership roles of Philippine Chinese leaders.

The basic materials used in this study are personal interviews with the eighty leading members of the Philippine Chinese elite.[1] Interviews covered questions on the socio-economic background and upbringing of the leaders, questions directed to their community activities, and questions concerning their attitudes toward inter-ethnic relations and community politics. Standardized data on the life histories of all leaders were collected: these form the basis of this article. Because of the sensitivity of the Chinese position in the Philippines, the researcher tapped elite attitudes and opinions only when respondents seemed willing to contribute such information.

A PROFILE OF THE PHILIPPINE CHINESE ELITE

We may develop a profile of the Philippine Chinese elite by looking at these variables: birthplaces and patters of immigration, educational levels and adaptiveness, and

economic positions. A review of these factors will preface our analysis of leadership assimilation.

Immigration Patterns

Although the majority of the Philippine Chinese population of 500,000 is Philippine-born (almost all Chinese under 20 were born in the Philippine islands), its elite is still basically an immigrant population. Only 15 leaders were born in the Philippines (19 percent). Of the remainder, 60 (75 percent) were born either in Amoy city or in counties adjacent to Amoy (Chin-chiang, T'ung-an, Lung-hsi, Huei-an); only four leaders were born in the Canton area, and one in North China.

The predominance of southern Fukienese in the Chinese population and in its elite is understandable upon consideration of the history of Chinese immigration to the Philippines and the geography of East Asia. Traders from southern Fukien province had arrived in the Philippines by the time of the Sung Dynasty; for several hundred years, traders plied regularly between Manila and the port city of Chuan-chou. During the period of Spanish colonization, regular trade was maintained between Amoy and Manila (for Chinese played a major role in the galleon trade).

Although most of the Chinese leaders (all are male whose average age is 57) were born in China, most have spent at least 75 percent of their total lives in the Philippines. (Only four men in the sample had spent less than 50 percent of their lives in the Philippines.) Lest this suggest that Chinese leaders have

---
*The author wishes to thank the Institute of International Studies at the University of California, Berkeley, for research grants which supported this project. I am grateful to two colleagues at CUNY, David Garza and Dorothy Guyot, who commented critically on earlier versions of the article. Of course, I bear sole responsiblity for the conclusions.

assimilated through residence, it should be noted that few leaders spent all of their formative years in the Philippines. Most of those born in China reached the Philippines in their mid- to late-teens. Thus, early environmental influences and key socializing agents were native Chinese.

When we consider the "generation" of these leaders, we find only thirteen men who could properly be considered "second generation", and two, "third generation" Chinese. Because of the peculiar nature of Chinese settlement in Southeast Asia, a simple generation index was not found useful in understanding Chinese attachment to the Philippines. Thus, in this sample, the fathers of 33 leaders had lived and worked in the Philippines, even though the leaders themselves were born in China. Another eight leaders were preceded by two generations (fathers and grandfathers) of residents of the Philippines. Consequently, a full 70 percent of the sample had previous patrilineal residence in the islands, even though they might not have been born there themselves.

When we consider the length of time the Chinese have been in the Philippines, it is interesting to note that the current Chinese leadership has little mixed ancestry. Only one leader had a Filipino mother. The rest of the elite were "pure Chinese", a factor which contrasts significantly with the general Chinese population in which a higher degree of mestizoization obtains (but less high than at the end of the nineteenth century [Wickberg, 1965]; the development of rapid and safe transportation brought the sex ratio near balance in Manila by the 1930s). That this sample represents business leaders whose enterprises are concentrated in Manila largely explains this factor.

Some of the leaders do have Filipino wives, however. The wives of eight leaders were either mestizas (children of a Chinese-Filipina marriage) or ethnic Filipinas. In several of these cases, however, the Filipina was one of several wives. (Ten leaders had two or more wives.) Despite the slight percentage of leaders born in the Philippines, 41 have Filipino citizenship. 23 of those with Chinese citizenship have sons or wives who hold Filipino citizenship. Thus, only 16 members of the sample (20 percent) are not covered by the legal protection of Filipino citizenship. This fact clearly sets this sample apart from the mass of adult Chinese working in the Philippines, who are far less likely to hold Filipino citizenship. (Less than 20 percent of the parents of a large sample of Chinese high school students questioned in 1969 possessed Filipino citizenship [McBeath, 1973].)

Educational Background

As an Asian minority elite, the Philippine Chinese leadership is relatively well-educated. Only four have had no formal or tutorial education; 55 (69 percent) have had some secondary education. The sample included eleven college graduates, four of whom had done graduate work. These data confirm earlier estimates (Williams, 1966) that the Southeast Asian Chinese elites are becoming increasingly well-educated, contrasting markedly with earlier community elites. In the Philippines, current leaders differ decisively from their own fathers, 52 (or 65 percent) of whom had no formal or tutorial education and only one of whom had finished college.

Most of the leaders had taken school work in more than one milieu. One typical China-born leader had taken some tutorial work in his home village and then attended a primary school in the nearby town. After four years, he emigrated to the Philippines and went to work in a relative's shop. During the evenings, he attended a Chinese night school (conducted in Chinese but teaching basic English, mathematics and bookkeeping). He than attended the "Overseas Chinese" high

school and upon graduation matriculated at a Filipino university.

Results from the whole sample show the following sites of education of leaders: 47 (59 percent) of those who had attended school had taken half or more of their work in mainland China; 27 (34 percent) had taken half or more of their work in Chinese schools in the Philippines; and only ten (12 percent) had done 50 percent or more of their work in Philippine schools.[2] One member of the elite had completed most of his work in the United States.

Since 59 (74 percent) of the elite had never attended Philippine schools, we can conclude that the educational milieu for most men was Chinese--whether this was in China or in the Philippines. They were socialized not only by Chinese families but in a Chinese school system.

These background factors partly explain the extraordinary support for Chinese education in the Philippines by the Chinese elite. At present, there are 160 Chinese schools in the islands, 45 of which are high schools. Philippine Chinese leaders are not boasting when they claim that any Chinese child may receive kindergarten to high school education, irrespective of his parents' ability to pay tuition. In fact, tuition costs for these schools rarely cover operating expenses, so community elites must supply the differential. Newspaper accounts verified the extent of this support: all members of the sample had made contributions to at least one school in the previous five years. Moreover, 30 members of the sample (37 percent) had served as either board members or chairmen of the boards of Philippine Chinese schools (i.e., they were responsible for the continued financial security of these schools).

We would be in error were we to suggest that Chinese leaders have supported only *Chinese* schools and are interested only in a Chinese-language education for their children. Two factors weaken the elite's support for exclusively Chinese-language education: pressures from the Philippine government, and the leaders' desire for quality education for their children.

The existence of Chinese schools in the Philippines has been protected since Filipino independence by the Sino-Philippine Treaty of Amity of 1947. Nevertheless, Chinese schools were soon thereafter attacked on two grounds. In the early 1950s, Filipino critics asserted that Chinese schools harbored communist teachers. Filipino Congressmen developed this accusation and added to it their concern over the maladaptation of the Chinese population.

This controversy produced an alteration in the Chinese school system. In a Sino-Philippine agreement signed in 1957, Chinese schools were required to register with the Bureau of Private Schools of the Philippine Education Department (Liao, 1964:335); additionally, all Chinese schools were to teach the basic Filipino curriculum. This latter stipulation produced a dual curriculum in all Chinese schools. Students attended two shifts daily; one copied that of Philippine public schools, and the second followed the pattern set by the Ministry of Education in Taiwan.

In the climate of anti-Chinese sentiments of the mid-and late-1950s, Chinese leaders became increasingly apprehensive over their connections with Chinese schools. Since many of the Chinese elite had taken Filipino citizenship, they were charged with duplicity for still enrolling their children in Chinese schools. Thus, during 1960 and 1961, many Chinese with Filipino citizenship withdrew their children from Chinese schools and enrolled them either in Filipino private academies or in the newly-created "Filipinized" schools (Jesuit academies for Chinese students which adopted Filipino curricula but maintained instruction in Chinese language and literature). Within this sample, 20 leaders who had taken Filipino citizenship had done so.

Concurrently, the Chinese elite had also begun to question the efficiency and quality of Chinese school education. Their children were required to attend two lengthy sessions, repeating much basic work. The instructors in the Chinese session were frequently ill-prepared (for the stringent visa policies of the Philippine government had made it impossible to train large numbers of Philippine Chinese teachers in Taiwan or Hong Kong). The English-language training in many schools was also deficient, so the students were poorly prepared for college studies.

The Chinese sample which the researcher interviewed was unanimous in its support for the best education for its children, more perhaps for its utilitarian (its use in occupational mobility) than for its intrinsic value. Only five leaders had children of college age who were not attending college. 20 leaders (25 percent) had supported their childrens' graduate education in the United States. One father of ten noted that all his children had graduated from college and five had completed their Ph.D.'s in the United States.

The site of their childrens' education reveals most clearly the current ambivalence of the Chinese elite. 51 of the 80 leaders (63.7 percent) had educated their children primarily in Chinese schools in the Philippines. But 17 leaders (21.2 percent) had placed their children in "Filipinized" schools for most of their education, and 14 (17.5 percent) had sent their children to Philippine private academies. In fact, only 13 leaders had kept their children in Chinese schools for all of their education.

These data reveal the dilemma currently faced by the Chinese elite. By leadership role, they are required to finance and defend a Chinese school system that has now come under annual attack in Congress and in the Philippine press. But as naturalized Filipinos and as parents desiring the best possible education for their children, they are disinclined to educate their children in Chinese schools.

Economic Position of the Elite

To survey the socio-economic position of the elite, let us first compare their current occupations with those of their fathers.

Table 1. -- Occupations of respondents and their fathers

Occupation List	Rs' Fathers		Respondents	
	No.	Per Cent	No.	Per Cent
Peasant	9	11.2	-	-
Laborer	2	2.5	-	-
Small-scale retail trade	23	28.7	-	-
Medium-scale retail trade	20	25.0	7	8.7
Large-scale retail trade	14	17.5	25	31.3
Large-scale import-export	-	--	6	7.5
Small-scale industry and manufacturing	1	1.2	2	2.5
Medium-scale industry	1	1.2	10	12.5
Large-scale industry	2	2.5	6	7.5
Banker	-	-	10	12.5
Government/community bureaucrat	1	1.2	3	3.7
Professional (teacher, doctor, editor)	7	8.7	11	13.7
TOTALS	80%	100.0%	80%	100.0%

This occupational chart tells us two things about the current Chinese elite. First, it is an entirely urban group, which should surprise no one familiar with the occupations and life-styles of the overseas Chinese. More significantly, only nine members of the elite had fathers who were peasants. The overwhelming majority of this sample were born into "business" families,

even though they themselves may have been raised in the countryside of China. When examining the background of respondents and fathers in terms not only of occupation but also of birthplace, it was discovered that only twelve respondents came from mainly or completely rural backgrounds. The rest were truly urban Chinese, even though many spent their early formative years in villages in the Amoy area. This finding then invalidates the commonly-held stereotype of Philippine Chinese as first generation entrepreneurs. The current entrepreneurial activity of the Philippine Chinese elite is founded on the activity of their fathers and grandfathers.

Second, and equally obvious, the Chinese elite is an upwardly mobile group. None operates a typical small retail shop--the *sari sari* variety store, found throughout the Philippines. These are mainly successful businessmen who have significantly increased the capital which they inherited. An independent check on the mobility of these leaders demonstrated that only one leader's economic position was entirely inherited.[3] The remainder of the leaders could be grouped into three classes, depending on the amount of assistance they received on their road to success.

The first group included 25 leaders (31.3 percent) who made their business success entirely on their own. Typical of this group was leader Chia, who came to the Philippines at age 14, during the American Commonwealth period. He had no close relatives in the Philippines, but a distant clan relative put him to work as an apprentice in a textile store. By sleeping in the store and working evenings in a restaurant, he was able to save ₱1,000 (then equivalent to $500) after five years. With this as his share of the capital, he then opened a new textile shop with friends. Their business prospered until the Pacific War, when the stores were confiscated by the Japanese and he joined a guerrilla branch operating in southern Luzon. After the war, American officials gave him scrip for his share of the confiscated stock. With this and a bank loan (given without collateral because of his reputation for trustworthiness and enterprise), he opened a yardgoods store independently. This enterprise also prospered, so that by the mid-1950s he was able to open a textile factory. When interviewed in 1969, Chia's two enterprises were returning a profit of $15,000 annually, and he had just opened a large import-export firm.

The second, also the largest, group of leaders (36 men, 45 percent) was composed of men who had become successful primarily on their own, but had had some assistance from relatives or friends. Leader Ting was typical of this group. Although his father had operated a small grocery store in Manila for twenty years, he had been born in Chin-chiang and remained there until 16. He then worked with his father and inherited the store after his father's death. Ting's stocks were also seized during the war, but he fled with considerable savings in gold. After the war, he reopened the store and simultaneously opened a small food products manufacturing company. During the period of controls on foreign exchange (which aided nascent industries), his factory on the outskirts of Manila tremendously expanded its volume of production and sales. Ting then bought rice mills in central Luzon, open an export firm in Manila with friends, and started a fertilizer plant. By 1969, Ting's net worth was well in excess of ₱ 1 million.

The third group of 18 leaders (22.5 percent) included men who inherited substantial wealth which they increased. Leader Yi is typical of this group. His father owned a medium-sized tobacco factory outside Manila and held considerable investments in land. Yi was born in the Philippines but returned to the mainland for his primary and part of his secondary education; with the advance of the Japanese armies in China, however, he returned to the Philippines. The Japanese stopped production in his father's factory when they arrived in Manila, and the family fled to the Bicol region. After the war, the factory was restored. At his father's death, Yi became owner-manager of the factory, which to that time had produced native cigarettes. Yi then began importing Virginia leaves from the United States, producing a better quality of cigarettes, and tripling his profits. During the early 1950s, he began a joint venture in a small steel mill, which also prospered. Shortly thereafter he invested in hotels in Taiwan and Hong Kong and established a commercial bank in Manila. When interviewed in 1969, he was one of the richest men in the Philippines and a widely respected leader.

Not all Chinese, by any means, have followed straight roads to success and fortune in the Philippines; nor have all community leaders been without financial reverses. During the period of the study, one leader was facing bankruptcy and two had recently lost a large part of their estates through intra-family disputes. Yet, by and large, the Chinese elite is a successful group. In fact, success in business is the most important criterion for community leadership--success measured by upward mobility and personal wealth. Among the 80 men of the sample, there were no poor Chinese: the panel of evaluators found only 16 (20 percent) who were not really wealthy, a group which included most of the professionals and medium-scale businessmen. 11 men (13.7 percent) were numbered among the richest 100 men in the Philippines and were several times millionaires. Another 32 (40 percent) were only slightly less wealthy; and the remaining 21 (26.2 percent) could be called "well-to-do". None of the men interviewed had any of the common man's "money worries". This financial security has given them an invulnerability which is highly valued in the sensitive Chinese minority community. More important, their financial resources are the *sine qua non* of continued operation of important community associations.

As an economic as well as community power elite, the enterprises of these leaders inform us about the changing patterns of the Chinese economy in the Philippines. While those over 60 years old in the sample tended to head traditional family financial empires, younger men were more likely to direct modern commercial empires and conglomerates. Five younger leaders held positions as board chairmen of large businesses listed on the Manila stock exchange in which Filipinos had invested substantial sums.

Most of the leaders, however, represented neither of these types. Instead, they were men with enterprises in one commercial or industrial line who had diverse holdings in myriad other concerns. The researcher's investigation was not conclusive in determining the motivation behind their investments. However, an exploratory survey of records at the Philippine Securities and Exchange Commission indicated that family connections among directors of the same company were no more prevalent than friendships (and neither seemed a more compelling motivation for investment than the profit motive).

No businessmen among the elite held interests in fewer than four concerns. This aspect is demonstrated simply in Table 2. The range and depth of enterprises held by Chinese individually compares favorably with those held by Americans in the Philippines and by Spanish-mestizos. However, as a community of some 500,000 residents, proportional Chinese wealth is far less. What the considerable elite holdings do suggest, however, connects with our closing comments in the previous section. Chinese leaders are far richer than ordinary

Table 2. -- Business interests of the Philippine Chinese Elite

Enterprise	No.	Per cent
Sugar milling and distribution (including the largest domestic sugar trading house)	5	6.3
Export or distribution of other local products--copra, abaca, rice, corn (the largest exporter of copra)	21	26.2
General import-export	23	28.7
General retail trade (including three of the largest department stores in Manila and two in Cebu)	28	35.0
Banking (including three of the five banking houses with the largest assets in the Philippines)	16	20.0
Insurance	6	7.5
Other investments, securities, brokerage houses	16	20.0
Manufacturing and processing industries (including the three largest tobacco factories, the largest lumber milling industry, two large food processing plants, numerous textile mills)	42	52.5
Services -- hotels, restaurants, theaters	13	16.2
Professions -- newspapers, schools	16	20.0

Chinese (who, in turn, are far better off than most Filipinos). Because of their wealth, they are accorded high status in the community's internal status system. Yet this wealth has isolated as well as protected the Chinese elite, frequently impairing their understanding of economic problems common to small tradesmen in the community.

COMPARATIVE RATES OF ASSIMILATION AMONG THE CHINESE ELITE

Having examined the composition of the Philippine Chinese elite, we now turn to a more significant issue—the status and role of the Philippine Chinese leadership in Philippine society. The Philippines is a "modernizing" society whose leaders are intent on establishing a state which is politically unified--in which all residents are allegiant if not participant. Those who have been most responsible for articulating Filipino nationalist values since the Philippine Revolution of 1898--the *ilustrado* class--have increasingly called for an ethnically homogeneous society--a Filipino *nation*--to guarantee political unity. In the modern Philippines, there is little support for the integration of all ethnic minority *groups* into a society in which lowland Filipinos would be merely the largest, but not the culturally dominant, force; nor is there support for group autonomy. On the contrary, the national cultural elite has directly encouraged (and many Chinese have argued that it has forced) the assimilation of minority *individuals* into Filipino society.

We do not consider "assimilation" to be the best solution for the problems of the Philippine Chinese community. In fact, the researcher has argued for an "integration" approach elsewhere (McBeath, 1973). Here, however, we consider the stages of assimilation represented by the elite as key indicators of their responses to the pressures of the Philippine environment. These responses, in turn, have clearly influenced Chinese community politics.

Cultural Adaptation

One measure of the cultural adaptation of the Chinese elite is its language use and preference. The Philippine Chinese are primarily immigrants from the Amoy area; within the elite, only six men (all Cantonese) were not fluent in Amoy. Community business (with the exception of Chinse embassy functions) is conducted in this language, as are many classroom sessions in the Chinese section of schools. Elite proficiency in Mandarin, English and Pilipino gives us further information about adaptation.

Table 3. -- Linguistic proficiency in Mandarin, English, Pilipino

Extent of Proficiency	Languages					
	Mandarin		English		Pilipino	
	No.	%	No.	%	No.	%
None	20	25.0	21	26.2	16	20.0
Fair	23	28.7	26	32.5	42	52.5
Fluent	37	46.2	33	41.2	22	27.5
Totals	80	100 %	80	100.0 %	80	100.0 %

Considering that 65 members of this group were born in China, the above figures for English and Pilipino use are quite surprising. The Chinese elite (except for those over 60 with limited education) is multi-lingual, speaking well the language of ethnicity, Mandarin (which is a second language for most), and the two national languages of the Philippines--English and Pilipino.

However, the linguistic *preference* of the elite is another matter. 42 indicated that they preferred to speak Amoy only--the language of their homes and ethnic community. 14 preferred to speak other Chinese languages (split between Mandarin and Cantonese), 9 preferred to speak English (all younger leaders and all born in the Philippines), and 15 indicated that they preferred to speak a combination of languages: Amoy *and* Pilipino *and* English or Mandarin, depending on the circumstances. While this response may have been given for the researcher's benefit, those expressing it were regularly exposed to situations requiring fluency in different languages. Thus, the Philippine Chinese elite has made substantial adaptation in language use toward its environment. (Those resisting change in this respect were older and could function in a linguistically homogeneous milieu.) We must hedge our bets when we consider the number who preferred to speak Amoy, however.

The reading preferences of these leaders also convey information about their adaptiveness. All but two read Chinese newspapers daily, but a large number also read the English press (56 men, 70 percent). More were likely to read English-language than Chinese periodicals, although fewer than half read either.

The aspect of religion also informs us about changes in clutural attitudes and beliefs of the elite. The Philippines is largely a Catholic society (notwithstanding the importance of the Protestant community, roughly 7 percent of the population, and of the Moslem community of Mindinao, approximately 5 percent). The religious beliefs of families of leaders, however, were either Buddhist, Confucian syncretist, or non-religious (in the Chinese sense). Only four leaders were raised in Christian families.

Leaders described their current religious affiliations in this way: 30 had no religion, 19 were Buddhists, 18 were Catholics, and 13 were Protestants. This seems to represent considerable adaptation toward the environment.

However, the respondents' own views of their religious beliefs indicated that for most, religion of any kind was simply not a salient factor in their lives. Only 15 attended services or participated with any degree of regularity. This sub-sample included many "true believers". One member of the elite is known throughout the community for his championship of Protestantism. He conducts Bible classes in his plant and is a church elder. Another distributes copies of the Bible and the Golden Rule.

Most of the sample, as community leaders, had contributed to the construction of churches or the support of sectarian schools in the previous ten years. But the prevailing attitude toward religion was best expressed by one leader who stated: "So far as Filipinos are concerned, I am a Catholic; but between you and me, I believe only in making money." While Filipinos familiar with this attitude have charged Chinese with hypocrisy, the attitude merely suggests that Chinese leaders (and most Chinese of the adult generation) have not yet adapted to either the style or substance of Filipino religiosity.

One final factor is of relevance to the cultural adaptation of Chinese leaders. In the Chinese community, and particularly in its press, Chinese leaders are all identified by their Chinese names. But five leaders use *bona fide* Filipino names in their dealings with non-Chinese. These five were born in the Philippines, and their use of Filipino names indicates their greater adaptation to the environment than that of those who do not use them. An additional 31 members of the sample have used Filipinized surnames with Filipino given names. (It is usually apparent to Filipinos that these surnames are partly sinicized.) Most commonly, the Chinese compound two or three characters (in romanization from the Amoy) producing a name such as Yuchengco or Uytachco. Some have added the name of a patron to their Chinese names, producing names such as Santos-Chua or Lopez-Ong. These changes in the use of Filipinized surnames have become increasingly popular; they do represent substantial adaptation.

Social Adaptation

When we turn to social relationships between Chinese leaders and Filipinos, we detect even greater changes in the pattern of behavior.

Because most members of the Chinese elite are well-to-do or quite wealthy, they can afford suburban residences. Early in this century, rich Chinese (including the community elite) resided within the Chinatown area. But at present, residences of the elite are dispersed throughout Manila (and Cebu) and have spread into the suburbs. This places members of the elite in proximity with the Filipino upper-middle and upper classes; it does not necessitate interaction, but it does predispose Chinese toward greater contact with Filipinos. Again, due to shared class interests, it has become common for Chinese and Filipinos to entertain one another and attend inter-ethnic social gatherings. However, residential integration is perhaps the weakest basis of Chinese-Filipino interchange at the elite level.

Of greater significance are Chinese elite relationships with those Filipinos who are needed to maintain or initiate business connections. All business leaders retained Filipino lawyers, and many used Filipinos as managers or "decorations"--office front Filipinos, as it were. But such contacts are less important than those which leaders have formed over the years with Filipino politicians. None of the leaders in business was without a Congressional ally. While interviewing, the researcher regularly viewed a gallery of politicians--autographed pictures of Presidents, Congressional leaders, Supreme Court justices--on the walls or desks of the offices of the elite.

It is easy to generalize about the motive for such friendships, but difficult to speculate on their depth or effect. Several of the elite have been protected by Filipino friends when discovered in illegal activities; surely, the need for protection is at least an unconscious motivation for those

Chinese who form friendships with actual or potential Filipino politicians. But the cases of genuine inter-ethnic friendships among this elite are legion. A former community leader, Dee G. Chuan, was a warm personal friend of President Quezon; and this example is still respected.

Some statistics support these impressions, but they tend to be somewhat misleading. Fifty men in the sample have moderate to extensive relationships with Filipinos, meaning they have Filipino friends and participate regularly in non-Chinese activities. Seventy (87.5 percent) have Filipino compadres.[4] 21 members of the elite are members of Filipino organizations such as the Lions Club, Rotary, Chamber of Industries, etc.

Analyzing the depth of sentiments toward Filipinos among the elite required concrete situations. In conversations with leaders, whenever possible the researcher asked about their attitudes toward inter-ethnic marriage. Seven members of the sample had Filipino sons- or daughters-in-law and were favorably disposed to inter-marriage. The other leaders regarded large-scale inter-marriage as inevitable in the future, but only a handful endorsed it or presented no objections to their child's possible marriage to a Filipino. This demonstration of cultural pride and social conservatism was the most convincing example the researcher found of the limits to social assimilation among the elite.

Analytical Types

Summarizing the socio-cultural assimilation of the Philippine Chinese elite requires an analysis of the co-variance of these variables: age, amount and site of education, birthplace and generation. A combination of these factors suggests these stages of assimilation among the elite:

1. *Partly Assimilated Leaders*

A small group of leaders (no more than ten) is fully assimilated socially to the Philippines, having receptive attitudes toward inter-ethnic marriage and extensive contacts with Filipinos. Although they are adapted culturally-speaking Philippine languages and ever preferring to speak English--not all are complete assimilated culturally (even though several in this group are considered more Filipino than Chinese).

The factors which explain this partial assimilation are the uniform Philippine birth of these leaders, their education in the Philippines during the Commonwealth period in English-language high schools and colleges, and a long family history of residence in the islands. Leaders of this type felt that their children would not be part of the Chinese community; two leaders in this group were originally reticent to participate in Chinese activities and have become partly re-sinicized through their participation.

2. *Accommodated Leaders*

A second, larger group of leaders (about 25) is fully accommodated, both socially and culturally, to the Philippine environment. (See Giok-lan Tan for the use of this term [1963].) These leaders speak Philippine languages fluently, but they still use Amoy in their homes and in community gatherings. Most of the leaders in this type are what Skinner called "virtual second generation" Chinese (1958). Although born in China, their fathers had worked in the Philippines, and they arrived in their early teens to help in the family business. Consequently, their educational milieu was partly Chinese and partly Filipino. Members of this group were more likely to have studied at Philippine colleges. Like the first group, they are now middle-aged men. Several of these have retained their Chinese citizenship, however; and most feel so at ease in the Chinese community--which gives them psychological as well as material satisfaction--that they would not opt for membership

in Filipino society even if they had the opportunity.

3. *Adapted Leaders*

The largest group (30) of Chinese leaders would fall in a third type: men adapted to the cultural forms and social system of the Philippines, but stalled on the path to assimilation either because of ethnic pride or resistance in the host society.

These men are also China-born, but are somewhat less likely to have been sons of businessmen in the Philippines. However, the chief difference between the adapted and accommodated leaders lies in two other areas. First, "adapted" leaders are less well-educated, having completed high school education at best. Second, they are wealthier, and are the best representatives of the *parvenu* Chinese. Community leadership has come to them as a consequence of their wealth; they take leading roles to protect and expand their personal holdings. As economic men, these leaders have paid less attention to matters of cultural change and assimilation. They have become sufficiently proficient in Philippine ways to advance their fortunes, but the motive for adaptation has been economic.

4. *Maladapted Leaders*

The last group of about 15 men is clearly not at all adapted to Philippine society. This group is composed of two sub-types: 1) several China-born leaders with limited formal education who came to the Philippines before the development of the Chinese school system; 2) several educators and editors who are well-educated, but whose training and community roles completely restrict their contacts with the Filipino population. This group is least wealthy and contains the oldest members of the elite (all are over 60). It includes most of the hard-core Kuomintang leadership and has been the chief guardian of Chinese traditions in the community.

THE STRUCTURE OF POWER IN THE PHILIPPINE CHINESE COMMUNITY

The above stages of assimilation are largely derived from social and cultural factors. But the elite is distinctive primarily because of its leadership role. This role is best understood through an examination of the major community organization and a separate treatment of the political attitudes and values of Philippine Chinese leaders.

The Federation as the Pinnacle of Power

The chief structure which articulates Chinese interests in the Philippines is the Federation of Filipino-Chinese Chambers of Commerce. Called the Federation (Shang-tsung), this association was formed in 1954 in response to both disintegration of Chinese associations and increasing pressures of nationalization upon the community. For ten years, the Federation vied with the Manila General Chinese Chamber of Commerce for the role of leading community association. After the death of the director of the Manila Chamber, the Federation absorbed the Chamber; its power has been uncontested since that time.

Since 1965, there has been a direct relationship between Federation membership (and position in the Federation's pecking order) and actual community power. Thus, the most important twenty leaders in the sample were all important Federation directors. The two most influential Philippine Chinese leaders held the No. 1 and 2 positions in the Federation at the time of this study. Only 23 of the leaders in the sample were not directors of the Federation; with only three exceptions (two editors and a school principal), these men formed the lower quartile of the sample with respect to community influence.

Although the Federation has enlisted powerful individuals as members, its membership consists largely of chambers of commerce (representing towns and regions throughout the Philippines) and trade associations (lines of business--e.g., lumber associations, *sari-sari* store associations, *etc.*). Thus, the Federation acts for Chinese economic interests throughout the Philippines, despite the concentration of its membership in Manila. Moreover, through an intricate pattern of interlocking membership, the Federation also includes the key members of the other major community associations: the Anti-communist League, the Philippine branch of the Kuomintang (Chinese Nationalist Party), the Grand Family Association, the Chinese Benevolent Association, the Chinese Schools Association, and numerous cultural, sports, and regional associations.

It is the Federation which responds to Philippine governmental pressures and initiates most actions taken by the Philippine Chinese as a community. Leadership of this body is determined by 80 directors selected at a biennial convention of all member units. These 80 directors then vote for the President, vice-presidents, and control officers. During the first 12 years of the Federation, these elections were colorless contests, merely endorsing that clique which had founded the Federation (a group of men closely associated with the Philippine Kuomintang branch who wished to superintend community politics).

But after the defeat of President Macapagal (who was supported by the Federation in the 1965 Presidential elections), an anti-party clique captured Federation leadership. The leader of this faction was a *compadre* of the new President, Ferdinand Marcos; he was a third generation Philippine Chinese (type 1) who had been substantially deculturated. The elections for Federation President in 1968 demonstrated vivid competition between party adherents and the anti-party clique (based on old members of the Manila Chamber) which wanted to reduce the party's influence in community affairs. The Filipino national elite intervened directly in these elections, not only to support Marcos' *compadre*, but also to ensure that the Federation would direct the major part of its electoral contributions to the President's party.

Although the anti-party faction succeeded in winning the 1968 Federation election, the post of president was restored to the party faction in 1970, where it remains at present. The fortunes of Federation leadership aspirants are thus intimately tied into national politics--a form of political assimilation of organizations--and to long-extant factional lines within the Chinese community.

Political Attitudes of the Elite
and the Question of Loyalty

The meaning of these organizational factors for individual members of the sample is more difficult to define. Let us look at the social attitudes of the elite and, from this basis, turn to an analysis of their political attitudes.

The community elite is by birth and inclination defensive of the Chinese population. Leaders uniformly expressed what Filipinos regard as chauvinistic views: they disparaged the state of education and the arts in the Philippines, they castigated the systematic corruption and misrule of the islands, and they frequently made unfavorable comparisons between Taiwan and the Philippines. All leaders but three agreed with the statement that China represented a "high" culture, and the Philippines - a nation without a long history or a significant cultural tradition - a "low" culture.

One might expect these socio-cultural attitudes to influence leaders' perceptions of Filipino institutions and political processes. While leaders tended to agree with the statement that Filipino politicians were commodities which could be bought or sold, they also respected the strength of Filipino political institutions. Thus, when questioned directly about nationalistic legislation passed by the Congress (in 1954, the Congress passed a Retail Trade Nationalization Act, aimed at crushing the Chinese monopoly position in retail trade; in 1959, Congress passed a Rice and Corn Nationalization Bill, which required operators of rice and corn mills and traders of cereals to hold Filipino citizenship), Chinese leaders resented the immediate effects of this legislation upon small Chinese entrepreneurs. But surprisingly, most felt that the long-term effects of this legislation would be advantageous to the Chinese community. Certainly, the personal security of none of the community leaders had been or would be threatened by such legislation. Moreover, considering the wealth of this elite, those without Filipino citizenship could either purchase it or work through fronts.

Leaders did not feel "alienated" from the political system of the Philippines, even though they frequently thought political processes were corrupt. Furthermore, most leaders seemed to feel highly "efficacious" about their own roles in Philippine society. Considering their community status, business success and personal wealth, these attitudes are not unusual. As will be seen below, such feelings have conduced toward elite Chinese support of the Philippine government and adherence to most of its regulations.

Such an analysis does not, however, inform us about the spread of factions in the community. Too, at a time when the Philippines is not only facing significant internal unrest but also re-evaluating its treaty relationships and diplomatic recognition of the Republic of China on Taiwan, we need to know more about partisanship among the elite.

To this end, the political views of the elite were ranked by a third panel of judges. This ranking defined those who were Kuomintang partisans (fully supporting the Taiwan government), those who at least publicly supported the KMT (although they might privately vacillate over issues such as trade with mainland China), and those who were "neutral" (refusing to support the Taiwan regime but also refusing to demonstrate loyalty to the People's Republic of China--either out of personal convictions or due to the conservative environment of Philippine national politics).

33 leaders (41.2 percent) were identified as Kuomintang partisans. These included most of the standing committee of the KMT in the Philippines, educators, newspaper editors and several leading businessmen. Many of these men were older and had been educated in Republican China. The Cantonese in the sample uniformly supported the KMT (Sun Yat-sen, the leader of the 1911 Revolution, was a Cantonese as well as an overseas Chinese).

But 34 leaders (42.5 percent) only "publicly" supported the Kuomintang. This group was composed mainly of middle-aged businessmen who had learned that to speak otherwise in the Philippines constituted political and economic suicide. Indeed, it is likely that the community leadership over-represents the number of KMT partisans in the community. The Chinese community is of course concerned with Chinese politics, but it has long disbelieved the "return to the mainland" promise of the Nationalist government on Taiwan. As an economic minority, Philippine Chinese--like those elsewhere in Southeast Asia--do not openly "talk about politics." In a situation that has not yet necessitated taking sides, it would be fool-hardy for either those in the community at large or in its leadership to openly advocate a policy line that differed from official government recognition policy.

The smallest group, 13 leaders (16.2 percent) could be labeled "neutralists." While some members of this group have been called "communists" by the rightist party newspapers in the community (the *Great China News* and the *Gong Li Press*), there is little basis to these charges. Real, visible communists did function among the Chinese in a guerrilla branch fighting against the Japanese during the war and relatively openly in the community from the end of the war until the early 1950s. Under conditions of the late 1960s and early 1970s, such overt activity has not been possible (notwithstanding the charges regularly appearing in the Philippine press that "rich Manila Chinese" have financed the Huks and the New People's Army). Nor have Filipino radicals been able to find candidates among the Chinese *elite* to articulate their viewpoints.

It is appropriate at this point to establish the relationship between the political rankings of the elite and the stages of assimilation represented above. The most direct relationship appeared between type 1 (partly assimilated) leaders and "neutralists". Eight of the ten leaders in type 1 were judged to be neutralists. The neutralist stance of these leaders seems a direct consequence of their assimilation into Philippine society. Yet these men, when interviewed, were not disinterested in Chinese national politics. Rather, they resented its intrustion into Philippine Chinese affairs and have been the mainstay of the anti-party clique.

Of the accommodated leaders (type 2), a slightly larger number (14) were "publicly pro-KMT" than KMT partisans. For these leaders, Chinese national politics are very salient, but less so for ideological reasons than for their occasional usefulness in maintaining community power and orthodoxy. However, as a group, these leaders have relied less on their party connections to hold office than have less well-adapted leaders. Those accommodated leaders who only "publicly" support the party have in recent years also supported the anti-party clique.

A larger majority of the adapted leaders (18 men) were identified as KMT loyalists. This type includes many newly-rich Chinese and as a consequence their political stance is somewhat suspect. The party label has been employed by many in this group to gain leadership, thus solidifying their economic positions.

Finally, the "maladapted" leaders (type 4) are primarily KMT partisans (11). Most of these leaders are not only politically concerned with the fate of Taiwan but also wish the Philippine branch of the party to play the commanding role in community politics. Their own interests are served by this connection; but they also win ideological rewards by it.

Despite the variance of these types, however, the Philippine Chinese elite is a politically conservative body (judges could locate only 13 "neutralist" leaders). This *elite* conservatism is founded on the aspects of socio-cultural traditionalism mentioned above. Conservatism is also a product of the economic interests of the elite, especially the Chinese role in the laissez-faire Philippine economy. Additionally, this attitude is supported by the conservatism of the Philippine political culture and ruling class.

But what can we say about the political loyalty of the Chinese elite? Several of the leaders in this sample demonstrated their loyalty to the Philippines by serving in guerrilla units, fighting Japanese during the occupation of the country in the Pacific War. However, at that time Chinese and Filipinos fought a common enemy, a power which invaded China as well as the Philippines.

The political loyalty of all Chinese has been a major concern of Filipino commentators since the Chinese communist liberation of the Chinese mainland in 1949; at a time of growing unrest in the Philippines, this concern has intensified. Membership in the KMT in the Philippine Chinese community (and in its surrogate agency, the Anti-communist League) and strategies for displaying the mon-communist nature of the Philippine Chinese population, and the reticence of community leaders to identify with mainland China have been the major strategies for displaying the non-communicst nature of the Philippine Chinese population, and protecting the community. A minor strategy, of course, has been a disclaimer of Chinese interest in Philippine national politics, issued on a periodic basis by community organs and officials.

These measures have not sufficed to defuse criticism, however. Since Filipino attacks are motivated by economic scapegoatism as well as by political concern, they have tended to increase when economic conditions have deteriorated--as they did following the corrupt and expensive 1969 elections. The interviews which the researcher conducted were far less useful in estimating politcal loyalty. The travel of leaders indicated that issues of political loyalty were probably unimportant for most. Over half of the sample travels to Taiwan and Hong Kong annually; eight maintain partial residence in Taiwan and three do so in Hong Kong. While much of this travel has been for purely economic (and possibly romantic) reasons, even this aspect has been castigated as a sign of political disloyalty. In 1968 Congressman Dupaya initiated a Congressional investigation of business investments and travel of naturalized Filipinos, accusing those with investments abroad of economic sabotage.

Certain of the leaders have traveled to mainland China; however, these trips were taken to visit old homes and living relatives. No leader in the sample had taken a directly political role--e.g., representing the community at the Canton trade fair. On the other hand, the Chinese elite has taken extensive, overt actions on behalf of the Taiwan government; but such actions could be construed as political disloyalty only if diplomatic relations were broken. Thus, our analysis must be inconclusive with respect to the issue of loyalty of the Chinese elite to the Philippine government.

CONCLUSION

This study has introduced relevant background data and information on attitudes of the present Philippine Chinese elite. The leadership of the Chinese community emerges from this investigation as an economic elite which maintains community power because of its material success and its skill in mitigating, if not eliminating, the pressures upon the community from the Philippine environment.

We have suggested that the elite is not representative of the Chinese community as a whole. Not women occupy elite roles, and wealthy businessmen are heavily overrepresented. The elite is middle-aged, and the youngest member is 39. Indeed, in these respects, there has been no change in the community's elite in the last fifty years.

It is their education, generation, and economic interest which separate these leaders from previous elites. Current Chinese leaders are far better educated than their fathers or earlier elites; they are far more likely to have spent most of their formative years in the Philippines; and their economic concerns are far less likely to be privatistic or family-oriented. In these important areas, the Chinese elite is not unlike the

Filipino national or economic elites.

These aspects are the basis permitting significant elite assimilation to the norms and behavior patterns of the Filipino elite. The majority of the Chinese elite is well adapted to Filipino society, for it has the requisite skills for participation in this society. This nearly uniform adaptation (with the exception of the small group of older, China-educated leaders) clearly distinguishes the elite from adult Chinese generally.

Of far greater import, however, are the consequences of this adaptation for leadership roles. What effect has this adaptation had upon community politics? Williams (1966) has suggested that the greater education and socio-cultural adaptation of overseas Chinese will lead naturally to "political assimilation"; that is, Chinese will participate in the government and politics of the Philippines (or be civically integrated in the nation-state).

By Williams' definition, the Philippine Chinese elite are certainly politically assimilated. Both Chinese elite connections with Filipino politicians and the involvement of national political actors in Federation recruitment demonstrate this. However, has the political assimilation of the elite created conditions for assimilation of the community?

The "adapted" members of the elite have attempted to change traditional Chinese customs and rituals--such as expensive, noisy funeral processions, elaborate, costly wedding feasts and the like. Also, the elite has conducted campaigns for contributions to Philippine charities and social welfare. But beyond this, there is little further positive empirical evidence.

Chinese leaders, as a group, have not attempted to address those problems of community morality which they are in the best position to resolve. The elite has not attempted to revise the Chinese educational system so that it would prepare Chinese children for productive lives in the Philippines. (In fact, those Chinese who conducted such a campaign have been ostracized by the community.) The elite has not altered (or even reviewed) those Chinese business practices and organizations which justifiably anger Filipinos. Nor has the elite, by personal example or official Federation policy, concerned itself with those social and economic problems in the Philippines which have undermined democratic institutions (even though these problems remain beyond the power of Philippine Chinese to resolve).

Interviews with the Chinese elite indicated, above all, the scarcity of far-sighted men in positions of community leadership. The sample included only two thinkers or intellectuals, men who were not regarded as powerful in community politics. A community elite based on economic skills and material success rarely bestows power on men of vision. Yet at this point in the development of Filipino-Chinese relations, it is clearly necessary for the Chinese elite to rethink the Chinese position and role in the Philippines, to move beyond defensive reactions to nationalization measures, and initiate bold and imaginative policies of internal change— whether these lead toward assimilation or integration.

POSTSCRIPT 1975

Since the above article was written in 1973, several major changes in Philippine politics have influenced the Philippine Chinese and their elite. President Ferdinand Marcos' assumption of martial law powers terminated the era of democratic, Congressional politics in the Philippines--invalidating alliances Chinese elites had formed with Congressmen and temporarily reducing prospects of additional nationalization of Chinese enterprises. (An early martial law decree allowed aliens to re-engage in rice milling and the cereal trade.)

Two martial law policies have had some impact on elite stability. A "get tough" policy on corruption (aimed principally at Marcos' political rivals) resulted in the detention for one day of the Federation's President and the flight from the Philippines of several prominent Chinese business leaders. Nonetheless, in interviews with elites during a trip to Manila in January, 1975, the author found that most leaders retained their old positions within the community hierarchy. (Deaths, retirements, forced departures from the Philippines accounted for changes in only nine elite slots.)

Changes in Philippine foreign policy have, to date, had a greater impact on community organization and elite dynamics. Mrs. Imelda Marcos' well-publicized trip to mainland China in September, 1974 initiated both a reversal in the direction of Philippine foreign policy (from anti-communism to peaceful coexistence with communist countries) and a Sino-Filipino detente that the Marcos administration hopes will reduce foreign support and domestic pressures of communist rebellion.

President Marcos travelled to Peking himself in June, 1975; he officially opened relations with the PRC and severed diplomatic ties with Taiwan. By the time of this trip, these changes had occurred in community structure: 1) the Chinese schools *system* was abolished. Although Chinese students could continue to attend schools whose faculty and student body were primarily Chinese, the Chinese-language session was eliminated. To remain accredited, directors, administrators, and faculty of these schools needed to possess Filipino citizenship. 2) During the first year of martial law, newspaper publication was suspended. Thereafter, two KMT-party newspapers consolidated their editions into one daily. The staff and supporters of the third (formerly neutral) paper purchased the printing plant of the fourth (pro-KMT) and began publication of a Chinese-English daily that endorsed the new Philippine foreign policy and China's developmental path. 3) The Chinese Nationalist party apparatus and supporting agencies ceased formal operations; however, they have been encouraged to retain informally their policing role in the community. 4) The Federation experienced difficulty in filling top offices after its 1974 directorate elections. It recruited as President a moderate, former KMT supporter; real power lay with the anti-KMT faction which now sought to "Filipinize" the entire directorate.

These changes are obviously of great import for the social and political assimilation of the Chinese elite. It is now impossible for leaders without Filipino citizenship to direct community activities. On the one hand, this further isolates the elite from those in the community who, despite liberalization of naturalization requirements, have not elected to assimilate civically. On the other hand, this strengthens the small chauvinistic sub-elite by presenting a viable alternative to assimilate (the PRC). Moreover, the recognition of the PRC has adjusted the orientation of community leaders from publicly pro-KMT to neutralist--adding legitimacy to the stance of those favoring closer ties to China without eliminating supporters of Taiwan. Thus, the relatively gradual process of assimilative change analyzed above has been disrupted. Intra-community political conflict now promises to add a new dimension to Philippine ethnic politics.

FOOTNOTES

1. The methodology of this study largely follows Skinner's work. 150 Philippine Chinese were asked to serve as "judges" and rank the "leaders" of the Chinese community

in two categories: *A* grade--the ten most important leaders in the community; and *B* grade--the fifteen next most influential Chinese. The judges were in all cases individuals who had lived in the community most of their adult years and regularly followed community politics. Many had served as members of major community associations. These rankings were tabulated, producing a list of 80 men whose leadership scores were significantly higher than others.

The list was then checked against a roster of participants involved in major community decisions in the previous ten years. No significant omissions were noted. During the time of research, the researcher established biographies for all members of the sample. These were based on reports of leaders' activities clipped from Chinese newspapers, records of their associational activity, records of conferences and organizational histories, and information provided by friends and relatives of the leaders.

Then, from January to June, 1969, the researcher interviewed the elite sample. All but four of the 80-member sample agreed to be interviewed; for those who refused, life histories were obtained from close relatives and friends. The researcher conducted all interviews himself, aided by a Philippine Chinese re earch assistant. The interviews ranged from 40 minutes to over three hours in length; they were carried on in the language in which the respondent was most proficient--whether Amoy (the speech-group of most Philippine Chinese), Mandarin, Cantonese, Pilipino (the Philippine national language), or English.

2. Figures total more than 100 percent, for some leaders divided their educational careers between China and Chinese schools in the Philippines.

3. Three bankers and financiers who were familiar with the career histories of all men in the sample rated the elite's career patterns.

4. The practice of co-parentage is an institutionalization of friendship. A *compadre* relationships is formed when one's children are baptized. The *compadre* guarantees the moral instruction or protection of the child and is also bound to a set of reciprocal relationships with the parent. See Guthrie (1968) for an account of its significance in Filipino society.

REFERENCES

Agpalo, Remigio E.
1962   The Political Process and the Nationalization of the Retail Trade in the Philippines. Quezon City: University of the Philippines.

Amyot, Jacques, S.J.
1960   The Chinese Community of Manila: A Study of Adaptation of Chinese Familism to the Philippine Environment. University of Chicago, Unpublished Ph.D. Dissertation.

Ch'en Lieh-fu
1968   Fei-lu-p'in ti Min-tzu Wen-hua yu T'ung-hua Wen-t'i (The Culture of the Filipino People and the Question of Chinese Assimilation) Taipei: Cheng-Chung Publishing Co.

Federation of Filipino-Chinese Chambers of Commerce
1965   Philippine Chinese Yearbook, 1964-65 Manila: Federation.

General Chamber of Commerce
1955   Fiftieth Anniversary Commemorative Album of the Philippine Chinese General Chamber of Commerce Manila.

Geertz, Clifford
1963   Old Societies and New States. Glencoe, Ill.: The Free Press.

Golay, Frank H.
1969   Underdevelopment and Economic Nationalism in Southeast Asia. Ithaca, N.Y.: Cornell University Press.

Gordon, Milton M.
1964   Assimilation in American Life: The Role of Race, Religion, and National Origin. New York: Oxford University Press.

Grossholtz, Jean
1964   Politics in the Philippines. Boston: Little, Brown and Co.

Guthrie, George M. (ed.)
1968   Six Perspectives on the Philippines. Manila: Bookmark.

Horowitz, Donald L.
1971   "Multiracial Politics in the New States." in Jackson and Stein (eds.) Issues in Comparative Politics. New York: St. Martin's Press.

Hunter, Guy
1966   Southeast Asia--Race, Culture, and Nation. London: Oxford University Press.

Jacob, Philip E. and
Toscano, James V. (eds.)
1964   The Integration of Political Communities. Philadelphia: J.B. Lippincott Co.

Liao, Shubert S.C. (ed.)
1964   Chinese Participation in Philippine Culture and Economy. Manila.

McBeath, Gerald A.
1973   Political Integration of the Philippine Chinese. Berkeley, Calif.: Center for South and Southeast Asia Studies.

Nevadomsky, Joseph, and
Li, Alice (eds.)
1970   The Chinese in Southeast Asia: A Selected and Annotated Bibliography of Publications in Western Languages, 1960-1970. Berkeley, Calif.: Center for South and Southeast Asia Studies.

Purcell, Victor W.
1965   The Chinese in Southeast Asia. London: Oxford University Press.

Shibutani, Tamatsu, and Kwan, Kian M.
1965   Ethnic Stratification: A Comparative Approach. New York: The Macmillan Co.

Skinner, G. William
1957   Chinese Society in Thailand. Ithaca, N.Y.: Cornell University Press.
1958   Leadership and Power in the Chinese Community of Thailand. Ithaca, N.Y.: Cornell University Press.

Tan Giok-lan
1963   The Chinese of Sukabumi: A Study in Social and Cultural Accommodation. Ithaca, N.Y. Southest Asia Program.

Weightman, George H.
1960   The Philippine Chinese: A Cultural History of a Marginal Trading Community. Cornell University, Unpublished Ph.D. dissertation.

Wickberg, Edgar
1965   The Chinese in Philippine Life: 1850-1898. New Haven: Yale University Press.

Williams, Lea E.
1966 The Future of the Overseas Chinese in Southeast Asia. New York: McGraw-Hill.

Wilmott, Donald E.
1960 The Chinese of Semarang: A Changing Minority Community in Indonesia. Ithaca, N.Y.: Cornell University Press.

Willmott, William E.
1970 The Political Structure of the Chinese Community in Cambodia. London: The Athlone Press.

PERIODICALS

Hsin-min Jih-pao (The Fookien Times). Manila, 1968-1972.

Hua-ch'iao Shang-pao (Chinese Commercial News). Manila, 1968-1970'

Kung-li Pao (The Gong Li Press). Manila, 1968-1969.

Shang-tsung Yueh-pao (Trade Journal). Manila: Federation of Filipino-Chinese Chambers of Commerce, 1968-1972.

Ta-chung-hua Jih-pao (The Great China Press). Manila, 1968-1969.

III. SOUTHEAST ASIA

After reviewing the cultural and traditional relationships between the Meo and the Lao, Andrianoff observes no weakening of the ethnic identity among the Meo tribes of northern Laos despite the devastating effects of the war and the eventual relocating into refugee camps. He attributes the economic foundations of Meo's sense of independence from low land people to their shifting swidden agricultural methods and their monopoly on opium production.

Denton examines the general interaction patterns between the Sen'ol Semai of West Malaysia, an aboriginal group of forest regions, and their rural Malay neighbors, utilizing the symbolic interactionist framework of sociology. The Semai's manipulations of stereotype images of the cambia here held by the Malayians for their own advantage, are described, and the modes of social boundary negotiations between the Semai and their neighbors are discussed.

Banks provides a historical review of the immigration of non-Malays and the ensuing development of intergroup relations among ethnically different poeple. He notices the pattern of rigid ethnic demarcations that developed in the centers of colonial powers spreading into inland. Resorting to the case studies of northern Malay where the non-Malay has been gradually but steadily become assimilated into the Malaysian culture, Banks claims that in those areas where the influence of the central government is weaker the assimilation process of the non-Malay has made gradual but steady progress. Banks also points out the middle man roles which the Chinese and Indonesians played under the colonial period in Malaysia.

Maxwell discusses the ethnic assimilation of Chinese in Thailand particularly through his case studies of medical students. He lists several key variables for assimilation; the willingness of the majority of the society to open socially valued positions to the minority group; willingness of the members of the minority group to move into more lucrative, higher status positions; the minority groups possession of qualifications for these positions. The Chinese communities in Thailand developed extremely comprehensive institutional networks: schools, hospitals, religious institutions, social and professional associations, etc. The Chinese are mainly urban and are in industry and commerce. In general, there is no sign of Thailand Chinese developing eagerness to assimilate into Thai society. Thai society displays a relative lack of ethnic exclusiveness. However, there is a growing pressure for Thai nationalism, and a national policy of a dominant Thai educational curriculum has been implemented. Many areas of government bureaucracies are closed to Chinese. In such a setting, a very high proportion of students in Thai medical schools are of middle or elite status Chinese origins. This is an indication of widespread interest of the Chinese into this socially desired occupation. Maxwell observes a general readiness of the Chinese students to assimilate into Thai society. However, he sees it as an example of a certain status group within an ethnic community moving into the majority society where openings for socially prestigious positions are made available. In general, Maxwell foresees only a moderate rate of assimilation of Chinese into Thai society.

van der Kroef surveys the history of the interaction between Papuans of West New Guinea and Indonesians: settlements of Indonesians as middle men for the colonial power during the Dutch rules, historical resentments of Papuans against Indonesians, Dutch encouragements of Papuans for nationalism and Indonesians contemp for locals and their Neocolonialism over Papuans. van der Kroef describes the steadily rising nationalistic movements among Papuans as having the goal of attaining a united independent nation of west and east New Guinea.

8

THE EFFECT OF THE LAOTIAN CONFLICT
ON MEO ETHNIC IDENTITY

DAVID I. ANDRIANOFF
Ithaca College

ABSTRACT

The present conflict in Laos, which has disrupted the lives and affected the culture of the Meo tribe, has not affected Meo ethnic identity. Leach's study of changing ethnic identity in Burma does not apply to the Meo of Laos, who are very conscious of their ethnic identity, and do not readily give it up. The Meo (and other higher elevation hill tribes in Southeast Asia) do not exhibit the same readiness to part with their ethnic identity, as the lower elevation hill tribes such as those in Leach's study. Throughout their history in China and, more recently in Southeast Asia, the Meo have maintained their distinct identity. Without giving up their identity, the Meo have made their own way within the Loatian political system. It is their control over opium production which is a significant factor in improving the position and prestige of the Meo vis-a-vis the Royal Lao Government. Today, most Meo live in heavily populated refugee centers, deprived of their traditional livelihood. Still, their ethnic identity has not been weakened--there is as yet no evidence that they have lost any of their identity as Meo as a result of their new identity as refugees. Whether the conflict has strengthened Meo identity has yet to be proven.

The Meo tribesmen of northern Laos have found their lives totally disrupted by the present conflict in that small country. Their traditional culture is undergoing a radical change. As a result of the conflict, the Meo have found themselves in refugee villages with other tribal peoples and cultures; no longer growing their swidden rice, corn, and opium, but totally dependent on United States air drops for their very lives. With its profound effect on Meo culture, how has the on-going warfare affected Meo ethnic identity? In an attempt to answer the question, the cultural and traditional relationships between the Meo and the Lao will be considered. Then, after a brief examination of the role which opium plays, the effect of the conflict on Meo refugees will be examined.

MEO-LAO ETHNIC RELATIONS

In his *Political Systems of Highland Burma*, Leach (1970) has provided an example of changing ethnic identity among the hill peoples of Southeast Asia. Leach proposes that Kachin and Shan classifications are not static. There is considerable mobility--with Kachin becoming Shan, and Shan becoming Kachin. The question under consideration is whether the same may be true of the Meo and Lao. Drawing on my own experience, this does not appear to be the case. Although the Meo have recently been resettled into villages with such other ethnic groups as Khmu, various Thai tribes, and Lao, they have retained their household, village and, frequently, district groupings. Their traditional patterns of leadership have been maintained even in these refugee villages (Barney, 1967).

The Meo are very conscious of their ethnic identity and do not readily give it up. I know of no instance in which a Meo has given up his Meo identity and become Lao. The Lao are no more likely to become Meo. Meo men frequently adopt Western dress; Meo women, less readily.[1] Only very rare and isolated instances of Meo adopting the Buddhist religion of the lowland Lao have occurred.[2] Most Meo men now speak Lao; however, they have not given up their Meo language, and many women who have lived in refugee villages on the Vientiane Plain for several years still do not understand any Lao.

It is not that cultural and ethnic mobility is absent in Laos: the Khmu, for example, who live on the mountain-sides at an elevation between the Lao and the Meo, frequently not only adopt Laotian culture, but also "become Lao".

How does one explain the discrepancy? Does the stoic maintenance of Meo identity mean that Leach's thesis is not typical for Southeast Asia, or is inconsistent? Or does it mean that the Meo are an isolated exception? Hinton (1969:4, 5) provides an explanation in his "Introduction" to *Tribesmen and Peasants in North Thailand:*

> It is probably significant that researchers who have been preoccupied with changing cultural identity have been students of the Thai, Karen, Lua', Thai Lue and Shan peoples . . . on the one hand, and Meo, Yao, Lahu, Lisu and Akha on the other and that it is dangerous to extend generalizations about patterns of intergroup relationships of the former to the latter societies. Probably the basic reason for this phenomenon is economic. Karen, Lua', Thai Lue and Shan are people who tend to live in the one place for extended periods.

As the lower-elevation hill tribes have taken up sedentary agriculture, they have found it necessary to seek accommodation with the neighboring communities. As a result, they make political as well as trade alliances with their neighbors and with the central authority. Kunstadter (1969) has observed, in Thailand, that a Northern Thai can "become Lua'" by marrying into a Lua' community, learning to speak Lua', and following a few Lua' customs. Assimilation, he says, can be completed in less than one generation. The Meo are in a different situation. As shifting agriculturalists, they live under the assumption that they will be in one particular area for a strictly limited time. Because of their residential mobility, they traditionally have had no incentive for coming to terms with the sedentary groups with whom they come into contact.

Although economy is an important factor in comparing the maintenance of Meo identity with that of the more assimilable people who live on the lower elevations, additional factors are involved. I refer to the basic difference in maintaining identity as the tribe's "ethos" (cf. Murdock, et at., 1961:12), in which I include such other factors as history, self concept, language-family and race. The Khmu and other lower-elevation hill tribes, for example, were forced into the hills by the conquering Lao and Thai cultures. Because of this they have felt the need to accommodate themselves to and identify with the rulers of the land. The Meo, on the other hand, came into Southeast Asia much later, and moved onto the mountain-tops--land in which the lowland rulers were not interested. As a result, neither the Lao nor the Meo felt any need to accommodate themselves to the other.

HISTORY

The Meo belong to the ancient races of China, first encountering the Chinese in prehistoric times (Bernatzik, 1970; Savina, 1924). Chinese accounts of the Meo relate rebellions and suppressions of rebellions. As a result of this warfare, the Meo were forced southward into Southeast Asia. Throughout many centuries, although the Meo have adopted many aspects of the Chinese culture, they have maintained their distinct identity as Meo.

Warfare forced the Meo into the region of what is now North Viet Nam in the late eighteenth and early nineteenth centuries (LeBar, et al., 1964:64-77). They entered Laos in the middle of the nineteenth century (Barney, 1967:271). Not only did French colonial rule rest heavily on the Meo of Laos, affecting their ethnic pride (in 1940, for example, under the French administration, not one member of a Laotian minority race had yet achieved a secondary education); but the Lao also have generally assumed their cultural superiority over the other ethnic groups. Even in 1946, writes the British historian Toye (1968:62):

> Little if anything was done to correct the balance
> in developement between the Lao and the hill
> peoples. The Meo . . . remained isolated in their
> mountain fastnesses. This was partly due to
> difficulty of access, partly to increased reluctance
> on the part of the Lao to share what few benefits
> there were with the backward tribal people. Now
> that political power was coming his way the Lao
> seemed particularly content that a lack of
> sophistication should continue in the hills.

Since World War II, the relations between the Lao and the Meo have changed radically. Lowlanders have penetrated tribal communities, and tribesmen have started taking a more direct role in lowland society. Although a few Meo did participate on both sides of the battle for Dien Bien Phu, and although they have fought with both sides in the struggles which have been going on within Laos since her independence, it has not been until the recent United States involvement that the Meo have actively participated in the military affairs of Laos. Since the early 1960s, when the Meo appeared ready to exploit the disorder among the Lao in order to create a "Meo state", the Meo in Xieng Khouang province have had virtual autonomy under their clan leaders (Fall, 1969).

ROYAL LAO GOVERNMENT

Even though no unified or cohesive national society exists in Laos, the ethnic groups cannot be considered independent entities. Increasingly, they are involved in the internal and international struggles of Laos. Many kinds of relationships between ethnic groups do exist and, indeed, form necessary parts of their socio-economic life. These relationships have become more important as the Meo have, recently, been forced onto the plains, and have made agreements with and accommodated themselves to the Lao rulers of the land. However, with their strong sense of race, they still pride themselves on the notion that they are better than the Lao. Having made their own way within the Laotian system (in spite of their disdain for the lowland Lao), the Meo maintain their distinct identity, and are reluctant to inter-marry with other ethnic groups.

Most of the ethnic groups in Laos, including the Lao, are parts of larger populations found across the borders of Thailand, China, and Viet Nam. Economically, politically, and socially the Lao are the dominant group in Laos, having always provided the ruling class. Although, as previously noted, some members of the minorities have "become" Lao, the Meo have managed to participate in the Laotian political system without giving up their identity. With their own political, economic, and cultural unity, the Lao have not been particularly interested in assimilating the non-Lao groups. However, the tribes--consisting of roughly half the population of Laos--have not been isolated. The Lao have maintained relations with non-Lao people through the official recognition of local village headmen and district chiefs. Still, there has until recently been no political integration as such. Laotian government officials have assumed that any integration will proceed on Lao terms: the ethnic minorities must become Lao in religion, language, dress, etc.

The common people of both the ethnic Lao and the hill tribes have little concept of the state as conceived by the Royal Lao Government; only the Lao elite understand Laotian government and politics. The larger part of the population is only vaguely aware of the constitution, political rights, or the role of the king; and only conditionally do they accept control from the central Laotian authorities. The possession of citizenship holds little significance for the diverse ethnic groups of Laos: membership in an ethnic group is a more important factor in self-identification.

The Lao have permitted certain Meo to obtain high positions in their government: Touby Lyfong has participated in the Royal Lao Government; another Meo, Vang Pao, is a power military commander. Another, Faydang, works with the Pathet Lao. All three have a following which is larger than the membership of their clans, and they have each organized the Meo for a purpose. None, however, occupy a political or social role which had already been established; and none has compromised his Meo identity.

As yet, one cannot determine whether the minority representation in the government is an honest attempt to fully represent these peoples, or whether it is a measure to stem the nationalistic tendencies of the Meo. The prestige and honor given to Touby and Vang Pao, the educational facilities increasingly being offered to the Meo, as well as other benefits now available to them are due more to economic than political considerations. Because the Meo control the opium production, it is expedient for the Laotian government to maintain good relations with them.

In spite of their unusual adaptability, initiative, and ability to organize themselves, controlling the territory which they inhabit, the Meo still are not a unified political entity, as are the Lao. The Meo will, however, play a vital role in any future Laotian developments. All sides in the present conflict, for example, recognize the Meo as the most suitable group for organization into political and military units. Therefore, they have received attention and aid to a much greater extent than have other tribal peoples.

A result of the strategic role which the Meo have played in the conflicts in Laos is that their position vis-a-vis the Laotian government has been greatly altered. As long as opium plays a significant role in Laotian politics, the Meo will maintain high prestige. The least likely motivation for the extensive Meo participation in the present conflict of the Royal Lao Government is a "love of royalty" or loyalty to the Royal Lao Government generally (Halpern, 1965).

OPIUM

Although th Meo brought opium production with them during their southward migration into Laos, it was the formation of the Meo opium monopoly by the French in

1939-1940 which began the legacy whose consequences are being reaped today. Not only has opium been behind the internal political disruptions in Indochina during the past decade, but much of the recent fighting and "see-sawing" in northern Laos is also timed to coincide with the opium harvest. All of the various Laotian government and Pathet Lao leaders have dealt extensively in opium.[3] According to Feingold (1970:339):

> Anyone who gets at all involved with the political economy of Laos ends up involved with opium. The French, Chinese, and the Vietnamese (North and South); the rightist, neutralist, and leftist Lao--all have traded and fought over opium in the past, and most of them continue to do so today.

Although the Laotian conflict is often difficult to understand, and the issues are cloudy even to those directly involved, the Meo know what they are fighting for--not Laos, but their opium crops. Meo economic priorities have changed as a result of the present conflict. Because of the high cost of transportation to and from their mountain villages, most cash crops are ruled out, leaving the Meo with two alternatives: opium and rice. They have traditionally placed their emphasis on rice which can be eaten if the market fails. But since they have been able to rely on Air America's regular rice drops for their food supply, the villagers have felt free to devote their energies entirely to opium production (McCoy, 1972:283).

Their involvement in opium has encouraged contacts and the forming of relationships with the Lao. However, the Meo have not, nor are they likely to compromise their position regarding the Lao. The new relationships formed between the Lao and Meo because of opium have not altered Meo ethnic identity.

REFUGEES

As the Meo are retreating from North Vietnamese invaders and United States bombs in northern Laos, they are nearing the end of the mountains and are reaching the limits of their strength. Their very survival has become a matter of concern. "Nomads of the highlands", they have been moving southward for centuries, slashing and burning their rice fields and moving on when they have exhausted the soil. At times, hostile pressure has speeded up their southward migration, but mountains have always been ahead of them. During the last decade, however, the Meo have been steadily driven to the south and west, till now, they find themselves approaching the end of the mountains: ahead of them is the Vientiane Plain; across the Mekong is the flat land of Thailand, and then the sea (Kamm, 1971). Used to mountain-top dwelling, the Meo have no taste at all for life in the communities of the oppresively hot plains. "The tropics are the ruin of the mountain peoples when they try to settle in the valleys" (Bernatzik, 1970:678).

Today, most Meo live in heavily populated refugee centers. During their resettlement movements, more than ten per cent of the population dies. The decade of fighting and fleeing has greatly reduced the Meo tribe of Laos. As USAID Director for northern Laos, Edgar "Mister Pop" Buell says:

> We have American doctors waiting for them with mosquito nets, malaria pills, pencillin, the works. But they die anyway. It is the move itself--the adjusting to a new area, different food and water. . . .
> . . . Just moving causes a kind of sickness. . . . I wouldn't go so far as to say they die of a broken heart or anything like that, but, yes--you can just

about say that for a lot of people, moving means dying (Greenway, 1971:10).

The Meo have two choices: They can remain in the mountains with the North Vietnamese and the bombs, or they can flee. They have, until now, generally chosen to flee. Kales (1970:76) explains the risk that the Meo take by remaining in an area under Communist threat:

> U.S. officials here [in Vientiane] appear to operate on a desperate assumption: that the only way to secure the people permanently from the Communists--and deprive the enemy of its manpower-is to remove them physically from Communist territory. From this point of view, the bombing is a broom, sweeping the refugees into the government safe towns.

The continuous warfare has totally disrupted the traditional economy of the Meo. Because roads in the remote mountain areas of the refugee centers are virtually non-existant, ninety percent of their necessary supplies are delivered by air. Deprived of their traditional livelihood, the Meo find themselves entirely dependent on United States air drops for survival.

It may be some years before the ultimate destiny of the refugees becomes clear. *If* the government succeeds in helping the dislocated hill tribes build satisfactory new lives, the Meo may find a new sense of national identity. It seems unlikely, however, that they will sacrifice their distinct ethnic identity.

CONCLUSION

In spite of the effects of the Laotian conflict, the Meo are still Meo--they are no more Lao than they were prior to the present conflict. Their ethnic identity has not been weakened. On the contrary, Halpern and Kunstadter (1967:248n) explain:

> The traditional Meo social structure has survived the rigors of continuous warfare and flourishes even in the refugee camps. This may well mean that the Meo will emerge with an even stronger sense of identity and better means for inter-village social organization than they had before the war.

Whether the conflict has indeed strengthened Meo identity has yet to be proven. There is as yet no evidence that the Meo have lost any of their identity as Meo as a result of their new identity as refugees.

What is quite apparent, however, is that Leach's thesis of changing ethnic identity among the hill tribes of Southeast Asia does not hold true for the Meo, who have maintained their identity in the face of such factors as a long history of ethnic encounters, increasing participation in the Royal Lao Government, control of the strategic opium production, and their tragic role as refugees in over-crowded refugee centers. Although I have used the Meo as an illustration, the Meo are not to be considered an isolated exception. What is true for the Meo may also be considered true for other higher-elevation hill tribes, such as the Yao, Akha, and Lahu. In order to determine more fully the effect of the Laotian conflict on Meo ethnic identity, additional field research is necessary.

FOOTNOTES

1. The adoption of Laotian or European dress by Meo women may be explained by their frequent resettlement. They are unable to take their traditional clothing with them, and Laotian clothing is cheaper and more easily obtained. Meo men adopt Western dress for the same reason, as well as to signify modernization.

2. Although Buddhism is the national religion, the Royal Lao Government makes no effort to proselytize the hill tribes. Such efforts at proselytizing the hill tribes by the government of neighboring Thailand has met with limited success (Kunstadter, 1967:76-77).

3. McCoy (1972) provides the details of the involvement in opium of various government leaders. McAlister (1967) briefly discusses the role opium played in financing Viet Minh operations in the early 1950s.

REFERENCES

Barney, G. Linwood
1967   "The Meo of Xieng Khouang Province, Laos." Pp. 271-294 in Peter Kunstadter (ed.), Southeast Asian Tribes, Minorities and Nations. Vol. 1. Princeton, N.J.: Princeton University Press.

Bernatzik, Hugo Adolf
1970   Akha and Miao. Alois Nagler (trans.). New Haven: Human Relations Area Files Press.

Fall, Bernard B.
1968   Anatomy of a Crisis. Garden City, N.Y.: Doubleday and Company, Inc.

Feingold, David
1970   "Opium and Politics in Laos." Pp. 322-339 in Nina S. Adams and Alfred W. McCoy (eds.), Laos: War and Revolution. New York: Harper and Row, Publishers.

Greenway, H.D.S.
1971   "Reports and Comments: Laos." Atlantic 228 (July):6, 10-14.

Halpern, Joel M.
1965   Government, Politics, and Social Structure in Laos. Yale University: Southeast Asia Studies Monograph Series Number 4.

Halpern, Joel M. and
Peter Kunstadter
1967   "Laos: Introduction." Pp. 233-254 in Peter Kunstadter (ed.), Southeast Asian Tribes, Minorities and Nations. Vol. 1. Princeton, N.J.: Princeton University Press.

Hinton, Peter
1969   "Introduction," Pp. 1-11 in Peter Hinton (ed.), Tribesmen and Peasants in North Thailand. Chiang Mai, Thailand: Tribal Research Centre.

Kales, Dale
1970   "The Refugees of Laos." The Nation (January 26):76-77.

Kamm, Henry
1971   "War in Laos Imperils the Survival of Meo Tribes." The New York Times (March 16):1, 12.

Kunstadter, Peter
1969   "Hill and Valley Populations in Northwestern Thailand." Pp. 69-85 in Peter Hinton (ed.), Tribesmen and Peasants in North Thailand. Chiang Mai, Thailand: Tribal Research Centre.

Leach, E.R.
1970   Political Systems of Highland Burma. Boston: Beacon Press.

LeBar, Frank M., et al. (eds.)
1964   Ethnic Groups of Mainland Southeast Asia. New Haven: Human Relations Area Files Press.

McAlister, John T.
1967   "Mountain Minorities and the Viet Minh: A Key To the Indochina War." Pp. 771-844 in Peter Kunstadter (ed.), Southeast Asian Tribes, Minorities, and Nations. Vol. 2. Princeton, N.J.: Princeton University Press.

McCoy, Alfred W.
1972   The Politics of Heroin in Southeast Asia. New York: Harper and Row, Publishers.

Murdock, George P., et al.
1967   Outline of Cultural Materials. New Haven: Human Relations Area Files, Inc.

Savina, F.M.
1924   Histoire des Miao. Hong Kong: Imprimerie de la Societe des Missions-Etrangeres.

Schanche, Don A.
1970   Mister Pop. New York: David McKay Company, Inc.

Toye, Hugh
1968   Laos: Buffer State or Battleground. New York: Oxford University Press.

Ward, James Thomas
1967   "U.S. Aid to Hill Tribe Refugees in Laos." Pp. 295-303 in Peter Kunstadter (ed.), Southeast Asian Tribes, Minorities, and Nations. Vol. 1. Princeton, N.J.: Princeton University Press.

9

IDENTITY AND ETHNIC CONTACT: Perak Malaysia, 1963

ROBERT K. DENTAN

State University of New York at Buffalo

ABSTRACT

This paper deals with the ways in which an aboriginal people, the Senoi Semai of West Malaysia, manipulate a constellation of "character traits" which they claim (or assert that non-Semai believe) constitutes their ethnic identity. This manipulation sets up a sort of "seduction scene" in which rural Malay neighbors of the Semai, who seek closer ties with them, can be received with all the forms of acceptance while the Semai themselves withhold any deeper relationship. Goffman's notions of human interaction are the foundation for the sort of analysis presented.

INTRODUCTION

Topic

This essay deals with how an aboriginal people, the Semai of southern Perak, Malaysia, perceived and responded to their rural Malay neighbors in 1963. The general thesis is that the quality of this relationship, whatever its historical basis, both rested upon and helped to define the social identity of the two peoples involved. By "social identity" I mean, roughly, the sort of answer people give to such questions as "Who are my people?" "Who is not one of us?" or "What makes us different from other people?"

The approach used derives so largely from the work of Erving Goffman (especially 1959, 1967, and 1971) that I have cited his work only when directly quoting from it. There are two reasons for using this synchronic and analytic approach rather than a culture-historical one. The first is that the historical record is fragmentary, and people's recollections seem slanted by the very contact situation which is under examination. The more important reason is that a social psychological approach underlines the fact that the relatively small expanse of time and space considered reflects more general identity problems inherent in confrontations between marginal and dominant peoples everywhere (cf., e.g., Harrington 1972). In fact, the ultimate question here is how a person comes to understand what sort of person he is. As Auden (1971:92) remarks:

> Must we--it seems oddly that we must--remind you that our existence does not . . . enjoy an infinitely indicative mood, an eternally present tense, a limitlessly active voice, for in our shambling, slovenly makeshift world any two persons, whether domestic first or neighbourly second, require and necessarily presuppose, in both their numbers and in all their cases, the whole inflicted gamut of an alien third, since, without a despised or dreaded Them to turn the back *on*, there could be no intimate or affectionate Us to turn the eye *to* . . .

Fieldwork

The fieldwork on which this presentation rests is a seven months residence in a Semai settlement in southern Perak. The Ford Foundation and the American Museum of Natural History provided funds for this work. My then wife and I spent a good deal of time travelling throughout southern Perak with our Semai friends and feel we know the Semai part of the area fairly well as it was in 1963. The year before, we had lived for seven months in a settlement of Semai and other Semai-ized aborigines in northeastern Pahang. The Pahang Semai lived a way of life quite different from that of the Perak Semai (see Dentan, 1968). It is worth noting, however, that

their feelings about Malays and about themselves were very similar to those apparent in Perak.

Cautions

At the very outset, four points must be stressed. First, the data presented here must not be construed as in any significant way exculpatory of Euroamerican treatment of "native peoples." The historical and technological circumstances, which space requirements prevent my detailing here, are qualitatively different. In fact, there is some evidence that British colonialism in the area and the concomitant expansion of Chinese economic power may have exacerbated pre-existing tensions between Malays and Semai.

Second, the phrase "rural Malays in southern Perak in 1963" is too cumbersome to use throughout this paper. But these are the Malays with whom this essay deals, and the phrase in quotation marks is intended to exclude, e.g., urban Malays at that time (except where specified), governmental policy at that time (except as set forth in Ministry of the Interior, 1961, and Carey, n.d.) and any other Malays or official programs in any other area or at any other time. This point merits stressing because, third, many Malays take justifiable pride in the efforts of their government to better the lot of the Malayan aborigines. The Department of Aborigines, the branch of the Ministry of the Interior responsible for aboriginal affairs, has since independence become a positive and activist force for the aborigines' economic betterment.

Finally, I realize that it may distress my Malay friends and acquaintances to hear, from a white, middle-class foreigner, that during my rather extensive travels among the Semai in southern Perak in 1963 the first topic that almost inevitably arose, without prompting from me, was how badly the local Malays were treating the Semai. To them I can only say that I wish the facts were different. I am convinced, however, that the following account of Semai attitudes in that area at that time is substantially correct. I regret that it was impossible for me to associate extensively with rural Malays during my stay without completely losing the confidence of the Semai community, although they were less suspicious of my occasional contacts with Chinese and Indians. Any judgement made in this essay about the accuracy of the Semai image of Malays rests primarily on casual conversations with Malays in and around the "neutral zone" of the town of Kampar. Even such judgements may be unconsciously tinged with Semai prejudice. After all, one cannot live nearly two years with a people and hope to remain completely neutral about a relationship which is central to their lives. Malignity can exist where the desire to malign is absent; if any such unintended bias has slipped into this paper, I apologize in advance. Nevertheless, I think the attitudes the Semai assigned to rural

Malays in southern Perak in 1963 were in at least some cases substantially correct. At the very best, the attitudes cited are those the Semai said they perceived in Malays.

The Peoples

Malay. Legally, the term "Malay" denoted such a heterogeneous category of people that the Malaysian government has fallen back on three criteria for "Malay-ness": (1) being a Moslem, (2) habitually speaking Malay and (3) following Malay customary law (adat). These criteria are nebulous enough so that anyone in the world, let alone in Malaysia, can qualify as a Malay (cf. Williams-Hunt 1952:10). Many formerly European colonialists have done so. Even Malays, sometimes perhaps for political reasons, often asserted that there was no significant difference between themselves and aborigines like the Semai (e.g., Mardiah Ahmad 1962). Moreover, the three criteria themselves, which at first glance seem straightforward enough, are also ambiguous in the Malaysian context. (1) Islam in Malaysia is much more tolerant and flexible than in other parts of the world. For example, males need not be circumcized to embrace Islam (Hughes 1896:5) although most rural Malays (and practically all Semai) seemed unaware of this fact and, indeed, considered male circumcision the outward and visible sign of the inward grace conferred by Islam. Similarly, although the Quran certainly does not enjoin female circumcision, it is widely practised (Collings 1949:106; Banks 1972). If one is Christian, one need not convert to marry a Malay, and so on. (2) Malay dialects are so heterogeneous that Malays from different parts of the peninsula often have difficulty understanding each other. Many of the Semai in southern Perak could readily speak the National Language, which has a definitely Indonesian tingg; the southern Perak dialect, which sounds like a nasalized Queens or Brooklyn American accent; and Chinese Malay, which, as in the American stereotype, transforms "r" sounds into "l" ones, etc..(3) Adat also varies widely from place to place, so that conclusions drawn from a study of one kampong (roughly, "settlement") may not apply to adjacent kampong. As one Malay proverb puts it, "Adat is real law; religion is ideal law."

It must be appreciated, however, that although the social identity of the Malays in rural Perak may not have been fixed vis a vis other Malays, nevertheless to the Semai and apparently to themselves in their dealings with Semai, they were just plain "Malays". A people's social identity need not be fixed or rigid, especially in Southeast Asia. In fact, most rural Malays seemed to feel that the three governmental criteria given above were at the heart of being Malay. It should perhaps also be re-emphasized for later reference that, although most rural Malays appeared rather ill-versed in the niceties of Islamic law, they were alert to the outward signs of Islam, notably male circumcision and food taboos.

Semai. Williams-Hunt, who was at the time he wrote the following quotations Member for Home Affairs of the Department of Aborigines, reports (1952a:9-10):

> The Perak Aboriginal Tribes Enactment of 1939 defines 'Aboriginal' as meaning a person whose parents were members of an aboriginal tribe and includes a descent through males of such persons.

He personally found this definition unsatisfactory and felt (1952a:10):

> that any community of Aboriginal descent which is converted [to Islam] but which retain any element of Aboriginal social organisation should be regarded as Aboriginal until all traces of its Aboriginal origin has disappeared.

My own attempt at definition (1968: 4) derives from a discussion by Karl Deutsch (1966:18-28 and passim), and is as unsatisfactory as either of the foregoing ones:

> First, the Semai all live in a definable geographic area. Second, they share a tradition of having been dispossessed and persecuted by non-Semai. Partially as a result . . . Semai tend to define their own ways of life as being not only different from but also opposite to non-Semai ways of life. Third, they have a common language which is unintelligible to non-Semai. Finally, they share a common attitude towards a great many things . . . As a result of these shared factors, they can communicate better, and over a wider range of topics, than they can with non-Semai.

Just how unsatisfactory these stabs at definition are emerges from applying the definition of "Malay" to Perak Semai. (1) In 1963 informants said there were at least two Semai communities in Kuala Kangsar, west of Ipoh, which had converted to Islam. Although they spoke disparagingly of the converts, they seemed to regard them as true Semai. Elsewhere there were scattered Semai converts to Islam, whom the Semai accepted as Semai, albeit with some reservations.

For example, in the village that served as our home base, a man had converted to Islam, allegedly "because he was told he would get money and land if he converted." He got neither. The villagers called him Mara' Gǝp (Venerable Malay) in the same sarcastic way they called the town toper Venerable Drunk. His house was just across the very small stream that divided the Semai village from a Malay kampong, but he did not seem welcome over there either. His daughter, raised as a Moslem, married a rather slow-witted, impoverished Malay, who lived in the Semai village but could not speak Semai. He also did very little visiting and would not eat Semai food (not eating food offered one is a serious insult for the Semai). His wife was also unpopular, and people reported saying to her, "You shouldn't visit us, because we eat any old thing [i.e., do not follow Moslem food taboos], and that's a sin for you." They added, "It's not that we reject her. It's just that she's become a Moslem."

Individual Malays occasionally settle down in Semai communities, "but only the ugliest and stupiest Malays come to live with us." Just as the Semai called Moslem Semai "our people", they called the Malay immigrants "Malays". The first two were purely practical (cf. Machado 1902:31). They did not like the idea of male circumcision ("I can't stand that cut, cut, cut," the slang word for Malay is "Clipped Person"). They did not like the idea of Moslem food taboos ("It'd kill us"), even though often in effect they followed them. The third reason is that they had their own form of worship, many of whose non-Moslem rituals they shared with Malays. They were interested in the religion of other peoples but detested the idea of being coerced to join a single one, a coercion they said the Malays practiced. (We saw no coercion applied at all). There was a widespread feeling that other people's religions were "other people's affair" (a completely dismissive Semai phrase). Jǝnang (roughly, Grandparent, God) did not care what organized religion you belonged to. Even the keramat, the localized spirits, could speak any language. Those few Semai who believe in the afterlife say that those who want it can be segregated by religion. They said that they respected the "wisdom" (ilmu) found in any religion and, at least in 1963, did not see how one form of "wisdom" could possibly exclude another, so that there were people who were simultaneously pagan (Semai-and Malay-style), Bahai, Moslem and Methodist. (2) Many younger people, especially from Ulu Bernam in the southeasternmost corner of Perak, speak Malay habitually and Semai only haltingly, a fact that other Semai found amusing but certainly not in any way disqualifying the Ulu Bernam people from being Semai. Of course such linguistic disability would not be a bar to marriage, since the Semai have traditionally accepted people of all races as sexual partners (see, e.g., Gibson 1928:43; Miklucho-Maclay, 1879:298, 211-12).

(3) In innumerable ways Semai adat seemed like that of the Malays. In some areas, e.g., Kinta, this resemblance is of long standing (e.g., Leach 1880:31; Williams-Hunt 1952b:58) For instance, in many Semai settlements a spouse who felt wronged was supposed to seek satisfaction from his or her spouse's mother's younger brother -- probably a sign of influence by the matrilineal Menangkabau Malays, since matrilateral preferences are not found among Semai less exposed to Malay influence. In fact, the *adat* of a given Semai settlement sometimes appeared closer to that of a given Malay settlement than the latter did to that of some more distant Malay settlement.

Conclusion. The question thus arises of how two such seemingly similar peoples, living almost side by side, legally and racially hard to distinguish from each other, managed to maintain discrete, even mutually opposite social identities. An anecdote may help illustrate how ambiguous the answer must be. According to a story told by Semai around Kampar, Major P.D.R. Williams-Hunt, whose book has been cited above and who had taken a Semai wife, one day stripped off his uniform, put on a loincloth and his major's insignia, picked up a blowpipe and marched through the town making the British and Malay soldiers salute him. The Semai, for whom the loincloth and blowpipe are symbols of Semai-ness, thought the situation hilarious. In 1963 people urged me to repeat this perhaps apocryphal performance. I agreed to do so, provided that two or three Semai men, similarly accoutered, would come with me. It turned out that there were no blowpipes or loincloths to be had, and I doubt that I could have persuaded anyone to come with me anyway.

This anecdote illustrates, I think, the complexity of Semai social identity. Loincloths and blowpipes are quintessentially Semai artifacts, rarely if ever used by their Malay neighbors. Blowpipes are especially highly valued tools, as symbols of virility and as marks of one's ethnicity. On the other hand, but by the same token, it was shameful for a Semai from a settlement in continuous contact with non-Semai to display these emblems. Apparently the Semai had taken to heart the sort of incident described by Maxwell (1880:50):

A Sakai [Semai] man followed by two or three girls . . . who had come to see the Penghulu [Malay headman], was literally hooted by all the small boys of the kampong, who ridiculed his accents, his dress (or rather his want of dress), his walk, and everything belonging to him . . . the aboriginal tribes are interesting to the Malays only so far as they are useful agents in clearing jungle, procuring gutta, or assisting in the more questionable pursuit of child stealing.

I do not know whether such a scene would have occured in 1963. I think probably not. But I think that such public humiliations helped create an ambivalence about the objective correlatives of Semai social identity, simultaneously "different" by preference and "inferior" by historical accident. If this surmise is true, than it should be no surprise that the way the Semai conceived of themselves and of Malays was so deeply ambivalent.

ENCOUNTERS

Introduction

If one thinks of the now benevolent relations of Malays with Semai as being a sort of attempt to "seduce" Semai from their traditional distrust of Malays, the following quote from Goffman (1971:207) about "seduction encounters" may be relevant.

Obviously it is social situations which provide the opportunity for relationship situations, this being especially true of . . . "open" occasions . . . where participation itself confers the right to initiate talk with anyone present and to be received in a freiendly manner. We can therefore anticipate a basic strategic design. The initiator exposes himself to rejection and to the judgement that he is undesireable, which judgement anyone who keeps his distance is allowed to avoid; the recipient exposes herself to providing evidence of another's desirability without obtaining the relationship that is the usual safeguard of this admission. The solution is strategic tact.

ENCOUNTER STRUCTURES

The Semai usually tended to construct any encounter with Malays in ways that conformed to their own social identity *vis a vis* that which they ascribed to Malays. The following table approximates the structure to which encounters tended to conform.

TABLE I SEMAI STEREOTYPES

RURAL MALAY	SEMAI
1. Arrogant, dominating	Self-effacing, fictitiously submissive
2. Cruel, aggressive	Kindly, timid
3. Dishonest (esp. about land)	Gullible (esp. about land)
4. Neglectful of own people	Concerned for own people
5. Rich	Poor
6. Market people (i.e., dom-esticated people, *orang jinak*)	Inland savages (i.e., "wild people," *orang liar*)

These points will be taken up in order, using as many Semai quotes as possible, in order to convey the flavor of their complaints about the Malays, justified or not.

1) Although the Semai say that they "bend with the wind like a lalang grass leaf," following whoever is in power, they resent the overt assertation of that power. A few examples of their response:

The Malays want us to call them "Tuan." Now, I call white people "Tuan." The English aren't like us. They have white skins and red necks. Their noses aren't like ours. The hair in their armpits--sometimes it's red, sometimes it's yellow, it's all colors. The Malays have dark skins and dark necks, like us. Their noses are flat, like ours. The hair in their armpits is mud-colored. They're just like us. I should call them "Tuan?" Excuse me, I don't want to.
I'll call them "Dato" or "Inche" [polite Malay titles] but "Tuan?" Sorry, I don't want to. When you write your report, you tell them I don't want to.
Why should we follow the Malays? If we follow the Chinese, they give us money for our work. We never get money from the Malays. There's no use following the Malays. [Cf. Skeat and Blagden

1906.I:230].

> The worst *kampong* in the world is Malay. (Q: But
> surely there are *some* good Malays?) In a hundred,
> there might be one who's OK.

There did seem to be some arrogance displayed by Malays
towards the Semai. For example, the government had
officially banned the use of the work "Sakai" and substituted
the politer phrase "Orang Asli", i.e., "aboriginal people." The
word "Sakai" means something like "bestial, unclean savage".
In counting, one spoke of *dua ekor Sakai* ("Two tails of
savages", as one would say "two tails of carabao"); but one
spoke of *dua orang melayu* ("two people of Malays").
Similarly, when they died, the Sakai *mampus* (died like an
animal), while the Malay *mati* (died like a person). Newspapers
were pressing the issue of not calling aborigines Sakai (e.g.
Robinson 1963). Nevertheless, the rural Malays were still using
the term, often, I believe, without realizing that they were
insulting the Semai, since, for reasons discussed below, the
Semai were careful to show Malays nothing but uninformative
"strategic tact."

2) We saw no acts of cruelty or aggression by Malays
against Semai, although we heard some almost certainly highly
exaggerated horror stories. The most aggressive act we saw was
the loitering by a few teenagers under a lamp post at the
entrance to our village. (The Malay kampong, separated, as I
have said, from our by a rivulet, had lighting at night; the
Semai did not). These teenagers teased the Semai women as
they came back from marketing, and several of the women
said that they were therefore afraid to be out of doors in the
Semai village after dark.

There have been acts of cruelty by Malays against the Semai
and other aborigines in the fairly recent past (e.g.,
Miklucho-Maclay 1878:42; Skeat and Blagden 1906, I:523,
527-31; Clifford 1925:79-104; Rathbone 1898:289). In an
official report dated 13 February, 1951, Williams-Hunt
reported that Malays were threatening to turn Semai men over
to the British as Communist sympathizers if the men could not
force their unwilling women to sleep with the Malays.

The Semai oral tradition of their relationship with Malays
made the written record look pallid. As a relatively mild
example, people said that Batu Berangkai, a Malay *kampong*
whose name means approximately "Stone with Chains on it,"
got its name from the fact that it was the spot where captured
Semai were chained to be sold as slaves, after all the men over
fifteen years old had been butchered. In short, although the
cruelty current in 1963 seemed negligible, the memory of
former cruelty and the elaborations time had probably worked
on that memory still tinged Semai-Malay relations.

2-3) Even during an amicable visit to our house by two
Malays from across the little stream, men who made every
effort to be polite to the Semai in our house, the Semai
present, themselves always cool but courteous, kept warning
us in the slang used when there were dangerous people present
who might understand a little Semai, e.g., "Nice mouth,
corrupt heart" or "Don't accept that cigarette; it's probably
got *rachun* in it; Clipped People are good at *rachun*, you
know." (*Rachun* is fatal, slow-working poison--see Gimlette
1971). After the Malays had left, one man made fun of them
imitating the formality of their departure, bowing low,
offering both hands and saying, "I must return, Tuan; I want
to offer maaany, maaany thaaanks." He continued until he
became too convulsed with laughter to go on, while the other,
more serious man kept shaking his head and saying, "Nice
mouths, corrupt hearts." This incident was far from typical.

3) Although we heard in almost every Semai settlement we
visited horrendous tales of Malays "cheating" Semai out Semai

land, my feeling is that most of the difficulty lay in the fact
that the Semai regarded their land as theirs because they lived
there and had buried their dead there. No one seemed to have
any idea of what the right of eminent domain was, nor that
the lands the Semai impassionedly felt to be their own were
classified as public.

In the past, there certainly have been unscrupulous Malays
who have bullied or cheated Semai out of land that was
rightfully Semai (cf. Machado 1900:263-64). H.D. Noone, the
first trained anthropologist to do significant work with people
who, like the Semai, speak Senoi languages, wrote a couple of
letters in the 1930's about Malay land grabs among the Perak
Semai. Excerpts follow:

> As is the case with most other surat kuasas
> [certificates of authority; see Dentan 1968:67-68]
> examined . . . this is merely a makeshift piece of
> paper designed to delude the Sakai into thinking
> they are secure, for already part of the Kiah area
> [an area "reserved" for aborigines] has been taken
> by a Mendiling Malay . . . with the aid it appeared
> of one Abdul Kadir when he was land collector at
> Tanjong Malim . . . It appears that $200 [about
> U.S. $66] was handed to Sagap, who said he did
> not want to sell, who received the money . . . He
> was told that he must accept the money and keep
> quiet . . . In any case, it appears that there were
> some 3,000 trees on the land taken which were
> not accounted for.

> The Ulu and Lower Behrang groups . . . have
> suffered a good deal in the past from expropri-
> ation by Malays. When the Behrang station road
> was made all the land south of the Behrang river
> was alienated to Malays. This land contained
> Semai rubber and dusuns [orchards]: Mr. C.H.
> Ryder of Slim River remembers the time when
> these still belonged to the families at Chenain and
> Kelan, some to Bagas . . . and some to Penghulu
> Muda whom [sic] Mr. Ryder recalls having planted
> rubber in these lost lands in 1928 . . .

In both these cases, it will be noted, the local government
conspired with the local people to get Semai land. The Semai
in 1963 rarely saw government, which they could not see. But
they could *see* rural Malays using the land they considered their
own, and they naturally put the blame on those they could see.

4,5,6) From a Semai viewpoint, Malays were rich. Many
lived in houses made of planks, whereas few Semai could
afford more than woven thatch and bamboo. Some Malays had
cars; no Semai we knew had a car.

> We stay poor and everyone else gets rich. The
> Chinese get rich. The Indians get rich. The Malays
> get rich. And they all get rich from the land of us
> Hinterland People. Is that fair?

Aside from the perennial emphasis on land-grabbing, the Semai
attributed Malay wealth to the fact that Malays were skilled in
the use of money, with which the Semai were relatively
unfamiliar. The only source of pride the Semai found in their
low economic status was the fact that there were no Semai
beggars. "If you look around, you'll see Indian beggars, Malay
beggars, even Chinese beggars, but you will never see a Semai
begging for alms. We look after our own people."

7) Even the fact that Islam was recognized as a source of
wisdom and that good Moslems were respected backfired
against the wall of Semai distrust of Malays. There was a very
definite feeling that, because of being Moslem, Malays should
be morally superior to the pagan Semai. Reportedly, part of
this belief had been drummed into the Semai by their Moslem
neighbors. The result is that the Semai expected the Malays to

live up to the dictates of Islam and were quick to notice any departure from the Moslem creed by any Malay. In other words, the Semai judged Malays negatively by Moslem standards as well as by their own.

"Nice mouths, corrupt hearts. They don't even follow the dictates of their own religion unless they're scared into it by the police." Thus a Malay may meet with condemnation for eating pork as a courtesy to the Semai (an infraction of Moslem food taboos) as well as for not eating pork proffered him by the Semai (a infraction of Semai rules of hospitality). Without the utmost finesse, a Malay simply has no way to act properly. Of course, many rural Malays were not very concerned to treat Sakai properly and simply dismissed the food offered them as *kotor* ("dirty").

Encounter Tactics

Semai: Flight: The traditional Semai way of treating Malays was to flee from them whenever possible (Cameron 1885:156; Wray 1890:161-162). There were special whistles that could warn of the arrival of a Malay raiding party, and the Semai cry to warn of strangers "was exactly like that of a wild beast" (Swettenham 1885:7; Clifford 1925:101, 102). By 1963, however, people merely tended to stay in their houses or to find business elsewhere. The women told my wife never to respond to remarks made to her by Malay women washing their clothes in the little stream that served to demarcate the two settlements. That tiny trickle of water could have been a wall. One man became very upset when my wife spoke to a ten year old Malay girl. While we were chatting with a gaggle of Semai children, some Malay children came by, and the Semai children closed the door so that "they won't come up and make trouble for us." Our first house was by the path that led to the Malay *kampong*. The Semai insisted that we move to a new place, because (a) the Malays might attack us and (b) the Malays could hear us talking and might understand that we were speaking in Malay. In brief, a subtler way of avoiding any encounters with Malays had evolved from the earlier headlong flight into the rainforest, an avoidance, however, which served its purpose almost equally well.

Semai: smart talk. Although the women were usually silent, those men emboldened *(berani)* enough to converse with Malay men usually used both of two tactics: a) cool politeness and b) what Americans call "the put-on." There is no hard and fast line between the two, since both are designed to obfuscate, manipulate and insult the Malay guest. An example of cool politeness might be neither proffering cigarettes to Malays nor accepting cigarettes proffered by Malays. Either action is much ruder in Semai terms than in Malay *adat*, and the Semai know it.

The men usually sat in a circle, with open arcs in the circle between the Malay and the Semai semicircles. Typically, the Semai kept their voices low and usually looked at the floor rather than at the Malays. My feeling, perhaps influenced by American behavior patterns, was that the Semai posture, soft voice and visual avoidance of contact reflected fear and perhaps contained agression-- "passive agression," as some psychologists call it.

Semai said that in dealing with Malays one had to be *cherdek* (roughly, "smart") and to *chakap politik* (roughly, "speak politically," i.e., deceptively and with a view to accomplishing one's own ends). The "smartest" thing to do was to act stupid, since informants said, "The Malays think we're dumb Sakai anyway." For example, one Semai boy asked his "uncle" what he should do about a threatened strike at a tin mine where he worked. His "uncle" told him just to say *"Tak tau lah"* (roughly, "Gee, I dunno"). For the Semai it was always better to play on the "stupid Sakai" stereotype than to risk getting into trouble.

One of the finest examples of the put-on I witnessed I will here summarize, although it is from Pahang and the abbreviation leaves out some of the finer points of Semai obfuscation. A dedicated young Malay from the Department of Aborigines, whom I shall call M, is trying to convince an influential Semai man (S) to move into a model village downstream. M has just made an eloquent argument in favor of the move. The parentheses are my comments.

S. (sits until everyone is quiet.) Well, I'm just an old man, deaf in one ear (shows which ear, in standard self-deprecation), but if our crops are growing up here, what are we going to eat?

M. The government will feed you, and they'll give you rubber seedlings.

S. Look, anyway, we don't know anything about rubber. We're just stupid Sakai. We live in the jungle like animals, we die in the jungle like animals.

M. But don't you want money?

S. Money? What do we need? No salt, no iron, and we'd weep. Otherwise, we just go around living like animals. Besides, it takes five years for rubber trees to mature, and I'm an old man. I'll be dead by then. (A slip: he had just said he knew nothing about rubber).

M. But what about your children and grandchildren:

S. We don't care about our children and grandchildren. We just live here in the jungle like animals . . .etc.etc.

M went away the next day, convinced, despite my telling him it was a put-on, that the Semai were "stupid, stupid, stupid." S, the same day, explained:

> You see what they want, these Malays. They want to get us downstream to that nice place with tin roofs and all. Then they grab our land up here, because we're not here. Then, when the rubber ripens, they take that. Then, what do we eat? Wood? Sorry, I'm not a porcupine.

Semai: violence. Of all the peoples of the world, the Semai seem to be among the least likely to incorporate violent action into their strategic design *vis a vis* Malays or anyone else. R.O.D. Noone, brother of the anthropologist H.D. Noone, allowed himself reluctantly to form an "aboriginal army", the Senoi Peraak. This troop became independent in 1958, and many people say it acquitted itself creditably (Miller, 1960). Although some of the less knowledgeable members of the Senoi Peraak thought it hysterically funny that I should associate their activities with killing people ("we just tend weeds and cut grass"), a few who were in active combat describe themselves as being in a situation akin to berserk (Dentan 1968:58-59).

One Perak man, not very bright and the village clown, said:

> It would have been better if our ancestors had made a deal with the Americans and got guns and airplanes and bombs and mortars. Then this would be a good place to live . . . If they really get us backed up against the wall, we'll fight. They're killing us whether we fight or not.

I am fairly sure that this little speech, the only one of its kind we heard, was mostly fantasy and fun; but there are depths of bitterness there that must be reckoned with. Semai children, playing with a blowpipe, played at "killing Malays".

Malay: counter-revolutionary. The British army, busily engaged in putting down the Communist and Nationalist revolution of the 1950's, belatedly realized that the Malayan aborigines not merely held control of the central part of the country but were also coming under revolutionary influence.

The government's slogan became "Win the aborigines and we win the war." The aborigines, as might be guessed from the foregoing pages, were not easily to be won to either side. To give a final quote from S, the Pahang Semai, even though there is probably a good bit of retrospective falsification in it,

> They'd come through looking for coolies, to guide them to Communist strongholds. I refused, saying, "For rubber, I'll take money; for chickens, I'll take money; for bananas, I'll take money; for blood, I'll not take money". . . . We Inland People gain nothing by mixing in the affairs of other groups; we only lose.

For an account of the social organization devised by the Semai to baffle both the government and the insurgents, see Dentan (1968:80-81).

At first, under the "Briggs Plan," the British dominated government tried to respond by bombing and starving the aborigines out of the rain forest into "New Villages" behind barbed wire. The aborigines were eventually allowed back into their homelands, under the protection of government "Jungle Forts." The Senoi Peraak, formed in 1956, did not become truly operational until 1958 (Miller 1960).

Malays: The Hand of Friendship. In 1963, there seemed to be several rural Perak Malays who genuinely wanted to be on good terms with the Semai. One man, from across the rivulet that separated the Semai from the Malay kampong, told my wife that he wanted to be friends with the Semai but that they did not want to be friends with him, that they rejected his overtures. He did visit us twice, and I thought he acted a bit patronizing and officious, e.g., making all the Semai line up so that he could get his pictures taken with them and us. At about the same time, the National Union of Teachers announced that it was "making every effort to recruit more aborigine teachers as members . . . Our attention is focused on aborigines teachers because we feel that they need the protection that can be afforded by the trade union movement" (Annon.b:3).

Such gestures towards the Semai could not hurt, although it is telling that they were necessary at all. I suspect, however, from my own stay with the Semai and from a few chats with rural Malays in Kampar who seemed kindly disposed towards the Semai, that many Malays with no particular claim to expertise felt that the Semai were their *adek*, "younger siblings", who should listen to the wisdom of their elders. Now the Semai respected wisdom, and they felt that it came with age, so that they generally respected and trusted an older Malay, especially a Haji, more than a younger one. But in 1963, most older Semai men, wise in the wisdom of their own years would be likely to regard a "youngster" *(litau)* with the gall to give them advice as a whippersnapper. Moreover, we were a bit concerned about the depth of the goodwill felt by those people on the local level who said they felt a sort of solidarity with the Semai. For example, when I, a white foreigner, stupidly asked in English why Semai-Malay relations seemed so strange, the Malay headman with whom I was talking glowered at me over his glass of beer and said, closing the subject, "We LOVE and RESPECT one another." But a few hours and beers later, while we were talking in Malay, he asked, "Isn't it hard to live with people as *kasar* as those Sakai?" *Kasar* means, approximately, "coarse, rough, unmannerly." A straw in the wind, perhaps.

But while affairs on the local level, the level of personal encounter, were tense in 1963, the government was following an increasingly progressive line towards the aborigines. A Department of Aborigines was formed in 1960-1961 (Ministry of the Interior, 1961) under R.O.D. Noone. It concentrated not merely on gathering information but, more importantly, on aiding the aborigines. Noone encouraged cottage industry on a small scale in the westernmost Semai villages of Perak, like Changkat Pinggan and Labu Kubong, and he set up a small shop at this headquarters in Kuala Lumpur to sell such artifacts. Although he has been accused of being an "ethnological museologist" in that he was strongly opposed to the Europeanization of the Semai, he did not object to their following Malay manufacturing styles and designs, with the result that it is, e.g., hard to tell a Semai basket from this area from a Malay basket. The main Semai objection to the program is the length of time between making something and getting paid for it. "If there's plenty of rice and fish, we'd make things for the fun of it; but if there isn't much rice and fish, it's hard to make things."

The medical program of the Department of Aborigines is, and has always been, a resounding success (see, e.g., Ng 1961, Moss 1962). Aborigine field technicians pack in medicines to the deep rainforest. No aboriginal village is more than a day's walk away from a helioport, maintained by the aborigines' own hospital at Gombak. By 1963, the army had come to recognize the effectiveness of the Department's policy, and had embarked on a similar program of its own (Tan 1963:5).

CONCLUSION

The governmental programs for the Semai, which had already been so much in evidence in 1963, seem to be progressing rapidly under the leadership of such dedicated men as Dr. J.M. Bolton and the new Commissioner on Aboriginal Affairs, the anthropologist Baharon Azhar bin Raffei. There is no question that all Malayan aborigines are much better off medically, economically and politically than in 1963 (cf. Ahmad Shaffie 1971). The land problem will of necessity be resolved in a way that the Semai do not like very much, although the enlightened current program (Ministry of the Interior 1961:14-17) and the sympathetic personnel of the Department of Aborigines should ease the transition. No group as small and powerless as the Semai can successfully claim so vast a territory on an increasingly crowded peninsula. There seems little danger here, for the Semai are too few and too nonviolent a people to form themselves into an independent revolutionary action group.

The real danger lies, as this paper has tried to stress, on the local level of face to face encounter. If, although legally equal citizens, the Semai remain despised by those they know; if they continue, rightly or wrongly, to believe that their neighbors look down upon them, either as inferiors or "our little brothers"; if they are ghettoized by force or choice; then the Department of Aborigines will need all its already remarkable and humane enlightenment to prevent the evils that follow such a social situation.

Traditional Semai society, even as it existed in 1963, is ultimately, perhaps even proximately, doomed. The loss of any way of life is like the loss of a species in an ecosystem; the fewer species, the more unstable and less viable the ecosystem. In the Semai case, the loss is inevitable, and our private grief should not blind us to the fact that, given that the government pursues its current policies, the Semai will probably continue to live a happier, healthier and freer life.

Nevertheless, even in settlements which seem, on cursory inspection, to be wholly engulfed by the Malay way of life, the Semai sense of their separate social identity seemed strong, even stronger, perhaps, than where contact with Malays was less frequent. A Semai, the identity formula seemed to run, was the opposite of a Malay--in some ways better, in some ways inferior, but opposite. This kind of social identity, defended by selective perception of differences and by self-fulfilling interpretations of those differences, may prove at least temporarily impervious to the changes that are making Semai more and more like Malays. To think of himself as a Semai, a Semai needs the concept of the Malay, that ultimate Other. The unresolved question is whether, after Semai and Malays become essentially indistinguishable to an outsider, the notion of Semai-ness can survive.

REFERENCES

JSBRAS: Journal of the Straits Branch of the Royal Asiatic Society

Ahmad Shaffie
1971   Temiar di Pos Brooke *Dewan Masharakat* (Oct): 32-35.

Anon. a.
1960   Aborigines: "British spy" allegation by P.M.I.P. is promptly denied. *Straits Times* (21 Dec): 7.

Anon. b.
1963   Union to recruit more aborigines as members. The Malay Mail (26 Feb.):3.

Auden, W.H.
1971   Selected poetry of W.H. Auden. New York: Random House.

Banks, D.
1972   Personal communication.

Cameron, W.
1885   Exploration of Pahang. JSBRAS 15:155-57.

Carey, I.Y.
n.d.   The Malayan Orang Asli and their future. Kuala Lumpur: Ministry of the Interior.

Clifford, H.
1925   In a corner of Asia. New York.

Collings, H.D.
1949   Malay notes. *Bulletin of the Raffles Museum. Series B#4:*104-112.

Dentan, R.K.
1968   The Semai. New York: Holt, Rinehart and Winston.

Deutsch, K.W.
1966   Nationalism and social communication. 2nd ed. Cambridge: MIT Press.

Gibson, A.
1928   The Malay peninsula and archipelago. London: J.M. Dent and Sons.

Gimlette, J.D.
1971   Malay poisons and charm cures. London: Oxford.

Goffman, E.
1959   The presentation of self in everyday life. New York: Anchor Books.

Goffman, E.
1967   Interaction ritual. New York: Anchor Books.

Goffman, E.
1971   Relations in public. New York: Basic Books.

Harrington, M.
1972   We few, we happy few, we bohemians:*Esquire* 78 (2): 99-103, 162-164.

Hughes, T.P.
1896   Dictionary of Islam. London: W.H. Allen and Co.

Leech, H.W.C.
1880   About Kinta, JSBRAS 4:21-33.

Machado, A.D.
1900   The hot springs of Ulu Jelai, JSBRAS 33:263-264.

Machado, A.D.
1902   A vocabulary of the Jakuns of Batu Pahat, Johore, together with some remarks on their customs and peculiarities. JSBRAS 38:29-33.

Mardiah Ahmad
1962   Orang[2] "asli" juga orang[2] Melayu. *Berita Harian* (I Be.):4.

Maxwell, W.E.
1880   The aboriginal tribes of Perak. JSBRAS 4:46-50.

Miklucho-Maclay, N.V.
1878   Dialects of the Melanesian tribes in the Malay peninsula JSBRAS 1:38-43.

Miklucho-Maclay, N.V.
1878   Dialects of the Melanesian tribes in the Malay peninsula, JSBRAS 1:38-43.
1879   Ethnological excursions in the Malay peninsula, November 1874 to October 1875 (preliminary communication). JSBRAS 2:205-221.

Miller, H.
1960   The fighting senoi, *Straits Time Annual* 1960:17-19.

Ministry of the Interior
1961   Statement of policy regarding the administration of the aborigine peoples of the Federation of Malaya. Kuala Lumpur: ministry of the Interior.

Moss, P.
1962   She patrols 400 square miles of high jungle. *Sunday Mail* (11 Nov.).

Ng Yook Yoon
1961   Science reaches the jungle folk. *Sunday Mail* (5 Nov.).

Rathbone, A.B.
1898   Camping and tramping in Malaya. London: Swan Sennenschein.

Roninson, A.K.
1963   Going into the jungle? Here are do's and don'ts *The Sunday Mail* (14 April):4.

Skeat, W.W., and
C.O. Blagden
1906   Pagan races of the Malay peninsula, 2v. London: Macmillan.

Swettenham, F.A.
1885   Journal kept during a journey across the Malay peninsula, JSBRAS 15:1-37.

Tan Tock Saik.
1963   Army out to win hearts and minds in the jungle. *Straits Times* (23 Feb.):5.

Williams-Hunt, P.D.R.
1952a An introduction to the Malayan aborigines. Kuala Lumpur: Government Press.

1952b Some Malay and aboriginal charms and methods of measuring weapons, *J. Malayan Branch, Royal Asiatic Society*, 25:56-61.

10
ASSIMILATION TO MALAYNESS: A Culture
Historical Perspective

DAVID J. BANKS
State University of New York at Buffalo

ABSTRACT

This essay deals with the problem of supposed "chauvinism" of Malay peasants, and attempts to place the picture of the dealings of Malays in court and kampong *in broader historical perspective. It suggests that current racial and ethnic problems in Malaya spread from early centers of intense colonial contact while in outlying areas processes of assimilation and orderly coexistence, probably ultimately moving in the direction of assimilation, proceeded gradually, much as they had in the past. Caste studies from North Malaya are used to illustrate the potential for harmony that is often neglected in treatments of ethnic relations in Malaya.*

INTRODUCTION

Phrases like 'Malay chauvinism' and references to irrational Malay racio-cultural nationalism have found a secure place in literature concerning inter-group relations in Malaya.[1] These statements have a long history in writings about Malays, and often imply more than a simple reaction by the Malay peasantry to the pressures of external forces which sought and seek to develop the peninsula: they imply a basic element of intolerance in the Malay psyche, a kind of cultural superiority complex expressing itself in non-rational behavioral practices with respect to other groups and a deeply ingrained unwillingness to accept them. The purpose of this paper is to place this evidence of Malayocentrism in historical perspective beside positive evidence of willingness of Malays to accept other peoples on their own terms and make concessions which would allow these peoples to be assimilated to Malay communities, or to a more Malay way of life. One cannot deny that there have been grave problems in racio-ethnic relations in the Malay Peninsula, as in most of the other areas of the globe in which peoples of greatly different cultural heritages have come into close contact, but, when conditions were favorable in the past, Malay rulers and peasants encouraged assimilation, and when this was not possible, they accepted coexistence on terms of mutual respect and integrity. I will identify and explore the circumstances that favored and those that discouraged assimilation, using historical sources as well as my own field data from the northwestern corner of the peninsula.

Those factors which seem to have been most destructive of good relations between Malays and other groups appear to have been connected with the loss of Malay political power in the 16th century, the rapid development of the peninsula during the 19th century, and the impact of British imperial expansion. These processes, which occurred over a period of nearly five centuries, shattered the framework which had fostered earlier amicable relations. Nevertheless, even during recent periods, there have been notable examples of Malay willingness to accept non-Malays into their local areas, if not into their communities. These more recent examples come from rural areas least affected by the impact of Malaya's growing economic and political ties with the modern world.

The Malayan case appears to provide more disquieting evidence of the wide-ranging effects of contacts with the West in the ethnohistory of Southeast Asia. Furnivall (1956) has described the ethnic characteristics of tropical countries made into dependencies as they have been brought into the modern world, and has suggested that the forces bringing different peoples in these areas into contact with the West created a plural society with 'economic forces exempt from social will', in which

. . . the society as a whole comprises separate racial sections; each section is an aggregate of individuals rather than a corporate or organic whole; and as individuals their social life is incomplete (1956:306).

His analysis implies that colonial societies were made into atomized wholes consisting of as many groups as were necessary for the functioning of the social and economic market places into which contact had changed them. Wertheim (1965), after expressing doubts about the applicability of the concept of pluralism in Furnivall's two colonial objects of study, Burma and Indonesia, suggests that the concept might be more fruitfully applied in Malaya (1964:65), and indeed, Freedman (1960) has made such an attempt. Freedman's analysis, however, falls prey to Wertheim's criticism that the concept of pluralism should be applied processually, for the Malayan evidence suggests that colonialism set forces in motion that went far further than setting apart the traditional Malayan ethnic groups - Malays, Indians, and Chinese - fostering cleavages within these groups as well. Furnivall's analysis, based upon crude economic determinist assumptions (that larger ethnic categories would become the basic sub-units of society, each fulfilling a basic economic function), suggests that differences within these categories would be minimal. This is, surely, implied in his comments on the loss of meaning of caste in the Indian community under the impact of British colonialism (1956:307).

I would suggest that, in Malaya, not only have differences between major categories been accentuated, but there has been no great incentive for complete homogenization within the major groups, so that their internal unity rests upon mutual antagonisms rather than upon common customs, patterns of behavior, and the ability to marry in all sections of one's own group. With respect to the Malay community, the greatest approximation to organic unity has been found in those states most recently brought under colonial rule, while the closer one moves toward the centers of foreign influence, the greater the internal differentiation of communities. This proposition appears to hold even when one allows that the ramifications of colonialism reverberated throughout the archipelago and into Thailand, a region notable for its lack of formal colonial rule.

Islam, usually considered an important obstacle in admission to the Malay way of life, appears to have played a chimerical, changing role in processes of assimilation or non-assimilation. On the one hand, it fostered a sense of cultural superiority in Malays over the other peoples who came to the peninsula or out of its forests, and had not yet embraced the faith and were hence *kafir* (infidels); on the other, it provided a medium for the acceptance of non-Malay

Muslims into Malay communities and also provided a medium through which non-Malays could demonstrate their willingness to become members of Malay village and trading families, enabling them to marry Malay girls and produce children who could be considered Malays. Generally, however, differences in language, dress and other culturally patterned behavior forms provided comparably severe obstacles if by assimilation one means adoption of the full range of behavior forms regarded as Malay by the inhabitants of an area. For assimilation, in this sense, normally implies a process spanning at least one generation, since, bearing in mind the subtleties that this strict definition implies, one would have to be born of parents who had made first steps in the direction of Malayness. To be a Malay appears to have always meant *to be born one*. In recent periods, both Islam and *adat* (custom) in general have gained in their power to exclude, especially in the major urban centers.

ETHNIC SCHISMS WITHIN THE MALAY COMMUNITY

In theory, one might expect the easiest adoption of Malayness among those groups that had already adopted Islam, and who had the same general physical type as Malays, or at least a physical type that was not markedly different from the Malay type, but this has not always been true. Wilson (1967) reports from Selangor - originally the scene of battles for sovereignty between Bugis and Malays in the 18th century, before the massive impact of Chinese tin mining in the 19th century - marked ethnic hostilities between Malay villagers (descendents of original inhabitants, and of other groups of early immigrants from Sumatra and other parts of the archipelago) and more recent, cohesive immigrant ethnic groups, in villages along the main trunk road from Kuala Lumpur south to Seremban. His work indicates that religion alone has not been a panacea. In the village that Wilson studies, Jenderam Hilir, there were members of three groups of Sumatran immigrants, one of which (Mandiling Batak) considers itself to be superior to other inhabitants and is considered pushy by the rest. Nevertheless, the author does not suggest that there are formal sanctions applied in cases of inter-marriage between Mandiling and other villagers. Minangkabau residents living in a nearby village in like fashion are described as even more snobbish, unwilling to give their daughters in marriage to other residents of the area. Having lived in Selangor for about a century, these Minangkabau no longer practice matrilateral inheritance but do speak an archaic dialect of Malay originating in Sumatra that is unintelligible (or poorly so) to other residents. Javanese, living in a different village, are said to be coarse and lax as Muslims, probably eating pork on some occasions, and are likened to the Banjarese, who are considered close to them culturally and who are accorded the lowest status within the general rubric 'Malay' (1967:15-37).

This case makes the influence of rapid growth and economic differentiation in the Malaysian economy clearly visible, for the Minangkabau seem pushy and snobbish to other groups because of their economic success in the world of Kuala Lumpur as clerical and other kinds of office personnel. The Javanese are also seen as having contributed excessive amounts of labor for low wages to the local economy, and hence have managed to succeed in a cruel world through the exercise of one virtue in an otherwise negative pattern of stereotypes. The issue that the author points to as bringing this congeries of people with different cultural origins together under the rubric 'Malay' is their mutual antipathy to the Chinese and Indians in Mayalsia, who are seen as interlopers combining many of the most despised of traits from the Malay point of view. Although Wilson perhaps overestimates the degree of mutual distrust between the major groups when he states that, in interpersonal relations, individual "Chinese....are always seen to represent the totality" (1967:23), his general description of inter-ethnic relations in rural Selangor highlights the destructive influence of the forces for economic development upon relations between Malays and other groups of 'outsiders' such as Chinese and Indians, *and* within the Malay community itself, which is a rather ill-defined congeries of peoples often having settled in the region fairly recently and, presumably as a result of expanded chances for livelihood, making more or less of their chances for contact with recognized 'Malay' inhabitants after arrival.

THE DEVELOPMENT OF ETHNICITY IN THE WIDER MALAYAN SOCIETY

In the distant past, under the Malay sultanate of Malacca, trade contacts did not lead to automatic acceptance of Muslims into the general Malay group, but it does appear that those traders from adjacent regions, converted to the faith, gradually formed a resident group that adopted a more Malay identity. Traders generally were male mercantile adventurers who came either without spouses and married local women, settling there, or who returned to their homelands later in life. All groups of foreigners in Malacca during the 15th century, reports Tome Pires, lived under the local authority of Shahbandars, officials appointed by the court from local ethnic groups to deal with problems within their own communities and with collection of taxes on trade carried out by their own group's members. Gujeratis formed one group and Bengalis and north Sumatrans another. There was another group for southern Sumatrans, Javanese and Moluccans and a fourth for Chinese and Indochinese traders (Kennedy, 1967:8). Local Malays were more important in the transporting of goods to neighboring ports, and this played a crucial role in making the Malay language a *lingua franca* for wide areas of the archipelago. There is little doubt that the sultans of Malacca encouraged the spread of Islam to neighboring states and to the local peoples living near their court city, but it appears that, despite probable pressures on traders who were not already Muslims to convert, conversion was not a necessary requirement of residence nor did conversion ensure any further assimilation to the ways of life of the peasant or urban Malays resident in the town (Meilink-Roelofsz, 1962:31, 36, 109).

Although it is difficult to determine the actual genetic constituents of any of the ethnic groups residing at Malacca even during early periods, it appears that there were genetic inputs through intermarriages between Malays of all social levels and all of the groups of traders that stayed in the area for considerable numbers of years as well as with so-called sea gypsies *(orang laut)* who were loyal para-military supporters of early sultans, enforcing their policies in neighboring ports, and doing some business of their own (often called piracy) on the side, who seem to have been admitted to the nobility along with other Proto-Malay groups (Meilink-Rolofsz, 1962:27-8, 109).[2] Despite this inter-breeding and intermarriage, there was a strong tendency for creolization, as Wertheim has described for Java (1965:64-65), rather than the adoption of a Malay identity. Rather than the trader becoming a member or active participant in the group from which he had gotten his woman, endogamous trading minority communities grew up which fiercely guarded their own cultural heritages even as these were gradually leached away by isolation from their homelands. Hence one finds a theoretically endogamous Chinese community in Malacca today which is probably much more endogamous now than it was before the 19th century when there was lesser availability of marriageable Chinese women in the Straits. These Chinese speak Malay with finesse in the home along with English and other Chinese languages, the Chinese languages serving to highlight their desire to preserve a social identity which is perceived in stark contrast to the prodigality of the Malays. In this regard, Newbold wrote in his *Political and Statistical Account of the British Settlements in the Straits of Malacca* (1839) with particular reference to Malacca:

> Education among the Chinese in the colonies, is at a much lower ebb than in the mother country. The reasons are the pressing nature of their avocations, and the non-emigration of females from China. Owing to the latter, the colonists are constrained to intermarry with the people among whom they settle; in the Straits generally with Malays and with their descendants; consequently the Malay language is the one commonly spoken in their houses, and becomes the vernacular of their children, to whom the later requirement of Chinese must become a matter of time and difficulty (vol. I, 172).

Portuguese rule during the 16th and 17th centuries, under the influence of an ecumenical church, encouraged the growth of a color conscious, Christian, western-oriented group in Malacca: the *Nasrani* (Ar. Nazarene) or Eurasians. The Eurasian community traditionally spurned any Asian identity in favor of relationship with the religion and culture of the West, their version of that culture commonly being several decades behind the fashions of the home country (cf. Purcell, 1951:17-38; Van Leur, 1955:110-13). Although the greater isolation of Malacca under Portuguese and Dutch rule did not foster easy identification of immigrant and indigenous communities, the influx of newer immigrants under British rule allowed a latent preference for light skin among all groups to manifest itself on a broader scale. 'Baba' (creolized) Chinese communities lightened themselves by importing girls from the Chinese mother country and identified their skin tones with the *purer* culture that accompanied them.

After the collapse of Malay sovereignty at Malacca, assimilation in other areas of the Malay peninsula appears to have depended upon entering the stratified Malay society at large, either at the level of nobility or as a peasant *(orang rakyat)* and if one entered as a peasant, whether one could enter a community which had sufficient numbers of one's own ethnic group to form an ethnic minority group village area distinct from the Malay group. In the latter case, further change seems to have been much slower and in at least one case (the Minangkabau of Negri Sembilan) did not make for significant enough changes over several centuries to earn them a completely Malay identity. Only a small group of 'Malay' traders (of various genetic origins) remained in Malacca town; their fortunes dwindled with the declining prosperity of the port itself (Newbold, 1971, vol. I:138-39).

The Minangkabau settlers of Negri Sembilan appear as a striking example of ethnic variation within the modern 'Malay' community, coming to the peninsula during the 15th and 16th centuries and adopting Islam there,[3] but consisting of sufficient numbers to accept local Malays into their own society, assimilating them (often described as aborigines or Proto-Malays who were not yet Muslims) to their own customary inheritance patterns, rather than the reverse. The area had its first Muslim ruler in Raja Melewar who was invited to accept the throne of the 'Nine States' in 1773. Islam in the Minangkabau mold was a curious and contradictory mixture of matrilineal *adat* laws of inheritance and a Muslim populace and a kingship with a patrilateral rule of succession. The Minangkabau presence, especially with a continuing relationship with southwestern Sumatra, probably did as much to discourage the further Islamization of the aboriginal peoples around Malacca as it did to consolidate and strengthen a separate ethnic identity for Minangkabau peoples coming to Malaya in recent centuries (see esp. Swift, 1965:8-25).

Marriages between local Malay rulers and royalty of other ethnic groups seem to have had a greater influence in encouraging assimilation at both the noble and peasant levels. Peasants were encouraged to follow the example of their rulers in making marriages that symbolized, on lower levels, the amity between the peoples concerned. The gradual incorporation of Bugis adventurers into the ruling families of Johore and Selangor during the 18th century provides an excellent example of this process. The Bugis, from Macassar in the Celebes, used weak Malay princes as levers in their attempts to break through the Dutch mercantile empire's monopoly on Malayan tin and other products. The typical policy was one of a Bugis intervention in a succession dispute after the Bugis had offered their good offices to several branches of the local dynasty. Bugis policy appears to have aimed at the expulsion of the Dutch from the archipelago and establishment of their own commercial dominance. Gradually, they had married Malay princesses and engaged their daughters to candidates for the thrones of both Johore and Selangor. Today, to say that one can trace part of his lineage back to Bugis is a symbol of royal parentage and indeed is a reason for pride in both states, indicating long and respected residence in Malaya. Gradually, the connection between Bugis and Macassar became less important commercially and militarily, their descendants adopting Malay language and culture through a gradual process of intermarriage and merger (see esp. Winstedt, 1962:14-58).

An indication of the great power of the model of the Malayan nobility over its subjects in assimilating foreign elements, versus the slower, 'natural' and voluntary processes of the urban trading towns, is indicated in the 19th century writings of Munshi Abdullah bin Abdul Kadir (1797-1856). These writings confirm the findings of Newbold during the same period. Abdullah, a literate and educated Malay writer of mixed Indian and Malay parentage,[4] found it necessary to break openly with the color consciousness and ethnocentrism of the Malaccan society of his day and embark upon a Malayocentric critique of the various communities residing in the Straits. Abdullah was always conscious of his Malay ancestry and professed pride in it, although he credited his frugality and life style to the severe disciplining that he had gotten from his father, who was of Indian ancestry. Abdullah's writings indicate that he felt the need for a movement toward positive symbols of Malay identity, scorning those communities that preferred to use other languages than Malay. He is considered the most significant forerunner of modern Malay literature (e.c. M. Taib, 1964:212-13; Ryan, 1967:113-14).

Abdullah's critique of the society of his day was a harbinger of the severity of Malaya's problems of racial and cultural differences. The history of the immigration of huge numbers of Chinese and Indian immigrants to Malaya has been well chronicled elsewhere (see Cowan, Jackson, Purcell). British intervention in the Malay States iced the cake of prosperity for closed, self-governing Chinese communities in Selangor, Perak and the Straits Settlements. Motivation of laborers coming to the Straits was almost wholly economic, and large numbers returned to China each year; but there was also a minority - and a substantial one - who stayed behind, becoming a new, resident and completely unassimilated community with all of the problems that tin mining and mercantile communities with huge surpluses of males with money in hand could create. Paramilitary *hui*, or secret societies, flourished, with their own rituals, armed forces and women controlled as property through quasi-legal means, even under British rule (see esp. Blythe 1969). Tamils, 'dark' minority who had been used for heavy labor and construction of roads from the time of the founding of Penang, were brought over in much greater numbers with the expansion of demand for natural rubber and the expansion of acreage under rubber after 1905. These laborers were given assisted passage to Malaya by the government of the by then Federated Malay States. The Malay element of the population was enriched by the migration of Indonesians from the Dutch territories seeking stable economic and political conditions, and the general prosperity that characterized Malaya relative to the rest of the archipelago until the Depression. The record of assimilation of Sumatran groups again appears better than that for Javanese and Banjarese (Vlieland, 1934:63-55).[5]

By 1941, the eve of the Japanese occupation, the government had restricted the immigration of Chinese and Indians to the Straits, and their percentages of the Malayan population were 44% and 14% respectively (Ooi, 1964:110-16). The pattern of Malayan race relations had been set: growing but essentially closed communities of resident traders, the majority being recent arrivals, virtually unassimilated; closed communities of similarly separate itinerant labourers; and a Malay peasant population, poorly represented outside of the agrarian sector of the economy. Education and the growth of Malay nationalism tended to modify barriers within the wider Muslim, indigenous community, but its effects were limited to the few who could attend growing numbers of government subsidized schools. One may also note, though probably a phenomenon of lesser significance, the growth of a Pan-Malayan nationalism uniting all sectors of the population regardless of ethnic origins (Ooi, 1964:116-20).

ETHNIC RELATIONS IN THE NORTHERN MALAY STATES

Patterns of ethnic relations in the northern Malay states of Pattani, Kedah, Kelantan and Trengganu appear to have differed from those in the southern, more developed areas due to several factors: first, the predominantly rural character of the economies of these states; second, their northward orientation towards Siam, and finally, the comparative lack of development of a prosperous mercantile sector in any of their economies. In this section we will look at the effects of these factors on the relations between Malays and Chinese in Tregganu and Malays and Siamese in Kedah. These cases do not give us perfect hindsight with respect to the pattern that ethnic relations might have assumed had all the Malay states remained isolated and autonomous, but they do give one a different perspective not possible in any of the cases of the southern areas.

L.A.P. Gosling (1964) has provided an extremely useful analysis of the factors making for the relatively smooth adjustment of late 18th century Chinese immigrants to the rural Malay society of fishing and rice cultivation in Trengganu. According to traditions, groups of Hokkien immigrants moved to the coast of Trengganu first as traders and then, with the declining fortunes of trade, decided to plant pepper, other garden crops and rice for subsistence. Their settlements gradually moved inland from Kuala Trengganu and Marang as a result of soil exhaustion, for they had to settle behind the pre-existing Malay settlements along the river banks, and the lands available had been heavily used by Malay hill padi farmers. Some of the communities found cash cropping, specializing in pepper cultivation, impossible in the areas that they could inhabit and so they adopted the local Malay system of mixed rice and garden crop cultivation and even more rapidly became less distinct from the Malay community at large than those who attempted to specialize and accumulate capital through cash sales of pepper crops. There appears to have been some competition with Malay communities in all areas as the Chinese settlers perfected the tools which they had acquired from their Malay neighbors. They were also required to make contributions to the sultan's tribute to the King of Thailand, as was the duty of all those occupying and using the lands of the Sultan of Trengganu.

As these 'Babas' migrated up the Marang and Trengganu Rivers, they adopted many extra-economic Malay culture traits in addition to the Malay traditional tools of cultivation and Malay knowledge about dealing with the local spirits of growth and the harvest. Houses are of the Malay style, oriented towards Mecca with verandahs under which pigs are kept. Patterns of dress are Malay, as are the majority of foods cooked and eaten. Little pork is eaten and there is no knowledge of the use of chopsticks. Their language is archaic Hokkien from the period when they first arrived but there is no literate indigenous Baba tradition, and inhabitants very commonly speak perfect Trengganu Malay both within and outside of the home so that it would be difficult to call Malay a second language. More recent Chinese arrivals in modern Kuala Trengganu shun the crude Hokkien of the inland villagers, while these villagers' Malay is up to date. There are Chinese good luck charms written in characters but these are not understood and are commonly translated into *jawi* (Arabic) script written on the charm.

One may account for the facilitation of this process of acquisition of a Malay style and the way of life by looking at objective historical factors. When trade lost its viability as a mode of livelihood, some trading families embarked upon attempts to do better in rural occupations in Malaya than they could have done in China. The traders and their coolies were levelled by the prevailing conditions, and all that stayed had to accept the fact of difficulty in securing Chinese brides. The population in early periods appears to have been heavily male and Malay girls provided a means of perpetuating communities of Chinese families with Chinese identities. Gradually, the weight of relations with the Malay society around them and the influence of Malay women within their groups resulted in 'Babaization'. Gosling suggests that there was also pressure from Malay brides for separate dwellings, breaking down the rural Chinese joint family ideal (1964:216).

The children of marriages between Malays and Babas soon differed little in appearance from the rest of the Malay population. It appears that the development of Muslim orthodoxy in the twentieth century introduced barriers to marriage between Chinese boys and Malay girls that did not exist in the past. The author makes the assumption (which seems probable) that the requirement that Malay children *masok jawi* (be circumcised) in order to wed was not as strictly observed in the past as in the present (1964:218). It was easy for a Chinese male to wed a Malay and marriages between important peasant Malay and Chinese families often occurred, as did the analogous marriages among poorer folk. Gosling suggests that there was always considerable loss in the populations of Baba communities due to the incentives to leave and marry Malay. The continuation of these alliances between filial groups in successive generations is a common Malay pattern: to 'keep the money in the family'. Gosling thinks that by far the majority of Baba genes became part of the Malay community by the 20th century, and thereafter, easier access to Chinese brides did something to slow the out-marrying trend. Recently, marriages between Baba girls and urban Chinese have taken the girls to the larger town, and it has been increasingly difficult to induce urban Chinese to join the rural community.

One may note with interest that, while the trend during two hundred years of rural life in Trengganu has been toward the gradual merger and dissolution of ethnic Chinese villages (even while these villages came more and more to approximate the Malay way of life), there have been, over the same period, groups of Baba families close to the town of Kuala Trengganu who have managed to maintain some connection with their trading past through access to Chinese females and to the outside world. Nor should one forget that, with or without such connections, the Chinese planters in Trengganu could not help but experience certain pressures from the surrounding Malay communities to Malayize themselves. Their keeping few pigs is probably as much an indication of their precarious political position in Malaya as of a lesser preference for pork. It is impossible to rule out the fear of Malay violence (which went further than simple sexual imbalance in accounting for outmarriage and inmarriage of Malays) as a potent factor in an active and probably sometimes conscious compromise between the two cultures.

The Thai-Malay or *Samsam*[6] of Kedah, Perlis and Satun appear to be the Siamese equivalent of the Baba Chinese in the eastern corner of the north. Communities of Muslims who spoke a mixed version of Malay and southern Thai were a much more conspicuous feature of the rural landscape in Kedah before the Second World War than more recently (e. g. Wells, pp. 188-89). There are various theories concerning the origins of the Thai-Malay. Some have argued that they have come from Malay populations moving north and adopting Thai language features while maintaining their own religion (Blanchard, 1958:62; Newbold, 1971:vol.I:420; Skeat and Laidlaw, 1953:133-34). This theory seems unconfirmed by the evidence, for it does not explain why these Malays have adopted Siamese language and certain cultural patterns while living in predominently Malay areas, nor does it account for the existence of Thai-Malay communities in Satun that are not Muslim (Abdullah Long Puteh, 1971:1; Archimbault, 1957:75-76; Seidenfaden, 1963:107).

A more convincing explanation of their origins is given in Crawford's Embassy to the Courts of Siam and Cochin China in 1821.

> The indigenous inhabitants of the territory of Queda, consist of four classes, namely; Malays, Samsams, Siamese, and Semangs; but chiefly the two former, among whom the second are said to be the most numerous. By Samsams, are meant people of the Siamese race, who have adopted the Mohammedan religion, and who speak a language which is a mixed jargon of the languages of the two people; a matter which, in the opinion of the latter, brings some reproach with it (1967:28-9).

Logan gives a similar explanation in his discussion of problems of law and order in Province Wellesley in 1867 when he describes them as:

> ...the descendants of rude inland Siamese of Kedah who, some generations back, were converted to Mohamedanism, a religion which still sits loosely on them. They form a majority of the inhabitants of many of the North-eastern villages, in which Siamese is still the current language, although, with few exceptions, they speak Malay also. Many of them are more stupid and ignorant than even the Malays in the same condition of life, and many are knavish, thievish, and addicted to gambling and opium-smoking (1885:200).

The Siamese origins of these mixed populations seem to accord well with the greater power of the Thai government over the western provinces of Malaya than in the east during more than two centuries. Like many of the Malays in extremely rural areas of the country, the Thai-Malay probably sought asylum in Kedah when they were unwelcome in the north while maintaining their Islamic faith in many cases (although not all have done so, either in Malaya or Satun).

The Thai-Malay are notable both for the long history of ethnic blending that their existence reveals and for the rapid assimilation and extinction on the Malayan side of the border of Muslim communities of Thai-Malay in the post-World War II period. In the district of Kedah (with which I am particularly familiar), Sik, there have been three principal areas of Siamese Muslim concentration: one in the eastern area, one in the northeastern area and the other in the southwest of the district, along the Muda River. The southwestern villages are at least as old as the beginning of the present century, and are mentioned in the accounts of the Skeat and Laidlaw expedition to the northwestern corner of Malaya. Oral reports of recollections of early periods reveal that the other area in the northeast of the district was inhabited during that period too, being one of the traditional stopping places of trader *mahouts* taking cargoes on elephant back to the Siamese border. It is also interesting to note that, in the area with which I am familiar (the northeastern one), none of the residents are classified as Siamese in government census information (Kedah, Population Census of 1957:7), although the settlement was originally a Siamese Muslim village in which orthodox Kedahnese rural Malay was spoken as a second language. For the purposes of the census, only Siamese Buddhists were classified as Siamese in the 'Others' category, and these Buddhists are found in the other areas along with Muslims, so that the approximately 1,800 recorded Siamese in the district (of a total of under 20,000 residents) does not reflect the total use of Siamese language and customs within the district.

Originally, this one small area of Sik, with no recorded Siamese inhabitants in recent censuses, was a completely Thai-Malay village, having only a few Malay residents who had married in from neighboring areas. After the Second World War and the rubber boom, others came to the village to settle, applying for land from the local district office. There was also a rise in population as a result of the influx of troops placed on duty during the Emergency and subsequently released at the close of the 1950s. Earlier, during the Depression years, in 1935, a road was finished from Sik town to the area of the village under consideration, thereby connecting it to the state capital at Alor Star and to the southern part of the peninsula via the main, north-south, trunk road. By the late 1960s, the original one village settlement consisted of three villages with headmen, surrounding the original Thai-Malay settlement. These changes have had the effect of making severe inroads on the comprehension and use of the mixed Thai-Malay vocabulary of the original inhabitants, and many of the older people find it difficult to accept their children's unwillingness to learn more than the most superficial aspects of their ancestral cultural bonds with Siam. With regard to circumcision, there is, as in Trengganu, no direct proof, but there are indications that in the past it was recommended (*sunat* means both recommended in religious law and circumcision) but not required. The Skeat and Laidlaw account states that marriage could take place in inland Kedah before circumcision and the authors give the case of a 17 year old male being circumcised. One of the informants on the same journey states that *Samsam* would commonly marry Malay girls and become nominal Muslims, not following Muslim dietary laws strictly (1953:134-43).

The most respected puppeteer of the district is a Thai-Malay from the area being discussed. He travelled to Bangkok during the Depression years to seek work, and returned, learning to speak proper Thai. He seems to have learned little about the art of puppetry there, though he finally inherited the puppets of his older brothers in the early 1960s. The stories that he performs before audiences of Malay and Thai speakers are but poorly known to him so that they must be whispered to him by a cohort of his late brothers. In performance, he alternates between Thai and Malay narration and dialogue, both being blends of 'proper' and rural dialects. The effects of Malay medium schools have also taken their toll in all areas formerly part of the Siamese-Malay cultural blend, and residents of Sik - both Siamese speakers and monolingual Malays - comment with some distaste upon the generally poor knowledge of even the basics of Siamese language throughout the area.

The Emergency had another important effect on ethnic relations in the area. Siamese Buddhist villagers close to the Thai border were resettled in areas closer to the main road and had to sacrifice much of their valuable land (covered with fruit trees and livestock) during an internship in closed camp areas before they were returned to new lands. This period of encampment has produced a bitterness between Buddhist and Muslim that has tended to compound the trend of assimilation to the Malay community at large. For the older Siamese Muslims, there is a kind of conflict of longings between their great respect for Thai cultural achievements, their affection for 'correct' Thai usages, and their knowledge that Thai engage in objectionable, dirty practices, as in the eating of pork and other animals, like lizards, unclean from the Muslim viewpoint. Monolingual Malays, particularly those recent settlers in the region, take a more unambiguously negative view of such practices. The children of Samsam more commonly identify with the Malay community, and express this in intermarriage with the children of monolingual Malay households, associating the old, rural Thai-Malay mixture with the boring backwardness of the isolated life of the past while modern, radio Malay is associated with the modern, urban life styles found in Alor Star and Kuala Lumpur.

In summary, it appears that the combination of a common rural lifestyle and residence in adjacent areas, due to isolation and lawlessness (see esp. Logan, 1885) have brought about the acceptance of Islam by a large number of Siamese, and closer cultural ties between all Siamese Muslims and Malays. The isolation of Sik (as in Trengganu) seems to have coincided with laxity in the enforcement of customary requirements for acceptance into the Muslim community. Intermarriage seems to have been an active force from at least before the beginning of the present century. These factors, combined in the post-war period, with equal treatment by the government and the swamping of Sik by excess population from coastal areas, have made for a closer identification of Thai-Malay with the

rest of the Malay population and the creation of a more distinct Siamese Buddhist group who are called 'real Siamese' *(Siam betul)*, some of whom have moved in the direction of providing Buddhist learning for their children and tightening links with kinsmen across the border. In the face of this growing polarization, modern informants do not think that it will be more than two generations before the old Thai-Malay language is little more than a memory, if that. Perhaps the making of the Hajj by an old Thai-Malay woman in Sik married to a Malay who 'knew some Thai' is a fitting symbol of the processes at work.

SUMMARY AND PROSPECTS

This brief survey has attempted to demonstrate the usefulness of an historical perspective in evaluating the evolving patterns of relationship between Malays and members of other groups on the peninsula in past and present periods. The entry of Malaya into the modern world made the Malay way of life a rural style of the hinterlands in an increasingly urban-oriented peninsula. The stratified, rustic Malay society had little power of attraction for other peoples ruled by others, supported by others, and not dependent upon Malays in any significant degree. Malay rule in the thriving center of Malacca did not succeed in creating a niche for Malays in the urban economy there that was capable of playing a dynamic role in the growth of the towns and cities of the 18th and 19th centuries (see Van Leur, 1955:112). The Portuguese conquest of Malacca, and the subsequent establishment of various national trade monopolies in the area, had the effect of moving whatever indigenous trade that existed up the river courses and into the hands of local chiefs or to the sultans themselves in small, generally coastal, court towns, with the remainder of trade falling to more or less Malayized trading minorities, usually Chinese, Baba Chinese, Indian or the Indian-Malay 'Jawi-pekan' groups (see esp. Roff, 1967:1-5; Gullick, 1965:126-127).[7] With the development of each successive non-Malay trading hegemony, the potential of the inchoate indigenous community for trade diminished. The Malay nobility taxed and administered trade while the commoners stayed on the land.

Even granting the shortage of women in the non-Malay, Asian trading communities in the peninsula, in-marrying females tended to be absorbed by the groups of their spouses, perpetuating distinctive trading minority communities in the Straits that were neither racially nor culturally equivalent to their mother cultures to the west or east, nor tied to a Malay peasantry that was largely barred from participation in the noble prerogative of trade. Although there were always, no doubt, individual traders even in the most developed areas, who entered the Malay population at large, assimilation of whole communities to the Malay way of life did not occur in urban centers like Malacca, Penang, Singapore or Kuala Lumpur. The implications of the western challenge for Malay society made Malays into more rural residents of Malaya than they had been before the Portuguese conquest. Later British colonial policy confirmed the equation of Malay and peasant which the Malay nobility had, if unknowingly, initiated (Roff, 1967:113-25).

This essay also indicates that in regions of greatest impact of external economic forces, schisms developed within the Muslim Southeast Asian community, through the maintenance over at least a century of distinctive 'Malay' groups whose ancestors, labourers of various groups, migrated from Dutch controlled Indonesia. Although these Indonesian immigrants stayed on in Malaya in greater proportions than either Chinese or Indian labourers and established ways of life similar to the traditional Malay mode, not all of them assimilated smoothly to the Malay community at large. Javanese and Banjarese were and are regarded as too much like Chinese to gain full acceptance. Minangkabau regard Malays as prodigal. The record has nevertheless been impressive with regard to acceptance of Sumatran groups into the Malay community and their acceptance of the Malay way of life. Sadka's historical materials concerning 'foreign Malays' in Perak would be startling to a naive Malay speaker visiting the area. Dialectical variation in the area would follow rural-ruban, hill-lowland differences, rather than following Sumatran dialect groups (see esp. Vlieland, 1934).

The greatest success of Malayization appears to have been in those areas least affected by the impact of the West and its entry into the social, political, and economic life of the Malay peninsula. Notable examples cited were in communities of Chinese and Siamese, neither of whom came from Muslin parent communities. Assimilation followed the adoption of a common way of life and was facilitated by ease in entering Islam and the concomitant access to Malay women by both groups and to women from both groups by Malays. Enclavement in Malay ruled and occupied areas also was a potent factor in the adoption of certain Malay patterns and in the elimination or modification of others, as in the lessening of consumption of pork and in the general respect accorded the local rites of the areas into which they moved. Indications from both areas in the north also point to the problems that the loss of isolation has posed for the continuing process of Malayization. In Trengganu the influx of large numbers of Chinese women has polarized a younger generation of Malayized Chinese into those who would stay behind in village areas and those who would leave them for more Chinese urban ones. Among those who stay behind inter-marriage proceeds. The continued viability of Baba communities may be lost as one price of the sharper division between Malayness and Chineseness which is a pan-Malayan phenomenon. In Kedah, the Emergency and the coming of Muslim orthodoxy have polarized the Malayan Thai population into a resurgent Buddhist faction and a rapidly assimilating one which identifies more closely with the mass of the Malay peasantry.

The general problem for and obstacle to assimilation to Malayness has been the generally urban orientation of the forces that brought immigrants to Malaya, and the essentially rural Malay way of life. The absence of an urban Malay life style through the concatenation of historical events and changes on the peninsula left a vacuum: a gap between the Malay peasant and the developing 'Malayan' styles in the urban areas in which Malays were and still are, to a considerable extent, marginal. There was no incentive for the urban merchant to think or act like a Malay as there was in Java, let alone become a Muslim in the absence of an intense personal commitment to do so, nor were there similar incentives for itinerant miners, construction or plantation workers. Normally those not assimilated were subject to livelihood were not Malay skills.

In conclusion, it appears that for future decades a major problem remains: the creation of an urban, indigenous Malay cultural style based upon development of urban roles for Malays. Government programs encouraging the entrance of Malays into urban occupations through study at home and abroad, loans for small businesses and for corporate enterprises, are aimed at filling the wide gap. Hopefully, too, they will remedy the image of the Malay urban dweller as a low level clerical employee or school teacher, a handyman, or other marginal resident, living in a squatter settlement (see

Hamzah, 1962; 1969:470). It is unlikely that there will ever be a Malay Malaya, if by that is meant a Muslim community with negligible cultural variation within. This is surely not the goal of government policy nor would it be feasible, but strides can be made toward a greater Malay presence in the emergence of Modern Malaysia.

FOOTNOTES

1. The tradition of anti-Malay, anti-Muslim bias in writings about Malaya is at least one hundred and fifty years old. Newbold, in his justly renowned *Political and Statistical Account of the British Settlements in the Straits of Malacca* presents a revealing picture of the prevailing prejudices:

   The Malays have several schools at Pinang, in which the Koran is taught and the principles of the Mohammedan religion. The following account of their system is from the Indo-Chinese Gleaner ... It affords a melancholy picture of the state of moral and intellectual darkness that every where attends the baneful influence of the tenets of Mohammed (1971, vol. I:87).

Writers who appear to be capable of objective description with respect to other groups have a noteworthy tendency to accentuate the negative when dealing with Malays. Very commonly, these writers' efforts are directed in behalf of the Malayan aboriginal peoples who are seen as victims of the depradations of an undifferentiated category - Malays - without considering backgrounds, character and interests of their informants and of the individuals said to be responsible for atrocious acts allegedly committed against aborigines. For these writers of the turn of the present century, aborigines represented a kind of pristine humanity amidst an ugly world of self-interested, bigoted Malayness. When Malays made accusations of theft or cheating against aborigines these accusations could be discounted while their reverse were treated with the greatest degree of seriousness. These excerpts from Skeat and Blagden present a good picture of the prevailing Anglo-Saxon opinions concerning the relations of migrating northern peoples and Malays:

   ... complaints are not infrequently made by Malays, and some countenance is even lent to these statements by the high authority of writers like Logan. There are, however, the gravest reasons for disbelieving, or at least heavily discounting, all tales of this kind, which it is never safe to accept without the strictest investigation ... there is as little likelihood of Malays being cheated by any of these wild races as there would be of the wolf of the fable being deceived by the lamb (1906, vol. I:523).

The authors add that the likelihood that the aborigines will be absorbed by the Malay population and be converted to Islam is unfortunate, notwithstanding the increasing number of conversions, for:

   ... rude and uncultivated as these people are, yet in some respects they are vastly superior to those races by whom they are likely to be absorbed--more honest, more truthful, less covetous, more free in every way of crime ... (1906, vol. I:524).

Following these general statements, the authors present a series of anecdotes which could give an impartial reader no clear picture of the state of relations between Malays and these ethnic groups. Malay adventurers are shown to have killed aborigines; Malays make work agreements with aborigines in outlying areas for the clearing of hill *padi* areas; Malays are said to have hunted and enslaved aborigines in the past; aborigines hate and disdain Malays; Malays hate and disdain aborigines (1906. vol. I:527-70).

W.E. Maxwell's account of a journey to hill regions in Perak and Kedah gives a vivid description of an inland freebooter Malay, whom he met in 1876, who seems typical of a group of fugitives (certainly atypical of Malay peasant villagers) in his open acknowledgement of commission of many crimes (1882: 20). Maxwell also records having seen an aboriginal girl who was adopted by a Malay household; Chinese and Malay and Siamese and Malay villages in close proximity in the hill region of Baling, all affluent; and the adoption of some aboriginal children into Malay homes as slaves, others presumably by simple adoption. The account indicates strong and effective administrative control of this rich trading area by a Malay official of the Sultan of Kedah (1882:43, 61, 63).

In Skeat's recently published journal of a trip to the northern Malay States of Kedah, Perlis and Setul - after having visited the Malay States in what is now Thailand (Skeat and Laidlaw, 1953) - there is ample evidence that Malays and aborigines could and did live in neighboring villages, even in the most remote regions of Kedah - Baling and Sik. One finds evidence of loose adherence to Islamic law and general amity, if not unity. In 1851, J.R. Logan commented upon the general similarity in appearance of Kedahnese Malays and the 'Negrito' populations of the area, especially with respect to the shape of nose and general facial contours (see Ahmad, 1967:5). It would seem that the relations between Malays and the various other indigenous inhabitants of the peninsula are complex ethnohistorical phenomena which belies the naive literal translation of statements by paid Malay informants (to white colonial officials or modern investigators) - that these peoples are 'animals' (Endicott, 1970:82).

Modern writers have modified their views somewhat, but the element of Malay irrationality is still present, as in the characterization of PMIP success in the northeastern states as a result of surfacing 'chauvinist nationalism' (Means, 1970:227), and Silcock's claim that

It is hysterical nonsense to claim that the Malays ever owned Malaya (in the sense of political ownership of the unoccupied land) in the same sense as the modern European state owns the territory it administers (quoted in Ginsburg and Roberts, 1958:238).

2. Hang Tuah, the famous Laksamana of the Malay Annals *(Sejarah Melayu)* is said to have been descended from Malay and 'Jakun' ancestors (Meilink-Rolofsz, 1962:53).

3. There is no positive agreement on when the Minangkabau adopted Islam.

4. Colonel Low wrote that:

A Jawi-pekan is the offspring of a man of Hindustan (India) and a Malayan woman (or a descendant of such a union). He inherits the boldness of the Malay and the subtlety, acuteness and dissimulation of the Hindoo (Indian). He is indefatigable in the pursuit of wealth and the most usurious in the employment of it when gained. Few employments come amiss to him. He cloaks ignorance where it exists, or makes up for it by pretence and zeal. His fingers seem to have a chemical affinity for the precious metals; he avoids downright theft, yet the transit of money or money's worth through the former is at a discount varying in amount to the calculations of detection. He is cringing to superiors, overbearing, and, where there is no check on his conduct, tyrannical to inferiors; like one of the feline tribe when it has changed quarters, he carefully obtains a perfect acquaintance with all the trapdoors, outlets and hiding crevices of the corner in which he is placed. Thus secured he makes the most of that position (quoted in Logan, 1885:197.).

Low's image of Abdullah's group should help the reader to understand at least part of the rationale for Abdullah's calling.

5. Emily Sadka reports:

The immigration of Malaysians was encouraged by rent remissions and small loans, but while settlement schemes were carried out on the initiative of individual district officers, there was no regular government assisted scheme of immigration. Families of settlers came singly or in small groups, sometimes independently, more often with the assistance of a leader who had previously negotiated with a district officer and secured land and an advance on the harvest, to be distributed among his followers. There was also a small intake of indentured labourers from Java and elsewhere in the archipelago, imported by coolie brokers and lodged in Colony depots before engagement, in the same manner as Chinese immigrants. They were employed chiefly in such work as felling and clearing, drain-cutting and road building, and frequently settled with their wives and families on the completion of their indentures. Malaysian settlers came from all over the peninsula and archipelago. Javanese settled in the Klang and Kuala Langat districts of Selangor, and in Lower Perak and Krian; Banjarese in Ulu Langat district and in Kinta where they were reported in 1894 to outnumber the indigenous Malays in the Kampar, Kuala Teja and Sungai Raya mukims... The largest Malay increase of all, both in absolute terms and in proportion to earlier figures, was in Krian, where the Malay population increased by 120 percent over 1879. Since five-sixths of the Malay population of Krian and Kurau was returned as 'foreign Malay' in 1879 (as well as the entire population of Selama) it appears that nearly all the Malays in this district in 1891 were born outside the state (1968:227-28; 230).

6. The term Samsam is said to be derived either from the Hokkien: *chamcham* or *sama sama* in Malay, which means, among other things, together (Archimbault, 1957:75). The term is an impolite one and although the writer found that all of his informants of mature age were familiar with it, none of them had ever used it in conversations with him until he himself had broached the topic.

7. Wan Ibrahim reports that during the reign of Sultan Abdullah Mukkaram Shah of Kedah, from 1762-1799, there were royal monopolies on elephants, tin, wax, iron, saltpeter, opium, salt, tobacco and cotton and that the selling of rice to traders for sale outside of the state was forbidden save for special exceptions. With the opening of the British port at Penang, the prosperity and royal revenues of Kedah fell considerably, although never below $80,000 (Wan Ibrahim, 1961:2-6).

REFERENCES

Abdullah Long Puteh
1971 Sejarah Negri Setol, Thailand (The History of Setol, Thailand), trans. from Thai by Wan Adnan Bin Wan Long, Alor Star (?).

Ahmad Saleh
1967 "Kedah Dalam Tahun 1851, Zaman Pemerentahan Sultan Zainal-Rashid I," Kedah Dari Segi Sejarah, Jilid 2, Bil. 1, May pp. 1-7.

Archimbault, C.
1957 "A Preliminary Investigation of the Sam Sam of Kedah and Perlis, Journal of the Royal Asiatic Society, Malayan Branch, vol. 30, pt. 2, pp. 75-92.

Blanchard, W.
1958 Thailand: its people, its society, its culture; New Haven: HRAF Press.

Blythe, W.L.
1969 The Impact of Chinese Secret Socieities in Malaya, Kuala Lumpur:Oxford.

Cowan, C.D.
1961 Nineteenth Century Malaya: The Origins of British Political Control, New York:Oxford.

Crawfurd, John
1967 Journal of an Embassy to the Courts of Siam and Cochin China, Kuala Lumpur: Oxford.

Endicott, Kirk M.
1970 An Analysis of Malay Magic, London:Oxford

Freedman, M.
1960 "The Growth of a Plural Society in Malaya, Pacific Affairs, vol. 33, no. 2, pp. 158-68.

Furnivall, J.S.
1956 Colonial Policy and Practice, New York:New York University. orig. 1948.

Ginsburg, Norton and G.F. Roberts
1958 Malaya, Seattle:American Ethnological Society.

Gosling, L.A.P.
1964 "Migration and Assimilation of Rural Chinese in Trenggenu," pp. 203-21 in Malayan and Indonesian Studies, Bastin, John and R. Roolvink, eds., London:Oxford.

Gullick, J.M.
1965 Indigenous Political Systems of Western Malaya, London:Athlone.

Hamzah Sendut
1962 "Patterns of Urbanization in Malaya", Journal of Tropical Geography, vol. 16, pp. 114-30.
1969 "The Structure of Kuala Lumpur, Malasia's Capital City," pp. 461-73, in Gerald Breese, ed., The City in Newly Developing Countries, Englewood Cliffs, N.J.:Prentice-Hall.

Jackson, R.N.
1961 Immigrant Labour and the Development of Malaya, 1786-1920. Kuala Lumpur:Government Press.

Kedah
1957 Population Census of 1957. Federation of Malaya, Kuala Lumpur.

Kennedy, J.
1967 A History of Malaya, London:Macmillan.

Logan, J.R.
1885 "Plan for a Volunteer Police in the Muda Districts, Province Wellesley, Submitted to Government by the Late J.R. Logan in 1867", Journal of the Royal Asiatic Society, Straits Branch, vol. 16, pp. 173-202.

McGee, T.G.
1963 "The Cultural Role of Cities: a case study of Kuala Lumpur," Journal of Tropical Geography, vol. 17, pp. 178-96.
1967 The Southeast Asian City, New York:Praeger.

Maxwell, W.E.
1882 "A Journey on Foot to the Patani Frontier in 1786," Journal of the Royal Asiatic Society, Straits Branch, vol. 9, pp. 1-67.

Means, Gordon
1970 Malaysian Politics, New York:New York University.

Meilink-Roelofsz, M.A.P.
1962 Asian Trade and European Influence in the Indonesian Archipelago Between 1500 and about 1630, The Hague:M. Nijhoff.

Mohd. Taib bin Osman
1964 "Trends in Modern Malay Literature," pp. 210-25 in Wang Gungwu, ed. Malaysia, New York:Prager.

Newbold, T.J.
1971 Political and Statistical Account of British Settlements in the Straits of Malacca, 2 vols., Kuala Lumpur:Oxford, (orig. 1839).

Ooi, Jin Bee
1964 Land, People and Economy in Malaya, London:Longmans.

Purcell, Victor
1951 The Chinese in Malaya, London:Oxford.

Roff, William R.
1967 The Origins of Malay Nationalism, New Haven:Yale.

Ryan, N.J.
1967 The Making of Modern Malaysia, Kuala Lumpur:Oxford.

Sadka, Emily
1968 The Protected Malay States, 1874-1895, Kuala Lumpur:University of Malaya.

Seidenfaden, Eric
1963 The Thai Peoples, Bangkok:Siam Society.

Skeat, W.W. and C.O. Blagden
1906 Pagan Races of the Malay Peninsula, 2 vols. New York:Macmillan.

Skeat, W.W. and F.F. Laidlaw
1953 The Cambridge University Expedition to Parts of the Malay Peninsula - 1899-1900, Journal of the Royal Asiatic Society, Malayan Branch, vol. 26, pt. 4.

Swift, M.G.
1965 Malay Peasant Society in Jelebu, London:University of London.

Van Leur, Jacob C.
1955 Indonesian Trade and Society: Essays in Asian Social and Economic History, The Hague:W. Van Hoeve.

Vlieland, C.A.
1934 "The Population of the Malay Peninsula, a study in human migration," Georgraphical Review, Vol. 24: 61-78.

Wan Ibrahim bin Wan Sulh
1961 Chara2 Mengutip Hasil Negri Dalam Masa Pemerentaham Sultan Abdullah Mukarram Shah, Sultan Negri Kedah, yang memerentah dalam tahun 1762 - 1799 bersamaan 1174 - 1212 Hijrah, Sharahan yang di-bori kapada Ahli2 Persatuan Sejarah Persekutuan Tanah Melayu (Chawangan Negri Kedah) dan murid2 Sultan Abdul Hamid College dan Sultanah Asma School, Alor Setar pada hari Ahad 18hb. Jun jam 8.00 - 9.00 malam.

Wells, Carveth
1925   Six Years in the Malay Jungle, New York:Garden City
       Publishers.

Wertheim, W.F.
1965   East-West Parallels, Chicago:Quadrangle.

Wilson, Peter J.
1967   A Malay Village and Malaysia, New Haven:HRAF
       Press.

Winstedt, R.O.
1962   A History of Malaya, Singapore:Marican.

11
THE ETHNIC ASSIMILATION OF CHINESE STUDENTS INTO THE THAI MEDICAL ELITE

WILLIAM EDGAR MAXWELL

*Bureau of Educational Research
and Department of Sociology
University of Illinois*

ABSTRACT

The arguments as to whether the Chinese are seeking or resisting assimilation in Thailand have ignored previous investigations which demonstrate that both processes are occurring. It is proposed that more relevant questions inquire as to the sectors of the Chinese community from which persons are assimilating, the rate of assimilation from each of these sectors, and the social destinations within Thai society toward which these persons are moving. Evidence is examined which shows that many of the students from Chinese homes who are in Thai medical schools manifest considerable identification with Thai society. Another large proportion of the students identify mainly with Chinese society.

The controversy over the ethnic identification of the Chinese in Thailand parallels the differences between two major theories of race relations. These contending points of view treat assimilation simply as either occurring readily between ethnic populations or almost not at all. Resolution of these questions awaits a more complex theory which allows for ethnic mobility in certain sectors of a population while not in other sectors. A modest development of such theory is proposed in this paper to account for whatever assimilation does or does not occur among Chinese students in Thai medical schools. This perspective contends that elements from both theories of assimilation and pluralism are applicable to ethnic phenomena among the Chinese in Thailand.

In contrast with the pre-World War II tendency of the Chinese to assimilate into Thai society, Coughlin (1955) finds little recent evidence of assimilation and concludes that the Chinese community will persist indefinitely. He describes Thai society as exclusive and reluctant to admit Chinese into government careers. Because Thai males are unlikely to work in business fields, the Chinese have been free to enter jobs where they could form their own occupational community outside the traditionally Thai domains of agriculture and government. Markedly different systems of values are attributed by Coughlin to the Chinese and Thai. However, Thai exclusiveness, occupational segregation and dissimilar values he considers as merely sufficient, not necessary, conditions for ethnic pluralism between the two groups. The fundamental premise of Coughlin's (1960:197-198) analysis, in common with most theories of pluralism (Furnivall, 1939; Glazer and Moynihan, 1963; Gordon, 1964), is the durability of the ethnic identification of the Chinese. The sense of identification with the Chinese culture and population, he concludes, is so strong that the ethnic community presently loses few of its numbers through assimilation and will long endure.

From his studies conducted in the nineteen-fifties, during the same period as Coughlin's research, Skinner (1957) finds much evidence of assimilation and concludes that the Chinese are probably assimilating more rapidly into Thai society than has been the case in other Southeast Asian societies. Similar to several theories of assimilation (Park, 1950; Shibutani and Kwan, 1965) Skinner (1957:300) assumes that ambitious Chinese, when given the opportunity, are likely to seek entrance into the elites of whatever country in which they reside. A significant difference between Thailand and other Southeast Asian societies is thus the opportunity for elite mobility. Skinner reports that many have gained access to high level positions within the Thai government. He describes the Thai as willing to accept as Thai any person of Chinese origin who conforms to Thai behavior norms. Skinner (1964:89-92) concludes that under the conditions of the late nineteen-fifties most of the Chinese population would assimilate into Thai society within two or three generations.

Neither Coughlin nor Skinner take adequate account in their theories of ethnic identification of the differentiation within the two ethnic groups. Each group is divided into several subgroups along the dimensions of status, class, and situs. A theory of ethnic mobility must ask "How much mobility into which level of the politically dominant ethnic group originates in which stratum of the subordinate ethnic group?" Skinner (1957:299-300) advances the hypothesis, relevant to this orientation, that the assimilation of the Chinese in Southeast Asia tends to be directed toward politically dominant elites. This hypothesis should be further elaborated to designate the social origins of the ethnically mobile Chinese as well as other possible destinations.

Status mobility into a more prestigious stratum is often the basis for movement between ethnic groups. Movement would not be expected between ethnic groups should it result in a net loss of status for the mobile. From these considerations we may advance the following general hypothesis concerning the destination of ethnic mobility: assimilation is likely to occur where movement between ethnic groups would also involve upward mobility between status levels. These considerations

*For assistance in collecting the materials for this report I am indebted to my colleagues, Jumroon Meekanon and Jirawat Wongswadiwat. Donald Dixon, Frederic K. Lehman, and Sumalee Paveanbampen discussed with me various versions of the manuscript. Advice and support were generously provided from the beginning of these studies by C. Wayne Gordon, Oscar Grusky, and Samuel J. Surace.

The research has been supported by grants provided by the Institute for Advanced Projects of the East-West Center, the National Science Foundation, the Midwest Universities Consortium for International Activities, the Center for Asian Studies and the Research Board of the University of Illinois.

The responsibility for the views presented is mine.

also suggest that the rate of assimilation is dependent upon the number of attractive positions vacant within the dominant group. Assimilation proceeds at a slow pace unless the number of these openings is many.

The racism in Western societies has affected the possibility of formulating and testing in the West alternative theories of ethnic identification. Given the conditions of discrimination and exclusiveness by a dominant ethnic group, both assimilationist and pluralist perspectives predict low rates of assimilation. It is only for a society where a prestigious dominant group is relatively free of ethnic exclusiveness that the two perspectives predict different outcomes. Thailand thus assumes special significance in comparative sociology if it is indeed a society in which the dominant ethnic group is little troubled by racism and is relatively open to ethnic mobility.

THE CHINESE IN MODERN THAILAND

For several centuries immigrant Chinese have figured prominently in the commercial centers in Thai society. Chinese constituted, however, only a miniscule part of the society until the nineteenth century when the trickle of immigrants from China swelled to a great torrent of fortune hunters seeking the attractive wages paid in rapidly modernizing and expanding sectors of the Thai economy. During the last one hundred years the commercial and industrial establishments of modern Thai society have developed almost completely under the initiatives of the Chinese and their descendants. The Thai have retained political control of the nation and through the government bureaucracy dominate all institutions within the society including those of commerce and industry. In addition to its ascendancy in the nation's class and political structures the bureaucracy is also pre-eminent in status, careers within it being considered as the most prestigious of any of the modern occupations in the society.

As intimately involved as they are in the urban economy of the nation, the Chinese are concentrated in the cities and provincial towns. A minority of the Chinese operate small general stores in the more prosperous villages of the countryside but almost none are engaged in farming. The Chinese were estimated by Skinner (1957:183) as numbering well over two million in the late 1950s and constituting about 10 percent of the total population of the society.

Chinese society and culture is different in many respects from that of Thai. Household structure, variant forms of Buddhism, occupational and other values differ between the two groups. Chinese communities maintain where possible separate schools, hospitals, religious institutions, and business and professional associations as well as the commercial zones dominated by their business establishments.

The Thai have historically welcomed the immigration of the Chinese and encouraged their acculturation into local Thai custom. It has only been in the last two decades that the Thai rulers have drastically reduced the rate of immigration, due to various domestic and international developments. The government has promoted the identification of the Chinese with the Thai culture and society especially through the medium of universal primary education in a distinctly Thai curriculum. Even in the private elementary schools operated by the Chinese the government requires that the majority of the curriculum be devoted to the nationally prescribed syllabus. Though the Thai voice some fears of the greatly increased Chinese power--economic and political--in Thai society, sharp conflict has occurred only in isolated incidents. History displays an unusual record of cooperation between the

Thai and immigrant Chinese. Several observers note that though both groups manifest some cultural prejudice towards the other, the Thai are not racist in their attitudes toward the Chinese (Skinner, 1957:381; Coughlin, 1960:81; Cowgill, 1968).

From the pluralist perspective, the distinctiveness of Chinese culture and the pride with which its bearers adhere to it suggest that the Chinese will resist assimilation in Thailand indefinitely (Carnell, 1955:277; Coughlin, 1955; Hanks, 1962:1257; Smythe, 1964:284-285). Furnivall (1939) and Coughlin (1955) describe the modernizing and burgeoning urban business of the society and the low interest of Thai males in commerce as conditions very favorable to the maintenance of ethnic pluralism. Coughlin (1960:124-125) reports that few Chinese are attracted to the professions or the Thai bureaucracy because so much more money may be gained by remaining within the expanding business sector. Because the few Chinese immigrants now permitted to enter Thailand comprise roughly equal numbers of males and females there is less necessity for intermarriage than formerly when male immigrants far exceeded the number of immigrating females. It is also suggested that since the Revolution of 1932 national policies of repression of the Chinese have deterred assimilation.

In contrast to predictions of pluralism, several observers report a disposition among many of the Chinese to assimilation. Many conditions in Thai society encourage entrance by the Chinese. The acculturation of the Chinese is encouraged by compulsory schooling in a Thai curriculum, Thai dominated mass communications, and convenient transportation facilities. A near absence of ethnic exclusiveness and an expanding government bureaucracy have afforded opportunities for ambitious Chinese to enter high levels of prestige among the Thai. Skinner (1957:381) reported that by the third generation almost all persons of immigrant origins are assimilated except in some cases where the individual has attended Chinese schooling. Both Guskin (1968:129) and Punyodyana (1971a:23-24) observed that the majority of the Chinese subjects in their surveys expressed a preference for education in the Thai universities and employment in the professions or government. From her questionnaire survey of second generation Chinese secondary school students Schumrum (1966) concluded that the majority of her subjects identified with Thai society and culture.

From these conflicting reports of Chinese assimilation two alternative hypotheses are drawn:

I.A. Few persons of Chinese origin seek to enter the Thai bureaucratic elite.

I.B. If given the opportunity many descendants of Chinese immigrants would attempt to assimilate into the Thai bureaucratic elite.

The findings of both Coughlin (1953:437) and Skinner (1957:307; 1958:227-247) imply that the elite Chinese are more likely to assimilate than are the others within the ethnic community. Useful theoretical implications may be drawn from this observation for assimilation processes among the great majority of Chinese, most of whom are not elites. The assimilationist perspective proposes that most Chinese would welcome an opportunity to occupy a prestigious as well as lucrative elite position within the Thai occupational structure. Thus Skinner observes the descendants of many of his sample of Chinese elites moving into the Thai elite. But of course most Chinese do not have the resources possessed by their leaders for gaining entrance into elite Thai occupations. These resources are the wealth required for private primary and secondary schools and informal social contacts with influential members of the elites. Accordingly, in Coughlin's predominantly middle status sample he found little mobility into the Thai elite. A Chinese is not likely to assimilate if his movement into Thai society would fail to maintain at least the occupational power and level of income of his origins. Most middle status Thai occupations are less lucrative than are many middle status Chinese occupations. It is then understandable that Coughlin found little evidence of middle status Chinese assimilating into middle status Thai positions.

Though several studies of Thai society have used the term to denote stratification in general, status is employed here in a more specific sense. Status is defined as the level of prestige attributed to occupational positions. In addition to the distribution of social honor in the occupational system status connotes in this study the stratification of occupational culture or style.

The theory of pluralism makes no allowance for the assimilation of either the elite or the middle status members of a subordinate ethnic group into the dominant group. Though Coughlin (1953:437) mentions the assimilation of the elite Chinese he does not explain this within the context of the pluralism he describes. With respect to middle status Chinese Coughlin (1960:124-125) found very few attracted to positions within the Thai government and professions. But this latter finding is contested by the reports from others (Schumrum, 1966; Guskin, 1968:123-130; Punyodyana, 1971a:23-25) concerning the aspirations of secondary school Chinese students and their parents.

These observations lead us to the following set of contending hypotheses:

II A. Though some persons of elite Chinese origin may assimilate into the Thai elite, few Chinese of middle or lower status origins are likely to seek assimilation into the Thai elite.

II B. Considerable assimilation into the Thai elite originates in both the elite and nonelite prestige strata of the Chinese community.

Analysis of ethnic mobility requires examination also of class origins. Consideration of both the status and class origins of Chinese entering Thai society permits a better estimate of the course and rate of assimilation because it facilitates a more focused designation of the subgroups within the Chinese population where ethnic mobility is likely to originate. Class is defined as occupational power with respect to the control a person has over his own work and over the work of others. The crucial boundaries between occupational classes are between three groups comprised of persons who control their own and other's work, those who control their own but not other's work, and those whose work activities are controlled by others. The first two groups may be considered as two kinds of elites, those who have power within the workplace. Because class has not been specifically examined in previous studies of Thailand's Chinese, it is difficult to deduce what previous analyses would imply on this matter. The distinction between the two main perspectives would probably concern, as it did with status, whether ethnic mobility originates only in the elites or at lower levels as well.

The two hypotheses implied in the matter of class origins are:

III A. Movement by Chinese into the Thai elite classes tends to originate within the elite classes of the Chinese community.

III B. There is considerable assimilation into the Thai elite classes of Chinese from both elite and nonelite classes.

To examine the above three sets of contending hypotheses the research reported in this study selected the Thai medical profession as a source of evidence. This profession is well suited for this purpose because it is one of the largest professions among university graduates in Thailand. Doctors enjoy a high status within the Thai elite and a very lucrative income. The profession is dominated by ethnic Thai culture. The government bureaucracy operates all of the medical schools and employs most of the latter's graduates. As a profession which has rapidly expanded with the continuing modernization of the society in recent decades it has provided an opportunity for mobility for both ambitious Thai and Chinese (Maxwell, 1971:50-54).

METHODS

The findings reported in this study are based upon evidence secured from two questionnaire surveys administered to medical students in the Thai language during classroom sessions. A survey was conducted in 1966 extending to each grade level of each of the nation's three schools. Responses were received from 87 percent (N=666) of the male students. An examination of the social characteristics of the 13 percent of the students not included indicated that the sample was highly representative (Maxwell, 1971:310-314). In 1971 a survey was conducted among the second year students of the newest medical school and of two of the three older schools. This survey obtained questionnaires for 98 percent (N=140) of the male students (Wongswadiwat, 1973:98-104).

For use in the 1971 survey an instrument was developed to measure identification with Thai society and culture. With the cooperation of a Thai social psychologist familiar with Chinese culture, a large pool of items was prepared in the Thai language. A panel of judges, consisting of Chinese who were considerably assimilated into Thai society, rated the items with respect to their relative weight as indicators of the general concept of ethnic identification with Thai society. The items selected by this procedure were then administered in a pretest and examined by item analysis methods common to summated ratings techniques. Items retained from the latter were included in the questionnaire survey after which a further item analysis was conducted in the following manner: the items were standardized, multiplied by their respective weights as earlier determined, and then examined for their correlation with both the total scale and a set of subscales representing various elements of ethnic identification.

Subsamples of students selected from the homes most identified with Chinese culture are used in several of the analyses. This emphasis upon distinctly Chinese origins is necessary to counter the possibility of findings of assimilation apparently occurring among students that in fact are simply a manifestation of the previous assimilation, particularly intermarriage, of the students' parents. An extreme criterion of the ethnic identification of one's origins is the language spoken at home (cf. Skinner, 1957:205 and Punyodyana, 1971b:234). Students are included in the select subsamples if they spoke either Chinese or a mixture of Chinese and Thai with their parents in the home. The item in the 1966 survey concerning language was phrased in terms of the language presently spoken with the parents rather than that spoken in the home as a small child. The 1971 survey used a questionnaire item addressed to the main language used in the home during childhood.

The occupational prestige of the fathers of the medical students was measured with the questionnaire data on the basis of operational assumptions in the index used by several American scholars to study Thai stratification (Skinner, 1957:300-310; Phillips, 1956:165-170). In addition to the dimension of the prestige of the father's occupation, the index includes the factors of reported family income, the number of the father's subordinates, and the father's education.

Two general occupational attitude scales are used from a factor analysis of questionnaire items from the 1966 survey. A correlation matrix for thirty-five items for 987 male and female students was introduced into a principal axis factor analysis. The commonalities were not estimated for this procedure. The resulting factors were rotated orthogonally by varimax procedures. Ten factors were extracted which accounted for about 55 percent of the variance in the principal axis analysis.[1]

FINDINGS

The medical school enrollment rates of students from various ethnic origins may be used as indirect evidence for hypotheses I A and I B concerning the desire of Chinese to enter the Thai bureaucratic elite. In 1968 28 percent of the male medical students spoke Chinese or a mixture of Thai and Chinese with their parents when at home. Another 4 percent designated both of their parents as ethnic Chinese. Eleven percent more of the students indicated the ethnicity of one of their parents to be Chinese. In addition to these several categories of Chinese families, another twenty-two percent of the students are from recently assimilated families in which both parents are ethnic Thai and at least one of their grandparents as born in China or having spoken Chinese. Considering these various categories of ethnic ancestry together, at least 65 percent of the male medical students are of families which include ethnic Chinese within the most recent three generations. The entrance of so many persons of recent Chinese origin into the medical schools indicates a tendency for Chinese to seek assimilation into elite occupations linked with the Thai culture. These data in themselves do not clarify, however, whether this ethnic mobility originates largely among the Chinese elite or in nonelite status levels as well.

Table 1. Occupational Status of Fathers of Male Medical Students By Ethnicity of Chinese Ancestors (1966 Survey)

Status	Both Parents Ethnic Chinese	One Parent Ethnic Chinese	One or More Grand-parents Ethnic Chinese
Elite	21	20	26
Upper-Middle	59	49	58
Lower-Middle	20	28	16
Lower	-	3	-
Total	100%	100%	100%
Number of Cases	(273)	(87)	(81)

Various kinds of evidence are presented in Tables 1 through 3 that bear on the second set of hypotheses concerning the status origins of Chinese ethnic mobility into the Thai elite. Table 1 displays the occupational status or prestige origins of the medical students from homes classified by the ethnicity of the parents and the language used. Many of the students are of elite Chinese fathers. The numbers of these elite Chinese students are disproportionately large when compared with the small Chinese elite (Skinner, 1957:301). Of greater interest is the finding that for each kind of ethnic origin a large majority of the students are from status levels below the Chinese elite.

Most of the Chinese students, 59 percent, from homes in which both parents are Chinese are from the upper-middle level of status. Another 20 percent are from a lower-middle level of status. Almost none of the students are from the lower status levels. The status distributions for the three groups of students distinguished by ethnic origins are essentially similar. In each group the great majority of the students are from the middle status levels.

Table 2. Zero-order Correlations between Ethstatus Origins Dichotomy (Elite Thai and Middle Status Chinese) and Various Scales of Thai Ethnic Attitudes

Content of Attitude Scales	Correlation Coefficient	Number of Cases	Survey Source of Data
1. Summary scale	.54*	(51)	(1971)
Language and educational attitudes			
2. Intentions for own children	.21	(51)	(1971)
Occupational attitudes			
3. Preference for Thai or Chinese colleagues and government employment	.49*	(51)	(1971)
4. Preference for non-government employment	.00	(666)	(1966)
5. Preference for foreign post-graduate training	.06	(666)	(1966)
Religious attitudes			
6. Practice of Thai Buddhism	.25**	(51)	(1971)
Attitudes toward other Thai customs			
7. Funeral, festival and animistic practices	.46*	(51)	(1971)
Marriage attitudes			
8. Inter-marriage and the marriage ceremony	.52*	(51)	(1971)

* Significant at p .0005, one-tailed test

** Significant at p .05, one-tailed test

Though a substantial number of students from middle status Chinese homes are entering Thai medical schools, where for the time of their training they must conform to Thai behavioral codes, there remains the question of the ultimate commitments of these students to Thai society and culture. To assess the extent or absence of assimilation among the middle status students of Chinese origin, comparisons with elite Thai students are presented in Table 2 on several scales and subscales developed to measure identification with the ethnic Thai. The comparisons are expressed in the form of Pearson correlation coefficients. The statistical analysis was conducted by selecting two categories of second year male medical students classified by their ethstatus[2] origins--middle status Chinese who had spoken a Chinese language with their parents and elite Thai--and correlating the resulting ethstatus dichotomy with each of the several ethnic attitude scales developed from the two questionnaire surveys. A moderate degree of correlation between ethstatus origins and the total or summary scale of Thai ethnicity is expressed in the coefficient of 0.54. There is considerable variation in the degree of correlation between ethstatus origins and attitudes having to do with specific ethnic institutions. A coefficient of 0.06 indicates that the students of Chinese origin have no more preference for employment in nongovernment institutions--e.g., private hospitals in Bangkok--than do the elite Thai students. Inspection of the questionnaire responses indicated neither category had a strong preference for private hospitals and that both are much more interested in working in the prestigious government hospitals. There is no difference between the two categories in the desire to travel abroad for postgraduate training (r = 0.07). Most students strongly aspire to such training. Almost as many students of Chinese origin expect to speak Thai with their children and school them in Thai schools as do the Thai (r = 0.21). Differences between elite Thai and middle status students of Chinese origin in their ideals and practice of Thai Buddhism are slight (r = 0.25). Stronger differences exist between these two categories of students in their preferences for Thai professional colleagues, their practice of various Thai festivals and traditions, and their readiness to marry an ethnic Thai woman.

While the statistical coefficients of correlation in Table 2 efficiently summarize many measures, the questionnaire responses[3] presented in Table 3 provide more detailed estimations of specific and illustrative attitudes of the students. This table compares second year male medical students from elite Thai families with students from Chinese speaking middle status families.

Table 3. Ethnic Attitudes of Male Medical Students by Ethstatus Origins, in Percentages (1971 Survey)

Questionnaire Item	Ethstatus Origins		Questionnaire Item	Ethstatus Origins	
	Elite Status Thai	Middle Status Chinese		Elite Status Thai	Middle Status Chinese
1. "Which language do you think you will speak to your children when alone with them at home?"			3. Ratio of Thai student friends to all student friends		
"Thai"	94%	85%	0% - 25%	39%	58%
"Chinese"	-	15%	40% - 49%	-	24%
2. "If the working conditions were equally good at each of the following places, where would you choose to work?"			50% - 80%	61%	18%
			4. "If you had your choice, with which of the following races would you prefer to marry?"		
"In a place where everyone is Chinese"	-	-	"Thai"	89%	58%
			"Chinese"	0%	21%
"In a place where the majority are Chinese"	-	6%	"No preference"	6%	15%
"In a place where the numbers of Chinese and Thai are equal"	17%	76%	5. "If you have a son, when he reaches maturity will you have him enter the monkhood for a while?"		
"In a place where the majority are Thai"	78%	15%	"Definitely" [or] "probably will do so"	61%	36%
"In a place where everyone is Thai"	5%	3%	"Not sure"	28%	27%
			"Probably" [or] definitely will not do so"	11%	33%
Number of Cases	(18)	(33)		(18)	(33)

In item number 1 it may be seen that almost all of the students from Chinese families, 85 percent, who themselves spoke Chinese as children with their parents now expect to converse with their children in Thai.

Two kinds of evidence concerning social interaction with ethnic Thai persons are indicated in items number 2 and 3. The questionnaire requested each student to designate as many as five of his closest student friends. For each friend so designated the respondent was requested to specify the person's "racial" ancestry. From these responses a sociometric ratio was computed for each student by dividing the number of Thai friends by the total number of friends for each student. The relatively large majority of Chinese students and the ease with which interethnic relations develop are

manifested in finding that not even one of the Thai students designates a circle of close friends entirely of Thai origin. A moderately large percentage of the students from Chinese families, 42 percent, find almost half or over half of their close friends among the Thai. Substantial differences do exist between the two categories in that within each category of ethstatus origins the majority of the students choose over half of their close friends from among their own ethnic origins. A relatively similar set of distributions is presented for item number 2 concerning the preferred ethnicity of future workplace colleagues. Students from Chinese origins are much less likely than the Thai to prefer an establishment where the majority are ethnic Thai. There is also evidence that few students from Chinese families tend to reject their ethnic origins in that only one of these students indicated a desire to work only alongside the Thai. A large majority of the students from Chinese homes, 76 percent, indicate an identification with both groups and choose neither ethnic group over the other. The relative lack of discrimination against Chinese by the Thai may be seen in that only one of the Thai students does not want to work among any of Chinese origin. However, most of the Thai prefer to work in a place that is predominantly Thai.

The potential for full assimilation of the Chinese medical students is indicated in item number 4 by the large number expressing an interest in marrying a Thai woman. To a variety of other questions concerning marriage the students from Chinese families expressed their interest in marrying someone from either ethnic origin. In response to an item questioning their reaction to the marriage of a sibling with a Thai, most of the students from Chinese homes expressed neutral feelings, many indicated pleased reactions but almost none thought they would be displeased.

Students from Chinese families tend to be less interested than the Thai elites in sending any sons they might rear to a temple for ordination and temporary stay as a Theravada Buddhist monk. Yet the differences between students of Thai and Chinese origin in the extent of this form of religious commitment seem not so great. On a variety of other items concerning religious practices the differences were even less.

The students of Chinese origin in Table 3 are only those who spoke Chinese with their parents. In the majority of these homes one or both of the parents were born in China and are quite unlikely to be much acculturated toward the Thai manner of behavior. The responses of the other Chinese students, who spoke Thai with their parents, to the same questionnaire items summarized in Tables 2 and 3 tended to manifest a greater degree of general identification with the Thai.

Table 4. Occupational Class of Fathers of Male Medical Students By Ethnicity of Chinese Ancestors (1966 Survey)

Class	Both Parents Ethnic Chinese	One Parent Ethnic Chinese	One of More Grandparents Ethnic Chinese
Employers and Executives	36	28	43
Independents	54	63	41
Middle Management	4	3	9
Independent Workers and Hawkers	2	-	-
Employees	4	6	7
Total	100%	100%	100%
Number of Cases	(235)	(71)	(69)

Though the status origins of the majority of the Chinese are middle level, most of the students are of fathers who enjoy an elite level of power in the workplace. The data in Table 4 describe the class origins of the students and are relevant for the third set of hypotheses. By the perspective discussed earlier, the elites are conceived to include all those with occupational autonomy and are represented in Table 4 by the categories of employers, executives and independents. The category of "independents" is comprised mainly of independent proprietors and includes a few professionals who are self-employed. While most of the merchant fathers of the students operate small businesses, typically family shops, the majority of these shops are prosperous by the standards of Thai society. The clearest finding emerging from Table 4 is that most ethnic mobility into the Thai medical profession does not originate in families where the father is subject to the direct control of superiors at his place of work. The fathers of most of these students are relatively autonomous and many of them exercise control over subordinate workers. An inspection of student questionnaire responses concerning family incomes indicates that most of the fathers are also relatively wealthy.

DISCUSSION

The evidence examined in this study generally tends to support the hypotheses associated with or drawn from the theory of assimilation presented earlier. The medical schools are open to persons of Chinese origin who conform to Thai norms of behavior. Given the highly selective processes which precede entrance into the medical schools, for so many of the students to be from Chinese homes there must be a relatively widespread interest among the Chinese in entering the Thai medical elite (cf. Punyodyana, 1971a:24). This mobility has not been restricted to Chinese of elite status origins. Indeed, the majority of the Chinese are from middle levels of occupational status. The status origins of the students are not widely distributed over the entire dimension of prestige, however. Almost no students are from lower status levels. Even more restricted is the range of occupational classes from which students enter the medical schools.

Proponents of the pluralist interpretation of Chinese ethnicity in Thailand might dismiss the medical students as an exceptional group. Their criticism might argue that not only does medicine comprise only a small number of persons but that it is also an occupation far more desirable to Chinese than are most positions in Thai society. Such an argument is inconsistent with what is the first premise of many pluralist theories, namely, the unyielding attachment to one's cultural identity. If the critical factor is not the durability of ethnic identity but instead the availability of attractive opportunities in the dominant group, then the assimilationist perspective seems more applicable. Pluralism, however, does exist in Thailand. The Chinese population is not speedily assimilating into Thai society. For example, of the marriages of third generation Chinese examined by Coughlin (1960:75) almost none involved intermarriage with Thai. Interpretations which claim the absorption of the Chinese community within a few generations have yet to furnish much evidence of rapid assimilation.

Pluralism and assimilation occur simultaneously among Thailand's Chinese. For large sectors of the Chinese community a course of movement into Thai society is very unlikely, while assimilation has regularly issued from other Chinese subgroups. Explanation of the rate and origins of this mobility depends upon the concept of opportunity. Occupational vacancies appear to be the most significant opportunities affecting the pattern of assimilation in Thailand. Such opportunities require tolerance by the Thai but tolerance is not a sufficient cause of assimilation. The jobs must in the first place exist and highly attractive jobs are, of course, in short supply in the elite and upper middle strata of an agrarian society. These higher levels of Thai society will not be able to absorb within their ranks all of the Chinese during the next two or three generations, if ever.

This study has been directed not to the overall rate of assimilation in contemporary Thailand but instead to the course and rate of movement into one domain among Thai elites, the medical profession. The research findings indicate this mobility is limited in origin mainly to families of middle status businessmen who manage their own firms. A smaller portion of the students are from elite status business families. Few of the students are of fathers who are employees or who have only average income. It appears that most of these students will not move into an occupational class level above that of their fathers in the sense that their fathers already exercise the high level of autonomy and social independence to which the medical students aspire as doctors. In this sense ethnic mobility for these students is not mixed with class mobility. On another dimension of class, that of income, some of these future physicians will earn more than do their shopkeeper fathers. The other students will simply retain the position of their fathers in an elite class level of wealth and property. For most of the students, entrance into the medical schools does involve upward status mobility whether or not this movement between status levels is accompanied by changes in ethnic identification. Both Chinese and Thai systems of stratification in Thailand accord higher status to modern physicians than to most shopowners.

Questionnaire responses concerning child rearing, religion, marriage and other cultural practices indicate no prevailing mode of assimilation. Many students plan to little involve themselves with the Thai beyond the workplace. Many others have already generally identified with Thai values and society. Almost all of the students plan to have their children acquire the practical cultural skills necessary for living among the Thai, including the Thai language and schooling. A sizeable minority do not plan to marry a Thai, however, and express only limited interest in Thai friends, work peers, religious and other practices, and other Thai institutions. Another group of students, approximately half of the students from ethnic Chinese homes, manifest a general commitment to Thai society. As many as 58 percent of the students from middle status Chinese families are interested in marrying a Thai. This identification with the Thai does not imply for most of these students a rejection of their Chinese origins. Most of them would readily continue to work and live among the Chinese as well as the Thai. For example, a majority indicated a preference for a workplace comprised of about equal numbers of Thai and Chinese.

Evidence from other studies suggests that in nonmedical elite sectors of the Thai bureaucracy ethnic mobility from Chinese families originates, in common with the medical students, among middle and elite status business families (Guskin, 1964:17, 18, 22; Maxwell, 1974). The approach taken by this study suggests that similar research be followed to learn if mobility originating in middle and elite status Chinese families is destined for any nonelite strata within Thai society. It may also be questioned as to whether a significant number of persons from lower status Chinese groups are assimilated by the Thai at any level of status.

The future ethnic identification of the students observed in this study depends very much upon the opportunities for continued involvement with Thai culture. Such opportunities include postgraduate training and employment within prestigious government institutions and the availability for marriage of desirable Thai or assimilated Chinese women. Impressionistic observations suggest that such opportunities are plentiful. Thus many of the medical students of Chinese origin, appear potentially assimilable. But future opportunities remain essential to their further assimilation.

For purposes of comparison with interethnic processes in other societies several features of the situation in Thailand must be recognized. There are some physical differences between the Thai and Chinese populations but these differences do not serve as much of a barrier to ethnic assimilation. These physical distinctions are so slight and unevenly distributed throughout the populations that appearance alone is not sufficient to identify the physical ancestry of many persons in the society. To the extent that there are physical differences between the two peoples each population is reported by Coughlin (1960:81) as considering the other as having an attractive appearance. Another set of differences between the Thai and Chinese which seems to pose minimal barriers to assimilation concerns religion. The Thai profess a Buddhism of the Theravada tradition while the Chinese are more influenced in their religious beliefs by Mahayana Buddhism. These are two traditions which have long advocated tolerance of the other. Second and subsequent generations of the Chinese in Thailand seem to readily adopt many of the Thai Buddhist practices and to make use of the Theravada facilities for worship (Skinner, 1957:313; Coughlin, 1960:92).

The specific character of the findings reported in this study must be recognized. One of the most serious failings of Western scholarship concerning the Chinese in Thailand has been the proliferation of unqualified generalizations to all of the Chinese and Thai populations from findings which concern only limited sectors of these populations. Though many sectors of the civilian bureaucracy readily accept persons of Chinese ancestry there are other sectors of the government which are adamant in their current opposition to recruitment from the Chinese community. However many of the Chinese observed in this study appear to be assimilating into Thai society, the theory invoked to interpret these findings suggests that of the total Chinese population few are likely to enter the Thai elite in a given generation and that the total amount of Chinese assimilation into any strata of Thai society is probably proceeding at present at no more than a modest rate.

FOOTNOTES

1. Scores for each student corresponding to each factor were computed by matrix algebra according to the following formula:

$$\text{Factor scores} = ZR^{-1}V$$

   Z = the matrix of standard scores for the thirty-five questionnaire items for each student.
   R^{-1} = the inverse of the correlation matrix for the thirty-five questionnaire items.
   V = the varimax rotated factor matrix.

2. An ethstatus group is defined as a group whose ethnic culture and identity may be distinguished from other cultures and as a group which is distinguished from other ethstatus groups within its own culture by the position of status it occupies. The index of status in this study is made up primarily of measures of occupational prestige. A similar notion, the concept of the "ethclass", is suggested by Gordon (1964:51).

3. For some of these items (no. 1, 4 and 5) not all the possible categories of response are listed. Thus the total percentage of responses for either the Thai or Chinese groups may be less than 100 percent. Some of the statistics represent categories of response which have been combined (on items no. 3 and 5).

REFERENCES

Carnell, Francis G.
1955 "The development of a middle class in Burma, Thailand, and Malaya." In International Institute of Differing Civilizations, Development of a Middle Class in Tropical and Sub-Tropical Countries, Record of the XXIX Session (September). Brussels.

Coughlin, Richard J.
1953 The Chinese in Bangkok, A Study of Cultural Persistence. Unpublished doctoral dissertation, Yale University.
1955 "The Chinese in Bangkok: A commercial-oriented minority." American Sociological Review 20:311-316.
1960 Double Identity. Hong Kong: Hong Kong University Press.

Cowgill, Donald
1968 "Social distance in Thailand." Sociology and Social Research 52:363-376.

Furnivall, J. S.
1939 Netherlands India, A Study of Plural Economy. Cambridge University Press.

Glazer, Nathan, and Patrick Moynihan
1963 Beyond the Melting Pot. Cambridge: Massachusetts Institute of Technology.

Gordon, Milton
1964 Assimilation in American Life. New York: Oxford University Press.

Guskin, Alan E.
1968 Changing Identity: The Assimilation of Chinese in Thailand. Unpublished doctoral dissertation, University of Michigan.

Hanks, Lucien M.
1962 "Merit and power in the Thai social order." American Anthropologist 64:1247-1261.

Maxwell, William Edgar
1971 Modernization and Mobility into the Elites among Medical Students in Thailand. Unpublished doctoral dissertation, University of California, Los Angeles.
1974 "The ethnic identity of male Chinese students in Thai universities." Comparative Education Review (in press).

Park, Robert Ezra
1950 Race and Culture. Glencoe: Free Press.

Phillips, Herbert
1956 "Social structure," in Lauriston Sharp (ed.), Handbook on Thailand. New Haven: Human Relations Area Files.

Punyodyana, Boonsanong
1971a Chinese-Thai Differential Assimilation in Bangkok: An Exploratory Study. Ithaca: Department of Asian Studies, Cornell University.
1971b "Later-life socialization and differential social assimilation of the Chinese in urban Thailand." Social Forces 50:232-238.

Schumrum, Tiparat
1966   The Psychological Assimilation of Second-Generation
        Chinese in Thailand. Unpublished master's thesis,
        Chulalongkorn University.

Shibutani, Tamotsu, and Kian M. Kwan
1965   Ethnic Stratification. New York: Macmillan.

Skinner, George William
1957   Chinese Society in Thailand: an Analytical History.
        New York: Cornell University Press.
1958   Leadership and Power in the Chinese Community in
        Thailand. Ithaca: Cornell University Press.
1964   "The Thailand Chinese: assimilation in a changing
        society." Asia 2:80-92.

Smythe, Hugh M.
1964   "Thailand minority groups." Phylon 25:280-287.

Wongswadiwat, Jirawat
1973   The Psychological Assimilation of Chinese University
        Students in Thailand. Unpublished doctoral
        dissertation, University of Illinois.

12

ETHNIC SELF-PERCEPTION AND POLITICAL ACTION:
The Papuans of Indonesian West New Guinea

JUSTUS M. VAN DER KROEF
State College of New York at Brockport

ABSTRACT

The 750,000 Papuans of West New Guinea (Irian Barat) constitute a distinct ethnic minority in Indonesia, with their own developing sense of national identity and political aspirations. The scattered, loosely structured pattern of indigenous Papuan societies has interacted with traditional Papuan hostility for the Indonesian, and with the nationalistically oriented character of the final Dutch colonial period in the territory. Papuan hostility to Indonesian rule has erupted, since 1962, in repeated armed uprisings, a stream of refugees into neighboring Eastern New Guinea, and in the agitation of Papuan emigre groups at the United Nations and among the African states. Officially, Indonesia views Papuan hostility as the result of the colonial period and as foreign (i.e. Dutch) inspired.

"I have been born in and for Melanesia and I shall die for Melanesia - One People One Soul - Melanesia for Melanesia, Polynesia for Polynesia, Micronesia for Micronesia, and Indonesia for Indonesia." These slogans are the closing sentences of a report issued at the end of 1971 by a group of Papuans who recently made their way out of Indonesian-controlled West New Guines (or Irian Barat as Indonesians call the territory).[1] Whatever their degree of bathos, the slogans and the report testify to a major unresolved ethnic-political conflict in Indonesia, namely, the anti-Indonesian struggle of some of the Papuan inhabitants of West New Guinea. This conflict, over the years, has repeatedly engaged the concern of the United Nations and of major powers in the Pacific area as well as of private humanitarian and civil rights groups. The National Association for the Advancement of Colored People (NAACP), for example, at its sixty-second congress held in Minneapolis in early July, 1971, adopted a resolution which declared that, in line with its principled opposition to the subjugation of any people, it urged the United Nations to provide all of the 750,000 Papuans of West New Guinea with an opportunity to express themselves freely and fully regarding their relationship with Indonesia. The resolution noted the fraudulent character of the so-called "act of free choice" held under U.N. auspices in West New Guinea in 1969, whereby Indonesian rule - "undesired" by the Papuan inhabitants - was confirmed over the territory. On January 4, 1972, Mr. Roy Wilkins, on behalf of the NAACP, again addressed a letter to the new U.N. Secretary General, Dr. Kurt Waldheim, to take new steps in defense of the rights of the Papuans and to give renewed consideration to the West New Guinea question in the United Nations.[2]

Meanwhile, varied (including official Indonesian) sources testify to continuing Papuan opposition, including armed resistance to Indonesian rule in West New Guinea. In September, 1971, for example, the Indonesian military commander of West New Guinea admitted that armed bands of the so-called "Free Papua Organization" (Organisasi Papua Merdeka-OPM) were creating a "disturbance" in the province, and noted the difficulty of dealing with these bands operating in the jungle border area near Australian-controlled Eastern New Guinea. At about the same time a Papuan officer in the Indonesian army in West New Guinea deserted, and began leading a new 200 man anti-Indonesian Papuan resistance movement. The flow of Papuans from West New Guinea, including whole families as well as the educated, such as teachers and medical personnel, who seek asylum across the border in Eastern New Guinea continues unabated. In early March, 1972, an Indonesian Defense department spokesman in Djakarta, while minimizing what he termed Papuan "terrorist" activity in West New Guinea, declared that in the preceding year 48 Papuan "terrorists" had been killed by Indonesian security forces and 133 had surrendered. He also estimated that "180 terrorists" remained, a figure generally considered from six to seven times too small by other (including Papuan emigre) sources.[3]

Particularly significant in recent years has been the growth of what may perhaps be called a "Pan-Papuan" sense of political unity, embracing both Indonesian-held West New Guinea and the two million inhabitants of the Australian administered Eastern half, the Territory of Papua-New Guinea (TPNG). This sentiment is not of recent vintage: in 1960, for example, when West New Guinea was still under Dutch rule, such political organizations there as the Democratic People's Party *(Democratische Volkspartij-*DVP) proposed a political connection between West and East New Guinea, to be called a "Melanesian Federation."[4] Nicolaas Jouwe, a noted earlier Papuan champion of a West New Guinea free from Indonesia, asserts that the future of his homeland lies in the coming together of East and West New Guinea, whose inhabitants "very much desire to be united".[5] In East New Guinea, similar sentiments are voiced, despite a realization of regional differences and even separatism in that territory.[6] As Wegra Kanu, chairman of the representative council of Vanimo, TPNG, has put it: "We were one. But that was before the whites came here. Since the Dutch, British, Australians, and Japanese came the land has been divided."[7] Pan-Papuanism often may seem unrealistic. But it is becoming a factor in the ethnic political nationalism of the island, and especially of West New Guinea, just the same. One Australian reporter, who visited West New Guinea in March, 1971, quotes the Roman Catholic Archbishop of Merauke, West New Guinea thus: "It's one island . . . If you have trouble in Rabaul (in East New Guinea) we will have trouble here. One island, one people. You can't stop it just by drawing a line on a map."[8] With TPNG steadily acquiring greater political autonomy and, possibly, complete independence in the very near future, Papuan nationalism in a West New Guinea that continues to be controlled by Indonesia is not likely to remain unaffected.

This Papuan nationalism in West New Guinea stresses racial distinctiveness and charges racial discrimination and hostility toward the Papuans on the part of Indonesia. For Jouwe and others in his movement, the "Papuans today" are being oppressed by an alien race, i.e., the Indonesians, and traditional folk Papuan tales known to Papuans from their early years, according to Jouwe, confirm the "many severe problems" which Papuans have had with "yellow-brown skinned people who always come from the direction of the sunset" (i.e. the Indonesians coming from the islands located West of New Guinea island), even before the arrival of the whites.[9] A "master-slave" relationship between the Javanese and Papuans, according to Jouwe, already developed during the pre-Western and pre-colonial history of the Indonesian region, when Indonesia and the rest of Southeast Asia engaged in "a busy slave trade" in which Papuan slaves were "an important commercial object".[10] Papuan nationalists maintain also that historic Indonesian attitudes of contempt for the darker-skinned Papuans of West New Guinea conditioned a split in the development of the Indonesian and Papuan educated elites, respectively, in the present century. In one brief sketch of the rise of Papuan nationalism published shortly before the Dutch agreed to surrender the territory to Indonesian control in 1962, one reads:

> The Nationalist Papuan Movement was started in 1907. The missionaries of the Netherlands Reformed Church soon found that the Papuan students (Johan Ariks and others) at the Seminary of the Protestant Mission at Depok near Jakarta were not liked by the Indonesian students. So the Papuan students were soon transferred to the Seminary at Tobelo on the island of Halma-heira. There, too, they were ragged and derided by the Indonesian students, so that finally the Rev. van Hasselt was compelled to start a Seminary for Papuans, which was opened in 1923 on the island of Mansinam. In 1925 the Seminary was transferred to Miei near Manokwari. Henceforth the Papuans received their training there. Consequently, West Papua is now electing as its leaders Papuans who studied at that Seminary.[11]

Ethnic distinctiveness between West New Guinea's Papuans and the Indonesians (as perceived by Papuans) is also accentuated by Papuan identification with Blacks, e.g. in a Papuan appeal phrased as coming from "the Negroids in the Pacific to the Negroids throughout the World", and in the characterization of New Guinea as "New Africa".[12] In an appeal to the "Organization of African Unity", in Addis Ababa, Ethiopia, Jouwe, on behalf of the "Freedom Committee of West Papua" (A Holland based organization of Papuan émigrés), identified his countrymen as "Papuan Negroes" and as "The Negro People of Western New Guinea", calling on "Brothers and Sisters in Africa" not to allow the extirpation of "a negro nation . . . from the earth."[13]

There is little question that this effort to give the Papuan independence movement a black racial image was actuated by political considerations, i.e., by the hope of arousing sympathy for the Papuan cause among the new African states and black minorities in other countries sensitive to lingering colonialism in the world. Moreover, on purely scientific grounds, it would be difficult to sustain fully the Papuan nationalist argument of the racial distinctiveness of West New Guinea's Papuans and other inhabitants of Indonesia. To be sure, the Papuans of New Guinea are basically Negroid, and in fundamental racial classification different from most Indonesians, who are Mongoloid. Yet, significant physical, anthropological variations prevail among the different Papuan groups. The origin of the Papuans as a whole, particularly as contrasted with New Guines's Negritos, remains a mystery, and distinctively Papuan or Negroid traits are frequently met with in Eastern Indonesia (e.g. on Timor, Flores and the Alor islands). West New Guines's flora and fauna do not yield unequivocal demarcations either, the former showing significant similarities to Indonesia's, the latter being more Melanesian and Australian. Linguistically, one must note first the incredible variety and complexity of the Papuan languages, showing important differences both from the languages of Indonesia and from those of the Australian-Melanesian language group and, secondly, the presence of Papuan

languages in Eastern Indonesia, e.g., in the interior of Timor and in Northern Halmaheira. Indonesian government spokesmen have emphasized, too, the similarity of certain aspects of customary law (such as in land use among Papuan and Indonesian ethnic groups), as well as the fact that Indonesia, quite apart from West New Guinea, is a melting pot of different ethnic segments of humanity and that racial considerations are alien to its concept of nationhood or public policies.[14]

The point is, of course, that it is not whether significant racial differences actually exist but whether they are perceived as existing, especially within a broader matrix of grievances and frustrations that can be readily politicized. So considered, a sense of racial distinctiveness also heightens the Papuan sense of discrimination and humiliation at the hands of Indonesians. According to Dutch anthropological sources, the "sense of superiority with which Indonesians treated Papuans dates from the beginning of their contacts", and the Indonesian expression *Papua bodoh* ("stupid Papua"), in which the adjective's tie to the noun is as indissoluble as that in "damn Yankee" for a Southerner, became only too common.[15] Indonesians deny that any policy significance can be based on such folk expressions, even if true. Still, in 1944, after American forces captured the Northern coast of West New Guinea from the Japanese, the Papuan population reacted by driving out local Indonesian teachers and officials, and by 1957, a Papuan delegation vainly petitioned the Dutch government of West New Guinea to drive out of the territory all inhabitants of Indonesian extraction.[16] The Indonesian government has always regarded such incidents as isolated occurrences, and has pointed to long patterns of intermarriage between East Indonesians and coastal Papuan communities.

But in 1971, the Indonesian government launched an official campaign to "civilize" the Papuan (the so-called *Operasi Koteka* which has as its major objectives (1) the wearing of "decent clothing", particularly pants and dresses, among Papuans, especially among those in the undeveloped interior of West New Guinea, and (2) bringing the Papuans "closer to social, economic, cultural and political progress" and "to the same level with that of their brothers in other parts of Indonesia."[17] The official Indonesian news agency, Antara, reported from Djakarta on December 9, 1971, that President Suharto had "symbolically handed over 800,000 pieces of clothing" to the West Irian government for distribution among the Papuans. Suharto, according to the same Antara report, also said on this occasion that "long term plans will persuade" the more isolated Papuans to leave their homes and settle instead in coastal areas or along rivers. However well intended, all these new campaigns designed officially to "civilize" the Papuan could not but re-enforce unfortunate Indonesian assumptions and stereotypes about Papuan backwardness. To Papuan nationalists, these schemes have become as repugnant as Indonesian President Suharto's proposal, at the close of 1969, to have some 200,000 Papuan children raised outside their West New Guinea homeland by Indonesian "foster" parents in order to facilitate the childrens' "Indonesianisation". The proposal created much adverse public comment, even in Indonesia, and subsequently Antara reported that Suharto had been "misunderstood". What Suharto really had had in mind, it was said, was to collect money for the education of Papuan children who would remain in their home territory. Little has come of this proposal, however. Meanwhile, Papuan nationalists today stress the isolated integrity of traditional Papuan societies, which, even though they have not changed "since the stone age", are said to reflect native Papuan wishes. As Jouwe puts it: "They (the Papuans) believe that the world in which they live is the most beautiful; that elsewhere no such beautiful world is to be found." (Nicolaas Jouwe, *De Stem van de Papoea's* Amsterdam, Uitgeverij C. de Boer, 1952, p. 12)

The real or imaginary Papuan humiliations among modern educated or nationalistic Papuans are also frequently related to contrasting Papuan experiences with the Dutch and other whites on the one hand, and with Indonesians on the other.[18] For example, in the initial expansion of Dutch missionary contacts with the Papuans, especially in the present century, Indonesians were frequently employed as teachers. These Indonesians became, in effect, intermediaries between the Papuans and the few Netherlanders in the New Guinea territory. The latter often had much less direct or continuous contact with the Papuans, with a correspondingly relative infrequency of conflict situations. Indirect rule, i.e., extensive use of indigenous nobility and headmen, had always been a cardinal principle of Dutch colonial policy in the rest of Indonesia. Even after they lost their Indonesian colonial possessions at the close of the Indonesian Revolution (1945-49), retaining only West New Guinea, the Dutch followed indirect administrative policies as much as possible in West New Guinea, developing and utilizing Papuan intermediaries. Unlike the Indonesians, the Dutch also derived certain benefits from Papuan traditions, such as the Papuan concept, typified in some legends, of having had white ancestors, as a result of which "one could expect from the whites not bad, but on the contrary many good things."[19]

The question as to what extent Papuan nationalist writers today rationalize these Papuan traditions to serve their own current political objectives becomes all the more acute when one considers that white, or more specifically Dutch, interest in West New Guinea came late and rather haphazardly, when compared to such interest in neighboring Indonesia. Indeed, it was not until after Holland had lost the rest of its Indonesian possessions, by the close of 1949, that the development of this "Forgotten Earth", as one Dutch colonial administrator termed West New Guinea,[20] was significantly taken in hand. Despite repeated and unsuccessful Indonesian attempts to get the United Nations to bring West New Guinea under Djakarta's sway, and notwithstanding a steadily mounting tension between Indonesia and Holland over the latter's continuing control over the disputed territory, the Dutch proceeded with an accelerating policy of modernization and controlled political emancipation avowedly directed toward giving the Papuans "their free choice about their future place in the world".[21]

Whatever the Dutch motives in doing so, and in ignoring or countering considerable Indonesian legal and political claims on West New Guinea, there is no question that, within the period of little more than a decade (1950-60), Papuan political self-consciousness and a sense of nationhood had significantly begun to develop. Whether the Dutch acted out of spite over the loss of their erstwhile colonial Indonesian possessions, or out of a genuine moral or political conviction that West New Guinea's future lay outside the orbit of Indonesian sovereignty, the net effect of Dutch policy was to encourage the Papuans, rightly or wrongly, to think of their future in essentially nationalistic and, certainly, in anti-Indonesian terms. This effect was achieved and, indeed, was even permitted to be accentuated, in the face of a mounting Indonesian bellicosity and determination to obtain control of West New Guinea. And within the Netherlands itself, well before the debacle of Dutch policy in 1962 and the agreement to transfer the territory to Indonesian control, there were voices asking whether Dutch emphasis on Papuan "self determination" was not in effect a mask for a covert form of Dutch "colonialism".[22]

Then, too, it might well be asked whether the original (i.e. pre-1945) pattern of Papuan-Indonesian hostility (with all its stereotyped imagery) was, in fact, any more intense than that prevailing among other diverse ethnic groups of the Indonesian archipelago. To this one must, however, add the query whether Dutch policy in West New Guinea did not, consciously or otherwise, unnecessarily deepen these antagonisms. In their historic interaction, many peoples of the Indonesian archipelago have developed certain ethnic stereotypes. (From his own earliest youth in Indonesia the present writer was exposed to such stereotypes, e.g., the Central Javanese being "lazy" or "refined", depending on the perceiver, the West Sumatran Minangkabau "restless" and "rootless", or "enterprising" and "resourceful", the Madurese "loudly bellicose" or "keen to defend his honor", the colonial Netherlander "coarse" and "aggressive", or an "energetic empire builder", and so on.) All observers are agreed that a segment of the Papuan population, particularly in the Radja Ampat area where Indonesian influences have historically been strong and intermarriages frequent, has always sympathized with the Indonesian national cause. Did Dutch policy not deliberately widen ethnic cleavages in West New Guinea, cleavages which elsewhere in Indonesia, under the influence of a successful nationalism and revolution, were notably beginning to narrow?

Any answer to this question must take into account the nature of Papuan indigenous society and the character of Dutch policy. It requires little elaboration to note, first of all that West New Guinea, even now, is among the least developed and, internally, least accessible and most isolated regions in the world. Of a total population of about 700,000 in 1961, the Dutch claimed only some 487,000 souls in the territory to be under *bestuursinvloed* or "government influence" (a rise from 359,600 in 1957).[23] For the remainder (i.e. nearly 30% of all inhabitants) the writ of administration, after a decade-long intensified development effort by the Dutch, remained all but unknown or, at best, a very fleeting, sometime thing. Since the Indonesian take-over of West New Guinea in 1962-63, there has been only a slow change. Some knowledgeable Indonesian sources today, in conversation with the author, claim no more than half of the estimated 750,000 Papuan population to be under direct administrative control, and point to Indonesian administrative neglect in the 1963-66 period and to limited financial resources as the reasons.[24]

Secondly, stress must be placed on the extremely scattered and fragmented character of Papuan society, which is typically village centered, but in which larger kinship or political-regional linkages, though not unknown, are undeveloped and functionally vague. The "absence of group formation, which makes possible the existence of larger political units than the village" is a "striking characteristic" of Papuan social life.[25] Moreover, of the 2,300 villages registered by the government, 60 percent have less than 100 inhabitants.[26] Anthropological and other observers have frequently commented not just on the weakness or, indeed, the absence of larger, overcapping and integrating social mechanisms in this isolated and fragmented Papuan existence, but also on the pervasive Papuan aversion to such integrating authority and on the strong Papuan tendency to simply move away with a small group whenever circumstances warrant, and to take up residence elsewhere in mountain valley or forest.[27]

These typical Papuan social characteristics contributed to the fact that as of the founding of the first permanent Dutch administrative posts (occurring not until 1898 in Manokwari and Fak Fak), West New Guinea was frequently exempted from the colonial laws and regulations applicable elsewhere in the Indonesian archipelago.[28] These exemptions further accentuated Indonesian-Papuan differences. The administrative and modernizing machinery in West New Guinea, having to be adapted to the Papuan geographic and social terrain, emphasized local integrative and development efforts which, presumably, pointed only gradually toward some kind of regional (and ultimately central) territorial unification. There can be little question of the acceleration of the development efforts in all fields of public service: by 1959, for example, the Dutch claimed the existence of 980 schools in the territory with more than 47,000 pupils, representing 12% of the total Papuan population then under direct administration.[29] Territorial budgets grew steadily (from about $10 million in 1950 to about $38 million in 1960), and of the more than 8,800 government officials in West New Guinea in 1961, about 4,950 were native Papuans, generally in lower and intermediate positions, to be sure, but evidence just the same of a steady political emancipation.[30] Creation throughout much of the territory (from the mid-fifties onward) of local urban and regional representative councils with elected and appointed memberships reflected central Dutch administrative policy concern for the growth of local "territorial communities, which can take care of their own interests" and manage "their own household."[31]

Despite this decentralized administrative focus, however, on April 5, 1961, the so-called "New Guinea Council", the territory's embryonic parliament, was opened, with a predominantly Papuan elected and appointed membership. Created in the face of an accelerating Indonesian campaign of so-called "confrontation" to acquire control of West New Guinea - a campaign accompanied by small scale Indonesian guerrilla infiltration into the territory, and an intensive Indonesian press campaign abroad designed to create the impression of the imminent outbreak of total war in the region - the New Guinea Council itself acted as an important catalyst for the political aspirations of the small but growing Papuan elite of teachers, petty officials, and a few entrepreneurs, and concurrently, on the acceleration of an unmistakable Papuan nationalism. Tacitly, and sometimes openly, Dutch policy encouraged this nationalism, that is, it encouraged a political process which, apart from its questionable wisdom in the face of bitter Indonesian opposition, also to a significant degree ran counter to the rest of its regionally focussed, essentially decentralized, territorial development effort. For by 1961, as has already been indicated, nearly a third of the territory's population was still outside regular governmental supervision.

The net effect of all this was to hasten the process of social bifurcation and uneven modernization in Papuan society, with a small elite of a few thousand being encouraged to experiment with political instruments totally outside the scope of knowledge of tens of thousands of others. Such a condition is, of course, hardly unique to West New Guinea. The point to be made, however, is that in reacting to Indonesian claims on the territory, Dutch policy not only greatly accentuated patterns of social and ideological distance between the Papuan elite and the mass but also, despite pronouncements on behalf of Papuan self-determination as the desired Dutch policy goal, in effect conditioned developing Papuan aspirations away from unity with the rest of Indonesia. In some urban, coastal pockets pro-Indonesian sentiments remained, not because of but despite this Dutch "free choice" policy principle. In the context of Dutch policy reactions to mounting Indonesian hostilities, Papuan development also was limited in an economic sense. While the participating indigenous

entrepreneurial groups in such fields as cash crop agriculture, shipping, and retail trade in West New Guinea were certainly significant, it was the public sector of the economy which was, and with the possible exception of petroleum production, remained the most dynamic, and in which investments continued to be the most significant by far.[32] The political controversy surrounding the territory's future greatly impeded private corporate investment. The consequence of this, in turn, was to make the Papuan elite in effect an adjunct of the Dutch colonial government structure and, therefore, obviously sensitive to its interests and policy preferences, particularly in relation to Indonesian claims on the territory.

While an analysis of these Indonesian claims falls outside the scope of these pages, it can be stressed here, in passing, that the basis of these claims is essentially, though not exclusively, an international legal one. The Republic of Indonesia, as a sovereign state, is viewed as the legitimate successor to the Kingdom of the Netherlands in its control over all the territory of what once was known as the Dutch East Indies. Exemption of the territory of West New Guinea (at the Sovereignty Transfer Conference in December, 1949, in The Hague) from being incorporated in the territory of the Indonesian Republic was viewed by the Indonesians as but a temporary political arrangement which did not absolve the Dutch from seeking ways to transfer the West New Guinea region to Indonesian authority in the future. Instead, the Dutch kept West New Guinea and, Indonesians charge, rebuffed all attempts at adjudication of the dispute. Needless to say, the Dutch contested this interpretation of the provisions of the 1949 Sovereignty Transfer Conference. Whatever the international legal questions involved, however, there is no denying that, in view of the Indonesian claims, the Dutch policy of emancipation in West New Guinea placed Papuan development under some unusually severe limitations.

And yet, these particular limits of its matrix notwithstanding, there could be no doubt by 1960 of the vigorous growth of modern Papuan political consciousness, expressed in part in the mushrooming of Papuan political parties, of various interest groups from trade unions to religious societies, and in the propagation of national Papuan symbols like the territorial flag, and so on. Elsewhere, the origins and programs of some of these Papuan political parties have already been detailed.[33] Suffice it to stress here the remarkable mixture of local and even ethnic-separatist interests with broader territorial or even Papuan "national" concerns in the objectives of these parties. Some of these groups clearly reflected the preponderant interests of certain population groups of the islands in the Geelvink Bay, another of the mountain dwelling Papuans of the Birds' Head Peninsula, yet another was obviously dominated by a traditional aristocracy of Indonesian extraction, while elsewhere other pro-Indonesian political sentiments were still influential. In some areas, even, new cargo cults and millenarian movements could be observed, traditional Papuan defense mechanisms against cultural change and political shock.

A few parties focused almost exclusively on immediate and local concerns (one party platform demanded for example that sugar and rice be sold in markets according to proper weight measurements and not merely in uncovered tins), not a few -- reflecting local missionary influences -- formally espoused religious principles (e.g., endorsing "God's sovereignty" and charity for all); others proclaimed lofty universal desoderata (such as "for peace against violence"), others again defined themselves as anti-Communist, and/or as striving for autonomy or independence in cooperation with the Dutch government (many urged broad propagation of Dutch as the common language), or called for development of foreign capital investment.[34] Despite such seemingly divergent emphases, a Papuan self-perception in terms of what perhaps may simply be called "development mindedness" clearly emerges as a common undertone in these party programs, along with a search for a Papuan national identity, not just anti-Indonesian, but also reaching out beyond the cocoon of Dutch colonialism.

In the organized political activity of the territory before 1962, perhaps no more than forty to fifty thousand Papuans were involved through these political parties, including in various elections for the local and territorial councils. Beyond them were not only the mass of inhabitants in directly administered areas (and those in irregularly supervised and isolated parts of the country as well), but also the Papuans of the sister territory of TPNG in the East, where an even more rapid political emancipation was underway. In and out of the U.N., Australia was one of Holland's staunchest allies in the crisis of Indonesia's "confrontation" policy to win control of West New Guinea. Through the developing Dutch-Australian administrative cooperation in the island, moreover, the dream of Pan-Papuan unification, and of a "Melanesian Federation", also began to root itself more strongly in the elite's political consciousness.[35]

Yet within a short period of a few weeks during the first half of 1962, the dreams of Papuan parties in West New Guinea were shattered, and the vision of Pan-Papuan unity particularly appeared doomed. Thanks largely to the pressures of the Kennedy administration, which was concerned to defuse the rising militancy of the Indonesian "confrontation" campaign and its destabilizing effects on Indonesian politics and the economy, the Dutch, by the middle of August, 1962, had agreed to transfer control over West New Guinea to Indonesia, after a brief United Nations interim administration.[36] The agreement provided that, before the end of 1969, Indonesia would give the Papuans an opportunity to participate in an "act of free choice" (the term "plebiscite" was carefully avoided) in order to determine whether they wished to remain with Indonesia. There were sharp Papuan protests and demonstrations against the agreement and, particularly, against the role which the U.S. had had in arriving at it (one common Papuan protest slogan, at this time reflecting a belief in an alleged American "sell out" of Papuan wishes, was "How many dollars for a Papuan, Yankee?"). Papuan leaders were particularly incensed that the decision to surrender the territory to Indonesian control had been reached with apparent total disregard for various resolutions adopted by the New Guinea Council in the previous months demanding Papuan self-government by 1970, and Papuan participation in any Dutch-Indonesian discussions about the future of the territory.

Scores of Papuan nationalist leaders subsequently left West New Guinea for the Netherlands, there to carry on their independence struggle, while over the following years hundreds of other Papuans sought refuge across the border in TPNG. These Papuans Indonesians were apt to characterize as "Dutch stooges" and "puppets". Also in violation of the West New Guinea transfer agreement, Indonesian authorities, acting on the basis of military and other emergency regulations prevailing throughout the rest of Indonesia, severely limited the rights of free speech, assembly and movement of the Papuans and, concomitantly, visits to the territory by foreign observers became more difficult. Still, enough information concerning conditions in West New Guinea trickled out to give something of an impression of the state of Papuan opinion and

reaction to Indonesian rule. One Australian journalist, a specialist on New Guinea, who visited West New Guinea early in 1963 -- as Indonesians were taking over control from the United Nations' Temporary Executive Authority (UNTEA) -- noted how some in the Papuan elite, with a sense of betrayal, now sought to ingratiate themselves with the Indonesians in their rush for jobs and patronage. But then he went on to note:[37]

> Nevertheless while leading Papuans, with the exception of a relative handful have set their hopes on Djakarta, the towns and urban villages around Hollandia, Manokwari, Biak, Sorong and Merauke remain far more divided than either UNTEA or the Indonesians admit. There are many incidents most of which concern either the Indonesian or Papuan flag ... The Papuan flag - a particularly forlorn symbol of unattained national sovereignty even in today's world - was given to West Papuans about 18 months ago. It became for a surprising number of them an emblem of unity to which, only half comprehending the notions of statehood and the world about them, they rallied. Many youths wear the Papuan flag sewn to the back of their multicolored sweaters or shirts. Some carry it on a stick or tacked to their bicycles. Others carry it in their pockets and whip it out daringly when they feel themselves unobserved.

About a year later, a noted Australian academic specialist on Indonesia also visited West New Guinea. After commenting on the occasionally exaggerated claims of some anti-Indonesian Papuans, he went on to observe:[38]

> I was jolted nevertheless. The Papuan nationalism of West New Guinea was clearly a more genuine and full blooded thing than I had expected. Every subsequent conversation with Papuans confirmed that conclusion.

Still, a year later (by May, 1965), one visiting British journalist had this impression of the character and effects of the Indonesian administration on the Papuans:[39]

> In the two years since the United Nations handed over administrative control of West New Guinea, Indonesian rule there has drifted, perhaps subconsciously, into something very like nineteenth century colonialism ...
>
> If one remarks on the absence of political rights and administrative responsibility for the West Irian people the classical colonial riposte come pat: they are uneducated, inexperienced, immature. And the Dutch, of course, are to blame ...
>
> There were signs that the local population is shrinking protectively from contact with their new Indonesian administrators. Around the main towns, fields that were once cultivated have now gone back to kunai grass and weeds, as the West Irianese continue to retreat to their jungle villages. Occasional indiscretions support rumors of growing West Irian resentment and sterner reprisals. Students have been forbidden to discuss, even among themselves, Indonesia's decision to abandon its agreement to allow the West Irian "an act of self determination" before the end of 1969.

Over the years, the appeals of Papuan nationalism in West New Guinea remained remarkably strong. By September, 1968, yet another Australian journalist, visiting the territory, commented that although there was not likely to be any foreign support for Papuan nationalism:[40]

Yet the lure of independence is nonetheless compelling. The "Free Papua Movement" clandestinely distributes its propaganda calling for "one people one soul" (One Papuan clergyman informant) also believes that a "United West Papua" movement for independence from Indonesia has widespread support.

Even in the Djakarta press, doubts were beginning to be voiced over Djakarta's legitimacy in West New Guinea. In September, 1967, for example, more than a year after the collapse of the Sukarno regime and the subsequent return of a modicum of press freedom in Indonesia, one leading Djakarta daily editorially noted that the conduct of Indonesian officials in West New Guinea reportedly had become "more repugnant" to the Papuans than that of the erstwhile Dutch "colonial rulers", and that "many people" returning from the territory were "pessimistic" that "should fair chances be given under the present conditions the local people would choose to remain in the Republic."[41]

The character of Indonesian policies, from the take-over in 1962 until belated improvements began to be instituted in 1967 after Sukarno's removal from office, appeared to be such as to aggravate unassuaged Papuan nationalist grievances. Economic development projects, initiated earlier, now stagnated, administrative controls soon broke down due to lack of financial and manpower resources, imports dwindled to a trickle, and "urban Papuans used to artificially high wages under the Dutch were forced to return to subsistence gardening in order to get enough food to eat."[42] On paper, Papuan education was intensified, and even a territorial university was opened, but in reality, resources remained all but unallocated, Indonesian teachers were very slow in making their appearance, and the university's reputation soon dropped to among the lowest in Indonesia. Worst, perhaps, was the heavy hand of the Indonesian territorial administration, much of it under the control of the Indonesian military. Looting of shops, and brutalization and harassment of Papuans, became only too common. As one Australian specialist put it: "The Indonesian Army carried out numerous beatings, shootings and goadings in order to ensure a passive population."[43] Though some of the major Indonesian political parties eventually opened branches in West New Guinea, local and territorial councils (the majority nationalists replaced by compliant Indonesian government appointees) continued to function, and while some token recruitment of Papuans in the territorial civil service took place, Papuan political assimilation with Indonesia was very limited, in part because of the strength of anti-Indonesian Papuan nationalism, and also because of the essentially military character of a suspicious Indonesian administration. E.J. Bonay, the first Indonesian-appointed Papuan territorial governor, soon found himself behind bars.

Already toward the close of 1962, during the UNTEA interim administration, there had been fighting between anti-Indonesian students and pro-Indonesian Papuan groups supported by Indonesian military.[44] In subsequent months, tensions heightened and conflicts increased, and in December, 1964, it came to sharp clashes between rebelling Papuan police and Indonesian military in the town of Manokwari.[45] It was not until May, 1965, however, that Indonesian authorities acknowledged the existence of an organized Papuan resistance movement, now generally called the *Organisasi Papua Merdeka* ("Free Papuan Organization" - OPM), operating initially in the Ajamaru region of the Bird's Head peninsula, but gradually spreading and developing a number of parallel organizations.[46] The fall of Sukarno in the wake of domestic Indonesian public

reaction to the abortive coup attempt in Djakarta and parts of Java on September 30, 1965, did not effect the mushrooming Papuan resistance movement in the slightest, except perhaps to provide increased press coverage of it. In November, 1966, for example, the Djakarta daily *Kompas*, published a series of articles by a reporter sent to West New Guinea, which emphasized that conditions were becoming critical in the territory. "Fights often break out between local people and government officials and it is not surprising that anti-Indonesian feelings are raging among the native inhabitants", *Kompas* declared.[47]

Meanwhile, delegations of Papuans began arriving in Djakarta to complain about Indonesian policies in the territory. Papuan spokesmen publicly excoriated allegedly rapacious Indonesian officials who were going to West New Guinea "for business and not to build the territory", as one of them put it.[48] By the beginning of January, 1967, new serious disturbances began to erupt in the town of Manokwari and other parts of the Bird's Head peninsula, disturbances lasting for several months. The territorial commander of Indonesian military forces in West New Guinea subsequently admitted that the Indonesian air force had strafed the town of Manokwari, killing at least 40 Papuans (other sources put the number of dead much higher).[49] The Indonesian military had acted in the face of a widening Papuan insurgency, centering around the proclamation of a "State of Free Papua" in Manokwari. Again and again, in appeals addressed to then United Nations Secretary General U Thant, Nicholaas Jouwe and other members of the Holland based "Freedom Committee of West Papua" charged Indonesian military in West New Guinea with mass killing and with severe maltreatment of Papuans.[50] Such appeals proved in vain, however, though at the same time their appeals were accentuated by a steady stream of Papuan refugees crossing the border into TPNG.

The new Suharto government in Indonesia countered all Papuan charges by pointing to the alleged Dutch colonial complexion of the Papuan emigre movement, while the U.S., among other Western powers, proved most reluctant to take to task a government which was proving so much friendlier to American security and financial interests than the preceding Sukarno regime. The American press kept a virtually total silence on the fighting in West New Guinea, though Asian media did not. The Netherlands, where the long dispute with Indonesia over control of West New Guinea had left bitter memories, and where similarly great economic advantages were expected from future dealings with the new Suharto government, also declined officially to take up the cudgels on behalf of the Papuan cause. Then, too, Suharto and his ministers in effect admitted that Indonesian policy in West New Guinea during the closing years of the Sukarno era had left much to be desired and promised to make amends, while urging the Papuans to help the local authorities.[51] Some prominent Papuan political prisoners were set free, limited quantities of imports into the territory were permitted, and ambitious development schemes to be funded by the Dutch and the United Nations were announced. On the central issue, however, i.e., a secession of West New Guinea from Indonesia, Suharto proved as implacable as his predecessor. Foreign observers agreed that the promised domestic stabilization efforts of the Suharto regime would come to nought if that regime's left flank were turned by a promise of Papuan independence.

Yet, the Papuan resistance refused to die, while from within the territory itself, as well as from Papuan emigre circles, reports of clashes in West New Guinea and Papuan appeals for independence continued to be relayed to the world. Papuan nationalist interests now focussed on the so-called "act of choice" which, under United Nations supervision, Indonesia had promised to grant the Papuans before the end of 1969, according to the terms of the 1962 Dutch-Indonesian transfer agreement. Initially, Indonesian spokesmen, from Sukarno on down, had declared such an act of self-determination to be unnecessary. But though the Suharto government subsequently agreed to implement the promised self-determination provisions, Indonesian spokesmen also made it plain that they would not countenance any Papuan secession.[52] Since the 1962 transfer agreement on West New Guinea left to Indonesia the method by which the "act of free choice" was to be carried out, there seemed little doubt that Indonesia would proceed to devise plebiscitary procedures in such a way that an outcome acceptable to Djakarta would inevitably result.

This, in fact, did occur. In July and August, 1969, a complicated, multi-tiered election process in each of the eight *kabupaten* or districts in West New Guinea resulted in a reportedly "Unanimous" Papuan vote to remain with Indonesia. On November 19, 1969, the U.N. General Assembly took note of and, in effect, endorsed a Dutch-Indonesian resolution accepting the report on the "act of free choice" made by the U.N. representative in West New Guinea, the Bolivian diplomat Dr. Fernando Ortiz Sanz. There were 30 abstentions in the U.N. Assembly voting, however, mostly coming from the African states where there were strong reservations about the fairness of the "act of free choice". A Ghanaian resolution, giving the Papuans another opportunity at an "act of free choice" by 1975, was defeated. In his report, Ortiz Sanz declared that despite his "constant efforts" the Indonesian government had not fully implemented the article in the 1962 transfer agreement providing the Papuans with freedom of speech, of movement and of assembly, and he added that "the Indonesian administration exercised at all times a tight political control over the population."[53]

Foreign journalists in West New Guinea amply documented Indonesian bribery and coercion of Papuans in the "act of free choice". Brian May, of Agence France Presse, noted that, due to tribal differences, the Papuans might well be unable to govern themselves; even so, he declared that "All foreigners whom I have met in West Irian are unanimous that if the choice were really free it would go against Indonesia."[54] Hugh Lunn, of the *Sydney Morning Herald*, reported from Manokwari in early August, 1969, on the "desperate fights" between young Papuans crying "alone, alone" (i.e. "independence"), with "baton wielding Indonesian and Papuan police" following the "act of free choice."[55] The present writer knows of no non-Indonesian and non-Papuan observer (whether journalist or U.N. official) of the self determination process in West New Guinea who has publicly concluded other than that, in the words of correspondent Geoffry Hutton, the process was "A shoddy script for the 'Act of No Choice.'"[56]

On June 27, 1969, the House of Assembly of TPNG passed a resolution expressing its "deep concern" over Indonesian policies in West New Guinea, as well as "deep dismay" over the U.N.'s failure to ascertain properly Papuan political wishes in West New Guinea. This resolution probably reflected earlier TPNG press comments that the members of the TPNY House of Assembly whould champion the cause of "their brothers, the West Irianese . . . ".[57] Moreover, in the weeks before and during the "act of free choice", there had been anti-Indonesian Papuan demonstrations in Djajapura, West New Guinea's capital, despite the rigid Indonesian military controls, as well

as several new Papuan uprisings (e.g., in Enarotali and Moanamani, in the Central Highlands of the territory), and armed clashed with Indonesian troops.[58] A Papuan underground resistance network, with base camps close to the TPNG border, also had begun to develop rapidly. One Australian observer reported:[59]

> "The underground West Papua freedom flag flies occasionally from jungle clearings and men carrying sticks for rifles perform military drill in preparation for an anticipated guerrilla campaign."

Since the "act of free choice", according to Papuan emigre circles, the Indonesians have continued to arrest prominent Papuan resistance figures. And while on the one hand the Indonesians have reported that groups of Papuan guerrilla fighters have surrendered, other resistance groups are taking the field, as was noted earlier at the beginning of this article.[60] Even now, groups of Papuan refugees also keep crossing into TPNG, where a careful examination of their bonafides has resulted in grants of political asylum for some, while other refugees have been persuaded to return to West Irian. The Australian government, it might be emphasized, has been most anxious to avoid a rupture with Djakarta over the refugee question.

It is quite clear that, since the "act of free choice", Indonesia has intensified her development efforts in the West New Guinea territory. The question arises whether this development is occuring fast enough to undercut Papuan frustrations. Specialists of the United Nations Development Program (UNDP) and of the United Nations Fund for the Development of West Irian (FUNDWI), fortified by an initial Dutch grant of U.S. $30 million, have assisted in the improvement of coastal shipping, air communications, and public transportation. A pilot saw mill project at Djajapura, a cattle project at Mindiptana, surveys for a new rubber industry and for the commercial export of indigenous artifacta all show long term promise. In these projects, the Indonesians are matching FUNDWI dollars on a two for one basis.

There is also some evidence that Papuan hostilities toward the Indonesians are, to a degree, beginning to lessen, but younger Papuans especially are still bitter over the undemocratic procedures of the "act of free choice".[61] It is these younger Papuans who, it may be noted *inter alia*, continue to flock to the banner of the West Papua nationalist resistance movement. The large number of unemployed or semi-employed Papuan youths, usually with primary or even secondary education, is becoming an increasing problem, the more so because Indonesian spokesmen in recent months have admitted that the development program for the territory is being severely delayed because of persisting transport problems, shortages of skilled labor, cumbersome financial procedures, lack of construction materials, and so on.[62] Meanwhile, Indonesian government reports speak of the steady growth in the number of Papuans enrolled in schools and of the widening of the public services to the Papuan citizenry,[63] both developments that are likely to heighten Papuan expectations and - in light of the sluggish pattern of economic growth - existing Papuan grievances. These grievances are further accentuated by the heavy influx of "Thousands upon thousands of sharpwitted Sulawesians from Makassar" into the territory, who, having seized control over much of the retail and other commercial life in some major urban areas (with the apparent encouragement of the Indonesian authorities), are beginning to cause new patterns of ethnic conflict. One reporter already commented last year:[64]

> "Some Indonesian government officials talked of 100,000 non-Irianese eventually arriving in the

province, using the paternalistic argument that the local people were unwilling to work or unable to learn how. But glaringly wherever I enquired I could find no evidence that efforts were being made to educate local people in the basics of business practice, thus enabling them to share in the economic development of the province ... So far Irianese anger has manifested itself physically only in market place disturbances--It is hard to believe that Djakarta government ... should be pursuing such an obviously incendiary policy."

Moreover, the steady influx of Makassarese and East Indonesians has thus far not hastened a general "Indonesianisation" process - if this was, in fact, Djakarta's intention - but rather has further accentuated the ethnic parameters and sharpened Papuan-Indonesian tensions. The "melting pot" strategy of the Suharto regime is not working, certainly not among the urban Papuan young. All things being equal, it seems but a matter of time before clashes between Papuan youth, and the Makassarese and other Indonesian groups will erupt into serious disturbances.

Still, one hastens to add that it has never been possible to consider Papuan aspirations in isolation. The critical significance of West New Guinea in contemporary Indonesian nationalism - legacy of the revolutionary struggle against the Dutch—remains, and it must be considered in any realistic assessment of West New Guinea's political future. In this connection, one cannot fail to note curious ambivalences in Indonesian attitudes. There is no denying the paternalistic, if not patronizing, attitude of Indonesian officialdom (and much of the Indonesian public) toward the supposedly backward Papuan, who must now be "civilized" by special Dajakarta policies (e.g., the previously noted *Operasi Koteka*).

On the other hand, the "liberation" of West New Guinea and of "our Papuan brothers" from Dutch colonialism will likely remain also a major chapter in the Indonesian nationalist mystique. In this mystique the Javanese, Makassarese and the Papuan, as well as the other ethnic groups of the Indonesian archipelago, are perceived as struggling in fraternal concord and equalitarianism toward a glorious, post-colonial, common destiny. Foreign criticism in the United Nations and in the press of Indonesian policies in West New Guinea, particularly in connection with the "act of free choice," was bitterly excoriated in some of the Indonesian media. Ortiz Sanz, for example, was accused of caring only about "the dreams of a few foreign stooges" in West New Guinea, and the role of such African countries as Dahomey and Togo in the U.N. debate on West New Guinea was dismissed as "ridiculous" by the Indonesian press.[65] Indonesia has also given prominence to a handful of prominent Papuans who have criticized Ortiz Sanz and defended the "act of free choice" and other Indonesian policies.[66]

Yet, as was noted earlier, there have also been serious misgivings in the Indonesian press and public opinion about the legitimacy of the Indonesian presence in West Irian, particularly in the face of rising Papuans nationalism. More than one Indonesian paper, in fact, has described the "act of free choice" as "a sham". deplored the obvious lack of free speech for the West New Guinea Papuans, or noted that the eruption of anti-Indonesian Papuan resistance was "due partly, or perhaps greatly, to our own errors and negligence".[67]

The dilemma of Papuan-Indonesian relations will, doubtlessly, deepen still further because of the future interaction of the two halves of New Guinea island, one of which, TPNG, is now steadily moving toward autonomy and political independence, while the other half, West Irian, remains under Indonesian - and from the Papuan nationalist point of view, under "colonial" - control. Whether, as has been asserted, the Papuans from TPNG "After achieving their independence ... will not remain indifferent to the calls for help across the border if West Papua were to remain under Indonesian occupation", remains of course to be seen.[68] There is no question of the strong, continuing sympathy for the West New Guinea population in many TPNG political circles, and some interest in a political unification of the whole island.[69] There is also a significant tribal and regional separatism in TPNG distrustful of a single independent TPNG state, although the observation that "Centrifugal tendencies, in fact, seem stronger than integrating forces" does seem to do less than justice to the Papuan sense of nationalism that is also steadily advancing in Eastern New Guinea.[70]

One factor that is likely to spur both anti-Indonesian sentiments among the Papuans of the Western half of the island, and demands for unification, is the comparatively more advanced level of economic development and the better employment opportunities in the Eastern half. As one veteran student of New Guinea has put it, "It would be unwise to underestimate over the coming decade the effect of (East) New Guinea's relative affluence on the West Irianese". Indeed, stories of such affluence may well have been an added or even principal inducement for West Irianese to cross the border to the East.[71] The allegedly "glaring differences" in living standards, public services, and other amenities between West and East are not likely to be overcome soon. Certainly, as far as the Papuans of the Western half are concerned, these differences are likely to accentuate a political amalgamation process.[72] On the other hand, in the more prosperous East, they may be a barrier to amalgamation.

In conclusion, it seems idle to speculate whether West New Guinea and the nationalist movement of its Papuan inhabitants would ever have become problems had the territory been transferred, in 1949, along with the rest of the former Dutch East Indies, to the government of the new Indonesian Republic. For if the Papuans and their nationalism might once have been considered casualties of a delayed "decolonization", today they are fast becoming casualties of a new unwanted "recolonization" (by Indonesia). The ethnic suspicions and animosities between Papuans and other Indonesians might well never have reached their present state had it not been for Dutch policy after 1949. The point is, however, that the Papuan's ethnic self-perception today is no longer just focussed on such traditional anti-Indonesian sentiments, but has gone on, not only toward a West New Guinea free from Indonesian control, but also toward a Pan-Papuan or "Melanesian" state, comprising both parts of New Guinea island. The viability of this new ethnic self-image remains to be seen.

FOOTNOTES

1. New Guinean (published by the "Workgroup New Guinea," Wageningen, Netherlands), February, 1972, p. 5.
2. On these NAACP efforts on behalf of the Papuans see the articles "NAACP-Resolutie over Rechten van Papoea's", and "Initiatief van Negerorgnisatie NAACP", both in Zelfbeschikking (Eindhoven, Netherlands), September-October, 1971, p. 3, and January-February, 1972, p. 3 respectively.
3. Antara Daily News Bulletin (Bonn), September 25, 1971 (vol. 23, no. 1285), p. I and March 8, 1972 (vol. 24, no. 1418), p. II; De Volkskrant (Amsterdam), September 20, 1971; Associated Press Dispatch, Port Moresby, Territory of Papua/New Guinea, September 20, 1971; "West Papua", Zelfbeschikking, November-December, 1971.

4. C.S.I.J. Lagerberg, Jaren van Reconstructie, Nieuw Guinea van 1949 tot 1961 (Diss., University of Utrecht; Zvid Nederlandsche Drukkerij, N.V.;'s Hertogenbosch, 1962), p. 187.

5. Nicholaas Jouwe, "Irian Irredenta. Papua's Worden door Vreend Ras Onderdrukt", Zelfbeschikking, January-February, 1972, p. 16.

6. In an interview with me on 1 April, 1969, Dr. John Guise, Speaker of the House of Assembly, TPNG, Port Moresby, declared that in his personal campaigns for a seat in the Legislative Council and the House of Assembly, TPNG, during the past decade he had advocated the political unification of the island of New Guinea, and that he continues to favor the idea.

7. Cited in A. Kamsteeg "Een Triest Verhaal Uit het Gresgebied van Nieuw Guinea", Zelfbeschikking, May-June, 1971, p. 6.

8. David Jenkins, "Irian After Free Choice", The Sydney Morning Herald, March 4, 1971.

9. Jouwe, Irian Irredenta", op. cit., p. 15.

10. Ibid, p. 15.

11. Voice of the Negroids in the Pacific to the Negroids Throughout the World. (Published by the "Papuan National Committee", 1962), p. 20.

12. Ibid., p. 3.

13. A Negro Race is Being Murdered. (Freedom Committee of West New Guinea, Delft, 1966), p. 1, 4.

14. On these racial, linguistic and ethnological aspects see Rapport van de Commissie Nieuw-Guinea (Irian), 1950. (Secretariaat van de Nederlands - Indonesische Unie, The Hague, 1950), part II, pp. 17-21, part III, pp. 28-42; J.P. Kleiweg de Zwaan, "The Papuans of Dutch New Guinea. A Physico - Anthropological Survey", Antiquity and Survival, 1956, no. 5, pp. 321-342; W.C. Klein, ed. Nieuw Guinea (The Hague, Staaksdrukkerij, 1953-54), vol. 2, pp. 191-275; Arend Lijphart, The Trauma of Decolonization. The Dutch and West New Guinea (New Haven and London, Yale University Press, 1966), pp. 25-27.

15. Rapport van de Commissie Nieuw-Guinea (Irian) 1950, op. cit., Part II, pp. 35-37; Tijdschrift van het Bataviaasch Genootschap van Kunsten en Wetenschappen, vol 79 (1939), p. 334.

16. J. van Baal, Het Nieuw-Guinea Vraagstuk. Een Opgave voor de Natie (Kampen, J.H. Kok, 1959), p. 10.

17. Antara Daily News Bulletin, October 16, 1971 (vol. 24, no. 1303), p. III.

18. O.J. Manusaway, "De Opinie leiders in Nederland en hun Invloed op de Publieke Opinievorming", New Guinean, February, 1972, pp. 7-9.

19. Ibid., p. 9.

20. Jan van Eechoud, Vergeten Aarde, Nieuw Guinea (Uitgeverij C. de Boer, Amsterdam, 1952).

21. Handelingen van de Tweede Kamer, vol. 2, 1959-1960 session, April 5, 1960, p. 2465.

22. A Averink, "Zelfbeschikkingsrechr als Camouflage voor Kolonisatie," Politiek en Cultuur, September, 1961, pp. 390-399. For the official Indonesian position on the West New Guinea question see West Irian. An Essential Part of Indonesia (Ganaco, Bandung, Indonesia, s.a.); Robert C. Bone, The Dynamics of the Western New Guinea (Irian Barat) Problem (Cornell University, Modern Indonesia Project Interim Reports Series, Ithaca, N.Y., 1958), and Justus M. van der Kroef, The West New Guinea Dispute (Institute of Pacific Relations, New York, 1958).

23. Ministry of the Interior of the Netherlands, Rapport Inzake Nederlands-Nieuw-Guinea Over Het Jaar 1961. Uitgebracht aan de Verenigde Naties ingevolge artikel73 e van het Handvest (Staatsdrukkerij, s.a.e.l., 1962?), pp. 1, 9.

24. For official Indonesian views on West New Guinea's development since the Indonesian take-over see Laporan singkat perkembangan kegiatan Pemerintah Daerah Propinsi Irian Barat Semendjak 1 Mei 1963 sampai dengan kwartal 1 tahun 1968 (Djakarta, Badan Koordinasi Pembangunan Daerah Propinsi Irian Barat; diperbanjak oleh Direktorat Irian Barat, Departemèn Dalam Negeri, 1968) 2 vols.

25. Nieuw Guinea Instituut (Rotterdam), Vademecum voor Nederlands-Nieuw Guinea 1956. (Drukkerij C. de Boer, den Helder, s.a.), p. 15.

26. Netherlands Ministry of the Interior, Papuans Building Their Future (Information Department, Netherlands Ministry of the Interior, The Hague, 1961), p. 7.

27. Compare the views of the noted Dutch anthropologist J. van Baal in Indonesië, January, 1952, p. 382.

28. Western New Guinea and the Netherlands (Netherlands Government State Printing Office, s. 1., 1954), pp. 12-13.

29. Papuans Building Their Future, op. cit., p. 13.

30. Rapport Inzake Nederlands - Nieuw-Guinea Over Het Jaar 1961, op. cit., pp. 22, 79-80.

31. Ibid., p. 18.

32. C.A. Cannegieter, De Economische Toekomstmogelijkheden van Nederlands Nieuw Guinea (Stenfert Kroese, Leyden, 1959), pp. 52, 54.

33. Cf.My "Nationalism and Politics in West New Guinea", Pacific Affairs, Spring, 1961, pp. 38-53, and "Recent Developments in West New Guinea", Pacific Affairs, Fall, 1961, p. 279-291.

34. See the party programs in Lagerberg, Jaren van Reconstructie. Nieuw Guinea van 1949 tot 1961, op. cit., pp. 228-232.

35. On Australian policy toward the West New Guinea question see, e.g., Henry S. Albinski, "Australia and the Dutch New Guinea Dispute", International Journal, Autumn, 1961, pp. 358-382, and Thomas R. Fennell, "Australian-Indonesian Relations as Affected by Events in New Guinea", East-West Center Review, June, 1965, pp. 23-45.

36. For details, see Justus M. van der Kroef, "The West New Guinea Settlement: Its Origins and Implications", Orbis, Spring, 1963, pp. 120-149. On U.S. pressure on the Dutch see also J.M. Luns, Ik Herinner Mij,. . . (A. Sijthoff, Leyden, 1971), p. 109.

37. Peter Hastings, "West New Guinea - the Big Sell-Out", The Bulletin (Sydney), March 2, 1963, pp. 13-14.

38. Herbert Feith, "Visit to West Irian", Nation (Sydney), April 18, 1964, p. 7.

39. Creighton Burns, "The Shutters Close Down on West Irian", The Straits Times May 17, 1965.

40. Peter Polomka, "The New Management's Onerous Task in West Irian", The Straits Times, September 9, 1968.

41. The Djakarta Times, September 22, 1967.

42. Peter Hastings, "West Irian - 1969", New Guinea (Sydney), September-October, 1968, p. 15.

43. Ibid., p. 16.

44. G. Zacharias Sawor, Ik Bèn Een Papoea (Uitgeverij de Vuurbaak, Groningen, 1969), pp. 34-35.

45. Cf the autobiographical account of the American missionary in New Guinea, Harold Lovestrand, Hostage in Djakarta (Moody Press paperback, Chicago, 1969), p. 15.

46. Cf. Warta Bhakti (Djakarta), May 25, 1965.

47. Cited The Straits Times, November 22, 1966.

48. For details see my "West New Guinea: The Uncertain Future", Asian Survey, August, 1968, pp. 691-707.

49. Sabah Times (Kota Kinabalu), April 28, 1967 and The Straits Times, March 17, 1967.

50. See e.g. the publication of the "West Papua Freedom Committee", Most urgent appeal of the Papuans of West New Guinea/"West Irian" to H.E. the Secretary General of the United Nations (s.1., 1967).

51. Sabah Times, December 24, 1966.

52. For details see my "Indonesia and West New Guinea: The New Dimensions of Conflict", Orbis, Summer, 1970, pp. 370, 373-374.

53. United Nations General Assembly, Twenty-Fourth Session, Report of the Secretary General Regarding the

Act of Self-determination in West Irian, A/7723, November 6, 1969, (mimeo), p. 70.

54. The Australian, June 4, 1969.

55. The Sydney Morning Herald, August 5, 1969.

56. Ibid., July 26, 1969. Reporting on the act of free choice the correspondent for The New York Times reported from Djakarta that "Jakarta's diplomatic community insists and members of the Indonesian government figures admit in private that the entire process is a meaningless formality", Philip Shabecoff in The New York Times, July 7, 1969.

57. "Spectator" in South Pacific Post (Port Moresby), March 24, 1969.

58. The Sydney Morning Herald, April 19 and July 11, 1969: The Australian, May 10, 1969.

59. Angus Smales in The Courier-Mail (Brisbane), December 16, 1968. See also "War in West Irian", Papua-New Guinea Tempo (Port Moresby), Febraury, 1968, pp. 1-2.

60. See e.g. Zelfbeschikking, September, 1970, p. 7, January-February, 1971, p. 14, and November-December, 1971, p. 13.

61. Preceding data in this paragraph from Bob Hawkins, "Irian the Forgotten Gets a Boost from President Suharto", The Sarawak Tribune, June 25, 1971. See also United Nations Development Programme. A Design for Development in West Irian (United Nations, New York, 1968).

62. Antara Daily News Bulletin, January 23, 1970 (vol. 22, no. 688) and De Volkskrant, February 17, 1971.

63. Departemèn Dalam Negeri, Irian Barat Membangun (Djakarta, 1971), and Departemèn Pendidikan dan Kebudajaan, Masalah Pendidikan dan Kebudajaan di Propinsi Irian Barat (Djakarta, 1970).

64. Bob Hawkins, "West-Irian. With the Utmost Sincerity", Far Eastern Economic Review, May 22, 1971, p. 67.

65. See, e.g., editorials in The Djakarta Times, November 13 and 15, 1969, and Radio Djakarta commentary on U.N. debate, November 17, 1969, 1210 GMT (FBIS).

66. Dinas Penerangan Propinsi, Irian Barat. Kebulatan tekad rakjat Irian Barat (Djajapura, 1969), and The Djakarta Times, November 15, 1969.

67. Warta Harian (Djakarta), May 9, 1969; Sinar Harapan (Djakarta), May 9, 1969, and Indonesia Raya (Djakarta), May 14, 1969, also cited in Peter Hastings' article "Indonesians Have Growing Doubts on West Irian Policy", The Australian, June 4, 1969.

68. P.A. Szudek, New Guinea. Danger Zone 1969 (The Anglo-Melanesian Aid Committee, s.1., 1969), p. 36.

69. For details see Justus M. van der Kroef, "Australian and the West Irian Problem", Asian Survey, June, 1970, pp. 496-498.

70. R.S. Parker, "The Embryo - Politics of New Guinea", Government and Opposition, Winter, 1969-70, p. 101. For other pessimistic assessments of TPNG's political future see the articles by R.S. Parker "Papua New Guinea. The Emergent State", and John Watts, Collision Course", pp. 35-51 and 52-57 respectively in New Guinea, January, 1972.

71. Peter Hastings, "West Irian - Papua - New Guinea", New Guinea, June-July, 1970, p. 67.

72. David Jenkins, "One Island: Two Worlds," The Sydney Morning Herald, March 3, 1970.

IV. SOUTH ASIA

In examining two ethnic groups, Parsis and Jews, in India, Schermerhorn argues that the nature and type of adaptation of these two groups to dominant culture is determined by their different arrival history: Jews came in small numbers, and they had to mix readily into local group; Parsis arrived in large numbers, and hence they were successful in keeping their pattern of endogamy. Schermerhorn delineates the major difference between the two groups: Jews were predominently oil-pressers during the period following their arrival and bureaucrats in the later colonial era (contrary to Becker's thesis of Jews as migrant traders); Parsis succeeded in industries and commerce, due to the protestant-ethnic-like features in their religion. Jews, due to their dominant position in middle echelon bureaucratic positions, had less of an emphasis upon higher education for their offsprings whereas, Parsis placed a high priority on higher education. Consequently, Parsis became more westernized than Jews and had a high literacy rate in English. Schermerhorn notes a marked tolerance accorded to both groups by their Hindu neighbors.

Johnson defines both the Neo-Buddhism of the Untouchables in India and the Black Muslims as revitalistic religions of protest. Both religions are this-world oriented, which is congruent with status-mobility aspirations of Untouchables of India and Blacks of the United States. Johnson, however, points out the difference between two religions: Neo-Buddhism is of indigenous adoption and is not in conflict with nation-state of India, consequently the followers are strongly encouraged to actively participate in politics; Black Muslim was adopted from outside the dominant religions of the nation-state, advocates the separation of Black nations and de-emphasises political participation by its followers.

Perinbanayagam and Chadda describe the history of conflict between Tamils (Hindu) and Sinhalese (Buddhist in Ceylon. They attribute the much deteriorated present relations between the two groups to inept Tamil leadership which repeatedly enforced a Sinhalese image of Tamils as potential enemies: by not supporting the Sinhalese resistance movement, by taking a lukewarm attitude toward the independence of Ceylon, and advocation of the '50-50' representation which ignored numerical minority positions of Tamil. Perinbayagam and Chadda are not optimistic in their predictions for the future of Tamil -Sinhalese relations in Ceylon.

13

PARSIS AND JEWS IN INDIA—A TENTATIVE COMPARISON

R.A. SCHERMERHORN
Case Western Reserve University

ABSTRACT

The purpose of this paper is to get below the stereotyped level of comparison between Jews and Parsis where only obvious similarities are stressed, i.e., that they are ethical monotheists, endogamous religious communities, and highly urbanized or Westernized merchant minorities. Although there are 3 groups of Jews in India, each with different background, only the overwhelmingly numerous (proportionately speaking) Bene Israel of Bombay are used in this comparison. Contrary to Howard Becker's thesis that these are migrating trading peoples, the paper raises serious doubts about middleman occupations for both Jews and Parsis on arrival in India and during early centuries of their life in the sub-continent. The author also emphasizes 4 major differences between the two minorities that become quite salient in the British period, presenting reasons for each. (1) Jews came to resemble the local population more than the Parsis did. (2) Parsis produced proportionately more entrepreneurs, the Jews more bureaucratic workers in the labor force. (3) The Parsis became more Westernized than the Jews: in speaking English, in levels of University education, and in emancipation of women. (4) Jewish communal leaders were eventually from the lower middle class, while among Parsis it was the industrialists who retained more power of decision in communal affairs. The two communities were alike, however, in being largely a-political, and in showing marked population decline (of different types, however). Both also enjoyed marked toleration and respect from their Hindu neighbors without noticeable discrimination.

At first glance, the Parsis and Jews of India share the kind of obvious similarities that put them in the same category, not only in popular opinion but in the views of certain scholars as well. Both groups are descendants of endogamous religious communities, ethical monotheists who migrated to India centuries ago in the wake of religious persecution. Both communities are now urbanized and Westernized with predominantly "middle class" occupation. This article takes a closer look at the two minority groups in order to discover how adequate this initial impression actually is.

First of all, it is necessary to recognize the three internal divisions of the Jewish community, each of which had its own distinctive but separate historical development in India: the Bene Israel, the Baghdadi Jews, and the Cochin Jews. Numerical ratios of the sub-groupings are so disproportionate, however, that demands of brevity make it unnecessary to consider them all. A chief authority on the subject estimates that there are 13,000 Bene Israel, 2,000 Baghdadi Jews and about 250 Cochin Jews in India (S. Strizower, 1971:5-6). Since the two latter sub-groups are so small, I shall disregard them in this paper and focus on the Bene Israel alone, comparing that branch of Jewry with the Parsis.[1]

A number of years ago, Howard Becker, discussing the case of the Jews as a minority group, came to the conclusion that they were not unique but only representative of a type of itinerant traders who settle in many lands where they continue their commercial occupations. For the many ethnic groups who fit this constructed type, Becker used the name "marginal trading peoples" and his examples are Jews, Armenians, Parsis, Greeks in Egypt, and border Scots.[2] (H. Barnes, H. Becker and F.B. Becker, 1940:31). Detailed analysis of both Jews and Parsis in India raises serious doubts about Becker's classification; as we shall see, it is really more applicable to the Parsis than to the Jews. Comparisons, too, if they are to be relevant, must be made at two points in time: at the period immediately following migration, and in the British period which crystallized the occupational structure for both minorities.

The Bene Israel migrated to the Konkan coast of India somewhere near the middle of the first millenium A.D., probably two or three centuries earlier than the arrival of the Parsis, who came to the west coast above Bombay in 716 A.D. We do not have sufficient evidence for either group to prove or disprove Becker's thesis that they were predominantly traders on arrival. By the time of confirmed historical reports of the Konkan Jewish community, many adults were in one of the lowliest occupations recognized by the Hindus, oil-pressing, while the rest were apparently in a few agricultural pursuits, with a sprinkling of carpenters (Strizower, *op. cit.*, 23-24). In the rural areas where the Bene Israel then lived, the great probability is that trading opportunities were rare and already appropriated by the Banias. Among the Parsis, the people remained rural dwellers too, for eight centuries after their arrival, and during these years they were "agriculturalists and toddy drawers". (D. Menant, ERE'IX, 642). In the pre-colonial period, the Parsis apparently entered a wider range of occupations than the Jews, but neither community was narrowly confined to trade, as Becker's thesis would suggest.

Discrepancy in numbers at the time of arrival had different consequences for Jews and Parsis. While there are no exact figures available, traditions of the Bene Israel relate that their ancestors were the scant survivors of a shipwreck off the Konkan coast--no more than seven couples altogether and that it is the descendants from this remnant that makes up their community today (Strizower, *op.cit.*, 13). While there are features of this story that are strangely like that accounting for the early, miraculous origin of the Chitpavan Bahmans of Maharashtra (B.J. Israel, 1963:4), there seems no reason to doubt the derivation of the Bene Israel from an extremely small group of entrants. On the other hand, the Parsis who first landed at Sanjon on the western coast in the 8th century were a sufficiently large company to have a Dastur (high priest) as leader and commander of the group and, by their very presence, to give the prince of the territory where they landed "some fear for the safety of his throne" (S.K.H. Katrak, 1965:109). A baker's dozen would hardly have aroused such apprehension. The initial number of Parsis, in all probability much more substantial, helps to explain some pheno-typical differences when Parsis and Jews are compared in the modern period.

I am assuming that any migratory group, if initially endogamous, will obey the rules for in-marriage only so long as the size of the group permits a choice of sexual partners within it. Below a certain numerical level of the group, any choice of in-group mates becomes impossible and other alternatives like temporary liaisons, concubinage, and intermarriage with or without incorporation of the spouse into the in-group (conversion, etc.) will take place. Once the community grows to a size that permits endogamy to operate normally, however, the traditional practice will be resumed. If the group is initially quite small, the process may take several centuries, during which the physical features of its members will resemble the surrounding population more and more. Strizower suggests that this process affected the skin color of Jewish migrant populations who became lighter in the trek north from the Middle East and darker in their journeys south (Ibid., 27-28). It seems plausible to infer, therefore, that if the Jewish arrivals were, at the outset, appreciably smaller than those of the Parsis, it was therefore far more difficult for the Jews to observe endogamous rules. As a result, they could be expected to have had more liaisons with those of the surrounding community than the Parsis would have. This hypothesis is corroborated by the development of internal semi-caste divisions within the Bene Israel, the Kala or dark Jews attributed to earlier mixed unions and the Gora or "white" Jews to endogamous marriages. However, since both Kala and Gora are today practically indistinguishable from other Maharashtrians or Gujeratis on the color scale, Strizower hypothesizes that "Kala are the offspring of mixed unions which for some reason or other have been *remembered*, while unions between the ancestors of the Gora and non-Bene Israel have been *forgotten*--perhaps the ancestors of the Kala contracted unions with non-Bene Israel later than did those of the Gorä"[3] (Ibid., 28).

As for the Parsis, the greater numerical size of their community at the time of migration made it possible to restrict marital unions to their own members in a way that was impossible for the Jews. In addition, the Parsis at the outset made a formal agreement with the Hindu ruler of the local province (Katrak, op.cit., 110) which had the result of setting up effective contractual boundaries between the two communities, thus reinforcing Parsi endogamy. Results show that Jews, in the long run, have come to resemble the surrounding population racially to a greater extent than the Parsis.

Arrival of the British, particularly on the west coast of India, opened up new economic opportunities in Bombay; by the middle of the 19th century, both Parsis and Jews were attracted to the city in such numbers that they have been dominantly urban ever since. However, the British trading colony had a different effect on the two communities, depending on the readiness of each to develop in a special direction. Robert Kennedy Jr. has shown in some detail that the religious values of the Parsis had much in common with the Protestant Ethnic as described by Max Weber and the ideology of the Puritans in 17th century England depicted by R.K. Merton. These values, which stressed the importance of accumulation rather than consumption of material goods, and the desire to maximize financial prosperity as a means of establishing a human order to match the divine order, provided the potential for entrepreneurship when proper occasions for its exercise arose. Even as early as the 11th century, the Parsis were among the leading traders of Cambay, and by the 15th century, outstanding Parsi men were coopted by rulers throughout western India as desais or tax farmers. As the Portuguese arrived in the 16th century, then the Dutch, and finally the English, all Europeans discovered to their advantage that Parsis were well suited to be their brokers (R.E. Kennedy, Jr., 1962; D.F. Karaka, 1885, 4,9). Rapid growth of these new occupations acted like a magnet, drawing in scores of recruits, and before long the process ceased to be a simple matter of cooptation; the Parsis, attracted by the wide variety of new

commercial and trading pursuits, sought them out with avidity and began to create new ones of their own. No longer content with dependence on British firms, the Parsis established companies of their own, and by the latter part of the 19th century made up 26 of the 46 shipbuilders in Bombay, while accounting for 33 of the 84 civil engineers (Karaka, op.cit., II 98). Other Parsi entrepreneurs utilized the larger ships of the British and opened up new trade connections with Burma, Calcutta, Persia, Arabia and China (Kennedy, op.cit., 17). By 1881, over 70 percent of the Parsi population were born in Bombay and more than a third were in commercial and industrial pursuits (Anil Seal, 1968, 82n. 3; Karaka, op.cit., I,99).

Entrance into business and trading pursuits occurred far less frequently among the Bene Israel who migrated to Bombay in the 18th and 19th centuries. It is possible that their employment as lowly oil-pressers in rural regions helped to delay their rise to higher positions with their transfer to urban residence, by lowering aspirations on the one hand, or stigmatizing them in public opinion on the other. Whatever the reason, the Jews reacted to the British presence by seeking out military and bureaucratic positions rather than those of entrepreneurship. A very large proportion of the Bene Israel, like the Anglo-Indians, gained a sizable number of posts in the railways, customs, postal and telegraph services and the like, positions which gave them security and a certain status (Strizower, op.cit., 139). This type of occupation became so common that the Jews were called a clerk caste and so referred to themselves. (Ibid., 77) Between 1750 and 1857, the Bene Israel enlisted in the Army in considerable numbers and would have continued this pattern of recruitment had not the policy changed so that regiments were formed by community after that date. Since the Bene Israel were not numerous enough to form regiments of their own they drifted into ancillary services[4], illustrated by the Aden contingent of 1872 in which they were "military accounts clerks and draftsmen, sub-engineers, overseers and mistries of the Public Works Department, Commissariat and medical service employees and skilled artisans such as masons and carpenters..." (S. Samuel, 1963, 60). Thus, the Bene Israel predominated more in bureaucratic positions in the new occupational hierarchies and had noticeably fewer business enterprisers, proportionally speaking, than the Parsis.[5]

Westernization seems to have made more rapid strides among Parsis than among Jews. This was partly due to the notably perservering efforts to learn the English language among the Parsis. An early impetus in this direction came when Parsis crowded into the ranks of the commissioned agents for British firms in the 19th century and were given the name of Dobhashias--a compound of Do (two) and Bhashas (languages), i.e., those who knew two languages. The British shortened the term to Dubash (Katrak, op.cit., 116), and it was reported in the census of 1881 that Zoroastrians had 146 out of a total of 159 dubashes listed among the commercial occupations. (Karaka, op.cit., I, 98-9). English medium schools, started in the early 19th century, were liberally attended by Parsis who later helped establish Elphinstone College; in this new center for higher education in English, Parsi enrollment equalled or surpassed that of the Hindus. Sir Jamshedji Jijibhai also contributed funds to establish a number of English medium schools at lower levels for deserving Parsi pupils (Karaka, op.cit., I, 281-3, 285, 288-90). Among the Jews, there has been considerable exposure to English education, beginning with the Mission of Dr. John Wilson in the early part of the 19th century. However, his influence emphasized instruction in both Hebrew and Marathi as well as

English, and later the communal school of the Bene Israel in Bombay used Marathi medium; if a student wanted more thorough English instruction he would have to seek it outside the Jewish community (Strizower, *op.cit.*, 40-41, 136). Comparative figures for Parsis and Jews point up the differences quite clearly: by 1931, for example the Parsis led all communities of India with the highest literacy in English--50.4 percent--almost twice as high as that of the next highest indigenous group who were the Jews, registering 26.4 percent (Kingsley Davis, 1951:185).

Another index of Westernization is the status of women. In this case there is also a differential between Parsis and Jews, though less marked. In both communities, female education began early in the 19th century with vernacular instruction preceding English--Gujarati for Parsis and Marathi for the Jews. Eventually, many Parsi ladies took the lead in female education, even extending to training in medicine. This had its repercussions in the greater freedom of movement outside the home for Parsi females (Karaka, *op.cit.*, I 123, 127, 129-30, 173, 299, 303, 324). Segregation of the sexes is sufficiently strict among the Jews to approach the Hindu norm. Thus Strizower comments,

> It would never do for Bene Israel girls to roam about as freely as do the boys--and most certainly not in the company of boys. Bene Israel say that girls found lingering about in the company of boys and chatting freely with them would damage their reputation beyond repair--'And who would offer for them then?' . . . For girls are expected to help their mothers in the home; and as they marry early--in their late teens--they are very soon occupied with their own household affairs. (Strizower, *op.cit.*, 149).

Parsi women, on the other hand, display far greater freedom of participation in community affairs, and have exhibited this quality quite openly since the late 19th century (Karaka, *idem*). On the other hand, it is reported that 14 percent of Jewish women in Greater Bombay were working for gain in 1961, a fairly high figure; the largest number of these are listed in the services which would include teachers and nurses as well as lawyers and doctors. This enumeration shows that a very sizable number of Jewish women have broken the traditional mold and family restrictions (B.J. Israel, 1963:22).

The freedom movement and its drive for independence gave rise to still other divergent trends. Even as early as the mutiny of 1857, Parsi leaders showed strong support for the colonial rulers, many of them suffering with the British at the hands of the mutineers (Karaka, op.cit., II 282). By 1885, the era of the moderates, the prominent Parsi leader, Dadabhai Naoroji, was elected the first President of the Indian National Congress. Stating the views of the Congress at the time, Naoroji declared that the best interests of India would be served by appealing to the British people directly, not against colonial rule but against the arbitrary and warped decisions of British authorities in India (Seal, *op.cit.*, 280). However, as more radical leaders like Tilak arose to demand independence by violent means if necessary, Parsi leaders in Bombay strongly opposed them. Being as loyal as most of the community to the Crown, Parsis as a whole did not go beyond a moderate nationalism, seeking greater representation in the existing councils (Sir Stanley Reed, 1952:167). The one firebrand who broke with this tradition, Madame Bhihaji Cama, regarded as quixotic, was expelled from England and died an exile in France in 1936 without having had any noticeable influence on her own community (Katrak, op.cit., 152-3).

These issues were kept behind the scenes among the Jews until 1917 and the convention of a communal assembly organized under the name of the Bene Israel Conference. During this meeting, the members split over the issue of including "politics" in their deliberations. Forces opting for non-political discussions won the vote in the assembly and, in protest, the opposing members withdrew and formed a rival organization calling itself the All-India Israelite League. At its meeting in Karachi in 1918, the League delegated eight members to present an address to Mr. Edwin Samuel Montagu, Secretary of State for India, supporting the scheme for reform proposed by the Indian National Congress and the All-Indian Muslim League, while opposing separate electorates for any community except the Muslims. This address received wide publicity and there is reason to believe that the Bene Israel Conference secretly sent a message to British authorities saying that the address did not represent the true wishes of the Jewish community. At any rate, the Bene Israel conference espoused a policy of neutrality on such political issues and this became the stance of the community as a whole. Significantly enough, such neutrality amounted, in effect, to support for the British, who could wish for nothing better than neutrality at the time. "Not to make political demands was to support the status quo and, in fact, the Bene Israel remained loyalists till 1947 and they genuinely regretted the departure of the British." (B.J. Israel, personal communication, 1972).

While both communities thus remained relatively non-political till the very eve of independence, the internal antagonism between two rival organizations within the Jewish community took a surprising turn, and one without parallel among the Parsis. Conflicts eventually became so bitter that the rank and file developed a widespread distrust of community leaders from the upper strata. Since these leaders were highly educated and the top business figures, bitter factionalism at these levels could, in the long run, gravitate downward and cause irreparable rifts in the community fabric. Reports suggest that the unseemly manoeuvres and counter-manoeuvres of the educated members of the community finally estranged their potential followers. Unable to believe any longer in the purity of motives within the educated section, the rank and file eventually decided to take over communal control (Strizower, *op.cit.*, 130). In the end, the clerks ousted both professionals and the business elite from positions of responsiblity in their communal organizations. Eventually, "it [was] the rank and file which [controlled] not only the synagogues but also the home for orphans and destitutes, the great part of the offices of the school and the cooperative society." (Strizower, *ibid.*, 130). The controllling element of Bene Israel communal life comes, therefore, from the stratum sociologically identifiable as the lower middle class. This is in marked contrast to the Parsis, among whom the wealthy members still retain dominant influence because of their philanthropic generosity (S.F. Desai, 1963:36-42). Conversely, the Bene Israel upper class is not well-known for its philanthropic efforts. The most notable philanthropies among the Jews come from the Baghdadis (Strizower, *op.cit.*, 42).

As already intimated, the educational level of the Parsis is generally higher than that of the Bene Israel. This is due in large part to Jewish acceptance of the ease with which they could step into jobs like customs, railway, postal or telegraph services under British auspices; for these, a university education was not needed. Eventually, this produced a tradition stressing intermediate education as the norm, and precluded the expectation of study in the upper levels of the educational system (Strizower, *op.cit.*, 139). Since the Parsis laid greater stress on attendance at the universities, the younger generation became more and more sophisticated. This has resulted in strong attacks by the young against ancient traditions and practices of the Parsis, and a division in the adult generation between orthodox and liberal (Katrak, *op.cit.*, 259-63). There seems to be no parallel split, religiously among the Bene Israel.

Both communities today are suffering a noticeable decline in population. For the Parsis, this process is gradual as the birth rate steadily declines and the families grow smaller. The failure of replacement is becoming more obvious with each passing year as shown quite clearly in the age of distribution: in India as a whole the younger generation ages 0-15 made up 40 percent of the population in 1961, while among Parsis it was as low as 18 percent. Conversely, only 6 percent of the all-India population was 51 years of age or over, while 30 percent of the Parsis were that old (S.F. Desai, 1964:30). While there are no comparable figures for the Bene Israel, it is well-known that their population has decreased more rapidly because of massive emigration to Israel. By 1971, Strizower reported that "the great majority of the 7,000 Bene Israel living outside India are to be found in Israel, and this is more than half the number left in India". (*op.cit.*, 58). The probability is that India will have a Parsi community long after the Jews have left the sub-continent.

In closing, I want to emphasize that the dominant Hindus in India have regarded both Parsis and Jews with toleration mixed with approval, since neither community is a proselytizing faith. This kept them free of oppression in the modern period and encouraged each one to develop a communal life in the way it thinks best. The reason for Jewish emigration is not mistreatment or harassment, but attraction to a homeland presented in somewhat utopian terms. But of all the settlers entering Israel, it is the Indian Jews alone who can report that they have not suffered discrimination or persecution in their former home.

FOOTNOTES

1. The 1961 census gives the total Parsi population of India as 100,772.
2. On Becker's hypothesis it is possible to add a number of others, i.e., Syrians and Lebanese in West Africa, Arabs on the Malabar coast, overseas Chinese in Southeast Asia, etc.
3. Italics added.
4. Personal communication from B.J. Israel.
5. This does not apply to the Baghdadi Jews who were much more successful as entrepreneurs.

REFERENCES

Becker, Howard
1940   "Constructive Typology in the Social Sciences," in Harry Elmer Barnes, Howard Becker and Frances Becker, eds., Contemporary Social Theory, New York, D. Appleton-Century Co.

Davis, Kingsley
1951   The Population of India and Pakistan, Princeton, N.J., Princeton University Press.

Desai, Sapur Faredun
1963   The Parsi Panchayet and its Working, Bombay, Privately Printed.
1964   "Statistics of World Zoroastrianism with Special Reference to Indian Zoroastrians," in The Second World Zoroastrian Congress, Report, Part II, Papers, Bombay.

Israel, Benjamin J.
1963   Religious Evolution Among the Bene Israel of India Since 1750, Bombay, Privately Printed.

Karaka, Dosabhai Framji
1884   History of the Parsis, Including their Manner, Customs, Religion and Present Position, London, Macmillan & Co. 2 vols.

Katrak, Sohrab D.H.
1965   Who are the Parsees? Karachi, Pakistan Herald Press.

Kennedy, Robert F., Jr.
1962   "The Protestant Ethnic and the Parsis," American Journal of Sociology 68 (July 1962) 11-20.

Menant, D.
1924   "Parsis," Encyclopedia of Religion and Ethnics, ed., James Hastings, New York Charles Scribner's Sons, Vol. IX, 640-650.

Reed, Sir Stanley
1952   The India I Knew 1897-1947, London, Odhams Press.

Samuel, Shellim
1963   A treatise on the Origin and Early History of the Beni-Israel of Maharashtra State, Bombay, Privately Printed.

Seal, Anil
1968   The Emergence of Indian Nationalism, Competition and Collaboration in the Later Nineteenth Century, Cambridge at the University Press.

Strizower, Schifra
1971   The Bene Israel of Bombay, New York, Schocken Books.

14

NEW-BUDDHISTS AND BLACK MUSLIMS: A Comparative
Analysis of Two Religions of Protest

SIPRA BOSE JOHNSON

State University of New York, New Paltz

ABSTRACT

Caste in India and the United States has been compared to yield insights into the functioning of both stratification systems. This paper examines similarities and differences in the life condition of Blacks and Untouchables and further explores two revitalistic religions of protest which have arisen in response to the conditions of deprivation faced by Untouchables in India and Blacks in the United States. Neo-Buddhism, *as the conversion movement to Buddhism among Indian Untouchables is called, and the* Black Muslim *movement among American Blacks are analyzed in regard to their origin myths, composition, their value systems, their leadership, and their political and social implications and impact.*

INTRODUCTION

Analysis of caste as a system of stratification has occupied the talents of many social scientists. While some see caste as being limited to India (cf. Dumont 1967:29, 1970: 214-216; Leach 1960:5), the recent literature indicates a widespread interest among anthropologists in treating caste cross-culturally. In particular the works of Berreman (1960, 1966a, 1966b, 1966c, 1967), De Vos (1966a, 1966b, 1966c, 1967) and Harper (1968a) have yielded important insights into the similarities of functioning of stratification systems designated as caste. Starting with the early popularization by John Dollard (1957 [first published in 1937]) of the term caste for Black-white relations in the United States, an examination of the similarities and differences in caste in India and the United States has drawn the attention of a variety of students of social structure (cf. Berremann 1960; Harper 1968a; Johnson and Johnson 1972).

The present paper is an attempt to critically compare the similarities and differences in the life situations of the Untouchables and Blacks in their respective societies. Consideration has been given both to the position of these two groups in the dominant culture and to the perception by these underprivileged groups of themselves and their attitudes toward their subordinate status in society. Further, I have tried to delineate some major methods of status mobility in each culture. In the second part of this paper I have examined two recent religious protest movements, Neo-Buddhism among Untouchables in India and the Black Muslim movement among the American Blacks, in an attempt to further our understanding of the stratification systems of India and the United States. In particular, I have examined in a comparative framework: (1) the rise of the movements; (2) their creation myths; (3) their composition; (4) their ideology; and (5) the characteristics of their leaders.

THE MYTH OF THE HAPPY UNTOUCHABLE

Shorn of power and status, the Untouchables who are 14.7 percent of the Indian population and the Blacks who make up 11.2 percent of the population of the United States both face discrimination in social and economic spheres. Such patterns as residential segregation, social segragation and relegation to menial or low-status jobs in both cultures are too well known to require elaborate documentation. However, whether untouchability can be said to exist in the United States as well as in India remains debated in the literature. Anant (1971:271-272) emphasizes the lack of the concept of untouchability in the United States while others such as Gould (1960:220), Harper (1968a:59) and Berreman (1966b:

293-295) seem to suggest that the notion of untouchability or pariah status exists in both cultures.

Berreman writes that "Pariah groups the world over share many characteristics, one of which is that they do the necessary but dirty, demeaning and unpleasant jobs for their social superiors. As a result they are contaminated, or perhaps because they are contaminated, they are given these jobs. In any case because they are defiled, *they are restricted in the contacts they may have with other members of society* (my emphasis). Frequently they are defined as "non-persons", a social definition that undoubtedly serves a number of social functions." (1966b:293).

In both India and the United States the maintenance of social distance between the high and the low then is a requirement for the operation of Untouchable status. The contexts in which social distance is maintained show some similarities and some differences. Common to both cultures are the culture traits of residential segregation, ban on intermarriage and restricted access by the underprivileged groups to public facilities. On the other hand direct bodily contact in such situations as the care of white children by Black nurses is possibly more prevalent in the United States. Permitted degree of bodily proximity and contact varies according to context in both cultures, for in India, too, some restricted contexts provide a greater degree of bodily proximity between the high caste and the low than would be permitted ordinarily. It is Mandelbaum's view, for example, that at harvest time members of all *jatis* or castes may work together and may come into physical contact with each other (1970:182). Harper has made a clearcut distinction between untouchability on the one hand and social segregation in public facilities on the other. He writes: "In India untouchability is carried to a further extreme than in the United States, while segregation in public facilities is carried to greater lengths in the United States" (1968a:59). It is not totally clear what Harper means by untouchability in this context. If by untouchability he is referring to the pattern of avoidance of bodily contact due to notions of purity and pollution, the clear distinction which he makes between untouchability and social segregation seems to me false. Social segregation in public facilities in the United States is simply a manifestation of untouchability rather than of a different

---

1. The final version of this article was completed in 1972. With the recent death of Elijah Muhammad, the Black Muslim movement has come under new leadership and seems to be taking some new directions which are as yet not entirely clear. The text of this article remains in its original form and does not include an analysis of recent developments within the Muslim movement.

order of phenomenon, for essential to both the Indian and American systems is the expression of social distance in a large number of contexts, sometimes through restriction on bodily contact but also through other symbolic means such as the American culture pattern of "entering by the back door". Social segregation in public facilities, indeed, can be considered an important context in which the concept of body separation arising from a concern with purity is expressed in American culture.

Sociologists, anthropologists and, indeed, well-informed citizens have been aware for some time of the bitterness and resentment with which Black Americans have faced their white adversary. What is curious is that the Indian Untouchable until very recently has been pictured as happy with his lot. In this traditional view of caste and the place of the Untouchables within it, the Untouchable is pictured as having swallowed the Caste Hindu interpretation that low status has befallen him due to the sins of the past and cheerful acceptance of one's role within the caste system is a religious duty. Thus the only acceptable path to upward mobility, according to this view, is through the slow process of transmigration and rebirth. Though this view that there is or was a value concensus among the high and the low on the Hindu concept of *Karma* is now questioned by some anthropologists (cf. Gough 1960:54; Mencher 1972:38; Beteille 1972:413), it retains a certain tenacious hold in the general literature on social stratification and underlies the static image of the caste system portrayed by otherwise sensitive, empathetic and well-known scholars of deprived peoples. For example, while C. Eric Lincoln in his excellent study of Black Muslims in America writes with keen understanding of human nature, "No healthy mind assumes that another healthy mind will welcome an inferior status or its degrading concomitants," (1961:39) he is not able to apply the same insight to India. In his view the Pre-Gandhian Indian caste system is characterized by "wholehearted acceptance of disparate social conditions" and "In such a society every group--high or low, favored or scorned--is felt to have a divinely ordained place in the sun" (1961:38). The earliest well known systematic statement, that of Berreman, which emphasized the essential similarities of deprivation of Untouchables and Blacks, appeared as late as 1960.

The recent anthropological literature is replete with cases of dissatisfaction of lower caste groups including Untouchables with their place in society. Efforts to raise the socio-economic, political and ritual status among specific Untouchable and other low status groups have been noted and analyzed by numerous anthropologists (cf. Cohn 1955; Mahar 1960; Rowe 1968; Bailey 1957; Harper 1968b; Lynch 1969). Most students of India are now agreed that Untouchable groups never accepted their position within the caste framework even if they accepted the rightness of the system. Where acceptance of the system existed, it may have been more pragmatic than ideological, for as new opportunities have emerged, Untouchables have shifted their strategy for status mobility from those based on an acceptance of the rightfulness of caste, i.e., processes such as Sanskritization (Srinivas 1956, 1965:30 [first published in 1952]) to those which negate the system such as modern political activities within the framework of the egalitarian Constitution. The Buddhist movement which is discussed below is of course also a rejection of the system.

Thus, no more than the American Black can the Untouchable be considered to be an enthusiastic supporter, or even a neutral observer, of the way in which caste has affected his life-chances. Berreman rightly points out that the functioning of the caste system is not necessarily based on consensus about the rightful position of particular groups but

more likely on force (1966b:228). Writing both of race relations in the United States and of caste in India, he explains: "Ultimately, I believe, the functioning of the systems depended upon considerations of relative power--upon enforcement, upon physical and economic sanctions at the disposal of the dominant groups" (1966b:228).

PATHS TO STATUS MOBILITY

Faced with rigid discrimination, the Untouchable and the Black have responded in some similar ways in an attempt to better their own conditions. Below we will consider some important avenues to status mobility which have been tried by both groups. These paths to mobility are not seen as mutually exclusive. The same individual or the same group often utilized a number of these methods at the same time.

"Passing" is a phenomenon known from both cultures but provides a satisfactory avenue to status mobility for relatively few in each culture. The assumption that greater possibilities for "passing" exist in India since Untouchables, unlike Blacks, do not have distinct physical characteristics to distinguish them as a group is unwarranted, since in the personalized, rural society the caste identity of individuals is a matter of public knowledge. In the urban area the Untouchable is hampered in "passing" by the fact that caste groups are marked by sharply differing life styles (for more details see Isaacs 1965:143-49). The cost to the individual of total disassociation from one's group which is the price for both Untouchables and Blacks who wish to "pass" is too high for most individuals in both societies. "Situation oriented passing" in the urban area such as in use of restaurants, public transportation and businesses, however, may have been more possible for the Untouchable than for the Black in the conservative American states of the pre-civil rights era. However, "situation oriented" passing was not a certainty for the Untouchables Sebring (1969) found in one area of Uttare Pradesh that tea shop owners are able to successfully establish the low caste identity of stranger clients through such cultural indicators as subservient and "rude" behavior as well as physical markers considered stereotypic of low caste. This, then, led to the denial of service to low caste individuals through a variety of pretexts.

Elite emulation or the attempt to raise status through taking on behavior of upper status groups is known from both cultures. Caste groups in India have attempted to raise their status through the twin processes of Sanskritization and Westernization (Srinivas 1956). In Sanskritization, one form of elite emulation (Lynch 1969:218), a low caste group chooses as its model of reference the more Sanskritic practices of higher caste groups. In this case the reference group or model is internal to the culture. In the process of Westernization there is the emulation of practices that are cultural imports. Both these processes are group-based. It is interesting to note that in the United States in the past the dominant model of elite emulation was the individually oriented process of emulation of white middle class culture. This can be described as the use of a reference group internal to the heterogeneous society of the United States. The recent trend toward Africanization in the popularity of African styles of names, dress, food and other culture patterns among Blacks in America, however, does not fit the model of elite emulation. Africanization is not an attempt to raise status in the context of the dominant society, for it does not assume that the taking on of these new patterns will validate higher status via a vis the dominant group. Rather, it is a tendency toward withdrawal from the symbols of prestige of the dominant society, substituting for them symbols meaningful to the subordinate group as evidence of cultural uniqueness. The aim of Africanization is an increase in the quality of cultural identity and self-respect. An increase in group self-respect may be seen by the group as an indispensable prerequisite to enhanced status in the dominant society. Africanizaion then is more akin to the nationalistic strategies of such groups as the Black Muslims who have emphasized the rewards of disconnecting from the dominant status system. Neither elite emulation nor separatist strategies have made significant changes in the life condition of the majority of Untouchables and Blacks.

The avenue of politics has also been utilized by Untouchables and Blacks in efforts to obtain a larger share of the resources of their respective countries. In both societies discrimination is outlawed through legislated or constitutional provisions (for a comparative analysis of governmental philosophy guiding policy toward Untouchables and Blacks, see Johnson and Johnson 1972. As the legal climate has changed, new opportunities have emerged for political action (for a comparative study of politics among Untouchables and Blacks see Verba et al. 1971). Political mobilization of Untouchables and Blacks is increasing in India and the United States.

RELIGIONS OF PROTEST

Underprivileged peoples in many parts of the world have often turned to religion for comfort. The recent developments of the Buddhist movement among Untouchables in India and the Black Muslim movement in the United States are religious movements arising primarily out of a need to protest the degraded status of Untouchables and Blacks. These religions of protest can usefully be seen to fall into the general category of movements called revitalization movements. Using Anthony Wallace's general definition of revitalization movements "as a deliberate, organized, conscious effort by members of a society to construct a more satisfying culture (1956:265)" we can class both Neo-Buddhism and Black Islam as revitalistic. Laue (1964) and Miller (1969) have examined these two movements in relation to the concept of revitalization in some detail. A brief comparison of Neo-Buddhism, Black Muslims and the Soka Gakkai movement of Japan as revitalization movements in complex societies has also been made by Fiske (1969:152-156). Other revitalistic religions of protest are found in India and the United States, but Neo-Buddhism and the Black Muslim movement are of particular significance in their widespread influence in India and the United States as strong critics of the dominant society.

Neo-Buddhism, as Buddhism among Untouchables is often called, is an attempt by some Untouchable individuals and groups in India to uncouple from the Hindu social system which is permeated with concepts of hierarchy, purity and pollution. In 1935 B.R. Ambedkar, the acknowledged leader of the Untouchables, declared, "I was born in the Hindu religion but I will not die in the Hindu religion" (Kharat quoted in Zelliot 1966:199-200) and thereby signaled the eventual conversion movement whose culmination came in the mass conversion ceremonies involving an estimated crowd of 300,000 to 600,000 people in October 1956 (Zelliot 1966:191). Since this time Buddhist conversion among Untouchables has continued in India.

The beginnings of the Nation of Islam are more difficult to pinpoint since it was an outgrowth of the Moorish-American Science Temple movement led by Noble Ali Drew and later by W.D. Fard but during the mid-1930s the movement came under the leadership of the present and most important leader of the Black Muslims, Elijah Muhammad, grew in membership and crystalized its organization and beliefs (Essein-Udom 1962:17-82; Lincoln 1961:10-17, 66, 72-74).

Both Neo-Buddhism and the Muslim movement had for their springboard the shared deprivations of a rigidly caste-organized society in which a respectable past was as foreclosed as a respectable present or future. The creation of a new past, then, came to be a prerequisite for the restructuring of the present and the future.

THE CREATION MYTHS

The creation myth valued by the Neo-Buddhists is embodied in the book by Ambedkar, *The Untouchables: Who Were They and Why They Became Untouchables?* (1948). Untouchables are portrayed as stray survivors of ancient tribes broken up by tribal warfare who struck a bargain with settled agricultural tribes to be the watchmen over their fields and cattle in return for food and shelter. These "broken men" came to live outside of the villages since kinship constituted the common bond required for habitation in a particular village. Being torn from the context of their own tribes these individual tribesmen had to form separate enclaves outside of the village. The "broken men" were ancient Buddhists who refused to change their religion to Brahmanism or Hinduism when it became ascendant. The transformation of these "broken men" into Untouchables was related to the long struggle for converts and power between Buddhism and Brahmanism. Brahmins, who were originally not only meat eaters but also beef eaters, took up vegetarianism and made the cow sacred in order to wean the masses to their faith and away from Buddhism which allowed meat-eating but not the killing of cows. At this point, the eating of cow meat came to be considered defiling and the "broken men" became Untouchables who, due to their extreme poverty, could not eliminate this offensive yet extremely important food from their diet.

The origin myth of the Black Muslims is embodied in an undated pamphlet written by Elijah Muhammad called the "Supreme Wisdom: Solution to the So-Called Negro's Problem". The major theme in this myth is that "The Original Man" or the first people, were Black members of the tribe of Shabazz and the procreators of all other races. Additionally, the "Original Man" was Muslim as are all Black men by nature. Blackness is divine and Blacks in the United States are the most righteous of all in the Black Nation. Whiteness as the antithesis of blackness is weak and immoral. White man was created by an ancient Black scientist through an experiement in human hybridization and has oppressed the Black man particularly through the "slave religion" of Christianity. However, the reign of white men is soon to end and Black men will again be supreme as in the beginning (Lincoln 1961:75-80; Essien-Udom 1962:131-142).

Despite obvious differences in the content of these two creation myths, they can be seen to be similar in that each attempts to portray a history which provides a link with the past when the group's status was much higher than in the present, and links the group to an orthodox religious tradition. Each myth pinpoints a people--Brahmins in the case of India and whites in the case of the United States--who were and are still the oppressors, and links each of these exploitive groups to a dominant religion. These religions, Hinduism and Christianity, respectively, are different from the original religious traditions of the oppressed.

The major difference between the Buddhist origin myth and the Black Muslim origin myth lies in the fact that Untouchables have claimed a connection to a religion which is indigenous to India while the Black Muslims claim ties with a religious tradition outside of American society, in the Middle East. This different has an important implication for the way that the Buddhists and Black Muslims relate to the Nations of India and the United States of which they are willingly or unwillingly a part. Neo-Buddhist reject Hinduism but consider themselves to be Indians while the Black Muslim identifies as a Muslim not only religiously but also nationalistically.

Origin myths of specific Untouchable *jatis* which claim past high status ordinarily accompany the process of Sanskritization in India. The origin myth of the Neo-Buddhists is of particular interest in that it claims a universal origin for all Untouchables in contrast to the specific myths of origin of particular Untouchable *jatis*. These points have important implications for the understanding of caste in India and the United States. While Harper (1968a:52) emphasizes the multi-caste nature of Indian society as opposed to the dual caste nature of American socity, others such as Berreman (1960) and Bhatt (1972), while recognizing the many caste groups, have sometimes utilized a dual caste model for India, finding it relevant for certain types of analyses. In this instance it can be seen that Neo-Buddhists are moving toward a dual caste model of Indian society comprised of Untouchables, the oppressed, the Brahmins representing the high caste oppressors. This dual model is of course very similar to the Muslim conception of the dual division between Blacks and whites in the United States and the world.

COMPOSITION OF BUDDHISTS AND MUSLIM

The actual numbers in the Muslim and Buddhist movement are difficult to pinpoint. In the early 1960s when the two major empirical studies of the Black Muslims were done Lincoln (1961:106) suggests that there were 100,000 members in the movement while Essien-Udom differentiates between levels of commitment to the movement and indicates "that there are at present between 5,000 and 15,000 registered followers, at least 50,000 believers and a much larger number of sympathizers" (1962:71). The movement has as a rule been secretive about the numbers of its following. The problem of estimating Muslim membership accurately is compounded by the fact that the recent U.S. census did not gather any information on religious affiliation. We can assume, however, that the United Nations figure for Muslims in North America which is given as 168,000 (Britanica Book of the Year 1972:613) includes very substantial numbers of Black Muslims though there are also other Islamic groups in North America.

In the 1961 census there were 3,250,227 Buddhists reported for India, of whom the majority are former Untouchables. One scholar puts the number of Buddhist converts among Untouchables at 3½ million in the 1966-1967 period (Fiske 1972:113). Uncertainties about actual numbers of Buddhist converts are primarily due to the fact that the benefits of the "protective discrimination policy", a system of government aid in education and employment, are extended most unambiguously to Untouchables who remain within the Hindu fold and, therefore, many who consider themselves to be Buddhists may not officially claim this status (Smith 1963:322-326; Isaacs 1965:117-119; Zelliot 1966:192-193; Lynch 1969:146-147; for an evaluation of the "protective discrimination policy" see the works of Dushkin 1961, 1967, 1972).

The Muslim membership can be characterized as young, mainly male, ordinarily lower class, predominantly comprised of ex-Christian American Blacks (Lincoln 1961:22-27). The essentially lower class composition of the Black Muslims is

seen in the fact that there were in the early 1960s only ten college graduates in the whole Nation of Islam (Essien-Udom 1962:183).

Conversion to Buddhism among Untouchables can be characterized as community-based. For example, 70 percent of the Mahars of Maharastra have embraced the new faith (Zelliot 1966:192). The Jatavs of Uttar Pradesh have been another caste drawn to Buddhism (Lynch 1969:129). Conversion seems to have occurred in castes which have already achieved, in comparison to other Untouchable castes in India, a degree of mobility and some access to the resources of wealth, education and privilege. For instance, in the early 1960s the Mahars, who comprise 35.1 percent of the scheduled caste or Untouchable population of Maharastra, were recipients of 85.5 percent of the "post-matric" scholarships set aside for Untouchable students in this state (Bose 1970:218), while the urban Jatav studied by Lynch (1969) had already experienced some general betterment of their economic and social conditions prior to conversion.

The clearest benefit of membership in both the Black Muslim movement and the Neo-Buddhist movement is a gain in self-esteem. Lincoln's statement that "to be identified with a movement that openly rejects the fundamental values of the powerful majority is to increase vastly one's self-esteem and one's stature among one's peers" (1961:29) applies equally well to the Muslim and the Buddhist. Zelliot has noted that recent converts to Buddhism "often say that they experience a sudden sense of release, a psychological freedom" (1966:205). For Black Muslims, this central reward of self-esteem may be coupled with various types of material gains. Muslims who have been genuinely open to the conversion of non-productive members of society such as the ex-convict have been able to provide economic opportunities for a growing number of its members in their own businesses. Muslims also have a record of ease in finding employment in the larger society as compared to Blacks who are not members of the movement (Lincoln 1961:24). Interestingly enough, this is probably due in large measure to the Muslims' strong emphasis on that set of white middle class values which can be subsumed under the title "the Protestant ethic". Muslims are prohibited from drinking, smoking, dancing, gambling, fornicating and enjoined to be diligent, honest, thrifty and sober in manner and in dress. A separatist stance, a search for a different cultural identity rooted in the Middle East has not meant a total rejection of the dominant values of the "successful" man in American Culture. Parenti has written: "If the Muslims reject the white man, they embrace the Protestant ethic. Nor should this appear as a paradox, for the very attempt to rise above the lower class Negro subculture requires some emulation of the standards of the dominant white community" (1964:185). The convert to Buddhism, however, may face serious problems of loss of governmental help earmarked for the Hindu Untouchable under the "protective discrimination policy" and the "reservation system". Since under this system a portion of government positions, legislative seats, university places and scholarships are reserved for members of the Untouchable castes, this is a serious loss indeed.

IDEOLOGY

The ideology of the Black Muslims and the Neo-Buddhists derives at least in part from the religious traditions of orthodox Islam and Buddhism. Neo-Buddhists and Muslims have tried to validate their position as parts of these orthodox communities and have met with a fair degree of resistance. While the orthodox traditions from which Neo-Buddhism and

Black Islam are drawn are quite divergent, seen as religions of protest, there are remarkable similarities as well as differences in their approach to the ultimate questions of man's relationship to man and to the supernatural. Both movements are basically secular and de-emphasize older-wordly concerns. Ambedkar drew upon an already established non-theistic strain in older Buddhism when he wrote the bible of the Neo-Buddhist movement, *The Buddha and his Dhamma* (1957). In this work he emphasized and reinterpreted in modern terms aspects of Buddhist thought which challenge Brahminical ideas forming part of the theological underpinning of the Hindu caste system. The followers of the New Buddhism also conceive of the religion as a system of "morality" which emphasizes the equality and dignity of man. They see Buddhism as this-world oriented (Fiske 1969:130-142).

The Black Muslim reinterpretation of orthodox Islam is perhaps more far-reaching, for " . . . the Movement is a religion with no distinct God, no after-life and no heaven. It is a religion of the here and now" (Lincoln 1961:248). Orthodox Islam, of course, has distinct notions of an after-life in which the individual is rewarded or punished for this life. The dominant religions in India and the United States, Hinduism and Christianity, respectively, place a strong emphasis on deferred reward in the next life. In Hinduism, the reward system is based on the notion of reincarnation into a higher caste, while in Christianity it is based on ideas of heaven and hell. Both Neo-Buddhists and Black Muslims have created ideologies that de-emphasize the possibility of reward in some other life and, thereby, have created ideologies congruent with their mobility-striving in this life.

Black Muslims differ greatly from the Buddhists in the separatist bent of their ideology. While the Buddhist in India looks toward integration into the larger society, the Muslims have a nationalistic, separatist ideology which accepts the racial system but asserts the superiority of Black men and looks forward to a separate Black nation. To the Black Muslim, therefore, citizenship in the United States tends to have little meaning and to be temporary. The Black Muslims, believing that white government and rule is corrupt and is soon to be replaced by the righteous rule of the Black Nation, shied away from political participation, particularly in the early days. The clearest indication of non-participation in the political arena prior to the 1960's, for example, was the reluctance of Muslims to vote (Lincoln 1961:18; Essien-Udom 1962:264-269). There is a good deal of evidence, however, that this early uncompromising and politically separatist posture has been softened in recent years, and that the movement has shown signs of accomodation to the larger society (Parenti 1964:187-191; Kaplan 1969:173). As a part of this accommodation, various types of political involvement, including voting, have come to be more acceptable in the Muslim culture (Parenti 1964:188-189). The Buddhists have been very energetic on the political front, and the Republican Party, an opposition party dedicated to the needs of the Untouchables, is primarily a party of Untouchable Buddhists in India (Zelliot 1966:207; Lynch 1969:95-96). The close relationship between the political party and the Buddhist movement is natural, since B.R. Ambedkar masterminded both efforts, and Lynch has shown the congruence between the goals of the Buddhists and the Republican Party which provide important reinforcement to the believer (1969:95-98, 143). It is ironic to note that recent court cases have ruled that Buddhists may not contest seats in parliament reserved under the "reservation system" for Hindu Untouchables (Dushkin 1972:200-201), and this has reduced the arena of effective political participation for the Buddhists.

THE LEADERS

The nature of the relationship between the two movements and the national societies in which they are found is also reflected in the kind of leadership that the Buddhists and the Muslims have had. While a number of important leaders have existed in both movements, I will here consider only the two leaders who have been considered to be the prophets of these faiths.

B.R. Ambedkar, who died shortly after the first mass conversion of Buddhists took place, remains in death as he was in life a culture hero to the Untouchables, and in particular to the Buddhists. An aura of the sacred is attached to him, since Buddhists have elevated him to the position of a Bodhisatva (Lynch 1969:Ch V 129-165; 1972). Born into the Untouchable Mahar community he achieved a degree of erudition and prestige rarely possible for Untouchables of his day. A prophet of the Neo-Buddhist faith and the first law minister of India, he helped to draft the Indian Constitution that struck down in law the traditional privileges of caste. He broke with tradition in his second marriage (to a Brahmin doctor) and exemplified the possibilities of mobility to his less fortunate and less gifted brethern. Ambedkar was not only a leader of the Untouchables and the Buddhists but also an important political leader in the dominant society. Indian society, particularly the governmental structure, is imprinted with his influence as well as that of other great leaders such as Gandhi and Nehru. The Buddhist acceptance of the new faith and their reaffirmation of the Untouchables as willing contributors and citizens of a new, modern India is symbolized in the person of Dr. Ambedkar.

Within the Muslim movement Elijah Muhammad, the "Prophet and Messenger of Allah", occupies a position similar to Ambedkar's as a charismatic religious leader. From a poor southern background, Muhammad received only a grade school education and came to show his skill as an organizer and leader within the context of the Muslim movement. Indeed, much of his appeal to the rank and file of the believers is that he is just like them, alienated from and discriminated against by the society at large (Essien-Udom 1962:79-80). Unlike Ambedkar, then, Muhammad is not an important leader of the "establishment" or the dominant society. The separatist nature of the Black Muslim movement is, of course, congruent with Muhammad's leadership role being limited to the movement.

SUMMARY

Neo-Buddhism and Black Islam are revitalistic religions of protest which are important movements in India and the United States. Arising out of a sense of deprivation in a caste oriented society, both are attempts to redefine the structural position of a group of people in a society. Each is an attempt to lay the blame for the present degradation of the group on a people and a dominant religion. Untouchables see their plight as due to the tyranny of the Hindu ideology and its Brahmin elite. Black Muslims rebel against the white man and his Christianity. Each group sees the society in which they live as essentially a dual caste society. This perception is reflected in the origin myth of each group and in their ideologies. Both movements bear testimony to the human effort to rebel against societal deprivation. The strength of the Neo-Buddhist movement among Untouchables in India is further indication adding to the mounting evidence that the Untouchables in India like the Blacks in the United States have not accepted the high caste interpretation of their inferiority as just and have used a variety of means to better their position in society. The secular, this-wordly ideologies of both religions have provided the ideological backing for status mobility aspirations of each group.

The major difference between these two movements which has been stressed in this paper is in the relation between Neo-Buddhism and Black Islam and the dominant secular societal context in which they are imbedded. Neo-Buddhism affirms its identification with the modern state of India. It does so in a variety of ways. The conception of Buddhism as an indigenous religion aids in Buddhist identification as Indians. The political participation by Buddhists in Indian society through the Republican Party is another way of expressing Indian identity. Dr. B.R. Ambedkar's leadership role in both the Buddhist subculture and in the dominant culture facilitated the identification of the Buddhists with the larger society.

The Black Muslims, unlike the Buddhists, have strongly stressed their separatism from the dominant culture and had done so prior to the emphasis on partial and voluntary separatism which has now become an important current in American Black culture. A de-emphasis of political participation in the larger society has been congruent with this separatist ideology. Elijah Muhammad's role as a leader has been confined primarily to the Muslim group and he has held no institutional leadership position in the dominant society. The separatist bent of Black Islam is symbolized in the restricted leadership role of Muhammad.

REFERENCES

Ambedkar, B.R.
1948   The Untouchables: Who are They and Why They became Untouchables. New Delhi: Amrit Book Company.
1957   The Buddha and His Dhamma. Bombay: Siddarth College Publication.

Anant, Santokh Singh
1971   "Caste Hindu attitudes: the Harijan's perception." Asian Survey. 11:271-278.

Bailey, F.G.
1957   Caste and the Economic Frontier. Manchester: Manchester University Press.

Berreman, Gerald D.
1960   "Caste in India and the United States." American Journal of Sociology. 66:120-127.
1966a   "Caste in cross-cultural perspective: organizational components: introduction." In George de Vos and Hiroshi Wagatsuma (eds.), Japan's Invisible Race: Caste in Culture and Personality. pp. 275-276. Berkeley and Los Angeles: University of California Press.
1966b   "Structure and function of caste systems." In George de Vos and Hiroshi Wagatsuma (eds.) Japan's Invisible Race: Caste in Culture and Personality. pp. 277-307. Berkeley and Los Angeles: University of California Press.
1966c   "Concomitants of caste organization." In George de Vos and Hiroshi Wagatsuma (eds.). Japan's Invisible Race. Caste in Culture and Personality. Pp. 308-324. Berkeley and Los Angeles: University of California Press.
1967   "Stratification, pluralism and interaction: a comparative analysis of caste." In A. de Reuck and J. Knight (eds.). Caste and Race: Comparative Approaches. Pp. 45-73. London: J.A. Churchill.

Béteille, André
1972   "Pollution and poverty." In J. Michael Mahar (ed.). The Untouchables in Contemporary India. Pp. 411-420. Tuscon, Arizona: University of Arizona Press.

Bhatt, Bharat L.
1972   "The distribution of scheduled castes and tribes as an element of regional social systems." Paper read at the Annual Conference of the Association of Asian Studies. New York.

Bose, A.B.
1970   "Educational development among scheduled castes." Man in India, Vol. 50, no. 3: 209-239.

Britannica Book of the Year
1972   Encyclopedia Britannica. Chicago, London, Toronto.

Cohn, Bernard
1955   "The changing status of a depressed caste." In McKim Marriott (ed.). Village India. Pp. 53-77. Chicago: University of Chicago Press.

De Vos, George
1966a   "Motivational components of caste." In George de Vos and Hiroshi Wagatsuma (eds.). Japan's Invisible Race: Caste in Culture and Personality. Pp. 325-331. Berkeley and Los Angeles: University of California Press.
1966b   "Essential elements of caste: psychological determinants in structural theory." In George de Vos and Hiroshi Wagatsuma (eds.). Japan's Invisible Race: Caste in Culture and Personality. Pp. 332-352. Berkeley and Los Angeles. University of California Press.
1966c   "Toward a cross-cultural psychology of caste behavior." In George de Vos and Hiroshi Wagatsuma (eds.). Japan's Invisible Race: Caste in Culture and Personality. Pp. 353-384. Berkeley and Los Angeles: University of California Press.
1967   "Psychology of purity and pollution as related to social identity and caste." In A. de Reuck and J. Knight (eds.). Caste and Race: Comparative Approaches. Pp. 292-315. London: J.A. Churchill.

Dollard, John
1957   Caste and Class in a Southern Town. Garden City, New York: Doubleday and Company.

Dumont, Louis
1967   "Caste: a phenomena of social structure or an aspect of Indian culture?" In A. de Reuck and J. Knight (eds.). Caste and Race: Comparative Approaches. Pp. 28-37. London: J. and A. Churchill.
1970   Homo Hierarchicus: An Essay on the Caste System. Translated by Mark Swainsbury. Chicago: University of Chicago Press.

Dushkin, Lelah
1961   "The Backward Classes: special treatment policy." Economic Weekly XIII, 1665-1668, 1695-1705, 1729-1738.
1967   "Scheduled caste policy in India: history, problems, prospects." Asian Survey VII, 626-636.
1972   "Scheduled caste politics." In J. Michael Mahar (ed.). The Untouchables in Contemporary India. Pp. 165-226. Tucson, Arizona: University of Arizona Press.

Essien-Udom, E.U.
1962   Black Nationalism. Chicago: University of Chicago Press.

Fiske, Adele
1969 "Religion and Buddhism among India's New Buddhists." Social Research. 36:123-157.
1972 "Scheduled caste Buddhist organizations." In J. Michael Mahar (ed.). The Untouchables in Contemporary India. Pp. 113-142. Tucson, Arizona: University of Arizona Press.

Gough, Kathleen
1960 "Caste in a Tanjore village." In E.R. Leach (ed.). Aspects of Caste in South India, Ceylon and Pakistan. Pp. 11-60. London: Cambridge University Press.

Gould, Harold A.
1960 "Castes, outcastes and the sociology of stratification." International Journal of Comparative Sociology. Vol. 1, 220-238.

Harper, Edward B.
1968a "A comparative analysis of caste: the United States and India." In Milton Singer and Bernard S. Cohn (eds.). Structure and Change in Indian Society. Pp. 51-77. Chicago: Aldine Publishing Company.
1968b "Social consequence of an 'unsuccessful' low caste movement." In James Silverberg (ed.). Social Mobility in the Caste System in India. Pp. 36-65. Hague, Netherlands: Mouton Publishers.

Isaacs, Harold
1965 India's Ex-Untouchables. New York: John Day Company.

Johnson, Sipra B. and M. Glen
1972 "India and the United States: divergent attacks on discrimination." Man in India. 52(2):113-122.

Kaplin, H.M.
1969 "Black Muslims and the Negro American's quest for communion." British Journal of Sociology. 20:164-176.

Laue, J.H.
1964 "Contemporary revitalization movements in American race relations: the Black Muslims." Social Forces. 42:315-323.

Leach, E.R.
1960 "Introduction: what should we mean by caste?" In E.R. Leach (ed.). Aspects of Caste in South India, Ceylon and North West Pakistan. Pp. 1-10. London: Cambridge University Press.

Lincoln, C. Eric
1961 The Black Muslims in America. Boston: Beacon Press.

Lynch, Owen
1969 The Politics of Untouchability. New York: Columbia University Press.
1972 "Dr. B.R. Ambedkar--myth and charisma." In J. Michael Mahar (ed.). The Untouchables in Contemporary India. Pp. 97-112. Tucson, Arizona: University of Arizona Press.

Mahar, Pauline M.
1960 "Changing religious practices of an Untouchable caste." Economic Development and Cultural Change. Vol. VII (3), 279-287.

Mandelbaum, David G.
1970 Society in India: Continuity and Change. Vol. 1. Berkeley, Los Angeles, London: University of California Press.

Mencher, Joan
1972 "Continuity and change in an ex-Untouchable community in south India." In J. Michael Mahar (ed.). The Untouchables in Contemporary India. Pp. 37-56. Tucson, Arizona: University of Arizona Press.

Miller, Beatrice Diamond
1969 "Revitalization movements: theory and practice as evidenced among Buddhists of Maharastra, India. In M.C. Pradhan et al (ed.). Anthropology and Archeology: Essays in Commemoration of Verrier Elwin 1902-64. Bombay: Oxford University Press.

Parenti, M.
1964 "Black Muslims: from revolution to institution." Social Research. 31:175-194.

Rowe, William
1968 "The new Cauhans: a caste mobility movement in North India." In James Silverberg (ed.). Social Mobility in the Caste System in India. Pp. 66-77. The Hague, Netherlands: Mouton Publishers.

Sebring, James M.
1969 "Caste indicators and caste identification of strangers. Human Organization, Vol. 28; no. 3, 199-207.

Smith, Donald E.
1963 India as a Secular State. Princeton: Princeton University Press.

Srinivas, M.N.
1956 "A note on Sanskritization and Westernization." Far Eastern Quarterly. Vol. XV (4), 481-496.
1965 Religion and Society among the Coorgs of South India. Bombay, New York: Asia Publishing House.

Verba, Sidney et al.
1971 Caste, Race, and Politics: A Comparative Study of India and the United States. Beverly Hills, London: Sage Publications.

Wallace, Anthony F.C.
1956 "Revitalization movements." American Anthropologist. 58:264-281.

Zelliot, Eleanor
1966 "Buddhism and politics in Maharashtra." In Donald Smith (ed.). Religion and Politics in South Asia. Pp. 191-212. Princeton: Princeton University Press.

15

STRATEGY OF INTERNAL RELATIONS:
An Examination of the Conflict in Ceylon

R.S. PERINBANAYAGAM AND MAYA CHADDA
Hunter College

and

MAYA CHADDA
Brooklyn College

ABSTRACT

Strategic considerations have been applied to the analysis of relationships between units within the internationsl system. Such applications were based on a general theory of strategy derived from - or at least connected to - an equally general social psychological theory. Hence the theory of strategy can be applied to any interactional system and process - interpersonal, inter-group, inter-community, inter-state or international. Such an application is made here to the relationship between two ethno-linguistic communities in Ceylon that have been in conflict for over two decades. It is argued that had the leadership of the communities thought in strategic terms *and prosecuted their interactions accordingly, certain manifestations of conflict could have been obviated. It is suggested that hence we can speak of clever and wise performers in leadership roles - those who anticipate the full implications of the activities they are pursuing at the moment, and stupid performers, who do not. In the language of game theory: it is incumbent on performers to distinguish between zero-sum games and mixed-motive games; to be unable to do so is to bring disaster on themselves and the causes they represent.*

I

A number of recent social theorists have developed a more or less related view that has been called variously "game theory" (Rapoport, 1960; Schelling, 1960) or the "dramaturgical perspective" (Goffman, 1954) or the "social psychological approach" (Scheff, 1967). Each of these labels are used to stress subtle variations in the model and perhaps also varying epistemologies; it however seems to us that the behavioral content of these approaches are the same. They all seek to understand and explain social phenomenon in terms of their "meaning" to participants -- meanings they themselves create in ongoing transactions.

This was certainly the seminal insight that George Herbert Mead bequeathed to sociology -- a notion that has had a variety of progeny. One makes a gesture, begins an act in the anticipation that another will make a corresponding gesture to complete the act and make it meaningful. The clear implication is that the respondent is willing and able to understand the gesture and respond to it; that is, to really appreciate the gesture. This is guaranteed, Mead argued, by the fact that the participants in a transaction exist in the same universe of discourse (Mead, 1934). This, it seems to us, while being an excellent general theory of symbolic communication, is deficient in expalining at least one special case: that of a relationship sustained by conflict rather then cooperation. One makes a neutral gesture, for example, that is deliberately interpreted by the respondent as a hostile one so that he can prosecute a conflict with the other. Another example would be a gesture that is fraught with a variety of likely significations, out of which the respondent selects the one most suitable to his purposes in the conflict. In other words, such opportunities for creating meanings over and above the ones intended is always present in human communications. If one adds the dimension of time to these aspects of communication, the opportunities for ambiguity in communication becomes more pronounced. Meanings are created not only in responsive discourse, but is maintained over a period of time, at any point of which period they can

be altered. It is this property of the development of meaning that lends substance to the conception of social life as drama. Langer writing of the similarity of life to drama observes, "Its basic abstraction is the act which springs from the past, but is directed toward the future and is always great with the future" (1953). The present however may be pregnant with the future, but it is for all that yet to be born, yet to unfold and may turn out to be something different from those anticipated by the participants of the present. However one comes to assess these participants in terms of their correct or foolish anticipations of the future events. Hence an awareness of the likely developments of an act and an anticipation of some of the more drastic consequences of an act are qualities that one expects from clever performers. An astute leader then is one who anticipates some of the more salient of the consequences of his act and measures their impact on his following and cause. A military tactician who makes his moves and destroys his whole nation is a foolish leader, however imperative his strategic moves may have been; a political leader who employs a strategy of whose multiple meanings he is innocent, may be rendering more harm to his followers than even their enemies could have done. Strategy then in a conflict may be viewed as an act that can have multiple consequences; it can solve immediate problems and create unsolvable problems for the future; it can be used to save face now, but may lead to the loss of the whole body some other time.

This perspective has been, in its many manifestations, very useful in analyzing international relations.[1] It is proposed here to examine relationships of two communities in conflict within a nation -- Ceylon, with this perspective. The two main ethno-linguistic communities in the island are the Sinhalese and the Tamils. Should they submerge sectarian differences and sacrifice some sectarian advantages and work towards the development of an economically and politically secure Ceylonese nation or should they conduct themselves in such a way that they would drift apart and lay the foundations of a festering area of conflict in South Asia? These, it seems to us, are two of the overwhelming questions in Ceylon's politics today. Presumably they can -- and could have, followed one or other of these paths and one of them would have been the wiser one. In short, if one can talk of the strategy of international relations, one can also talk of the strategy of internal relations.[2]

II

THE BACKGROUND

An examination of the minority problem in Ceylon must perforce begin with a historical account of the origin of the various groups now resident in Ceylon, though one can seriously talk of the minorities as a political problem only with the emergence of the trappings of the modern nation-state in the shape of universal adult franchise, representative government and a centralized administration and bureaucracy. It is proposed here to give a brief historical account of the origins of Ceylon's different ethnic and religious groups and then pinpoint the circumstances under which they -- individually and severally became units in a structure of conflict and confrontation that has been the political life of Ceylon for several decades now.

The dominant group in Ceylon is the Sinhalese who constitute about 70% of the population. Their origin myth has it that they immigrated from nothern India and settled in Ceylon about 2500 years ago. The language of the Sinhalese lends support to this thesis insofar as it is an Indo-European language. However it also seems certain that racially the current Sinhalese group underwent heavy admixture with the neighboring Dravidian element. Further many migrant Dravidian groups from Southern India were also sinhalized over time and contributed their numbers to the Sinhalese stock (Obeysekera, 1970). In any case, they constitute a more or less homogenous ethno-linguistic group and are mainly Buddhists. This combination of ethnicity, linguistic community and religious identification give them a certain rigidity as well as a sense of destiny. No doubt it is a source of their great psychological and political strength.

The next significant group in Ceylon -- the main minority group, are the 'Ceylon Tamils' -- so called to distinguish them from the Indian immigrants of later vintage. The Ceylon Tamils are mainly descendant of Tamil immigrants over the centuries -- mainly of those who came with the South Indian invasions that characterized Ceylon's earlier history. They occupy the northern and eastern part of the island today and were constituted as an independent kingdom at the time of the European take-over.

The South Indian immigrants are the descendants of indentured laborers brought to Ceylon by the British to work in the coffee and later the tea plantations. They number a little over a million today and during the British rulership and immediately thereafter were treated as an integral part of the Ceylonese community.

In addition to these groups there are the 'Burghers' -- descendants of Portuguese and Dutch settlers from the days when these two powers ruled Ceylon. The Burghers have for the most part imigrated to Australia, the U.K. or Canada and do not constitute a part of the problem of the minorities.

If the foregoing can be said to be a description of the minorities from an ethnic and/or linguistic basis, we must yet focus on the problem as one of religious conflict as well. The Sinhalese are mainly Buddhist and the Tamils are predominantly Hindu. However the European conquest of the island created a large number of Christians-Protestants and Roman Catholics, and they were a privileged minority during the British occupation. These groups are drawn from both the Sinhalese and Tamil ethnic groups, though naturally most of them are Sinhalese. In addition to thse groups there are also substantial number of Muslims -- descendants of Arab and Moorish merchants and traders.

When Ceylon was finally conquered by the British in 1796, the Portuguese and after them the Dutch had ruled the coastal regions for nearly 300 years. However the British consolidated their power in the island by conquering the inland kingdom of Kandy as well and brought the entire island under a central administration. The island--hitherto consisting of a western coastal kingdom, a central kingdom and the northern kingdom was effectively unified despite the linguistic, religious and cultural differences among them. In an important sense, this was the first step towards the eventual emergence of a nation-state. In any case, whilst doing this, they also laid the foundations for the structures of conflict that were to emerge a hundred years later. Thus unified, the Sinhalese in South and Central Ceylon and the Tamils in the North and East of Ceylon began to accommodate themselves to the new situation. One of the important consequences of such accommodation was the emergence of an English-educated elite. The establishment of English schools and the opening of positions in the administrative services to the natives resulted in this emergence and the British lost no time in trying to co-opt this strata into its imperial framework. The instrument of this co-optation was the "Legislative Council"--a body that consisted of nominated Ceylonese and English representatives and whose task was to advise the Governor on the proper administration of the country. The British government was so pleased with this arrangement that it decided to extend its powers--at least to make it elective. By making it elective, it also decided to give additional weightage to the minorities--particularly the Tamils by creating "communal electorates", thereby giving the Tamils a sense of power in the country's affairs not warranted by their numbers. In addition, such a step was a tacit admission that a Ceylonese nationalism was still far from a reality.

In any case, the Legislative Council was abandoned in 1931 and rather revolutionary constitutional changes were introduced--The Donoughmore Reforms. Communal representation was abolished and territorial representation with universal, adult franchise to a new State Council with both legislative and executive powers was introduced. This was a truly extreme step, when one considers the bitter struggles that were going on in India at this time for similar reforms. The Tamils boycotted the elections to begin with, on the grounds that the reforms were not far-reaching enough. And the Sinhalese proceeded to take advantage of the absence of the Tamils to form a Pan-Sinhalese Ministry.

The State Council, with its program of partial self-government, functioned till the eve of Independence in 1948--The Soulbury Reforms of 1947. The minorities returned to the Council chambers and in the Second State Council of 1936, Tamils were given responsible positions. When independence came in 1948, it appeared that despite the cries of some Tamil representatives, organized in the Tamil Congress, a certain measure of harmony among the various groups in Ceylon had been established. Indeed it is doubtful whether independence would have come so easily and so readily had not the Sinhalese leadership of the time given assurances, in word and deed, that a unified *Ceylonese* nation, in which no ethnic or religious group would claim special privileges was the goal of all responsible Sinhalese opinion. The constitution of Ceylon in fact embodied these assurances in the form of numerous provisions to safeguard the rights of the minorities in Ceylon (Wilson, 1958). Indeed various Tamils were co-opted into the cabinet that was formed after the 1947 general elections and the ruling political party--the United National Party was composed of all ethnic and religious groups and was apparently interested in pursuing the objectives of a secular national-bourgeois state. Even the dissident Tamils in the Tamil Congress seemed to agree when they joined the UNP government soon fafter independence.[3]

The calm and the harmony was however only on the surface. Unbeknownst to most observers and to the leadership, a cauldron was simmering, to soon boil over in 1956. It is customary to give credit to Mr. S. W. R. D. Bandaranaike for having given the final spark for this to happen. In any case, the UNP was a party of the English-educated and westernized elite, elected to office on account of a support received from a semi-feudal electorate, blind to its very interests. Soon the electorate realized that its interests--economic, socio-cultural and political were not in the hands of the UNP but in the newly formed *Sri Lanka Freedom Party* and its leadership. This party was able to articulate the aspirations of the Sinhalese masses--that its language should receive preference to English, that its religion and culture should receive support and recognition--and indeed the slogan of the moment was Language and Religion. For too many years have Sinhalese and Buddhism been the step-children of the State and it was time to dethrone English and Christianity. It was indeed a powerful rallying cry and it was destined to change the subsequent story of Ceylon irrevocably. For the Tamils and the Christians it was a cry of alarm and the unity and sense of participation with the Sinhalese Buddhists they were beginning to feel, was to erode soon. The SLFP and its allies won the election of 1956 and soon enacted the 'Sinhala Only' legislation and pledged to give "Buddhism its due place". The Tamils united under the leadership of the 'Federal Party', a party pledged to some form or other of separation of the 'Tamil speaking areas' from the rest of Ceylon. In other words, both the Sinhalese and the Tamils were suddenly shoved apart and moved to extreme positions.[4]

As can be seen from the foregoing, the Ceylonese population was divided--divided into structures of identity and associations that were at odds with the assumptions and objectives of a nation-state. These structures were seeing themselves as having different and conflicting interests which, generally speaking, could be realized only at the expense of the interests of the others. How had this come about? The answer to this question has always been given in terms of historical, political, and economical factors. It is proposed here to examine it in historical, political as well as in social psychological terms.

III

PATTERNS OF FAILURE: TAMIL STRATEGY IN CEYLON POLITICS

In a retrospective examination of the politics of Ceylon, it is fairly obvious now that the Tamils having been traumatized by the abolition of communal representation by the Donoughmore reforms, somehow took the wrong turn. Ever since then they have been taking turns that compounded their error and made retracement difficult. The days before Donoughmore were halcyon days with Tamils in leadership in every sphere--including the political sphere, and the illusion was fostered, and it now appears, entrenched, that they could somehow overcome their numerical limitation. The years since have been years in which the Tamils have been emancipating themselves from this illusion, albeit rudely and without charity from the Sinhalese.

What happened after the Donoughmore Reforms? The Tamils were now being represented by Mr. G. G. Ponnambalam a flamboyant orator with, it seems, little political and social thought to inform his leadership. Every political issue was for him a legal problem and the only thing to do was to prepare a good brief and make a plea to the proper court. The entire period between the Donoughmore reforms and the Soulbury reforms was then spent in trying to undo the disadvantages suffered by the Tamils as a result of the introduction of territorial representation based on adult franchise. In other words, Mr. Ponnambalam was seeking to overcome the fact that his followers, the Ceylon Tamils, were only about 12% of the population. The strategy that the Tamil Congress adopted to accomplish this was to bring other smaller minorities in Ceylon like the Muslims and the Burghers under one banner and demand "balanced representation" for the minorities.

The utter simplicity of this scheme to destroy the electoral strength of the Sinhalese must have awed many a minority follower of Mr. Ponnambalam's. Though the alliance of minorities did not last, it must be said to Mr. Ponnambalam's credit that he did cement one briefly with the leaders of the Muslim and Burgher communities. In a sense, this was the real beginning of communal politics in Ceylon and almost certainly the first step towards the impasse in which the Tamils find themselves today. The formation of a ministry consisting entirely of Sinhalese despite the presence of many talented Tamils was provocation for such a step, but certainly it is possible to say now that the mistake made by the Sinhalese was compounded by the steps taken by the Tamils: it had the cumulative effect of driving the two communities further apart. The doctrine of balanced representation began to gain favor among the minorities and when the Soulbury commission came in 1946 to Ceylon, they were ready: they wanted balanced representation between the Sinhalese on the one hand and the minorities on the other (Tamils, Muslims, Burghers) and they also wanted Britain to send a commission every ten years to investigate the operation of this scheme.

Meanwhile, of course, the Sinhalese leaders as well as a handful of nationalistic Tamils (along with most other political leaders in colonial territories) were arguing for independence in one or another of its many forms. Of course Lord Soulbury and his associates rejected out of hand Mr. Ponnambalam's demands and established parliamentary government based on territorial representation: the attempt of the Tamils to transform themselves into a basis of numerical equality failed, but much more was lost in these transactions than balanced representation, as will be shown later.

The defeat at the hands of the Soulbury Commissioners did not daunt Mr. Ponnambalam and his followers; they proceeded to fight a virulent communal campaign to get elected to Parliament, and were noticeably lukewarm towards the coming of independence soon after. However, the dynamics of parliamentary government finally gripped Mr. Ponnambalam and an awareness of the blind alley into which he was leading the Tamils together took him into an alliance with the Senanayake government in 1948. Nevertheless, the lessons of isolationism and the capacity to lead his followers into a world of political fantasy were only too carefully learned by some of his henchmen that they broke away and formed an organization that called itself the Federal Party. Obscure though this party was in the beginning, it has since become the voice of the Tamil people as a result of the "language issue."

The language issue broke on the scene in 1956 a few months before the impending general election. This was perhaps the most ambiguous political event in the recent history of Ceylon. To explicate: English had remained the official language of Ceylon even after independence though there were vague promises to make the national languages official languages sometime or other. So that a movement to make Sinhalese the official language was initially an attempt to dethrone English; in addition it was an attempt to dethrone the English-educated elite and elevate the Sinhalese-educated to an elite status; it was further an attempt to dethrone the Tamils who had benefitted most by English education. Finally it was an expression of a genuine cultural revival of the sort that gripped parts of India decades earlier. Hence it is fallacious to interpret the Sinhala only movement in its general manifestation as an exclusively racist, anti-Tamil movement. No doubt the Sinhala only movement had many benighted racists in it and some of them quite prominent, but it is generally a mistake to interpret a mass social movement in terms of single causes or individual participants: to do this is to ignore the complex and emergent properties of a social movement.[5]

In any case, the Tamils as a whole were only too willing to see the Sinhala only movement as a direct and calculated attack on their rights and privileges: decades of communal propaganda had done their proper work. The Federal Party, which up to now was not conspicuously on the side of the national languages replacing English, were there to fight for Tamil anyway and their way was to reorganize the government of Ceylon on a federal basis -- the Tamil-speaking areas and Sinhalese-speaking areas being the units of the federal state. Once again the Tamils and their leaders were unwilling or unable to see the complexity of the situation and responded by making a demand that was calculated, dramaturgically speaking, to increase Sinhalese hostility and suspicion: a demand for near separation in the context of Ceylon's politics was immediately associated with attempts to undermine Ceylon's sovereignity vis a vis India or specifically Southern India and an irritating indifference to the fact that a majority of the Tamils were living in scattered pockets outside the so-called Tamil speaking areas.

The final chapter in this review of the developments is the strategy of the Tamils to have its demands met by assisting one or the other of the major political parties in Ceylon to capture parliamentary power. In accordance with this strategy, they were open to bargains from both the SLFP and the UNP and did in fact conduct negotiations with the SLFP in 1960 and 1965: however the SLFP considered the price asked by the Federal Party too high and so the UNP became the willing buyer. The price it turned out was a bill making for the reasonable use of Tamil, and a more far-reaching demand for regional autonomy for the Tamil speaking areas. The leadership of the UNP in time showed itself willing to fulfill these promises: the first one was fulfilled without great strife and dissension, but the attempt to fulfill the latter threatened to destroy the popular foundations of the UNP that it hastily retracted the Regional Council Bill. This was anathema to the Federal Party who now stood exposed and dishonored before their own popular base--a fact that the opponents of the Federal Party were not slow in pointing out. It was really a matter of time before the Federal Party bowed itself out of the government and it came in September 1968--three years after a general election and two years before another: another strategic move had turned to dust and the Tamil leadership was once again trapped in its own illusions. The UNP was not in a position to pay the agreed price and the SLFP was not even in the market.

Since the failure of that strategy, the Tamils have effectively been outside the political processes in Ceylon. The SLFP returned to power in 1970 with an overwhelming majority and has since proceeded to formulate a new constitution. The main representatives of the Tamil community refused to participate in the proceedings of the constituent Assembly and the Tamil Parliamentarians have in fact kept aloof from the affairs of the nation. Very lately the leadership of the Tamil people--the Federal Party--has called for a 'united front of the Tamil people' to launch a struggle against Sinhalese domination. This is yet to make its impact on the political scene.

What went wrong? Where did they take the wrong turns and why were these in fact wrong turns? In other words, what were the strategic shortcomings of the attempt of the Tamils to secure their fundamental rights in a country where they were unquestionably legitimate citizens as well as industrious and capable producers? In examining the developments outlined here, one is struck by the total dedication and clarity with which the Tamil leadership took the wrong step at critical moments in the emergence of the Ceylonese people. In the days before the fateful Donoughmore Reforms, the political leadership in Ceylon was already beginning to think in terms of forging a Ceylonese people out of the several groups in Ceylon, while some of them were even modelling Ceylon on the example of England. D. S. Senanayake in post-independence times made a valiant attempt to keep the nation together and for a brief moment, from 1947-55, it looked as though he and the UNP might pull it off.

However the abolition of communal representation and the creation of the "Pan-Sinhalese Ministry" had started a process that was unfortunate as it was unforeseen. The two communities--the Sinhalese and the Tamils now looked upon each other as contestants and competitors rather than as partners. The drama of conflict for presumed scarce goods had begun once again and steps taken by either side tended only to aggravate the conflict and continue the drama: each party was only too willing to define the other as the villain. However, the argument of this paper is that the Tamil leadership took steps that were incommensurate with its minority position and secondly that it successfully validated its image as the villain in the drama by measures that were easily construed as either traitorous or thoughtlessly selfish. The Sinhalese, on the other hand, responded to ancient myths of "Tamil danger" and in thoughtless attempts to right wrongs of three hundred years in a few years, paid little heed to concepts of pluralistic societies and nations and demonstrated little interest in understanding the legitimate grievances of Tamils that were masked by their rhetoric and postures.

The minority community in a society or a nation needless to say has a number of handicaps to overcome. Its very minority status somehow makes it a victim of the majority community's patronage and superciliousness. The Tamils of Ceylon were no exception. Notwithstanding this the Tamils were beginning to multiply in the professions and government service, out of all proportion to their number in the population. Of course the Tamils were not to be either blamed for this or be held responsible for it in any way: they merely won out in the competition. However the image this created in the awareness of the Sinhalese community was one of an avaricious and monopolistic tendency to get all the fat of the land: the moment demogogic leaders were found to articulate this image, the casting of the Tamils in the role of the villain was complete. But how do the Tamils, in particular, their leaders respond? The fruitful strategic course would have been to attempt a recasting of the role assigned to the Tamils, to wit, to win the confidence of the majority of the people of

Ceylon and erase these suspicions. But what does Mr. Ponnambalam do? He demands balanced representation in the legislature. Clearly, from the point of view of the Sinhalese, the Tamils were being unreasonably avaricious, almost sinfully attached to certain privileges that had after all fallen to them rather fortuitously. In terms of strategy, nothing could have been more calculated to make the Sinhalese think (or continue to think--it really does not matter) of the Tamils as greedy villains. Dramaturgically speaking, the Tamil leadership really cast themselves in this role with nary a hesitation. The very staging of the Tamil response to rising Sinhalese social movements was to demand a privileged status quo for the Tamils at the expense of the Sinhalese.

In the second place, the Tamil leadership at this stage did not see that the trend in the rest of the colonial world was towards independence. Even in Ceylon where the nationalist movement was very underdeveloped and the leaders indifferent to the struggles going on in India, the Sinhalese leaders were beginning to think in terms of independence. At this critical moment, however, the Tamil leaders were busy once again casting themselves as villains and worse by demanding that Britain send a commission every few years to examine how Her Majesty's loyal subjects--the Tamils, were doing. No other demand could have been more out of date, out of place and out of mind: to really demand that Britain continue her suzerainty just when she wanted to leave the island to its destiny. The Tamil leadership however was concerned only with the support of the Tamil electorate, seemed unaffected by this stupidly unhistorical and politically indefensible move. However, the critical issue seems to have been, once again, the capacity of the Tamils to choose the role of aliens or outsiders to the Sinhalese and Ceylonese cause.

History gave another opportunity to the leaders of Ceylon to show themselves as in fact rational leaders of *Ceylon* and once again the opportunity was lost. The Senanayake government disenfranchised workers of Indian origin on the plantations in one fell swoop and the response of the Tamil leaders was to view this as another attack on "the Tamils": all agitation on the score conducted by the Federal Party of the Ceylon Tamils, was in terms of this interpretation. Yet a rational analysis must admit that the disenfranchisement, while being excessively harsh and inclusive was also an attempt to help the long suffering Sinhalese peasantry. The critical point being made here is that this step could have been seen as a complex problem which demanded sympathy for the Kandyan Sinhalese *as well* as the Tamil Indians. It is suggested that the response could more wisely have been presented by the Tamils in nationalistic terms: the strategy should have been to accept the just aspirations of the Sinhalese and demand the elevation of the people of Ceylon. The ensuing

The ensuing conflict was therefore waged over this kind of emotionally charged misconstructions and misconceptions, all hopes of a significant dialogue were quashed and both sides continued to talk past each other. The Sinhalese and the Tamils both claiming to the citizens of Ceylon were now thoroughly entrapped in the thoughtways of conflict and confrontation.[6]

IV

PATTERNS OF ARROGANCE:
THE SINHALESE IN POWER

How did the Sinhalese define the situation and organize their responses in view of their emergence as a political force with the grant of universal adult franchise? It can be described as a posture of definsive arrogance and foolhardy determination to construct a Sinhala Buddhist Ceylon. This

was patently impossible to achieve -- and could lead only to dissension in the country and costly deviations from the goals of modernization, economic development and national consolidation. But the roots of these attitudes lay deep and have to be examined to understand them fully.

The most obvious place to begin is in the myth and legend as well as history of the Sinhalese people. The key element in these versions of the life of the early Sinhalese people is a certain ambivalence towards India: they claimed origin from an Indian migration and at the same time wanted to be different from India. They were also frightened of Indian political power. 'India', in the early days, meant mainly South Indian Tamil kingdoms. This ambivalence has dominated Sinhalese consciousness to this very day and recent events in India and Bangladesh have made some of these misgivings about India more pronounced. However, the recorded history of the Sinhalese, highly poeticized and garbled no doubt, is contained in various chronicles written by Buddhist monks and a persistent theme in these chronicles is the venality of the "Dammilas", i.e., the Tamils.[7] The Tamil power in South India had conquered Ceylon and made it a part of their empire. At other times, South Indian kings have intervened in dynastic disputes and territorial conflicts in Ceylon. In short, Sinhalese history is permeated with the image of a villain -- the Tamils, who at various times, interfered in local matters, desecrated Buddhist places of worship, etc. To be sure this was all true; nevertheless it must be remembered that it was not Tamils as an ethnic-linguistic group that was responsible for this, but a Tamil Kingdom which fought against a Sinhalese Kingdom.

This then is part of the heritage of the Sinhalese: the Tamil is an enemy, and an enemy with good reason. The myths and exaggerations that are contained in the chronicles represent, among other things, a desperate attempt to preserve Sinhalese hegemony intellectually and otherwise[8], in a Dravidian sea. The Sinhalese are about 8-10 million people, surrounded by Tamils in North Ceylon and South India. Hence they felt an abiding sense of insecurity and suspicion in the face of a civilization that was both vital and had numerous representatives. When the British conquered Ceylon, they consolidated the Sinhalese areas and the Tamil areas into one administrative unit and it has remained so ever since. And as long as the people of Ceylon were not effective contenders for political power, the Sinhalese and Tamils lived in relative amity. The moment this changed, was also the moment when the amity began to break, leading to the present state of hostility, suspicion and discrimination. Though the legislative council was the first, more or less, representative body in Ceylon, it was nevertheless based on ethno-linguistic electorates. This gave a taste of ethnic representation to the minorities which they were not willing to forego without protest. But the damage it worked was deeper than that: it underlined and gave legitimacy to the notion of differing ethno-linguistic communities having differing interests to be represented in the council. But it is with the coming of the Donoughmore Reforms that the Sinhalese began to feel the full weight of their political power and demonstrate a determination to exercise it ruthlessly, if need be. The Tamils boycotted the elections to the State Council of 1932 and the Sinhalese members proceeded to form the infamous Pan-Sinhalese ministry. A delay in the elections of the ministries, a little attempt to understand the position of the minorities, a refusal to take advantage of the absence of the Tamils from the council, perhaps even a show of solidarity with the Tamils who were after all boycotting the elections because they thought the Reforms did not go far enough, would have been the gesture in the direction of building a united Ceylonese nation -- let alone considerations of charity and magnanimity. But no, the Pan-Sinhalese ministry was formed and Tamils learned a lesson -- one that was perhaps not fully intended by anyone: don't trust the Sinhalese. Soon however the Tamils entered the State Council and the breach was apparently healed and after the elections to the State Council in 1936 Tamils found themselves in positions of power. It was during the lifetime of this Council that a resolution to make Sinhalese the official language of the country was moved; an amendment to make Tamil and Sinhalese was accepted by the mover of the original resolution and passed without division by the Council. These were indeed far off days. This spirit of harmony was to continue till the coming of independence -- at least from the point of view of the Sinhalese leadership of the time, there was no cause for complaint or alarm at the deprived position of the Sinhalese. It must be remembered that an English speaking elite, some of them educated abroad in England, owning large allotments of land and other forms of property, were in control. As pointed out earlier, they were dethroned in the elections of 1956 and it was then that the final destruction of the unity and communal harmony in the island was initiated. The fact that Ceylon had people who spoke no Sinhalese and were not Buddhists was ignored by the emerging leadership; and the fact that only a commitment to a pluralism, however qualified, and a secularism, however diluted, was the only hope of constructing a nation of relative stability and internal harmony was lost sight of. The language policy of the government was sloganized as "Sinhala Only" in 1956. Subsequently, various concessions have been made to the Tamils, the principle one contained in a piece of legislation, called with a touch of irony no doubt, the "Reasonable Use of Tamil Act". But to all intents and purposes, Sinhalese is the official language of Ceylon and the Tamils remain a dispossessed and embittered minority. The demands of the Buddhists was sloganized as the "Rightful Place for Buddhism", which meant a departure from secularism. The Christians and to some extent the Hindus were alienated by many of these moves, some of them indeed are rather silly and childlike (Obeyesekera, 1970) though others were well warranted. In treating themselves as "Sinhalese" who alone had inalienable rights in the island of Ceylon and as "Buddhists" who had a mysterious divine right to supremacy in the island, the majority community displayed an unhistorical and unnationalistic arrogance that has succeeded in creating irroconcilable structures of conflict -- "Sinhalese", "Buddhists" on the one hand and "Tamils" and "non-Buddhists" on the other.

anything else. The strategy of isolation and aloofness was a fruitless one, based on fantasy of Tamil strength in Ceylon politics. A further error in this respect was imagining that other minorities in Ceylon would come to the aid of the Tamils. The Muslims were probably more afraid of being dominated by the Tamils than the Sinhalese and even the Indian Tamil leadership was noticeably lukewarm. The leadership of the Tamils then successfully isolated the Ceylon Tamils and thus contributed really to more facile exploitation by Sinhalese chauvinism.

The second strategic failure of the Tamil leadership was in its failure to anticipate all the consequences of their acts and activities. However the issues between the Sinhalese and Tamils are eventually settled, the overwhelming fact of the presence of each other in lives of the Sinhalese and the Tamils can never be gainsaid: they can neither be wished away or willed away. In a unitary Sinhala Only Ceylon, just as much as in a Federal Ceylon, the Tamils have to live with the Sinhalese: they are both deeply involved in each others lives. The Tamil leadership however has acted as if though this was not true. They refused to support the independence movement; they refused to support the Sinhala renaissance and they have also refused frequently to support the economic and social legislation passed by various governments. They have in fact acted throughout the post-Donoughmore days as if they had no stake in the country. This was a second more grievous error in the strategic thinking of the Tamil leaders. Everytime the Tamil leadership took the steps outlined earlier, its impact was much different than the one the Tamils intended and the effect was to confirm the impression that the Ceylon Tamils were in fact uninterested and unconcerned with the people of Ceylon, if not openly hostile to it.

The Sinhalese on the other had have conducted themselves in the rather blind belief that an ethno-linguistic group, on account of its numerical supremacy, has a prior claim to the fruit of the land. This is not only an indefensible position but can be enforced only with violent and repressive measures. It is also self-defeating in so far as having an embittered minority within the confines of a nation-state is always wasteful and problematic. Finally one may say that it violated the charters and principles established in recent years to defend the rights of minorities.

The drama of the confrontation then was played out in these confused terms and misappropriated roles which neither side was willing to take the initiative in changing; they were only concerned with working out the equation: them or us? Sadly, it was, as recent events testify, all of us or none at all.

V

In summary then, what can we say of the strategies and programs the Tamil leadership adopted since the time of the Donoughmore Reforms? It seems that it could safely be said to have followed a path of fantasy and self-destruction in which they were unaware of the limits of their power and taken steps, the multifarious meanings and consequences of which they neither recognized nor anticipated. The Tamils of Ceylon in an age of universal adult franchise were a small minority in terms of governmental power and attempts to wage a political conflict based on a meager parliamentary strength was fore-doomed to failure. Hence to have built a political party and an ideology entirely on the Tamil base, spurning all Sinhalese organizations alike was the epitome of folly. However forcibly the Tamil leaders wished and dreamed, their numerical inferiority could not be transformed into

FOOTNOTES

1. See Glen, Johnson, Kimmel and Wedge, (1970), for an excellent example.
2. In our article we have avoided the use of the technical vocabulary of game theory or international relations.
3. See Weerawardana (1951) for a full version of the events recounted here.
4. For a detailed discussion of these issues see: Robert Keaney (1967) and S. Arsaratnam (1967).
5. See B.H. Farmer (1965) for a discussion of this.
6. The ideas about conflict and its resolution and containment found here and elsewhere in this article are discussed persuasively in Arne Naess (1956).
7. The main chronicles are the *Mahavamsa* and *Culavamsa*.
8. See Obeyesekara, (1971) for further discussion of this point.

REFERENCES

S. Arsaratnam
1967   "Nationalism, Communalism and National Unity in Ceylon" in India and Ceylon, Unity and Diversity, 260-278, P. Mason Ed., New York: Oxford University Press.

B.H. Farmer
1964   "Social Basis of Nationalism in Ceylon", Journal of Asian Studies, XXIV, 3, 431-40.

Edmund S. Glenn, Robert N. Johnson,
Paul R. Kimmel and Bryant Wedge
1971   "A Cognitive Interaction Model to Analyze Culture Conflict in International Relations", Journal of Conflict Resolution, Vol. XIV, I, 35-48.

Erving Goffman
1959   The Presentation of Self in Everyday Life, New York: Doubleday Anchor.

Robert Keaney
1967   Communalism and Language in the Politics in Ceylon, Durham, North Carolina: Duke University Press.

Susanne K. Langer
1953   Feeling and Form, New York: Charles Scribner Sons.

G.H. Mead
1934   Mind, Self and Society, Chicago: University of Chicago Press.

Arne Naess
1956   "A Systematisation of Gandhian Ethics of Conflict Resolution", Journal of Conflict Resolution, Vol. II, No. 2, 140-154.

G. Obeyesekara
1971   "The Gajabahu Synchronism" in Ceylon Journal of Humanities, Vol. I, No. 1, 25-56.
1970   "Religious Symbolism and Political Change in Ceylon", Modern Ceylon Studies, Vol I, No. 1, 43-63.

Anatol Rapoport
1960   Fights, Games and Debates, Ann Arbor: University of Michigan Press.

Thomas Scheff
1967   "Towards a Sociological Model of Consensus", American Sociological Review, 32, I, 32-45.

T.C. Schelling
1960   The Strategy of Conflict, Cambridge: Harvard University Press.

I. D. S. Weerawardana
1951   Government and Politics in Ceylon, Colombo: Ceylon Printers Ltd.

A. J. Wilson
1958   "Minority Safeguards in the Ceylon Constitution" in Ceylon Journal of Historical Studies, Vol. I, No. 1.

NAME INDEX

SUBJECT INDEX

ABOUT THE CONTRIBUTORS

DAVID ANDRIANOFF is lecturer in the anthropology department at Ithaca College.

DAVID J. BANKS is associate professor in the department of anthropology of the State University of New York at Buffalo. He has done field research among Malay peasants in Kedah and is the author of several articles on Malay kinship. Currently, he is editing a volume entitled *Changing Ethnic Identities in Southeast Asia*.

MAYA CHADDA teaches political science at the School of Contemporary Studies, Brooklyn College, New York. Her main interests are in international relations and political sociology. She is currently working on a monograph on Indo-Soviet Relations. She was educated at the University of Bombay and the Graduate Faculty of the New School for Social Research, New York.

WALKER CONNOR is a professor of political science at SUNY, Brockport, and research associate of the Harvard University Center for International Affairs. His research has been focused upon ethnonationalism as a global phenomenon.

DAVID M. DEAL is an assistant professor of history at Whitman College. His current research interests include policy toward national minorities in Southwest China during the twentieth century and the problem of political integration in Modern China. He completed his Ph.D. degree in modern Chinese history at the University of Washington in 1971, studied political theory under a NEH grant at Stanford University during the summer of 1972 and social anthropology at Harvard University under a Graver Award during the summer and fall terms of 1973.

ROBERT K. DENTAN has a joint appointment in anthropology and American studies at the State University of New York at Buffalo. His "field work" includes work in East Africa, Malaysia, and Erie County (N.Y.). His current research interests are in the differential distribution of power in Erie County, the American revolutionary tradition, Semai ethnography, and ethnomethodology. He is author of *The Semai*.

LUCIE CHENG HIRATA is assistant professor of sociology and acting director of the Asian American Studies Center at the University of California, Los Angeles. She received her Ph.D. from the University of Hawaii. Her research interests are contemporary Chinese society and overseas Chinese communities. Among her publications are the articles "Novelists and Social Scientists: A Study of Social Typing in China," "Mental Illness Among the Chinese, Myth or Realty?," and "The Asian American in Sociology."

SIPRA BOSE JOHNSON is an associate professor in anthropology at SUNY, New Paltz, where she teaches courses on cultural anthropology including the culture of India. Her research interests include comparative stratification with a special focus on the Untouchables in India and Blacks in the United States. Professor Johnson has pursued this topic both in teaching and in research. In the fall of 1973, she was a visiting lecturer at Yale College, where she taught a seminar on "Study of Comparative Patterns of Discrimination: India and the United States." Sipra Johnson is the co-author with M. Glen Johnson of "India and the United States: Divergent Attacks on Discrimination," which appeared in *Man in India* June 1972.

TAI S. KANG is an associate professor of sociology at SUNY, Buffalo. His major areas of current interest are cross-cultural study of nonverbal communication, minority relations in Asia, and cross-cultural study of social systems of the underworld.

YONG MOK KIM is assistant professor of history at California State University at Los Angeles. He specializes in the intellectual history of modern Japan, particularly Japanese Marxism, and also in Asian minorities in America and is currently working on a history of the Korean minority in America and a social history of Japanese women.

GERALD A. McBEATH is associate professor of government at John Jay College of Criminal Justice, City University of New York. His article reflects his continuing interest in minority Chinese communities. His earlier work in this field is reflected in a monograph recently published: *Political Integration of the Philippine Chinese*. He is now working on a book about comparative ethnic leadership.

DON MARTINDALE is professor of sociology at the University of Minnesota. He has authored over a dozen books and contributed numerous articles in professional journals and has edited books. His interests in inter-group relationships and ethnic group formation are reflected in his development of a general theory of community and application of this general theory to the processes of guest community formation in several different host societies. A few selected titles of his books are: *The Nature and Types of Sociological Theory* (1960); *American Society* (1960); *Community, Character and Civilization: Studies in Social Behaviorism* (1963); *Social Life and Cultural Change* (1962); *American Social Structure: Historical Antecedents and Contemporary Analysis* (1960); *Small Town and the Nation: The Conflict of Translocal Forces* (1969); *Psychiatry and Law* (1973).

WILLIAM EDGAR MAXWELL is an associate professor in the bureau of educational research and department of sociology at the University of Illinois at Urbana-Champaign. He is interested in the comparative study of effects of occupational and educational opportunities on class and ethnic stratification.

R.S. PERINBANAYAGAM teaches sociology at Hunter College in New York City and is mainly interested in social psychology and the sociology of conflict. He is currently working in the area of language and social interaction. He had his education at the University of Ceylon and the University of Minnesota.

R.A. SCHERMERHORN, emeritus professor of sociology, Case Western Reserve University, has had a major interest in ethnic and race relations for many years and, in addition to numerous journal articles, has published two well-known books on the subject: *These Our People, Minorities in American Culture* (1949), and *Comparative Ethnic Relations* (1970). As a result of two and a half years of teaching and research in India, he is now in the process of preparing a volume on the minorities of that country to be entitled *Ethnic Plurality in India: Selected Profiles* (forthcoming). His article on Parsis and Jews in this book is a reflection of his research in that larger work.

JUSTUS M. VAN DER KROEF is Charles Anderson Dana professor of political science and chairman of the department at the University of Bridgeport, Connecticut. He holds his Ph.D. from Columbia University and has served as visiting professor of Asian studies in universities in Singapore, the Philippines, and Ceylon. A specialist on Indonesian politics and social problems, he is the author of *The West New Guinea Dispute* (New York, Institute of Pacific Relations, 1958) and *Indonesia After Sukarno* (University of British Colum-bia Press, Vancouver, 1971). From 1968 to 1969 he was a post-doctoral research fellow in the University of Queensland, Brisbane, Australia, engaged in research on Australian policies toward New Guinea.

HIROSHI WAGATSUMA is professor of anthropology at the University of California at Los Angeles. Born and raised in Japan, he was educated in both Japan and the United States. He has taught in both countries and done research in Japan. His major areas of interest are the comparative studies of minority/ethnic relations and of ethnic/national/group identity and the study of Japanese intellectuals in the context of modernization.

LOUIS L'AMOUR

KILLOE

KILLOE

A Bantam Book | May 1962

2nd printing .... May 1962	6th printing ...... March 1969
3rd printing .. November 1962	7th printing .. September 1969
4th printing .... June 1967	8th printing .... February 1970
5th printing .... February 1969	9th printing .... June 1970

New Bantam edition | August 1971

2nd printing .. November 1971	9th printing .... August 1975
3rd printing .... April 1972	10th printing .... January 1976
4th printing .. September 1972	11th printing .. February 1977
5th printing ...... January 1973	12th printing .... August 1977
6th printing .. September 1973	13th printing .... April 1978
7th printing .. November 1973	14th printing .... January 1979
8th printing .. September 1974	15th printing .... October 1979

ISBN 0–553–13622–4

Published simultaneously in the United States and Canada

Bantam Books are published by Bantam Books, Inc. Its trade-
mark, consisting of the words "Bantam Books" and the por-
trayal of a bantam, is Registered in U.S. Patent and Trademark
Office and in other countries. Marca Registrada. Bantam
Books, Inc., 666 Fifth Avenue, New York, New York 10019.

PRINTED IN THE UNITED STATES OF AMERICA

To Bill Tilghman: Frontier Marshal
WHO SHOWED ME HOW IT WAS DONE
WITH A SIX-GUN

KILLOE

CHAPTER ONE

Pa came down to the breaks along the Cowhouse where I was rousting out some steers that had taken to the brush because of the heel-flies.

"Come up to the house, boy. Tap has come home and he is talking of the western lands."

So I gathered my rope to a coil and slung it on the pommel of my saddle, and stepping up to the leather, I followed Pa up through the trees and out on the open grass.

Folks were standing in the breezeway of our Texas house, and others were grouped around in bunches, listening to Tap Henry or talking among themselves.

It was not a new thing, for there had been argument and discussion going on for weeks. We all knew that something must be done, and westward the land was empty.

Tap Henry was a tall man of twenty-seven or -eight and we had been boys together, although he was a good six to seven years older than me. A hard, reckless man with a taste for wild country

1

and wilder living, he was a top hand in any man's outfit, and a good man with a gun.

You couldn't miss Tap Henry. He was well over six feet tall and weighed a compact one hundred and ninety. He wore a freshly laundered blue shield-style shirt with a row of buttons down each side, shotgun chaps, and Spanish boots with big California spurs.

He still packed that pearl-handled six-shooter he had taken off a man he had killed, and he was handsome as ever in that hard, flashy way of his. He was our friend and, in a sense, he was my brother.

Our eyes met across the heads of the others as I rode up, and his were cold and measuring. It was a look I had seen in his eyes before, but never directed at me. It was the way he looked when he saw a possible antagonist. Recognition came suddenly to his eyes.

"Danny! Dan, boy!" He strode through the crowd that had gathered to hear his talk of the lands to the west, and thrust out a hand. "Well, I'll be forever damned! You've grown up!"

Stepping down from the saddle, I met his grip with one of my own, remembering how Tap prided himself on his strength. For a moment I matched him, grip for grip, then let him have the better of it, for he was a proud man and I liked him, and I had nothing to prove.

It surprised me that we stood eye to eye, for he had always seemed very tall, and I believe it surprised him too.

Almost involuntarily, his eyes dropped to my belt, but I was wearing no gun. My rifle was in my saddle-boot and my knife was in its sheath.

"We're going west, Danny!" His hand on my shoulder, we walked back to where Pa now stood with Aaron Stark and Tim Foley. "I've scouted the land, and there is grass enough, and more!"

Pa glanced curiously from one to the other of us, and from the shadow of the breezeway Zebony Lambert watched us, a strange light in his green eyes. Zeb's long brown hair lay about his shoulders, as carefully combed as a woman's, his eyes level and hard under the flat brim of his Spanish hat.

Zebony Lambert was my friend, but I do not think he had many friends, for he was a solitary, self-keeping sort of man little given to talk. Of medium height, his extraordinarily broad shoulders made him seem shorter, and they were well set off by the short Spanish jacket he wore, and the buckskin, bell-bottomed breeches.

Lambert and Tap had never met until now, and it worried me a little, for both were strong men, and Tap was inclined toward arrogance.

"Is it true, then?" I asked Pa. "Is it decided?"

"Aye . . . we're going west, Dan."

Tim Foley was our neighbor who ran a few cows of his own, but occasionally worked for us. A square-built man with a square, honest face. "And high time," he said, "for there is little grass and we have those about us who like us not at all."

"How far is it, then?"

"Six hundred miles or less. Right across Texas and into New Mexico. If we do not go on, it will be less."

Pa looked at me. More and more he was paying mind to my judgment, and listening to what I had to say. He was still the boss . . . I knew that and he knew it, but he had respect for my judgment, which had grown since he had been leaving the cattle business to me.

"How many head, Dan? What can we muster?" Pa put the question and I caught a surprised look from Tap, for he remembered me as a boy, and a boy only.

"Fifteen hundred at least, and I'd say a bit more than that. Tim will have a good three hundred head under his own brand, and Aaron nearly as many. When all are rounded up and the breaks swept clean, I would say close to three thousand head."

"It is a big herd, and we will be short of men," Pa commented thoughtfully.

"There will be three wagons, and the horse herd," I added.

"Wagons?" Tap objected. "I hadn't planned on wagons."

"We have our families," Tim said, "and there are tools we must take."

There began a discussion of what to take, of trail problems and men, and I leaned against the corral rail, listening without paying much attention. In every such venture there is always more talk than is necessary, with everybody having his say, but I knew that when all was said, much of it would be left to me, and I would do as seemed best to me.

There is no point in such endless discussion, except that men become familiar with their problems. Long ago, when the first discussion of such a move began, I had also begun thinking of it, and had made some plans I thought necessary. Lambert, a thoughtful man, had contributed a few pointed and common-sense suggestions.

We could muster barely a dozen men, far too

few for the task that lay ahead. Once the herd was trail-broke, four to five men might keep it moving without much trouble, but until then it would be a fight. Some of these old mossyhorns had grown up there on the Cowhouse and they had no wish to leave home.

There would be the usual human problems too, even though the people who would be accompanying our move would all be known to us. And once away from the settlements, there would be Comanches.

It was a risk, a big risk. We were chancing everything.

We might have fought it out where we were, but Pa was no hand for a fight, although he had courage enough for two men, and had seen his share of fighting in the Mexican War and with Indians. He had grown up in the Five Counties and knew what feuding meant. It was Tap who had suggested going west, and Pa fell in with it.

But there was risk connected with everything, and we were hard men bred to a hard life in a hard land, and the lives that we lived were lonely, yet rich with the voice of our singing, and with tales told of an evening by the campfire.

What pleasures we had were created by ourselves or born of the land, our clothing was made by our own hands, our houses and corrals, also. Those who rode beside us knew the measure of our strength as we knew theirs, and each knew the courage of the other.

In that country a man saddled his own broncs and fought his own battles, and the measure of his manhood was that he did what needed to be done, and did it well, and without shirking.

Me? I, Dan Killoe, was born in a claim cabin on Cowhouse Creek with the roar of buffalo guns filling the room as Pa and my Uncle Fred beat off an Indian attack. I let out my first yell in a room filled with gunsmoke, and when Ma died I was nursed by a Mexican woman whose father died fighting with the Texans at the Alamo.

When I was six, Pa met Tap's Ma on a trip to Fort Worth, and married her, bringing her west to live with us, and they brought Tap along.

She was a pretty woman, as I recall, and good enough to us boys, but she wasn't cut out for frontier life, and finally she cut and run with some no-account drifter, leaving Tap to live with us.

Tap always pulled his weight, and more. He took to cow country like he was born to it, and we got along. He was thirteen and doing a man's work and proud of it, for the difference between a man and a boy is the willingness to do a man's work and take a man's responsibility.

Being older than me, he was always the leader, no matter what we were doing, and a few times when we had a chance to attend school, he took up for me when I might have taken a beating from bigger boys.

When Tap pulled out the first time he was seventeen and I was a bit more than ten. He was gone most of a year, working for some outfit over in the Big Thicket.

The next time I saw him he was wearing a pistol, and we heard rumors he had killed a man over near Caddo Lake.

When he was at home he worked like all get-out, but he soon had the name of being a good man to let alone. Pa said nothing much to him, only dropping a comment now and then, and Tap always listened, or seemed to. But he was gone most of the time after that, and each time he came back he was bigger, tougher, and more sure of himself.

It had been three years since we had last seen Tap, but now he was back, and at the right time, too. Trouble was building along the Cowhouse and neighbors were crowding in, and it was time we moved west and laid claim to land.

We would be leaving mighty little on the Cowhouse. When Pa moved into the country a body couldn't live there at all without neighbors and they bunched up for protection. Some died and some were killed, some drifted and some sold out, but the country changed and the people, and now it was building into a fight for range.

Some of the newcomers had no cattle, and from time to time they would kill a beef of ours. Pa was no one to keep a man's youngsters from food, so he allowed it. The trouble was, they turned from killing a beef for food to driving them off and selling them, and trouble was cropping up.

A couple of times I'd caught men with our brand on some steers they were driving, and I drove them back, but twice shots had been fired at me.

The old crop that worked hard and fought hard for their homes were gone. This new lot seemed to figure they could live off what we had worked for, and it was developing into trouble. What we wanted was land that belonged to us—land with boundaries and lines drawn plain and clear; but due to the way everybody had started out on the Cowhouse, that wasn't true here.

There was talk of moving west, and then Tap rode in, fresh from that country.

Pa was a farmer at heart, more interested in crops than cattle, and of late I'd taken to running the cattle business.

"It is a bad trip, I'll not lie about that," Tap was saying. "But the time of year is right, and if we start soon there will be grass and water."

"And when we get there?" Foley asked.

"The best grass you ever saw, and water too. We can stop on the Pecos in New Mexico, or we can go on to Colorado."

"What would you suggest?" Foley was a shrewd man, and he was keeping a close watch on Tap as he questioned him.

"The Pecos country. Near Bosque Redondo."

Karen Foley came to stand beside me, her eyes watching Tap. "Isn't he exciting?" she said. "I'm glad he will be with us."

For the first time I felt a twinge of jealousy, but it was a small twinge, for I liked and admired Tap Henry myself, and I knew what she meant.

Tap was different. He had come riding back into our lives wearing better clothes than we could afford, riding a fine chestnut gelding with a beautifully hand-tooled saddle, the first one I had ever seen. Moreover, he carried himself with a kind of style.

He had a hard, sure way about him and he walked and moved with an assurance we did not have. You felt there was no uncertainty about Tap Henry, that he knew what he wanted and knew how to get it. Only faintly, and with a twinge of guilt, did I think that perhaps he cared too little for the feelings or interests of others. Nevertheless, I could think of no better man on a trip of the kind we were planning.

Karen was another thing, for Karen and I had been walking out together, talking a little, and a couple of times we had taken rides together. We had no understanding or anything like it, but she was the prettiest girl anywhere around, and for a girl out on the Texas plains she got herself up mighty well.

She was the oldest of Tim Foley's three children. The other two were boys, fourteen and ten.

It was plain she was taken by Tap Henry, and one thing I knew about Tap was that he was no man to take lightly where women were concerned. He had a way with them, and they took to him.

Pa turned around. "Come over here, Dan. We want your advice."

Tap laughed as I walked up, and clapped a hand on my shoulder in that way he had. "What's the matter, Killoe? You taking advice from kids now?"

"Dan knows more about cattle than anybody I ever knew," Pa said quietly, "and this won't be his first trail drive."

"You?" Tap was surprised. "A trail drive?"

"Uh-huh. I took a herd through Baxter Springs last year. Took them through to Illinois and sold them."

"Baxter Springs?" Tap chuckled. "Lost half your herd, I'll bet. I know that crowd around Baxter Springs."

"They didn't cut Dan's herd," Foley said, "and they didn't turn him aside. Dan took them on through and sold out for a good price."

"Good!" Tap squeezed my shoulder. "We'll make a team, won't we, boy? Man, it's good to be back!"

He glanced over toward the corral where Karen

was standing. All of a sudden he said, "Well, you understand what's needed here. When you are ready for the trail, I'll take over."

He walked away from us and went over to where Karen stood by the rail. Tim Foley glanced after him, but his face revealed nothing. Nevertheless, I knew Tim well enough to know he disapproved.

Foley turned and went into the house and the others drifted away, leaving Pa and me standing there together.

"Well," Pa said, "Tap's back. What do you think of him?"

"We're lucky to have him. He knows the water-holes, and he's a good hand. Believe me, Pa, before this drive is over we'll need every man."

"Yes, that we will." He seemed about to say something more, but he did not.

Pa was a canny man and not given to unnecessary talk, and I knew that if he had something on his mind he would say it soon enough. Something was bothering him, however, but all he said a minute later was, "Do you remember Elsie?"

Elsie Henry had been Tap's mother, and I did remember her. She was the only mother I'd ever had, but somehow she never seemed like a mother . . . more like somebody who came to stay for a while and then went away. Yet she was good to Tap and me and, looking back on it, I knew she had done a lot of thinking before she broke loose and ran off.

"Yes, I remember her."

"She wasn't cut out for this life. She should not have come west."

"I often wondered why she did. She was a pretty woman with a taste for pretty clothes and fancy living. Seems to me she would have been happier back east."

"Character," Pa said, "is the thing, whether it's horses, dogs, or men. Or women, for that matter."

He walked off without saying anything more, and I took my horse to the corral and stripped off the outfit and hung it up. All the time I was thinking of what Pa had said, and wondering what lay back of it. Pa had a way of saying things that left a lot unsaid, and I was wondering just how far he wanted that comment to go.

But with the trip coming up, there was very little time for thinking of that. Or of anything else.

It was spring . . . hot and dry. There had been some good winter rains, and there should be water along the trail to Horsehead Crossing on the Pecos.

Squatting on my heels near the corral, I gave thought to that. Karen and Tap had wandered off somewhere, but right now I was thinking about horses. We would need a cavvy of fifty or sixty head, and with all the horses we could round up between us, including those belonging to Tim Foley and Aaron Stark, we would be short about twenty head.

Two of the wagons needed working on and there was harness to mend. Also, we must get a lot of lead for bullets, and cast enough at least to get us started in case of Comanche trouble. And we would need some additional barrels for carrying water.

Zebony Lambert strolled over and dropped to his heels beside me. He was smoking tobacco wrapped in paper, a habit some of the Texans were picking up from the Mexicans. Most of us smoked cigars, when we smoked.

"So that's Tap Henry."

He spoke in a peculiarly flat tone, and I glanced around at him. When Zeb spoke in that voice I knew he was either unimpressed or disapproving, and I wanted them to like each other.

"We spent a lot of time together as boys, Zeb. He's my half brother, stepbrother . . . whatever they call it."

"Heard that."

"When his Ma ran off, Pa let him stay on. Treated him like another son."

Zeb looked across the yard to where Tap was laughing and talking with Karen.

"Did he ever see his mother again?"

"No. Not that I know of."

"He fancies that gun, doesn't he?"

"That he does . . . and he's good with it, too."

Zeb finished his cigarette, then pushed it into the dirt. "If you need help," he said, "I stand ready. You'll need more horses."

"You see any wild stuff?"

"Over on the Leon River. You want to try for them?" Zeb was the best wild-horse hunter anywhere around. The trouble was there was so little time. If we wanted to travel when there was water to be found we should be starting now. We should have started two weeks ago.

Zebony Lambert never worked for any man. Often he would pitch in and help out, and he was a top hand, but he would never take pay. Nobody understood that about him, but nobody asked questions in Texas. A man's business and his notions were his own private affair.

"Maybe we can swap with Tom Sandy. There's a

lot of young stuff down in the breaks, too young for a trail herd."

"He'll throw in with you if you ask him."

"Sandy?" I could not believe it. "He's got him a good outfit. Why should he move?"

"Rose."

Well, that made a kind of sense. Still, any man who would leave a place like he had for Rose would leave any other place for her, and would in the end wind up with nothing. Rose was a mighty pretty woman and she kept a good house, but she couldn't keep her eyes off other men. Worst of all, she had what it took to keep their eyes on her, and she knew it.

"She'll get somebody killed."

"She'll get Tom killed."

Zeb got up. "I'll ride by about sunup. Help you with that young stuff." He paused. "I'll bring the dogs."

Zebony Lambert had worked cattle over in the Big Thicket and had a bunch of the best cattle-working dogs a man ever did see, and in brush country a dog is worth three cowhands.

He went to his horse and stepped into the saddle. I never tired of watching him do it. The way he went into the leather was so smooth, so effortless, that you just couldn't believe it. Zeb had worked with me a lot, and I never knew a better coordinated man, or one who handled himself with greater ease.

He walked his horse around the corral so he would not have to pass Tap Henry, and just as he turned the horse Tap looked up.

It was plain to him that Lambert was deliberately avoiding him, for around the corral was the long way. Tap laid his eyes on Zeb and watched him ride off, stepping around Karen to keep his eyes on him.

The smell of cooking came from the house, where Mrs. Foley was starting supper.

Karen and Tap were talking when I approached the house. He was talking low and in a mighty persuasive tone, and she was laughing and shaking her head, but I could see she was taken with him, and it got under my skin. After all, Karen was my girl—or so everybody sort of figured.

Tap looked up. "You know, Karen, I can't believe Danny's grown up. He used to follow me around like a sucking calf."

She laughed, and I felt my face getting red. "I didn't follow you everywhere, Tap," I replied. "I didn't follow you over the Brazos that time."

He looked like I'd slapped him across the mouth, but before he could say something mean, Karen put a hand on his sleeve. "You two are old friends . . . even brothers. Now, don't you go and get into any argument."

"You're right, Karen," I said, and walked by them into the house.

Mrs. Foley glanced up when I came in, and then her eyes went past me to Tap and Karen. "Your brother is quite handsome," she said, and the way she said it carried more meaning than the words themselves.

For three days then we worked sunup to sundown, with Tap Henry, Zeb Lambert, and Aaron Stark working the breaks for young stuff. Pa rode over to have a talk with Tom Sandy about a swap, and Tim Foley worked on the wagons, with his boys to help.

Lambert's dogs did the work of a dozen hands in getting those steers out of the brush and out of the overhang caves along the Cowhouse which gave the creek its name.

Jim Poor, Ben Cole, and Ira Tilton returned from delivering a small herd to San Antonio and fell in with us, and the work began to move faster.

Every time I had the chance I asked Tap questions about that route west. The one drive I'd made, the one up through Kansas and Missouri into Illinois, had taught me a good deal about cattle, but that was a sight better country than what we were heading into now.

The corn grinding was one of the biggest jobs, and the steadiest. We had a cornmill fixed to a post and two cranks on it. That mill would hold something around a peck of corn, but the corn had to go through two grindings to be right for breadbaking. We ground it once, then tightened the mill and ran it through again, grinding it still finer.

We wanted as much corn ground as possible before the trip started, for we might not be able to use the grinder on the road without more trouble than we could afford. Between grinding the corn and jerking beef, there was work a-plenty for everyone.

None of us, back in those days, wore storebought clothes. It was homespun or buckskin, and for the most part the men dressed their own skins and made their own clothes, with fringe on the sleeves and pants legs to drain the rain off faster. Eastern folks usually thought that fringe was purely ornamental, which was not true.

For homespun clothes of either cotton or wool, the stuff was carded and spun by hand, and if it

was cotton, the seeds were picked out by hand.
Every man made his own moccasins or boots, re-
paired what tools or weapons he had, and in some
cases made them from the raw material.

Down among the trees along the Cowhouse the
air was stifling. It was a twisty creek, with the high
banks under which the cattle took shelter, and it
was hot, hard work, with scarcely room to build a
loop.

A big brindle steer cut out of the trees ahead of
me, and went through them, running like a deer,
with me and that steeldust gelding right after him.
Ducking a heavy branch that would have torn my
head off, I took a smaller one smack across the face,
making my eyes water. The steer lunged into a six-
foot wall of brush and that steeldust right after him.
Head down, I went through, feeling the branches
and thorns tearing at my chaps. The steer broke
into the open and I took after him, built a loop, and
dropped it over his horns.

That old steeldust sat right back on his haunches
and we busted that steer tail-over-teakettle and
laid him down hard. He came up fighting. He was
big, standing over sixteen hands . . . and he was
mad . . . and he weighed an easy eighteen hundred.

He put his head down and came for me and that
steeldust, but that bronc of mine turned on a dime
and we busted Mr. Steer right back into the dust
again.

He got up, dazed but glaring around, ready for
a fight with anything on earth, but before he could
locate a target I started off through the brush at a
dead run and when that rope jerked him by the
horns he had no choice but to come after us.

Once out in the open again and close to the herd, I shook loose my loop and hazed him into the herd.

It was heat, dust, sweat, charging horses, fighting steers, and man-killing labor. One by one we worked them out of the brush and up onto the plain where they could be bunched. Except for a few cantankerous old mossyhorns, they were usually content as long as they were with others of their kind in the herd.

That tough old brindle tried to make it back to the brush, back to his home on the Cowhouse, but we busted him often enough to make a believer of him.

Tap, like I said, was a top hand. He fell into the routine and worked as hard as any of us.

We rolled out of our soogans before there was light in the sky, and when the first gray showed we were heading for the brush. We wore down three or four horses a day, but there are no replacements for the men on a cow outfit.

Breakfast was usually beef and beans, the same as lunch, or sometimes if the women were in the notion, we had griddle cakes and sorghum . . . corn squeezings, we called it.

Morning of the third day broke with a lowering gray sky, but we didn't see that until later. We had two days of brutal labor behind us, and more stretching ahead. Usually, I slept inside. Pa and me occupied one side of the Texas, Tim Foley and his family the other side; but with Stark's wife and kids, we gave up our beds to them and slept outside with the hands.

Rolling out of my soogan that third morning, it took me only a minute to put on my hat—a cowhand always puts on his hat first—and then my boots and buckskin pants.

The women had been up and we could hear dishes a-rattling around inside. Tap crawled out of his blankets and walked to the well, where he hauled up a bucket of water and washed. I followed him. He looked sour and mean, like he always did come daybreak. With me it was otherwise—I always felt great in the morning, but I had sense enough to keep still about it.

We went up to the house and Mrs. Foley and Karen filled our plates. That morning it was a healthy slab of beef and a big plate of beans and some fried onions.

Like always, I had my bridle with me and I stuck the bit under my jacket to warm it up a mite. Of a frosty morning I usually warmed it over a fire enough to make it easy for a horse to take, and while it wasn't too cold this morning, I wanted that bronc of mine to be in a good mood.

Not that he would be . . . or ever was.

We sat on the steps or squatted around on the ground against the wall, eating in silence. Karen came out with the big pot and refilled our cups, and took a mite longer over Tap's cup.

None of us was talking very much, but Zebony moved over beside me when he had finished eating and began to make one of those cigarettes of his.

"You been over to the Leon?"

"No."

"You and me . . . we take a *pasear* over there. What do you say?"

"There's plenty of work right here," I said. "I don't see—"

"I do," Tap interrupted. "I know what he means."

Zeb touched a delicate tongue-tip to his thin paper. "Do you think," he said to me, "they will let you drive your cattle away?"

"They belong to us."

"Sure—there are mighty few that don't. Those others . . . the newcomers . . . they have no cattle, and they have been living on yours. By now they know you are planning a drive, and are cleaning out the breaks."

"So?"

"Dan, what's got into you?" Tap asked irritably. "They'll rustle every steer they can, and fight you for the others. How many men have we got?"

"Now? Nine or ten."

"And how many of them? There must be thirty."

"Closer to forty," Zeb said. "There's tracks over on the Leon. They are bunching your cows faster than you are, and driving them north into the wild country."

"I reckon we'd best go after them," I said.

Tap got up. "I reckon we had," he said dryly. "And if you ever carried a short gun, you'd better carry one when you go after them."

It made sense. This lot who had squatted around us had brought nothing into the country except some beat-up horses and wagon outfits. Not more than two or three had so much as a milk cow . . . and they had been getting fat on our beef, eating it, which Pa never minded much, and even selling it. And not one of them had done a tap of work. They had come over from the east and south somewhere—a bedraggled bunch of poor whites and the like.

That did not make them easy. Some of that outfit had come down from Missouri and Arkansas, and some were from the Five Counties, where there had been fighting for years. Pa was easy-going and generous, and they had spotted it right off.

"Don't tell Pa," I said. "He's no hand with a gun."

Tap glanced at me briefly as if to say, "And I suppose you are?" But I paid him no mind.

Tim Foley saw us bunched up and he walked over. That man never missed a thing. He minded his own affairs, but he kept an ear to the ground. "You boys be careful," was all he said.

The sun was staining the sky with rose when we moved out from the place. As we rode away, I told Ben Cole to keep the rest of them in the bottoms of the Cowhouse and to keep busy. They knew something was up, but they offered no comment, and we trailed it off to the west, then swung north.

"You know who it is?" I asked Zeb.

"That Holt outfit, Mack, Billy, and Webb—all that crowd who ride with them."

Tough men, and mean men. Dirty, unshaven, thieves and killers all of them. A time or two I'd seen them around.

"Webb," I commented, "is left-handed."

Tap looked around at me. "Now that," he said, "is a good thing to know."

"Carries his gun on the right side, butt first, and he draws with either hand."

We picked up their trail in a coulee near the Leon River and we took it easy. They were driving some twenty head, and there were two men. Following the trail was no trick, because they had made no attempt to hide it. In fact, they seemed to be inviting trouble, and realizing how the odds figured out, they might have had that in mind.

We walked our horses up every slope and looked around before we crossed the ridges or hills. We kept to low ground when we could and just managed to keep the trail in sight.

If we moved our cattle out of this country the rest of that ragtag and bobtail would have to move out or starve to death. Cattle were plentiful in most parts of Texas and it wasn't until later that folks began to watch their beef. For a long time, when a man needed beef he went out and killed one, just as he had buffalo, and nobody paid it no mind.

In those days cattle were good for their hides and tallow, and there was no other market. A few drives had been made to Louisiana, to Shreveport, and over into Alabama, but cattle were a drug on the market. However, this far west the wild cattle had begun to thin out, and fewer were to be found.

This was the frontier, and west of us there was nothing but wide, unsettled country. In those days the settler furthest west in Texas was a farmer who was about four miles west of Fort Belknap, and that was away off north of us, and a little west.

Cattle liked the country further east or along the river bottoms where the grass was thick. Zeb Lambert told me he had seen a few over on the Colorado, west of us, but they were strays that had somehow found their way there. Nobody lived in that country.

The coolness remained in the morning, clouds were heavy, and there was a dampness as of coming rain. Despite the work we had to do, we hoped for it. Rain in this country meant not only water in the water-holes and basins, but it meant grass on the range. In a few days our lives would depend on both.

Zeb Lambert pulled up. "Dan," he said, "look here."

We both stopped and looked at the trail. Two riders had come in from the east and joined the two we were trailing. The grass was pushed down by their horses' hoofs and had not straightened up —they could have joined them only minutes before.

Tap Henry looked at those tracks. "It could be accident," he said.

"What do you mean?" I asked him.

"Or it could be that somebody told them we were riding this way."

Zebony said nothing, but he started building himself one of those cigarettes he set so much store by.

"Who would do a thing like that?" I asked. "None of our crowd."

"When you've lived as long as me," Tap said shortly, "you won't trust anybody. We were following two men . . . now two more come in out of nowhere."

We rode on, more cautiously now. Tap was too suspicious. None of our folks would carry word to that bunch of no-account squatters. Yet there were four of them now, and only three of us. We did not mind the odds, but it set a man to thinking. If they were tipped off that we were moving against them there might be more of them coming.

Tap suddenly turned his head and saw Zeb cutting off over the rise.

"Now what's got into him?" he demanded.

"He'll be hunting sign. Zeb could track a coon over the cap-rock in the dark of the moon."

"Will he stand?"

"He'll stand. He's a fighter, Tap. You never saw a better."

Tap looked after him, but made no comment. Tap was riding tall in the saddle this morning, head up and alert, ready for trouble. And Tap Henry was a man who had seen trouble. There had been times before he left us when he had to face up to a difficulty, and no telling how many times since then.

Suddenly, we smelled smoke.

Almost at the same moment we saw our cattle. There must have been three hundred head bunched there, and four men were sitting around the fire. Only one of them got to his feet as we approached.

"Watch it, Tap," I said, "there's more of them."

The hollow where they were was long, maybe a quarter of a mile, and there were willows and cottonwood along the creek, and here and there some mesquite. Those willows shielded the creek from view. No telling what else they might hide.

The remuda was staked out close by. My eyes went to the staked-out horses. "Tap," I said, "five of those horses are showing sweat."

Webb Holt was there, and Bud Caldwell, and a long, lean man named Tuttle. The fourth man had a shock of uncombed blond hair that curled over his shirt collar, and a chin that somehow did not quite track with his face. He had a sour, mean look about him.

"Those cows are showing our brand," I said mildly. "We're taking them back."

"Are you now?" Webb Holt asked insolently.

"And we're serving notice. No more beef—not even one."

"You folks come it mighty big around here," Webb commented. "Where'd you get the right to all these cattle? They run loose until you came along."

"Not here they didn't. There were no cattle here until my father drove them in, and the rest came by natural increase. Since then we've ridden herd on them, nursed them, dragged them out of bogs, and fought the heel-flies and varmints.

"You folks came in here with nothing and you've made no attempt to get anything. We'd see no man go hungry, least of all when he has young ones, so we've let you have beef to eat. Now you're stealing."

"Do tell?" Holt tucked his thumbs behind his belt. "Well, let me tell you something. You folks want to leave out of here, you can. But you're taking no cows."

"If you're counting on that man back in the brush," I said, "you'd best forget him. He won't be able to help you none."

Holt's eyes flickered, and Bud Caldwell touched his tongue to his lips. The blond man never turned a hair. He kept looking at Tap Henry like he'd seen him some place before.

"I don't know what you're figuring on," I said, "but in your place I'd just saddle up and ride out. And what other cattle of ours you have, I'd drive back."

"Now why would we do that?" Holt asked, recovering some of his confidence. "We got the cows. You got nothing. You haven't even got the men."

"The kind we've got," Tap said, "we don't need many."

Holt's eyes shifted. "I don't know you," he said.

Tap jerked his head. "I'm Dan's stepbrother, you

might say, and I've got a shooting interest in that stock."

"I know him," the blond man said suddenly. "That's Tap Henry. I knew him over on the Nueces."

"So?"

"He's a gunfighter, Webb."

Webb Holt centered his attention on Tap. He was wary now. Bud Caldwell moved a little to one side, spreading them out. My Patterson revolving rifle lay across my saddle, my hand across the action, and as he moved, I let the muzzle follow him ... it seemed to make him nervous.

Tap kept his eyes on Holt. We knew there was a man out there in the brush, but we—at least I did—depended on Zeb to take care of him. It was a lot of depending, yet a man can do only so much, and we had four men there in front of us.

"You're going to have a choice to make," Tap said, "any minute now. If you make the right choice, you live."

Webb Holt's tongue touched his lips. He knew he was looking right down the muzzle of Tap's gun, and if Tap was faster then he was, Webb was dead. I had let my horse back up a mite so I could keep both Bud and that blond man under my eyes.

"You can catch up your horses and ride out," I said. "You can start any time you're of a mind to."

Suddenly Zebony Lambert was standing on the edge of the brush. "You boys can open the ball any time you like," he said. "There's nobody out there in the brush to worry about."

You could see them start to sweat. It was three to four now, and my rifle was laid right on one of them. Bud was a tough enough man, but he wasn't going to play the hero. Not on this fine spring morning. Until a few minutes ago he had been complaining the weather was mighty miserable; now any kind of a morning was a fine morning.

"You kill that man?" Holt demanded.

"He didn't make an issue of it," Zeb replied.

Nobody said anything for about a minute, and it was a long minute. Then I stepped my horse up, holding that rifle muzzle on Caldwell.

"Case you're interested," I said, casually, "this here is a Patterson revolving rifle and she shoots five shots . . . .56 caliber."

"Webb . . . ?" Bud Caldwell was kind of nervous. That Patterson was pointed right at his stomach and the range was less than twenty feet.

"All right," Webb Holt replied, "we can wait. We got forty men, and we want these cows. You folks take 'em along now—you won't keep them."

"Webb?" Tap's voice had an edge to it that raised the hair on the back of my neck. "You and me, Webb. Those others are out of it."

"Now see here!" Webb Holt's face was touched with pallor.

"Forty, you said." Tap was very quiet. "I say thirty-nine, Webb. Just thirty-nine."

Bud Caldwell reached for the sky with both hands and the thin man backed up so fast he fell over a log and he just lay there, his arms outspread.

The blond man stood solid where he was. "He called it," he said loudly. "It's them two."

Webb Holt stood with his feet spread, his right side toward Tap Henry. His gun butt was on his right hip, the butt end to the fore and canted a mite.

"Look," he said, "we don't need to—" He

grabbed iron and Tap shot him twice through the chest.

"Lucky you warned me about that left hand," Tap said. "I might have made a mistake."

We rounded up those cattle and drove them home, and nobody said anything, at any time.

Me, I was thinking about those other thirty-nine men, and most particularly about Holt's two brothers.

It was time we pulled out, and pulled out fast.

CHAPTER TWO

We were there when the country was young and wild, and we knew the smell of gunsmoke and buffalo-chip fires. Some were there because they chose the free, wild way, and some were born to it, and knew no other.

To live with danger was a way of life, but we did not think of it as danger, merely as part of all that we must face in the natural order of living. There was no bravado in our carrying of guns, for a man could no more live without a gun in the Texas of the 1850's than he could live without a horse, or without food.

We learned to live like the Indians, for the Indians had been there first and knew the way of the land. We could not look to anyone for help, we must help ourselves; we could not look to anyone for food, we must find our food and prepare it ourselves.

Now there was no more time. Westward the land was open, westward lay our hopes, westward was our refuge. Those were years when half the world grew up with the knowledge that if everything went wrong they could always go west, and the West was foremost in the thinking of all men. It was the answer to unemployment, to bankruptcy, to adventure, to loneliness, to the broken-hearted. It was everybody's promised land.

We pointed the cattle west into the empty land, and the brindle steer took the lead. He had no idea where he was going, but he intended to be the first one there. Three thousand five hundred head of mixed stuff, with Tap Henry and Pa away out there in front, leading the herd.

The wagons took the flank on the side away from the dust. Tim Foley's boy was driving a wagon, and his wife drove another. Aaron Stark's wife was driving a third, and Frank Kelsey was driving Tom Sandy's big wagon.

Tom and Rose Sandy were coming with us. Zeb Lambert had been right about Sandy, for when he heard of our move he promptly closed a deal on an offer for his ranch, sold all his stock but the remuda and some three hundred head of selected breeding stock, and threw in with us.

He brought two hands with him. Kelsey had been with him ever since Tom Sandy had come to Texas riding a sore-backed mule, and the other hand was Zeno Yearly, a tall Tennessean.

Tilton, Cole, and Poor rode one flank, and two of Pa's other hands, Milo Dodge and Freeman Squires, the other.

We had been making our gather before Tap Henry returned, so getting on the road was no problem. Above all, speed was essential. Now that we had determined to leave, there was no sense in delaying and awaiting an attack, if it came.

We started before sunup, and those first few miles we kept them moving at a trot. We hoped that if we could keep them busy thinking about keeping up they would have less time to worry about where they were going.

We had two scouts out, Tim Foley away on the left, and Aaron Stark to the north, watching for any of the Holt crowd.

Zebony Lambert and me, we ate the dust of the drag, hazing the stragglers back into the herd, changing the minds of any that took a notion to bolt and run for their old home on the Cowhouse.

We made camp fifteen miles out that first night, bedding them down on about six acres in a bottom where the grass was good and there was water from a small stream that flowed toward the Leon River.

Ben Cole and Jim Poor took the first guard, riding around the herd in opposite directions. The rest of us headed for the chuck wagon where the women folks had prepared a meal.

From now on, the routine would vary little unless we headed into trouble. We would be lucky to make more than fifteen miles a day with the herd, and most of the time it would be closer to twelve. We were short of horses, having about five horses per man, when a drive of that kind could use anywhere up to eight or nine per man.

A herd of that size would spread out for a mile along a stream when watering, and when bunched for the night would browse a good bit; when actually bedded down they would use a good six acres. After they had fed they would sleep, and about midnight, as if by some secret order, they would rise, stretch, usually browse a little, and finally go back to sleep. Maybe a couple of hours later they would get up again, stretch, and then go back to sleep. Some of them might browse a mite during that second stretch. But by dawn they were all up and ready to move. In ordinary weather two men could keep guard over that many cattle. If there was a storm brewing it might take every hand.

Going to the fire with my cup and a tin plate in my hand, I could hear Ben Cole singing them to sleep. Singing was not just a way of keeping himself company; partly it was that the sound of a human voice—most cowpunchers sounded somewhat less than human when they sang—had a quieting effect. Also, it served notice to the cattle that the shadow they saw out there was a man, and therefore all right.

Karen filled my plate and cup. "You riding all right, Karen?"

She nodded, and her eyes went beyond me to where Tap was sitting. "He's a good man," I said dryly.

Her chin came up defensively. "I like him." Then, she added, "After all, he is your brother."

Taking my grub, I walked over and dropped to the ground where Tap was sitting. "How you coming, kid?" he asked.

After that we ate in silence, and I expect all of us were thinking about what lay behind us as much as about what lay ahead. There were long, dry miles before us, but the season was early, and our chances were good. At least as far as Horsehead Crossing on the Pecos.

When I had cleaned the Patterson, I turned in and stretched out. Nothing better than turning in after a hard day's work. I slept a little away from the rest of them so I could listen better, never wanting anything to come between me and the night.

The clouds had drifted off and the sky was clear. Somewhere over on the bluffs a coyote was talking it up, and from time to time a bird called in the night.

Next thing I knew a hand was shaking me and it was Ira Tilton. He and Stark had relieved Ben Cole and Jim Poor on first guard.

Rolling out, I put my hat on and slid into my boots. Tilton still stood there, chewing tobacco. He started to say something, then turned and walked off toward the fire, which was burned down to coals.

Hitching my chaps, I took the Patterson and went to the fire. Tap, who was sharing my night guard, was already squatting there, cupping his hands around the warm cup, and sipping coffee. He glanced up at me, but said nothing, and neither did I.

Tom Sandy had taken on the job of wrangling horses, and he was up and had a *grulla* caught up for me. Of a right, a hand usually caught up his own mounts, but Tom was not sleeping much these days. Seemed to me Tom should worry less and spend more time in bed, with problems like his.

The night was cold. Glancing at the Dipper, I saw it was after three in the morning. I swallowed another belt of black, scalding coffee and went over to that *grulla* and stepped into the saddle.

He unwound in a tight circle, crow-hopped a few times, and then we started off for the herd, both of us feeling better for the workout.

Tilton had little to say. "Quiet," he said, "quiet so far," and he rode off.

He was a puzzling man in a lot of ways. He had worked for us upwards of three years and I knew him hardly better than when he first came. Not that that was unusual. Folks those days said little about their personal affairs, and many a man in Texas had come there because the climate was not healthy where he came from.

In Texas you did not ask questions about a man's past—that was his business. A man was judged by what he was and how he did what there was to do, and if he had been in trouble elsewhere, nobody paid it any mind. And that went for the law, too, where there was law. The law left you alone, no matter how badly you might be wanted elsewhere, so long as you stayed out of trouble where you were.

As far as that goes, there were several men working for Pa who might have had shady pasts, but they did their work and rode for the brand, and we expected nothing else.

That coyote off on the ridge was talking to the stars. And he was a coyote, too, not an Indian. Once you've heard them both, a body can tell the difference. Only a human voice echoes to any extent, and next to the human the coyote or wolf, but an owl or a quail will not echo at all.

Off across the herd I could hear Tap singing low. He had a good voice, and he was singing "Brennan on the Moor," an old song from the old country about an Irish highwayman. Circling wide, I drew up and listened.

The coyote was still . . . listening to Tap, most likely . . . the stars were bright. There was no other sound, only the rustling of the water in the stream nearby.

A big steer stood up and stretched, then another
and another. A faint breeze stirred and the big
steer lifted his head sharply. Now, a man who
trusts to his own hearing only is a fool . . . you
learn not only to look and listen, but to watch the
reactions of animals and of birds, for they will often
tell you things you would never sense otherwise.

Something was moving out there. That steer
faced around, walking a step or two toward the
north. My Patterson lifted a mite and I eased back
on the hammer. The click was loud in the night,
and that big steer flipped an ear at me, but kept his
eyes where they were.

Tap was across the herd from me, but he was
coming around, walking his horse. The herd was
uneasy, so, risking revealing myself to whatever was
out there, I commenced talking to them, speaking
low and confidently, working my horse in nearer to
them.

And I walked my horse toward the trouble.

The big steer kind of ducked his head, and I
could almost see his nostrils flare as he moved up a
step. He was full of fight, but his attitude puzzled
me.

Cattle did not like the smell of Indians, and were
apt to get skittish if they came around . . . maybe it
was the wild smell, or the use of skins so many of
them wore, but the herd did not act like they would
if Indians were out there.

They would not get excited if a white man was
approaching, nor were they as nervous as if it was a
bear or a cat. In those days grizzlies often were
found down on the plains in Texas, in the Edwards
Plateau country, and there were a good many lions
around.

Walking that *grulla* ahead, I eased my rifle forward in my hand, then listened.

The big steer had kept abreast of me. He was not frightened, but full of fight. Nevertheless, he liked the company.

And then I heard it.

Straining my ears into the darkness at the edge of the bottom where the cattle were, I heard a faint dragging sound.

It stopped, but after several minutes it began again.

Suddenly, Tap was beside me. "What is it, Dan?" he whispered close to my ear.

"Something dragging. Cover me, Tap. I'm going into the brush for a look."

He caught the reins of my *grulla* when I passed them to him. "Careful, kid. Might be an Indian."

On cat feet, I went into the brush. All my life I'd lived in wild country, and this was second nature to me. Over the years I'd become like any cat, and could move in the night and through the brush making no sound.

A few feet, and then I listened again. Squatting down, I peered under the brush, but it was too dark to see anything. And then I heard that faint dragging sound again, and a panting . . . a gasping for breath.

Lifting the Patterson, I put the muzzle on the spot and spoke in a low, conversational voice. "You're covered with a five-shot Patterson. If you're in trouble, tell me. Start anything and you get all five shots."

There was a sort of grunt, almost as if somebody tried to speak and couldn't, and then there was no more sound at all.

I eased through the brush and found a long sort of aisle among the willows. There was a faint gray light there, for it was getting on to four o'clock, and lying on the grass was something black.

"Speak up," I said, just loud enough.

No reply. Suddenly there was a faint stirring beside me and a low growl. It was one of Zeb Lambert's dogs.

"Careful, boy." I whispered it to him, but he was going forward, sniffing and whining.

It was no animal. I knew that. Cautiously I went forward, and suddenly I stood over a dim figure. It was a man, and he was badly hurt.

"Tap?" I called, keeping my voice down. "It's a man, and he's in bad shape!"

"I'll get Milo," he said quickly.

Milo Dodge was a cowhand who'd had a good bit of experience with wounds and such, and one of the best men in any kind of sickness or injury that I'd ever known. On the frontier we were mighty scarce on doctors. In fact, here I was pushing twenty-three and I'd never even seen one, although there was one down to Austin, and I think they had a doctor or two in San Antonio. When sickness came, or wounds, we naturally cared for our own, and had nowhere else to turn.

Seemed like only a minute or two until Milo and Tap were back there, and meanwhile I'd put together a mite of fire to give us light.

The injured man was a Mexican, a slim handsome man with a fine black mustache, but you never did see a man more torn up than he was. His fancy shirt and jacket were soaked with blood and his pants all the way to his knees were covered with blood and soaked with it. He'd dragged himself a long distance, you could see that, but he had a knife in his hand, gripped so hard we couldn't get it loose.

Milo indicated the ripped and torn sleeves of the wounded man's jacket. "Wolves been at him." He pointed at the lacerated condition of the man's wrists. "He fought them with the knife. Must have had one hell of a time."

"I'll get back to the cattle," Tap said. "You help Milo. Free Squires is out at the herd."

The Mexican stirred and muttered as we cut away his bloody clothing. As we examined him, the story became clear.

Somewhere, several days ago, he had been shot and had fallen from his horse. Obviously his horse had stampeded with him and dragged him at a dead run over the rough country. Somehow the Mexican had held onto his gun long enough to shoot his horse . . . which was one reason guns were carried, for a man never knew when he might be thrown from one of the half-broken wild horses.

Then he had probably started to crawl, and the wolves had smelled blood and had come after him. He must have used up what ammunition he had, and sometime later they had grown brave enough to rush in on him and he had fought them off with a knife.

"He wants to live," Milo said dryly; "this one really put up a fight."

"I wonder who shot him?"

Milo glanced at me. "I was wondering about that. My bet is that he came from the west."

We heated water and bathed his wounds and his body. The bullet wound and the drag wounds were several days old and some of them were festering. The teeth marks had all come later.

The bullet had gone all the way through him and was pressed against the skin of his back. Milo made a slit with his Bowie knife and took the bullet out. Then he made a poultice of ground maize and bound it on both bullet holes.

It was broad daylight by the time the wounds were dressed, and one of the wagons had pulled alongside to receive the wounded man.

We were the last to move out, for the cattle had already started, and the wagons had all gone but the one into which we loaded the Mexican, bedding him down in the wagon on a mattress Tim Foley had found he could spare.

The day was clear and bright. The cattle had moved off at a good pace with only a few of them striving to turn back.

Lingering behind, I watched them trail off, and then rode my horse up to the highest bluff and looked off across the country. As far as I could see, the grass moved lightly under the wind, and there was nothing else. In the distance a black object moved out of a draw and started into the plain, then another followed . . . buffalo.

Searching the plain, I thought I could see the track that must have been made by the Mexican, for grass that is damp does not immediately straighten up when pressed down, and this track had been made, in part at least, during the night.

Holding the Patterson rifle in my right hand, I rode down the slope and scouted the vague track I had seen. Even when I was on the ground and close to the track, it was scarcely visible, nevertheless I found it.

There was blood on the grass.

As I walked the horse along, I saw so much mute evidence of the man's courage that I felt hatred swell within me for whoever had done this to him. Yet I knew that there were many men in Texas, some of them close to me, who believed any Indian or Mexican was fair game.

Whoever the man was, he had come a long way, and he had come with courage, and for that I had only respect. Courage and bravery are words too often used, too little considered. It is one thing to speak them, another thing to live them. It is never easy to face hardship, suffering, pain, and torture. It is always easier to die, simply to give up, to surrender and let the pain die with you. To fight is to keep pain alive, even to intensify it. And this requires a kind of courage for which I had only admiration.

And that Mexican, crawling alone and in darkness, had come a long way, and against fearful odds. I thought of him out there in the darkness, stalked by wolves, close to death, yet fighting back, stabbing, thrusting, fighting with the knife clutched desperately in his fist. This was a man I wanted for a friend, for of his kind there were too few.

Dipping into the coulee, I rode my horse up the other side and followed the herd.

What was it that drove the man on? Was it simply the will to live? To survive in spite of everything? Or was there some other reason? Was it hatred of those who had shot him from the saddle? The desire to live and seek revenge? Or something else?

When I rejoined the herd Pa was working the drag with Zeb.

"Milo says he's in bad shape," Pa said. "Did you see anything?"

"Only that he crawled a long way last night," I said.

The cattle were strung out in a long column, all of half a mile from point to drag. Moving up behind them with Pa, we started bunching them a little more, but keeping them at a good pace. What we wanted now was distance between us and the Cowhouse; and also the faster we got into dry country, the better.

Yet they were settling down, and fewer of them were trying to make a break for their home on the Cowhouse. Nor was there any sign of the Holt crowd or any of that renegade bunch. When nightfall came we had another fifteen miles behind us, and we bedded them down in the shelter of a bluff near the Colorado.

Through dust and rain we made our way westward, and by night the cattle grazed on the shortgrass plains and watered from the Colorado River of Texas. Each day with the sun's rising we were in the saddle, and we did not stop until shadows were falling across the land.

The rains were few. Brief showers that served only to settle the dust, but left no pools along the way. The river water ran slack, and Tap's face was drawn with worry when he saw it, but he said nothing, and neither did Pa.

But we had staked everything on this westward move, and all of us knew what lay ahead, and we had all heard of the eighty miles of dry country across which we must take the herd.

It was a hard, grueling business. Alkali dust whitened our faces, dusted over our clothing and

our horses. Sweat streaked furrows through the
dust, turning our faces into weird masks. Throughout the day the children dropped from the slow-
moving wagons to gather buffalo chips for the
nighttime fires. These were carried in a hammock
of cowhide slung beneath each wagon.

Our trek had taken us north further than we
might need to go, because we wished to strike a
known trail sooner, a trail where the difficulties,
being known, could be calculated upon and
planned for.

We reached that trail below Fort Phantom Hill,
and turned south and west again.

We were followed . . . we saw their dust by day,
sensed the restlessness of our horses by night, and
we knew they were near.

We did not know whether they were Comanches
prowling to steal ponies and take scalps, or whether
they were the renegades from the banks of the
Brazos and the Cowhouse.

Tap Henry killed a buffalo, and the meat was a
welcome thing. Later he killed an antelope, and
reported Indian sign. The further we went, the wilder the country became. We were striking for
Horsehead Crossing on the Pecos, used by the
Comanches on their raids into Mexico. Named, it
was said, for the skulls of the horses that died there
after the wild runs up out of Mexico.

Occasionally we found tracks. The old idea that
an Indian always rode an unshod horse and a white
man a shod one did not hold true, for Indians often
stole shod horses from ranches, and the white man
often enough rode an unshod pony.

Cracked mud in the bottom of water-holes worried us. The river still had water, but it ran shallow. There had been few rains and this was spring— what would it be like in a few weeks more with the sun baking the land?

There was almost a feeling of doom hanging over us that quieted our songs and stilled our voices. The herd was our all. On this move we had staked our futures, perhaps our lives.

Off in the front was Tap, usually riding with Pa, guiding our way through the wild, dry country. At night we heard the wolves. By day occasionally we saw them slinking along, watching for a chance to pull down a calf.

We carried our guns across our saddle-bows, and we rode high in the saddle, ready for trouble. Tempers grew short; we avoided each other, each man guarding himself against the hot words that could come too easily under the circumstances.

Karen ignored me. Before Tap returned we had walked out together, danced together, gone riding together. Now I hardly saw her; every moment she could spare she was with Tap.

On this day she was driving the Foley wagon and, breaking away from the herd, I rode over to her. She kept her eyes on the road ahead.

"I haven't seen much of you lately," I said.

Her chin went up. "I've been busy."

"I noticed that."

"I don't belong to you. I don't have to answer to you."

"No, ma'am, you surely don't. And Tap's a good man. One of the best."

She turned and looked right straight at me. "I am going to marry him."

Marry *Tap?* Somehow I couldn't see it. Tap was

a drifting man . . . or that was how I thought of him.

"Didn't take you long to make up your mind," I commented. "You haven't known him a week."

"That's neither here nor there." Her temper flared suddenly. "He's a man! A *real* man! That's more than most people can say! He's more of a man than you'll ever be!"

There did not seem reason to be mad about it, except that she was expecting criticism and was all wound up for it.

"Maybe," I agreed. "Tap's a good man," I said again, "no question about it. Of course, it depends on what makes a man. If I was a woman I'd give a lot of thought to that. Now, Tap is a man's man . . . he's strong, he's regular, he does his work."

"So?"

"He's like a lot of men, he doesn't like to stay hitched. I don't think he will change."

"You'll see." But her tone was less positive, and I wondered if she had given it any thought at all. Many a time when a girl gets herself involved with romance she is so busy being in love she doesn't realize what it can lead to. They are all in a rosy sort of glow until suddenly they find out the man they love was great to be in love with, but hell to be married to.

Well, I just drifted off, feeling a sort of ache inside me, and angry with myself for it. Seems to me folks are foolish about other people. Karen and I had walked out together, and folks had come to think of her as my girl, but as a matter of fact, we were scarcely more than good friends. Only now that it seemed I'd lost her, I was sore about it. Not that I could ever claim I'd had a serious thought about her, or her about me.

Moving over to the drag, I hazed a laggard steer back into the bunch, and ate dust in silence, feeling mean as a grizzly with a sore tooth.

Yet through it all there was a thread of sanity, and I knew that while there had been nothing between Karen and me but conversation, Tap was all wrong for her. Karen and me had known each other quite a spell, and she knew the others around. Tap Henry was different: he was a stranger who came riding into camp with a fancy outfit and a lot of stories. It was no wonder she was finding something in him that she had been looking for.

Truth to tell, all folks dream, old and young, and they picture in their minds the girl or man they would like to love and marry. They dream great dreams and most of them settle for much less. Many a time a man and wife lie sleeping in the same bed, dreaming dreams that are miles apart and have nothing in common.

Only Tap Henry was a drifter—yet maybe not. Maybe Karen was the answer to his dream, too, and maybe he was going to settle down. It seemed unlikely, but it was none of my business.

Milo Dodge rode back to the drag. "Talked to that Spanish man. He wants to see you."

"Me?"

"You found him. You fetched us to him."

"Where's he from?"

"He won't say. Except he kept asking me about a man with a spider scar on his cheek, a big, dark man with a deep indentation in his cheek and little scars radiating out from it, like a spider's legs."

We made camp on Antelope Creek where the

water was clear and sweet. Large oaks and pecan trees grew along the banks, and the place we found to locate was a big open meadow of some thirty or forty acres. The cattle scattered along the creek to drink, then wandered back into the meadow to feed.

Pa came back to where I was sitting my horse in the shade of a big pecan. "Good country," he said. "It tempts a man."

"It does," I said, "and it might be a good thing to hold up here another day and let the cattle fatten up and drink their fill. From now on, according to Tap, the country gets drier and drier."

Tap rode up to join us, and Zeb Lambert followed. The wagons were bunching in a rough circle near the bank of the stream. A faint breeze stirred the leaves of the trees. Tap glanced across the Concho at the bluffs beyond the river. Close to where we sat, the Antelope joined the Concho, and the Concho itself pointed our way west.

"I don't like those bluffs," Tap commented, "but we're as safe here as anywhere, I guess."

Pa told him what we were thinking, and he agreed. We couldn't have chosen a better place to stop, for we had some shelter here from any wind that might blow up, there was good water, and there was grass. The youngsters were already rousing around in the leaves and finding a few pecans left over from the previous fall.

Switching saddles to a line-back dun, I rode over to the wagon where the Mexican was riding. He was propped up a little, and he had some color in his face.

"I'm Dan Killoe," I said.

He held out a slender brown hand and smiled;

his teeth were very white. "*Gracias, amigo.* You have save my life, I think. I could go no further."

"You'd crawled a fair piece. I don't see how you did it."

He shrugged. "It was water I needed, and a place to hide." He grew serious. "*Señor,* I must warn you. By sheltering me you will make the enemy . . . even many enemies."

"A man who makes tracks in this world makes enemies also," I said. "I figure a few more won't matter."

"These are very bad . . . *malo.* They are the Comancheros."

"I've heard of them. Some of your people who trade with the Comanches, is that it?"

"*Si* . . . and we do not approve, *señor.* They found me in their country and they shot at me. I escaped, and they pursued . . . I killed one Comanchero, and one Comanche. Then they hit me. I fell, they caught me with a rope and dragged me. I got out my knife and cut the rope and I took that man's horse from him and rode . . . they pursued again. My horse was killed, but they did not catch me."

This Mexican was something of a man. In my mind's eye I could see that drag and that chase. The only way he could get that horse was to kill its rider, and after that horse was killed he had dragged himself a far piece.

"You rest easy," I told him. "Comanchero or Comanche, nobody is going to bother you."

"They will come for me." He hitched himself to a better position. "You give me a horse and I shall ride. There is no need to risk."

"Let them come." I got down on the ground. "The Good Book says that man is born to trouble.

Well, I don't figure on going against the Bible. What trouble comes, we will handle as we can, but nobody in my family ever drove a wounded man from his door, and we aren't about to."

That line-back dun was a running horse. He was also a horse with bottom. Leaving off the work that had to be done, I started for the Concho, and Zeb Lambert fell in alongside me.

This was Indian country, and we were expecting them. We scouted along the river for some distance, mainly hunting tracks, or signs of travel, but we found none.

Across the river we skirted the foot of the bluffs, found a faint trail up, and climbed to the top.

The wind was free up there, and a man could see for a long distance. We sat our horses, looking over the country. Zeb's brown hair blew in the wind when he turned his head to look.

The country away from the river was barren, and promised little. But no matter how we searched the country around we saw no movement, nor any tracks. Finally we circled back to camp.

They were out there somewhere, we were sure of it. But where?

The fires were ablaze when we rode in, and there was the good smell of coffee and of steaks broiling. Ben Cole and Freeman Squires had taken the first guard and were already with the cattle.

The herd was still feeding, relishing the fine, rich grass of the meadow. A few head had returned to the creek to drink again. Somewhere out on the plains a quail called.

Tap Henry came over to where I stood with Pa. "We'd best double the guard tonight," he said. "I've got a feeling."

"We've been lucky so far. The way I see it," Pa said, "that outfit back on the Brazos decided to let us get far enough out so they can blame it on Comanches."

Tap looked around at me. "Who's your Mexican friend?"

"He had trouble with the Comancheros. Says the man after him had a spider scar on his cheek."

Tap gave me an odd look. "Maybe we'd better give him the horse," he said, and then he got up and walked away.

"Now, what's the matter with him?" Pa asked.

It was unlike Tap to say such a thing, or to shy from trouble with anybody. "He must know something we don't," I said. "I'm getting curious about that man with the scar."

We ate, and I caught myself a little shut-eye, spreading my soogan under a pecan tree and lying half awake, half asleep, listening to the bustle around the camp.

All too soon, Zebony came to call me. He was pulling on his boots and, sitting there beside me, he said, "It's quiet out there . . . too quiet. You better come loaded for bear."

Milo Dodge was at the fire, and so was Aaron Stark. They were drinking coffee, and Stark had his Sharps repeater beside him.

Stamping my feet into my boots, I walked over to the fire. Once I had got to sleep I'd slept sound . . . so sound it worried me, for I did not like to get into the habit of sleeping so soundly I could not be awakened by the slightest move.

The coffee was strong, and hot as hell. Pa came to the fire and handed me a cold biscuit, which I ate with my coffee.

"You boys be careful, now. I never knew Tap to be jumpy, but he surely is tonight."

Tom Sandy had the line-back dun ready for me, and when I stepped into the saddle I glanced over at Tap's bed. The bed was there, but Tap was not.

"You seen Tap?"

Tom turned away. "No, I haven't!" he said, almost snapping the words at me.

Once we were away from the firelight, the night was dark, for the area was partly shielded by the bluffs and the trees. We rode out together, the four of us, scattering to places about the herd.

At such a time all the little noises of the night become intensely clear, and sounds which one has always known are suddenly strange and mysterious. But the ears of men accustomed to the wilderness and the nighttime silences and sounds choose from among the many small noises those which are a warning.

A bird rustling among the leaves, a small animal in the grass, a branch rubbing against another, the grunts and gasps and breathing of the cattle, the click of horns accidentally touching—all these are familiar.

We scattered out, circled, and then fell into pairs. As always, I rode with Zebony.

It was very still. Some of the usual noises we did not hear, and this in itself warned us that something was out there, for the small animals and birds become apprehensive at strange movements among them.

"What do you think, Zeb?"

"They'll try to get close."

Milo Dodge and Stark rode up from the other side. "Milo," I whispered, "Zeb and me, we're going to move out into the edge of the trees. We'll try to meet them before they get to us."

"All right," he said, and watched when I pointed out where we would be.

We never got the chance. There was one brief instant of warning, a rushing in the grass, and then they came with the black loom of the bluff behind them so that we could catch no outline at which to shoot.

They came charging, but in silence, and then the first shot was fired.

It was my shot, fired blindly into the blackness, as much as a warning to the camp as anything.

There was an instant burst of firing in reply, and I heard a heavy fall somewhere near me, and the grunt of a man hitting the ground. A spot of white . . . a man riding a paint horse showed, and I fired again.

The horse swerved sharply and then we were all firing. The surprise had been mutual. They came unexpectedly from the night, but they charged when all four of us were almost together, and our fire smashed them back, caused them to swerve. Shouting and yelling, they bore down on the herd.

The cattle lunged to their feet and stampeded down the valley and away from camp.

Catching the momentary outline of a man against the sky, I fired again, and then again. Hastily I reloaded and started after them. But as suddenly as it had happened, it was over. The attackers were gone and the herd was gone.

Zeb came riding up out of the night. "Dan! *Dan?*"

"Yeah . . . somebody's down."

There was a rush of horsemen from camp, and Pa yelled out, "Dan? Are you all right?"

Zeno Yearling spoke from nearby. "Here he is. I think it's Aaron."

Pa struck a light. Aaron was down, all right. He was shot through the chest and he was dead.

"They'll pay for this," Pa said. "By the Lord Harry, they'll pay!"

We circled warily, hunting for other men who were down. We found two of theirs. One was a man named Streeter, a hanger-on who had drifted to the Cowhouse country from over on the Nueces after trouble with the Rangers. The other man we had seen around, but did not know.

"Two for one," Tap said.

"Two, hell!" Pa exploded. "I wouldn't swap Stark for ten of them! He was a good man."

"We'll wait until daylight," I said, "then go hunting."

We rode back to camp with Aaron across a saddle. Nobody was feeling very good about it, and I didn't envy Pa, who would have to tell his widow.

There was no talking around the fire. Picking up some sticks, I built the flames up. We checked around, but nobody else had been hurt.

"Two doesn't seem right," Zeb said. "I know we hit more of them. They came right at us, close range."

Karen and Mrs. Foley were at the fire, making coffee. Taking the Patterson, I cleaned it carefully, checked the loads, and reloaded. Then I went out and looked the line-back dun over to see if he'd picked up any scratches. He looked fit and ready, and I knew him for a tough little horse.

The day broke slowly, a gray morning with a black line of trees that slowly took on shape and became distinct. With the first light, we saddled up again.

Tim Foley, despite his arguments, was forced to stay behind with the wagons, and Frank Kelsey stayed with him.

"You'd better stay, Tom," Pa said. "We've lost one married man already."

"Be damned if I will!" Sandy replied testily. He hesitated. "We should leave another man. Suppose they come back?"

"Free"—Pa looked over at Squires—"you stay. You stood guard last night."

"Now, look here!" Squires protested.

"As a favor," Pa said. "Will you stay?"

Freeman Squires shrugged and walked away. The rest of us mounted up and moved out.

The trail was broad enough, for they had followed the herd into the night, and the herd had taken off into the broad, empty lands to the south.

This was Lipan country, but the Lipans, of late, had been friendly to the white man.

We rode swiftly into the growing light, a tight bunch of armed horsemen, grim-faced and bitter with the loss of Aaron Stark and our cattle. No longer were we simply hard-working, hard-riding men, no longer quiet men intent on our own affairs. For riding after lawless men was not simply for revenge or recovery of property; it was necessary if there was to be law, and here there was no law except what right-thinking men made for themselves.

The brown grass of autumn caught the golden light of morning, and the dark lines of trees that marked the Concho fell behind. Our group loosened, spread out a little to see the tracks better.

Among the many cattle tracks we searched for those of riders.

Away off on the flank, I suddenly came upon the tracks of a lone rider whose mount had a magnificent stride. Drawing up, I checked those tracks again.

It was a big horse—far larger and with a better gait than our cow ponies—and it carried a light burden, for the tracks indicated the weight upon the horse must be small.

The tracks came from the northwest, which did not fit with those we followed, unless they were being joined by some scout sent on ahead. Yet why would such a scout be sent? And who among the renegades who followed the Holts could possibly have such a horse?

The tracks had been made the night before, or late the previous afternoon, and I followed them, but kept my own party in sight.

Suddenly the tracks veered sharply west, and I drew rein, looking in that direction.

There was a clump of black on the prairie . . . mesquite? Cautiously, rifle ready, I walked the dun toward it. The size grew . . . it was a clump of trees and brush almost filling a hollow in the plain.

The edge broke sharply off in a ledge of rock, and the tops of the trees barely lifted above its edge. The tracks I followed led to the edge and disappeared into the copse. Warily, I followed.

Then I heard running water, a trickle of water falling into a pool. A wind stirred the leaves, then was still.

My horse, ears pricked, walked into a narrow trail where my stirrups brushed the leaves on either side. After some thirty yards of this, there was a sudden hollow under the arching branches of the live oaks, and an open space some fifty feet in diameter, a pool a dozen feet across, and a magnificent black horse that whinnied gently and pricked his ears at my dun. There was coffee on a fire, and bacon frying, and then a voice spoke, "Stand where you are, señor, or I shall put a bullet where your breakfast is."

My hands lifted cautiously. There was no mistaking the ominous click of the cocking gun . . . but the voice was a woman's voice.

CHAPTER THREE

She was young and she was lovely, and the sun caught and entangled itself in the spun red-gold of her hair, but the rifle in her hands was rock-steady, its muzzle an unwinking black eye that looked at my belt buckle.

A flat-crowned Spanish hat lay upon her shoulders, held by the chin strap which had slipped down about her throat. She was dressed in beautifully tanned buckskin, the skirt was divided for easy riding—the first I had seen, although I'd heard of them before this.

"Who are you? Why are you following me?"

"Unless you're one of the cow thieves that ran off our herd last night, I wasn't following you until I came across your tracks out there."

The rifle did not waver, nor did her eyes. "Who are you? Where do you come from?"

As she talked, I was getting an idea. Maybe a wild one, but an idea.

"The name is Dan Killoe, and we're from over on

the Cowhouse. We're driving to New Mexico. Maybe to Colorado. We're hunting new range."

"You spoke of cow thieves."

"They ran our herd off last night. The way we figure, it's a passel of thieves from back on the Cowhouse. If we leave the country with our stock, they've all got to go to work."

She watched me with cool, violet eyes. Yet it seemed to me she was buying my story.

"You must have heard the cattle go by a couple of hours back," I added. "Now may I put my hands down?"

"Put them down. Just be careful what you do with them."

Carefully, I lowered them to the horn of the saddle. Then I glanced around. "Seems to me you're a long way from home," I said, "and you a woman alone."

"I am not alone," she said grimly. "I have this." She gestured meaningfully with her rifle.

"That's a mighty fine horse you've got there. Fact is"—I pushed my hat back on my head—"that's one reason I followed you. I wanted to see that horse."

She lowered her rifle just a little. "Have some coffee?" she suggested. "It will boil away."

Gratefully, I swung down. "I'd like a cup. Then I'll have to follow after the others and lend a hand. I figure in about an hour we're going to have us a scrap with those thieves."

My own cup hung to my saddle-horn and I helped myself and looked again at her. Never in all my born days had I seen a girl as pretty as that.

"Now," I said, "I've got an idea. You wouldn't be looking for somebody, would you?"

She glanced at me quickly. "Why do you ask that?"

"Wondered." I took a swallow of hot coffee. "Do you know anything about the Comancheros?"

Oh, I'd hit pay dirt all right, that was plain enough from the way she reacted. "I know about them," she said.

"We picked up a maverick a while back, and he was in mighty bad shape. He had been shot and he had been dragged, and the Comancheros had done it."

"He's alive? He's all right?"

"Friend of yours?"

"Where is he? I am going to him."

"He's in bad shape, so you take it easy. We found him out in the brush, and the wolves had been at him. He'd fought them off, but he was chewed up some." I swallowed the last of the coffee and rinsed my cup at the stream. "He's got nerve enough for three men. How he ever crawled so far, I'll never know."

She gathered her meager gear. "I am going to him. Where is your camp?"

"Ma'am, that boy is in bad shape and, like I said, he had some rough treatment. I don't know you, and for all I do know you might be one of his enemies."

"I am his adopted sister. After my father was killed, his family took me into their home."

It was time I was getting on, for I'd already lost too much time, and the Kaybar outfit was riding into trouble. "You ride careful when you get to camp. They are expecting trouble, and you might collect a bullet before they see you.

"You ride north from here. The camp is on the

Antelope near where it empties into the Middle Concho. Tell them Dan Killoe sent you."

Mounting up, I rode up to the plain and swung south. Keeping to low ground, I rode swiftly along, coming up only occasionally to look for the trail of torn earth where the Kaybar crew had passed.

They had been moving slowly, so I figured to overtake them before they ran into trouble. But I was almost too late.

When I finally saw them they were fanned out, riding toward a bluff. The country beyond that bluff stretched out for miles, and I could catch glimpses of it. Suddenly, just as I slowed down so as not to rush among them, the grass stirred between them and me and a man reared up, rifle in hand.

Intent upon making a kill, he did not notice me, and my horse made little sound with his hoofbeats on the plain's turf. Not wishing to stampede their horses by rushing among them, the dun was walking at a slow pace when the man rose from the brush.

He came up with his rifle and lifted it, taking a careful sight on Tap, and I slapped the spurs to the dun. I was not a rider who used his spurs, and the startled dun gave one tremendous leap and then broke into a dead run.

The ambusher heard the sound of hoofs too late, and even as he brought the rifle into position to fire, he must have heard that rushing sound. It could not have been loud, for the turf was not hard and there was short grass, but he turned quickly, suddenly, but I was fairly on top of him and he had no chance. I fired that Patterson of mine like you'd fire a pistol, gripping it with one hand and holding it low down close to my thigh.

He was slammed back by that .56-caliber bullet as though struck by an axe, and then I was over and past him and riding up to join the others.

As if on order, they all broke into a run, and when I reached the ridge they had been mounting, I saw the camp that lay below.

At least two dozen men were lying about, and my shot must have startled them, for they evidently had jumped up and started for their guns, those who didn't have them alongside.

There were several men with the herd, and my first shot went for the nearest guard. It was a good shot, for he left the saddle and tumbled in a heap, and then we ripped into that camp.

We were outnumbered two to one, but our coming was a complete surprise and we made the attack good. I saw Tap wheel his horse and come back through a second time, blasting with a six-shooter. Then he tucked that one away and started blasting with a second one, and unless I missed my guess, Tap would be carrying at least two more.

In those days of cap-and-ball pistols many a man when fighting Indians—and some outlaws too—carried as many as six pistols into action because of the time it took to reload. And some carried extra cylinders that could be placed fully loaded into the pistol.

A big man with a red beard and red hair all over his chest jumped at me, swinging a rifle that must have been empty. The dun hit him with a shoulder and knocked him head over heels into the fire.

He let out an awful yell and bounded out of that fire with his pants smoking, and sticks and coals were scattered all over the place.

We swept on through camp and started those

cattle high-tailing it back to the north, and if we picked up a few mustangs in the process, we weren't taking time to sort them out, even if we'd been a mind to.

We got off scot-free.

Ben Cole had a bullet burn alongside his neck, and he grumbled all the way back to the Concho about it. Fact is, it must have smarted something fierce, with sweat getting into it, and all. But you'd have thought he had a broken knee or a cracked skull, the way he took on.

Zeno Yearly rode back alongside me. He was a long-legged man with a long face, and he didn't look like he could move fast enough to catch a turtle in a barley field. However, out there when the fighting was going on, I'd noticed he was a busy, busy man.

Tap fell back beside me. "Where'd you drop off to?" he asked. "I figured you'd taken out, running."

"Had to stop back there to talk to a girl," I said carelessly. "She offered me coffee, so I stopped by."

He looked at me, grinning. "Boy, any girl you find out in this country, you can have!"

"Prettiest girl you ever did see," I commented, "and she'll be back at camp when we get there."

"You're funnin'!" He stared at me, trying to make out what I was getting at. The idea that the girl actually existed he wouldn't consider for a moment, and in his place I wouldn't have believed it either.

"Too bad you're getting married," I said. "Puts you out of the running."

His face flushed. "Who said I was getting married?" he demanded belligerently.

"Why, Karen. She allowed as how you two were looking for a meeting house."

His face flushed a deeper red under the brown. "Nothing to that," he protested. "Nothing to that, nothing at all."

"She seemed mighty positive," I said, "and you know how folks out here are, when it comes to trifling with a good woman. Tim Foley is a mighty handy man with a shotgun, Tap. I'd ride careful, if I were you."

He grinned. He was recovering himself now. "Now, don't you worry, boy. Nobody ever caught old Tap in a bind like that. Karen's a fine girl . . . but *marriage?* I ain't the marrying kind."

Whether it was what I'd said or something else, I can't say, but that night I noticed Karen sitting by herself, and she wasn't liking it, not one bit.

The red-headed girl was there, and she was the center of quite a bit of fuss by the women folks. Most of the men hung back. She was so beautiful it made them tongue-tied, not that any of them, unless it was Tap, would have won any prizes in an elocution contest.

Me, I hadn't anything to say to her. She was the prettiest girl I'd ever seen, and to ride out there by herself took a lot more nerve than most men would have, riding right through the heart of Comanche country, like that.

Two or three times she looked over at me, but I paid her no mind. Most of the time she spent talking to the Mexican or fixing grub for him.

Karen's face was pale and her lips were thin. I'd never noticed how sharp and angular her face could get until that night, and I knew she was mad, mad clean through. Tap, he just sat and joked with the men, and when he got up Karen would have cut him off from the bunch, but he stepped into the saddle and rode out to the herd.

Tom Sandy came up to the fire for more coffee, and for the first time I saw he was wearing a six-shooter. He favored a rifle, as I do, but tonight he was packing a gun. Rose was at the fire, too. A dark, pretty woman with a lot of woman where it mattered, and a way of making a man notice. She had those big dark eyes, and any time she looked at an attractive man those eyes carried a challenge or an invitation. Or something that could be taken that way. Believe me, she was no woman to have around a cow outfit.

Sandy looked across the fire at her a few times, and he looked mean as an old razor-back boar.

Rose dished up some beans and beef for Tom and brought them to him, and then she turned to me. "Dan, can I help you to something?"

I looked up at her and she was smiling at me, and I swallowed a couple of times. "Thank you, ma'am. I would like some more of those *frijoles.*"

She went to the fire for them, giving her hips that extra movement as she walked away, and Tom Sandy was staring at me with a mean look in his eye.

"Hot," I said, running a finger around my shirt collar.

"I hadn't noticed," he said.

Pa came over and dropped down beside me. "Tap figures we'd better get on the road right away in the morning, before daybreak. What do you think?"

"Good idea," I said.

Tom Sandy walked off, and Pa looked at me.

"Dan, you aren't walking out with Rose Sandy, are you?"

"Are you crazy?"

"Somebody is. Tom knows it and he's mad. If he finds out, there'll be a killing."

"Don't look at me. If I was planning to start something like that, she wouldn't be the one."

At sunup we were well down the trail and moving steadily westward. Away from the stream the land was dry and desolate, and showed little grass. It was a warning of what lay ahead.

So far we had done well. Despite the driving off of our cattle and our recovery of them, we seemed to have lost none, and we had gained by half a dozen horses that had been driven off with the cattle when we recovered them.

We saw little game. There were the usual prairie dogs and jackass rabbits, and when we camped that night Zeno caught us a mess of catfish which offered a change of diet.

Out on the plains away from the river there was prickly pear, greasewood, and sage brush, but mighty little else. Here and there in a bottom or at a creek crossing we found a few acres of grama, and we took time out to let the cattle eat. It was a scary thing to think of the long marches ahead of us with grass growing less and less.

We all knew about the eighty miles of dry march ahead of us, but we preferred not to think of it. Each night we filled our barrels to have as much water as we could for the day to come. But all of us knew there might be a time when there would be no water, not even for ourselves and our horses.

We nooned at a pool, shallow but quite extensive,

but when we left, it was only a patch of muddy earth churned by the feet of our cattle.

While there, I went up to the Mexican's wagon to see how he was . . . or at least, that's what I told myself.

When I spoke, the redhead drew back the curtain, and her smile was something to see. "Oh, please come in! Miguel has been telling me how it was you who found him."

"Just happened to be first," I said, embarrassed.

"If you had not found me," Miguel said, "I should now be dead. That I know. Nobody else had come to see what lay out there, even if they heard me."

"Your name is Dan Killoe?" she asked. "I am Conchita McCrae. My father was Scotch-Irish, my mother a Mexican."

"You had nerve," I said. "You must have ridden for days."

"There was no one else. Miguel's father is dead, and there is only our mother . . . his mother. She is very old, and she worried about her son."

Well, maybe so, but it took nerve for a girl—or a man for that matter—to ride into Comanche country alone. Or even to drive through it, as we were. She had a fast horse, but that isn't too much help when the Comanche knows the country and is a master at ambuscade. There was very little about hunting or fighting that the Indian did not know, and what he did not know, he learned fast.

Conchita McCrae stood tall in my estimation, and I liked the way she looked straight into your eyes and stood firmly on her small feet. That was more of a woman than I had ever seen before.

"The Comancheros," Miguel said, "I do not approve of what they do. They are some of my people

who trade with the Comanche, and it is a profit-
able trade, but they sell the rifles with which to
kill, and they kill our people, and yours also."

He paused to catch his breath, and then said,
speaking more slowly, "They believed I was spying
when I was only hunting wild horses, for they knew
me as one who did not approve. I had hoped to
avoid trouble with them, but there are men among
the Comancheros who are worse than the Comanches themselves."

"The man with the scar?"

The skin around his eyes seemed to draw back.
"He is the worst of them. He is Felipe Soto. You
know of him?"

I knew of him. He was a gunfighter and a killer.
It was said he had killed more than twenty men in
hand-to-hand battles with knife or gun. How many
he had killed in fights of other kinds, no man could
guess.

In a few short years the man had become a
legend, although so far as I knew he had appeared
east of the Pecos on only one occasion. He had
crossed the Rio Grande from Matamoras and killed
a man in Brownsville.

He was an outlaw, but he was protected by many
of his own people, and among them he had been
guilty of no crimes. A big man, he was widely
feared, and even men who might have faced him
with some chance of winning did not care to take
the risk such a meeting would involve.

"Where did they find you?"

"Ah! There is the trouble, *amigo!* They find me
just as I have come upon their . . . shall we say,
rendezvous? It is a word you know?

"There is a canyon to the north, a great long,

high-walled canyon, and in the bottom there is rich, green grass. They were there . . . the Comanches and the Comancheros. This place I have seen is a secret place, but I had heard of it. It is the Palo Duro Canyon."

"They will follow him, Mr. Killoe," Conchita said. "They will not let him live now. The Comancheros are men of evil. If they do not find him now, they will come searching for him when he is home again."

"What they do then is no business of mine," I said, "but we won't let him be taken from us. I promise you that."

There was a movement behind me. "Don't make any promises you can't keep."

It was Tap Henry. His features were hard, and there was a kind of harsh impatience in his eyes that I had seen there before this.

"I'll keep the promise, Tap," I replied quietly. "I have made the promise, and it will stick."

"You'll listen to me," Tap replied shortly. "You don't know what you are walking into."

"I have made my promise. I shall keep it."

"Like hell you will!" Tap's tone was cold. "Look, kid, you don't know what you're saying."

He paused, taking a cigar from his pocket. "We've got enough to do, getting our cattle west, without borrowing trouble."

"Please," Miguel had risen to one elbow, "I wish no trouble. If you will loan me a horse, we can go."

"Lie down, señor," I said. "You are my guest, and here you will stay."

"Who's leading this outfit, you or me?"

"I thought Pa was," I said dryly. "When it comes to that, we're both working for him."

His face stiffened a little. "Well, we'll see what Pa has to say, then!" he said sarcastically.

We walked together toward where Pa stood by the fire. Zeb Lambert was there, squatting on his heels, and Zeno Yearly was there too. Ira Tilton had come in from his guard for coffee and I saw his eyes go quickly to Tap Henry.

"Pa," Tap said, "the kid here has promised those Mexicans that they can have our protection all the way into New Mexico. Now, we know the Comancheros are hunting them, and that means trouble! They can muster fifty, maybe a hundred white men and more Comanches, and we're in no shape to stand up to that kind of a crowd. I say we let them shift for themselves."

Zeno glanced up at Tap, but his long horse-face revealed nothing.

Pa glanced at me. "What do you say about this, Dan?"

"I told them they were our guests, and they were safe with us."

Pa looked at Tap. "What's wrong with that?"

Tap's face darkened, and his eyes were cold. "Pa, you don't know what you're saying. Neither you nor the cattle nor any of us will get through if that outfit tackles us! I heard that Mex say he knew where their hide-out was, and that's the best-kept secret in this part of the country. They dasn't let him live."

"We will try to see that he does," Pa said quietly.

Pa was a square-faced man with carefully combed gray hair and a trimmed gray mustache. No matter how bad times got or how busy we were, Pa was always shaved, his hair was always trimmed.

And I do not recall ever seeing Pa lean on anything —he always stood on his own two feet.

He looked steadily at Tap now. "I am surprised, Tap. You should know that I would never leave a man—least of all a man and a woman—out here on the plains alone. If we have to fight to protect them, then we shall have to fight."

Tap Henry stared at him with sullen eyes. "Pa, you can't do that. These folks are nothing to you. They are—"

"We took them in. They needed help. So long as I live, they will have it from me. I have never turned a man from my door, and I never shall."

Tap Henry drew a deep breath. "Pa . . ." He was almost pleading. "These Comancheros . . . they're worse than Comanches. Believe me, I know—"

"How do you know, Tap?" Pa asked mildly.

Tap shut up and turned sharply away. That he believed us all to be a pack of fools was obvious, and maybe he was right. Pa was not a man who ever preached to anyone, least of all to his boys, but he had taught us always to stand on principle. I say taught us, but it was mostly example. A man always knew where Pa Killoe stood on any question, and no nonsense about it.

Not that we had any doubts about the trouble we were in. The plains were alive with Comanches, and the Comancheros were as bad, if not worse, and Tap was right—they would be hunting Miguel.

An idea that was sheer inspiration came to me of a sudden. More than likely they already believed Miguel to be dead, but suppose they wanted to see the body before they believed?

"Pa . . . I think we should bury him. Miguel, I mean."

Pa glanced around at me; and Conchita, who had come down from the wagon, stood stock-still, listening. "We should bury him right here," I said, "and put a marker over the grave."

Zeno Yearly walked over to the wagon and took a shovel from the straps that bound it to the wagonside where it would be handy. Without any further talk, he walked off to one side and stuck the spade into the ground. Getting another shovel, I joined him.

We dug the grave four feet deep then dropped in a layer of big rocks, then another. If they were curious enough to open the grave they might not be curious enough to lift out all those rocks. We filled in the dirt and put up a marker.

"Name?" Yearly asked.

"No," I said, "we don't want them to think he talked. Just make it: *Unknown Mexican Died on This Spot April 16, 1858.*"

After a short nooning, we rolled our wagons again, and the herd moved on.

Tap had nothing to say, but he was short-tempered as a rattlesnake in the blind, which is the way they refer to a snake when he is shedding his skin. At that time a rattler won't rattle—he simply strikes at anything that moves.

But Tap was wary. He rode far out much of the time, scanning the hills. The word got around, of course, and most of the hands went out fully armed and loaded for bear. We kept the herd moving late, and five miles further on we crossed the South Fork, sometimes called the Boiling Concho. This was real water—deep, clear, and quite rapid in some places, and the herd spread out along the banks for water while we hunted a place to ford it.

Tap found the spot he was looking for—a ledge of rock under the water that gave sure footing for the cattle and was wide enough to take two wagons abreast. We crossed over, moving them slow, and started across some flat country dotted with mesquite and occasional live oak. The grass was good. We crossed Dove Creek, filled with rushes, and pushed on to Good Spring Creek.

The water was clear and cold, the grass good, and there was plenty of wood and buffalo chips. It was coming on to dark when we rounded the cattle into position and circled our few wagons.

Zeno Yearly got out his tackle and threw a bait into the creek. By the time the sun was gone he had six black bass, all of them good. Those fish were so hungry and so unfamiliar with fishhooks that they could scarcely wait to grab.

The fish tasted good. Nobody was saying anything but our grub wasn't holding up like we had hoped. We had figured to kill more game, and we just hadn't seen any, and we didn't want to kill a steer because we would need all we had. Aside from the steers, we were depending on the rest for breeding stock.

Nobody talked very much, and we ate quickly and turned in for a rest. Ben Cole and Zeno Yearly took the first guard, but Tap Henry was awake, too. He smoked near the fire for a while, then got up and walked out beyond the wagons. He was still standing out there alone when I dropped off to sleep.

Tom Sandy woke me. He looked thinner, and he was rough waking me. I got out of my blankets into the cool night and put on my hat, then my boots.

Tom had walked off to the fire without saying anything, but he looked mean and bitter.

Zebony was at the fire, and he glanced up at me. "Did you see Tom?"

"I saw him."

"Trouble's riding that man. Something's chewing on him."

Glancing over at Tap's bed, I saw him there, sleeping. We mounted up and rode by and out to the herd. We were relieving Kelsey and Squires.

"Quiet," Kelsey said.

They rode off toward the fire and Zebony started away. From where I sat by the edge of the herd I could see Tom Sandy huddled in his blankets near the wagon. My eyes strayed to Tap's bed, but somehow it did not seem occupied. Bushes obscured it somewhat, however, and it was none of my affair.

Slowly, I started around the herd. I was riding a big roan horse that was hard-riding but powerful, and for his size, quite fast.

My mind went suddenly to the blond gunman who had accompanied Webb Holt on the day Tap killed him. That man worried me. He had taken the whole affair too calmly, and I had a feeling we would see more of him. And Bud Caldwell, too, for that matter.

It was almost an hour later and the cattle had gotten to their feet for a stretch, and some had begun to graze a little, when suddenly a big longhorn's head came up sharply. Looking where he looked, I saw only the blackness of a patch of live oak.

With the Patterson ready in my hand, I walked the roan toward the trees. Trust a longhorn to spot trouble, for although they were considered domestic cattle, actually they were wild things, reacting like wild things, and most of them lived wild all their lives.

Suddenly, from the corner of my eye, I saw movement in the blackness, and caught a gleam of light on a gun barrel.

Somebody else was searching that patch of woods, somebody from our camp. Stepping the roan around a patch of brush, I took him into the darkness. He was curious, and he could sense danger as any mustang would, so he stepped light and easy.

There was a stir of movement, a low murmur of voices and then a woman's soft laugh.

An instant there, I stopped. I could feel the flush climb up my neck, for I knew what I would find in there . . . and in the same instant I knew who that other man was.

Instantly, I pushed the roan through the brush. It crackled, and I saw the man across the small clearing lift his rifle. Slapping spurs to the roan, I leaped him ahead and struck up the gun before it could be fired. Grasping the barrel, I wrenched it from the hands of the startled man.

There was a gasp of alarm, and then a cool voice said, "Turn him loose, boy. If he wants to come hunting me, give him his chance."

"Give me the rifle, Dan." It was Tom Sandy. Only he was not the easy-going man I had known back on the Cowhouse. This was a cold, dangerous man.

"Give me the rifle," Sandy persisted. "I shall show him what comes to wife-stealers and thieves."

"Let him have it," Tap said coolly.

Instead I laid my rifle on Tap. "You turn around,

Tap, and you walk back to the herd. If you make a move toward that gun, I'll kill you."

"Are you crossing me?" He was incredulous, but there was anger in him, too.

"We will have no killing on this outfit. We've trouble enough without fighting among ourselves." I saw Tom Sandy ease a hand toward his shirt front where I knew he carried a pistol. "Don't try it, Tom. That goes for you, too."

There was silence, and in the silence I saw Rose Sandy standing against a tree trunk, staring at the scene in fascinated horror.

Others were coming. "Turn around, Tom, and walk back to camp. We're going to settle this, here and now. You, too, Rose."

She looked up at me. "Me?" Her voice trembled. "What—?"

"Go along with him."

Tap Henry stood watching me as they walked away. "You'll interfere once too often, boy. I'll forget we grew up together."

"Don't ever do it, Tap. I like you, and you're my brother. But if you ever draw a gun on me, I'll kill you."

The late moon lit the clearing with a pale, mysterious light. He stood facing me, his eyes pinpoints of light in the shadow of his hat brim.

"Look, you damned fool, do you know who you're talking to? Have you lost your wits?"

"No, Tap, and what I said goes as it lays. Don't trust your gun against me, Tap, because I'm better than you are. I don't want to prove it . . . I don't set store over being called a gunfighter like you do. It's a name I don't want, but I've seen you shoot, Tap, and I can outshoot you any day in the week."

He turned abruptly and walked back to camp. Pa was up, and so were the others—Tim Foley and his wife, Karen, her face pinched and tight, and all of us gathering around.

"Free," I said to Squires, "ride out and take my place, will you? We've got a matter to settle."

Pa was standing across the fire in his shirtsleeves, and Pa was a man who set store by proper dress. Never a day but what he wore a stiff collar and a necktie.

Tap walked in, a grin on his hard face, and when he looked across at Tom Sandy his eyes were taunting. Tom refused to meet his gaze.

Rose came up to the fire, holding her head up and trying to put an impudent look on her face and not quite managing it.

Pa wasted no time. He asked questions and he got answers. Tap Henry had been meeting Rose out on the edge of camp. Several times Tom Sandy had managed to see them interrupted, hoping Rose would give up or that Tap would.

Karen stood there listening, her eyes on the ground. I knew it must hurt to hear all this, but I could have told her about Tap. As men go he was a good man among men, but he was a man who drew no lines when it came to women. He liked them anywhere and he took them where he found them and left them right there. There would have been no use in my telling Karen more than I had . . . she would believe what she wanted to believe.

Worst of all, I'd admired Tap. We'd been boys together and he had taught me a good deal, but we were a team on this cow outfit, and we had to pull together if we were going to make it through what lay ahead. And every man-jack on the drive knew that Tap Henry was our insurance. Tap had been over the trail, and none of us had. Tap knew the country we were heading toward, and nobody else among us did.

Tap was a leader, and he was a top hand, and right now he was figuring this was a big joke. The trouble was, Tap didn't really know Pa.

Tom Sandy had heard Rose get out of the wagon, and he knew that Tap was gone from his bed, so he followed Rose. If it hadn't been for that old longhorn spotting something in the brush, Sandy would have unquestionably killed one of them, and maybe both. He would have shot Tap where he found him. He said as much, and he said it cold turkey.

Tap was watching Sandy as he talked, and I thought that Tap respected him for the first time. It was something Tap could understand.

"What have you to say for yourself?" Pa asked Tap.

Tap Henry shrugged. "What can I say? He told it straight enough. We were talking"—Tap grinned meaningly—"and that was all."

Pa glanced over at Rose. "We're not going to ask you anything, Rose. What lies between you and your husband is your business. Only this: if anything like this happens again, you leave the drive . . . no matter where we are. Tom can go or stay, as he likes."

Pa turned his attention back to Tap. His face was cold. "One thing I never tolerate on my drives is a trouble-maker. You've caused trouble, Tap, and likely you'd cause more. I doubt if you and Tom could make it to the Pecos without a killing, and I won't have that, nor have my men taking sides."

He paused, and knowing Pa and how much he cared for Tap, I knew how much it cost him. "You can have six days' grub, Tap, and a full canteen. You've got your own horse. I want you out of camp within the hour."

Tap would not believe it. He was stunned, you could see that. He stood there staring at Pa like Pa had struck him.

"We can't have a man on our drive, which is a family affair, who would create trouble with another man's wife," Pa said, and he turned abruptly and walked back to our wagon.

Everybody turned away then, and after a minute Tap walked to the wagon and began sorting out what little gear he had.

"Sorry, Tap," I said.

He turned sharp around. "Go to hell," he said coldly. "You're no brother of mine."

He shouldered his gear and walked to his horse to saddle up. Ira Tilton got up and walked over to him, and talked to him for a minute, then came back and sat down. And then Tap got into the saddle and rode off.

Day was breaking, and we yoked up the wagons and started the herd. The river became muddy and shallow. We let the cattle take their time, feeding as they went, but the grass was sparse and of no account.

We had been short-handed when we started west, and since then we had buried Aaron Stark and lost Tap Henry. It wasn't until the wagons were rolling that we found we had lost somebody else.

Karen was gone.

She had slipped off, saddled her pony, and had taken off after Tap.

Ma Foley was in tears and Tim looked mighty grim, but we had all seen Tap ride off alone, and so far as anybody knew he had not talked to Karen in days. But it was plain enough that she had followed him off, and a more fool thing I couldn't imagine.

Pa fell back to the drag. "Son, you and Zeb take out and scout for water. I doubt if we will have much this side of the Pecos. There's Mustang Ponds up ahead, but Tap didn't say much about them."

We moved out ahead, but the land promised little. The stream dwindled away, falling after only a few miles to a mere trickle, then scattered pools. Out on the plains there was a little mesquite, all of it scrubby and low-growing. The few pools of water we saw were too small to water the herd.

The coolness of the day vanished and the sun became hot. Pausing on a rise where there should have been a breeze, we found none. I mopped my neck and looked over at Zebony.

"We may wish we had Tap before this is over."

He nodded. "Pa was right, though."

At last we found a pool. It was water lying in a deep hole in the river, left behind when the upper stream began to dry out, or else it was the result of some sudden, local shower.

"What do you think, Zeb?"

"Enough." He stared off into the distance. "Maybe the last this side of Horsehead." He turned to me. "Dan, that Pecos water is alkali. The river isn't so bad, but any pools around it will kill cattle. We've got to hold them off it."

Suddenly he drew up. On the dusty earth before

him were the tracks of half a dozen unshod ponies, and they were headed south. The tracks could be no more than a few hours old.

"As if we hadn't trouble enough," Zeb commented. He squinted his eyes at the distance where the sun danced and the atmosphere shimmered.

Nothing . . .

"I wonder what became of Tap?"

"I've been wondering if that Foley girl caught up with him," Zeb said. "It was a fool thing for her to do." He glanced around at me. "Everybody thought you were shining up to her."

"We talked some . . . nothing to it."

We rode on. Sweat streaked our horses' sides and ran down under our shirts in rivulets. The stifling hot dust lifted at each step the horses took, and we squinted our eyes against the sun and looked off down over the vast empty expanse opening before us.

"If the women weren't along . . ." I said.

We had come a full day's drive ahead of the herd, and there was water back there, water for a day and a night, perhaps a little more, but ahead of us there was no sign of water and it was a long drive to Horsehead Crossing.

"We'll lose stock." Zeb lit a cigarette. "We'll lose a-plenty, unless somewhere out there, there's water."

"If there is, it will be alkali. In the pools it will be thick, and bad enough to kill cattle."

Removing my hat to wipe the hatband, I felt the sun like a fire atop my skull—and I carry a head of hair, too.

Once, dipping into a hollow, we found some

grass. It was grama, dead now and dry, but our horses tugged at it and seemed pleased enough.

From the rim of the hollow we looked again into the distance toward Horsehead.

"Do you suppose there's another way to drive?" I asked.

Zeb shrugged. "It ain't likely." He pointed. "Now, what do you think of that?"

In the near distance, where the road cut through a gap in the hills, buzzards circled. There were only two or three of them.

"First living thing we've seen in hours," Zeb commented. "They must have found something."

"If they found anything out there," I said, "it's dead, all right."

We walked on, both of us shucking our firearms. I held the Patterson with light fingers, careful to avoid the barrel, which was hot enough to burn.

The first thing we saw was a dead horse. It had been dead all of a day, but no buzzards had been at it yet. The brand on the shoulder was a Rocking H, the Holt brand.

Topping out on the rise, we looked into a little arroyo beside the trail. Zebony flinched, and looked around at me, his face gray and sick, and Zeb was a tough man. My horse did not want to move up beside his, but I urged it on.

The stench was frightful, and the sight we looked upon, even worse. In the bottom of that arroyo lay scattered men and horses . . . at first glimpse I couldn't tell how many.

The men were dead, stripped of clothing, and horribly mutilated. That some of the men had been alive when left by the Comanches was obvious, for there were evidences of crawling, blind crawling, like animals seeking some shelter, any shelter.

We walked our horses into the arroyo of death, and looked around. Never had I seen such a grim and bloody sight. What had happened was plain enough. This was some of the outfit that had followed us from the Cowhouse—some of the bunch that had stolen our cattle, and from whom we had recovered the herd.

They must have circled around and gotten ahead of us and settled down here to ambush us when they were attacked. Obviously, they had been expecting nothing. They would have known they were far ahead of us, and they had built fires and settled down to prepare a meal. The ashes of the fires remained and there were a few pots scattered about. There were, as we counted, eleven dead men here.

What of the others? Had they been elsewhere? Or had some of them been made prisoners by the Indians?

Hastily, we rode up out of the arroyo, and then we got down and pulled out rocks and one way and another caved in the edge of the arroyo on the bodies to partly cover them.

"Wolves won't bother them," Zeb commented. "We haven't seen any wolves in the past couple of days."

"Nothing for them to feed on but snakes. According to Tap Henry, this country is alive with them."

We turned away from the arroyo, both of us feeling sick to the stomach. They had been our enemies, but no man wishes that kind of fate on anyone, and a Comanche with time on his hands can think of a lot of ways for a man to take time to die.

Circling the scene of the ambush, we found the trail of the departing Indians. There must have been at least forty in the band—the number could only be surmised, but it was at least that large.

Their tracks indicated they were going off toward the north, and it was unlikely they would attempt to remain in the vicinity, because of the scarcity of water. But they must have crossed this terrain many times, and might know of water of which we knew nothing. Judging from the arid lands around us, though, it was doubtful.

We had started back toward the herd when we saw those other tracks. We came upon them suddenly, the tracks of two horses.

"Well, she caught up with him," Zeb commented, indicating one set of tracks. "That's Tap's paint . . . and those other tracks belong to that little *grulla* Karen rode off. I'd know those tracks anywhere."

They had come this way . . . after the massacre in the arroyo, and they were headed due west. Before them lay the eighty miles or so to Horsehead Crossing . . . had Karen taken any water? They would need it.

We camped that night by the deep pool in the river bed—the last water of which we knew.

CHAPTER FOUR

The deep pool was gone. Where the water had been was now a patch of trampled mud, slowly drying under the morning sun.

"All right, Dan," Pa said to me, "I'm no cattleman, and I have the brains to know it. You take the drive. I don't need to tell you what it means to all of us."

"There's eighty miles, or close to it, between here and Horsehead." I was speaking to them all. "But as we get close to the Pecos we may come up to some pools of water. I'll have to ride ahead, or somebody will, and spot those pools before the cattle can get wind of them, and then we'll have to keep the herd up-wind of that water.

"It's death if they drink it. Water in the pools is full of concentrated alkali, and they wouldn't have a chance.

"This is a mixed herd, the toughest kind of all to drive. From now on, anything that can't keep up will have to be left behind—any calves born on the drive must be killed.

"You know the best day we've had was about fifteen, sixteen miles. On this drive we will have to do better than that, and without water.

"The first night out, we will go into camp late and we'll start early. From that time on every man-jack of you will be riding most of the day and night."

"I can ride." Conchita McCrae stood on the edge of the group. "I've worked cattle since I was a child. We want to pull our weight, and Miguel isn't up to it yet."

"We can use you," I replied, "and thanks."

Nobody said anything for a few minutes, and finally it was Tim Foley who spoke. "There's no water for eighty miles? What about the Mustang Pools?"

"We don't know, but we can't count on them. Maybe there is water there, but we will have to think like there wasn't."

Pa shrugged. "Well, we have been expecting it. Nobody can say we weren't warned. What we had best do is fill all the barrels, jars, everything that will hold water, and we had best be as sparing of it as we can."

Zebony led off, his long brown hair blowing in the wind, and after him came the brindle steer, still pointing his nose into God knows where, and then the herd.

Ben Cole and Milo Dodge rode the flanks; and behind them, Freeman Squires and Zeno Yearly.

Turning, I walked my horse back to where Tim Foley was getting ready to mount the seat of his wagon. His wife sat up there, her eyes fastened on distance.

"Everything all right, Tim?"

He turned around slowly. "No . . . and you know it isn't. Karen's gone, and you could have kept her, Dan."

"Me?" It was not at all what I'd expected from him. "Tim, she wouldn't have stayed for me. Nor for anyone, I guess."

"We figured you two were going to marry," Tim said. "We counted on it. I never did like that no-account Tap Henry."

"Tap's a good man, and there was no talk of marriage between Karen and me. We talked some, but there weren't any other young folks around . . . just the two of us. And she fell hard for Tap."

"He'll ruin her. That is, if she isn't lying dead out there already."

"She's with him. We found their tracks. She caught up to him and they are riding west together."

This was no time to tell them about the massacre. I had told Pa, and some of the boys knew, because I wanted them to look sharp . . . but it might only worry the women folks.

If had a wife now, well, I'd tell her such things. A man does wrong to spare women folks, because they can stand up to trouble as well as any man, and a man has no right to keep trouble from them, but this was Tim Foley's wife and Aaron Stark's widow, and there was Rose Sandy.

The wagons rolled, their heavy wheels rocked and rolled down into the gully and out on the other side, and we moved the cattle westward. Dust lifted from the line of their march, and the rising sun lit points of brightness on their thousands of horns. Somebody out along the line started up a song, and somebody else took it up, and glad I was to hear them, for they needed what courage they had for the long march that was ahead.

The cattle lowed and called, the dust grew thicker, and we moved on into the morning. Sweat streaked their sides, but we moved them on. Every mile was a victory, every mile a mile nearer water. But I knew there were cattle in this herd that would be dead long before we came to water, and there were horses that would die, and perhaps men, too.

The way west was hard, and it took hard men to travel that way, but it was the way they knew, the way they had chosen. Driving increases thirst, and the sun came hot into the morning sky, and grew hotter with the passing of the hours. The dust mounted.

Twice I switched horses before the morning was over. Working beside Jim Poor, I handled the drag, with Pa off in front with Zebony Lambert.

And when at last the cool of night came, we kept them moving steadily westward until at last we camped. We had made sixteen miles, a long drive. Yet I think there was a horror within us all at what lay ahead, and Conchita looked at me with wonder in her eyes. I knew what she was thinking.

We were mad . . . mad to try this thing.

We cooked a small meal and ate. We made coffee and drank, and the cattle were restless for water and did not lie down for a long time. But at last they did.

The burden was mine now. Carefully, I looked at the men, studying their faces, trying to estimate the limit of their strength.

It was late when I turned in at last, and I was the first awake, rolling my blankets and saddling the dun. Zeno Yearly was squatted by the fire when I came up to it.

He gestured at the pot. "Fresh made. He'p yourself."

Filling my cup, I squatted opposite him. "I ain't a talking man," Zeno commented, out of nowhere, "so I've said nothing about this. Especial, as Tap is your brother."

Swallowing coffee, I looked at him, but I said nothing.

"This here range Tap located—how come that grass ain't been settled?"

"Open country. Nobody around, I reckon."

"Don't you be mistook. That there range was settled and in use before you were born."

Well, I couldn't believe it. Tap had told about that range out there, free for the taking. Yet Zeno was not a talking man, and I had never known him to say anything but what proved true.

"Tap found it for us," I protested. "He left a man to guard it."

"Tolan Banks?"

"You know him?"

"I should smile. That's a mean man, a mighty mean man. I heard Tap call his name, and I said nothing because I'm not a gun-fighting man and wanted no part of Tap unless he brought it to me. That Tolan Banks is a cow-thief and an outlaw."

So there it lay. We were headed west across some godawful country, running risk of life and limb, thinking we were bound for fresh and open range, and now I found that range belonged to somebody else and we would be running into a full-scale range war when we arrived.

They say trouble doesn't come singly, and surely

that was true of ours. So I drank coffee and gave thought to it, but the thinking came to nothing. For all I could see was that we were committed, and we would arrive faced with a fight—and us with starving, thirsty cattle, and folks that would be starved also.

"Zeno, you keep this under your hat. This is something I've got to study about. Seems to me, Tap should have known better."

Zeno he put down his coffee and filled his pipe. He was speaking low, for fear we would be overheard. "Meaning no offense, but it seems to me that Tap Henry is a self-thinking man. I mean, he would think of himself first. Now, suppose he wanted that land, but had no cattle? To claim land in this country you have to use it . . . you have to run cows on it.

"So what better could he do, knowing you folks were discontented and talking the West? I think you will ride into a full-fledged range war, and you'll be on the side of Tolan Banks . . . which puts you in a bad light."

"It isn't a good thought," I said. "I don't know this Tolan Banks."

"Like I say, he's a mean man. He will fight with any sort of weapon, any way you choose, and he's killed a lot of men. Some folks say he was one of that Bald Knob crowd, up there in Missouri. On that I couldn't say, and it seemed to me his voice sounded like Georgia to me."

We moved our herd on the trail, and they were mean. They had nothing to drink, and had not had anything the night before, nor was there water in sight.

We moved them out before the light and walked

them forward, moving them steadily. And this day we worked harder than ever before. Now that water was gone, these cow-critters began thinking back to the Cowhouse or the Middle Concho, and they had no notion of going on into this dry country. First one and then another would try to turn back.

Again, I worked the drag. Nobody was going to say that because I was in charge that I was shirking my job. At noontime we found a sort of bluff and there was shade along it for a good half-mile. We moved the herd into that shade and stopped, lying up through the hot hours.

Miguel was sitting up when I went to the wagon. "I shall be able to ride soon," he said, "and I shall help."

Glancing out, I could see nobody close by. "Miguel," I said, "we are heading for land in New Mexico."

"*Si*, this I know."

"Do you know the Mimbres Valley?"

"*Si*." Miguel's face had grown still, and he watched me with careful attention.

"Is it claimed land?"

Miguel hesitated. "*Si* . . . most of it. But there is trouble there. However, the valley is long—perhaps it is not the place of which I speak."

"And Lake Valley?"

"*Si* . . . I know it. There is much trouble there, from the Apache . . . but from white men also, and from our own people, for some of them are bad, like Felipe Soto."

"Do you think we will have trouble there? We were told the range was open. It is not open, then?"

"No . . . and you will have much trouble." Miguel

paused. "Señor, I regret . . . I wish I could ride. I know how hard it is for you."

"Have you been over this road?"

"No . . . I came from the north. I was trying to escape, and then when hurt I tried for water on the Concho."

As it grew toward evening, we started the herd once more, and Conchita was in the saddle at once, and riding her big horse. Surprisingly enough, it proved a good cutting horse, and it was needed.

Now every rider was needed. The herd slowed and tried to turn aside or turn back, but we worked, keeping them moving, pointing westward into the starlit night. At last we stopped, but the cattle would not settle down. They bawled continuously, and finally I gave up.

"Pa, let's move them. They aren't going to rest, so they might as well walk."

Once again we started, and we sagged from weariness. The men around me were bone-tired, their eyes hollow, but we pushed them on. And the white dust lifted from the parched plain, strangling, stifling, thick.

When the morning came there was no rest, no surcease. The sun rose like a ball of flame, crimson and dark, and the air was still. No slightest breeze stirred the air, which lay heavily upon us, so that our breathing required effort. And now the cattle wanted to stop, they wanted even to die, but we urged them on.

Here and there one fell out, but they had to be left. The horses slowed, and stopped, starting again with a great effort.

At the nooning the ribs of the cattle stood out, and their eyes were wild. The brindle steer stared about for something to attack, and the weary ponies had scarcely the agility to move out of the way.

We made coffee, and the riders came back to the fire one by one, almost falling from their horses, red-eyed with weariness. Yet there was no complaint. Conchita was there, her eyes great dark hollows, but she smiled at me, and shook her head when I suggested she had done enough.

Foley came to me. "Dan," he said, "we're all in. The horses, I mean. We just made it here."

"All right . . . let's load everything into two wagons."

Miguel hitched himself to the tail-gate of the wagon. "I can ride," he said. "I prefer to ride."

Nor would he listen to anything I said, and in truth it was a help to have him on horseback, although he would be hard put to take care of himself, without trying to help us. The goods, which had thinned down owing to our eating into the supplies, were loaded into two wagons, and the team of the abandoned wagon was divided between the other two.

The bitter dust rose in clouds from the feet of the cattle, the sun was a copper flame in a brassy sky, the distance danced with heat waves and mirage. The cattle grew wearier and wearier with each succeeding mile; they lagged and had to be driven on, slapped with coiled riatas and forced back into the herd.

Here and there an aging cow fell out of the herd, collapsed, and died. Our throats burned with thirst and inhaled dust, and our shouts mingled with the anguished bawling of the thirsty cattle. And there was no respite. We pushed on and on, finding no convenient place to stop until hours past noon.

We stopped then, and a few of the cattle fell to the ground, and one horse died. The sky was a ceiling of flame, sweat streaked our bodies and made strange signs on the dusty flanks of the cattle.

As the suffering of the cattle increased, the tempers of the men shortened. Here and there I lent a hand, moving twice as much as any other hand, working desperately, the alkali dust prickling my skin, my eyes squinted against sun and trickling sweat.

It was brutal work, and yet through it all Conchita was busy. She did as much as any hand, and asked no favors. At times I even saw Miguel hazing some steer into line.

Wild-eyed steers plunged and fought, sometimes staggering and falling, but we pushed them on, and then I began moving out ahead of the herd, scouting for the poisonous water-holes of which I had been warned by Tap Henry.

A thousand times I wished he had been with us, a thousand times I wished for an extra hand. For three days we did not sleep. We gulped coffee, climbed back into the saddle, rode half blind with sweat and dust, fighting the cattle into line, forcing them to move, for their only chance of survival lay in moving and getting them to water.

The brindle steer stayed in the lead. He pushed on grimly, taking on a fierce, relentless personality of his own, as though he sensed our desperation and our need for help.

And every day the sun blazed down, and long into the night we pushed them on.

Cattle dropped out, stood with wide-spread legs and hanging heads beside the trail. How many had we lost? How many horses worked to a frazzle?

We lost all idea of time, for the cattle were almost impossible to handle, and we fought them desperately through the heat and the dust.

Pushing on alone, I found the Mustang Ponds, but they were merely shallow basins of cracked dry mud, rapidly turning to dust. There had been no water here in months. It was the same with the Flatrock Holes, and there was nothing else this side the river, except far and away to the northwest what were known as the Wild Cherry Holes . . . but they were off our route, and of uncertain nature.

Staring into the heat waves, it came upon me to wonder that I was here. What is it that moves a man west? I had given no thought to such a thing, although the loneliness of the far plains and the wide sky around move a man to wonder.

We had to come west or be crowded. As for the Holt crowd, we could have fought them better there than on the road. Was not this move something else? Maybe we just naturally wanted to go west, to open new country.

There have always been wandering men, but western men were all wandering men. Many a time I've seen a man pull out and leave good grass and a built house to try his luck elsewhere.

Twice I came upon alkali ponds, the water thick with the white alkali, thicker than thick soup, enough to kill any animal that drank from it.

I pushed on, and topped out on a rise and saw before me the far dark thread of growth along the Pecos. My horse stretched his neck yearningly toward the far-off stream, but I got down and rinsed my handkerchief twice in his mouth after soaking it from my canteen. Then we turned back.

We turned back, the dun and myself, and we had

only some sixteen or seventeen miles to go to reach the herd.

It was a sickening sight, a dread and awful sight to see them coming. From a conical hill beside the trail I watched them.

Pa was off in front, still sitting straight in his saddle, although I knew the weariness, the exhaustion that was in him. Behind him, maybe twenty feet, and leading the herd by a good fifty yards, was that brindle steer.

And then Jim Poor and Ben Cole, pinching the lead steers together to keep them pointed down the trail.

Over all hovered a dense cloud of white dust. Alkali covered them like snow. It covered the herd, the riders, their horses . . . it covered the wagons too.

Back along the line I could see cattle, maybe a dozen within the range of my eyes. Two were down, several were standing, one looked about to fall.

But they were coming on, and I walked the dun down the steep slope to meet them.

"Pa, we'll take the best of them and head for the river. I dislike to split the herd, but if we can get some of them to water, we can save them."

Most of them were willing to stand when we stopped, but we cut out the best of them, the ones with the most stuff left, and, with Pa leading off, four of the boys started hustling them toward Horsehead on the Pecos.

The day faded in a haze of rose and gold, great red arrows shot through the sky, piercing the clouds that dripped pinkish blood on the clouds below. The vast brown-gray emptiness of the plain took on a strange enchantment, and clouds piled in weird formations, huge towers of cumulus reaching far, far into the heavens.

Many a time I had heard talk of such things, the kinds of clouds and the winds of the world, and I knew the wonder of it. But no evening had I seen like that last evening before Horsehead, no vaster sky or wider plain, no more strange enchantment of color in the sky, and on the plains too.

Pulling up alongside the wagons, I told Mrs. Foley, "Keep it rolling. No stops this side of Horsehead!"

She nodded grimly, and drove on, shouting at the tired horses. Frank Kelsey mopped the sweat from his face and grinned at me. "Hell, ain't it, boy? I never seen the like!"

"Keep rolling!" I said, and rode back to where Miguel was coming along, with Conchita holding him on his horse. "You, too," I said. "Pay no attention to the herd. If you can, go on to the river."

The crimson and gold faded from the sky, the blues became deeper. There was a dull purple along the far-off hills, and a faint purplish tone to the very air, it seemed. We moved the remaining cattle into the darkening day, into the slow-coming night.

Under the soft glory of the skies, they moved in a slow-plodding stream, heads down, tongues lolling and dusty. They moved like drunken things, drunken with exhaustion, dying on their feet of thirst, but moving west.

The riders sagged wearily in their saddles, their eyes red-rimmed with exhaustion, but westward we moved. The shrill yells were gone, even the bawling of the cattle had ceased, and they plodded on through the utter stillness of the evening.

A heifer dropped back, and I circled and slapped her with the coiled rope. She scarcely flinched, and only after the dun nipped at her did she move, trancelike and staggering. More cattle had fallen. Twice I stopped to pour a little from my canteen into the mouths of fallen cows . . . both of them got up. Some of the others would be revived by the cool night air and would come on because they knew nowhere else to go.

And then the breeze lifted, bringing with it the smell of the river.

Heads came up, they started to walk faster, then to trot, and of a sudden they burst into a head-long run, a wild stampede toward the water that lay ahead. Some fell, but they struggled up and continued on.

There was the hoofs' brief thunder, then silence, and the smell of dust.

Alone I rode the drag of a herd long gone. Alone, in the gathering night. And there was no sound then but the steady *clop-clop* of the dun's hard hoofs upon the baked ground, and the lingering smell of the dust.

The stars were out when I came up to the Pecos, and there our wagons were, and our fire.

When the dun stopped, its legs were trembling. I stepped down heavily and leaned for a moment against the horse, and then I slowly stripped the saddle and bridle from him and turned him loose to roll, which was all the care most mustangs wanted or would accept.

Zebony came in to the fire. "They've drunk, and we're holding them back from the river."

"Good . . . no water until daybreak." Sitting down near the fire I took the Patterson from its scabbard and began to clean it. No matter what, that Patterson had to be in shape.

"I want a four-man guard on those cattle," I said, "and one man staked out away from camp, to listen. This is an Indian crossing too. The Comanches used it long before any white man came into this country, and they still use it."

Mrs. Stark brought me a cup of coffee. "Drink this," she said. "You've earned it."

It was coffee, all right, laced with a shot of Irish, and it set me up somewhat. So I finished cleaning my rifle, then went to the wagon and dug out my duffel-bag. From it I took my two pistols. One I belted on, the other I shoved down behind my belt with the butt right behind my vest.

When I came back to the fire, Pa was there. He looked at that gun on my hip, but he said nothing at all. Tom Sandy looked around at me. "Never knew you to wear a hand-gun," he said, "you expecting trouble?"

"You're tired, Tom," I said, "but you get mighty little sleep tonight. I want all the barrels filled now."

"Now?" Tom stared at me. "You crazy? Everybody is dead-tired. Why, you couldn't—"

"Yes, I can. You get busy—every barrel full before we sleep."

And they filled them, too.

It was past one o'clock in the morning when I finally stretched out, slowly straightening my stiff muscles, trying to let the tenseness out of my body, but it was several minutes before I could sort of let myself go . . . and then I slept.

The first thing I heard when I awoke was the water, the wonderful, wonderful sound of water.

Even the Pecos, as treacherous a stream as ever was ... but it was water.

The sky was faintly gray. I had been asleep almost two hours, judging by the Big Dipper. Rolling over, I sat up and put on my hat. Everything was still.

I pulled on my boots, belted on my gun, and walked over to the fire.

What I had believed to be trees and brush along the line of the Pecos was actually the shadow cast by the high bank. The river at this point was destitute of anything like trees or shrubs. The only growth along it was a thin line of rushes. It lay at the bottom of a trough that was from six to ten feet deep. The river itself was about a hundred feet wide and no more than four feet deep at the deepest point. The plain above was of thin, sandy soil, and there was only a sparse growth of greasewood, dwarf mesquite, and occasional clumps of bear grass.

Zebony came up to the fire and sat his horse while drinking a cup of coffee. It was quiet ... mighty quiet.

The cattle, still exhausted, were bedded down and content to rest, although occasionally one of them would start for the river and had to be headed back.

"You going to lay up here?"

"No."

Tim Foley looked around at me. Tim was a good man, but sometimes he thought I was too young for my job. Me, I've never seen that years made a man smart, for simply getting older doesn't mean much unless a man learns something meanwhile.

"We're going to finish crossing, and then go up

stream a few miles." I gestured around me at the row of skulls marking the crossing, and at the crossing itself. "We don't want to run into Comanches."

Zeb started to turn his horse and stopped. "Dan . . . !"

Something in his voice spun me around. A party of riders were coming toward us. Near as I could make out, there were six or seven.

"You wearing a gun, Tim?"

"I am."

"I'm holdin' one." That would be Zeno Yearly.

Behind me there was a stirring in the camp. I glanced across the river where the herd was lying. Four men would be over there . . . but what about the fifth man who was staked out? Had he seen these riders? Or had they found him first?

Conchita was suddenly close by, standing half concealed by a wagon wheel.

My eyes fastened on the man in the lead. He rode a powerful bay horse, and he was a huge man. This, I knew at once, was Felipe Soto.

He rode up to the edge of camp and I saw him look carefully around. I do not know how much he saw, for we looked like a sleeping camp, except for the three of us standing there. Foley was across the fire from them, and Zeb on his horse some twenty feet off to one side. I was in the middle, and intended it that way.

My Patterson lay on the rolled-up blankets of my bed about a dozen feet off.

"I look for Miguel Sandoval," the big man said. "Turn him over to me, and you will have no trouble."

Taking an easy step forward, I took the play away from him. "What do you mean, no trouble?

Mister, if you want anybody from this outfit you've got to take them. As for trouble, we're asking for all you've got."

He looked at me with careful attention, and I knew he was trying to figure how much was loud talk and how much was real trouble.

"Look, señor, I think you do not understand." He gestured behind him. "I have many men . . . these are but a few. You have women here, and do not want trouble."

"You keep mentioning that," I said quietly, "but we're as ready as you are. We've had a mean drive, and we're all feeling pretty sore, so if you want to buy yourself a package of grief, you just dig in your spurs and hang on."

His men started to fan out and Zebony spoke up. "Stand! You boys stand where you are or I'll open the ball," he said coolly. "If there's to be shooting we want you all bunched up."

Soto had not taken his eyes from me, and I do not know if he had intended to kill me, but I know I was ready. Whatever notion he had, he changed his mind in a hurry, and it was Zeno Yearly who changed it for him.

"You take the big one, Dan," Zeno said conversationally. "I want the man on his right."

Soto's eyes did not leave mine, but I saw his lips tighten under the black mustache. They had not seen Zeno, and even I was not sure exactly where he was. They could see three of us . . . how many more were there?

There was no use losing a good thing, so I played the hand out. "Zeno," I said, "you've gone and spoiled a good thing. Between you and the boys on the river bank, I figured to collect some scalps."

Soto did not like it. In fact, he did not like it even a little. He did not know whether there was any-body on the river bank or not, nor did he like what he would have to do to find out.

He knew there must be men with the cattle, and that, had they seen him coming or been warned in time, they might easily be sheltered by the high bank and waiting to cut Soto and his men to doll rags.

"I regret, señor"—Soto smiled stiffly—"the short-ness of our visit. When we come again there will be more of us . . . and some friends of ours, the Co-manches. You would do well to drive Miguel Sandoval from your camp."

"There was a grave back yonder," I said, "of a Mexican we found and buried."

Soto smiled again. "A good trick . . . only we turned back and opened the grave. There was no body."

He turned his horse and walked it slowly away from camp, but we knew he would come back, and we knew we were in trouble.

"All right," I said. "A quick breakfast and then we move out."

During the night several steers and a cow had managed to make the river, and rejoined the herd. There was no time to estimate the loss of cattle on the drive, although obviously several hundred head were gone.

We pushed on, keeping up a steady move, paus-ing only at noon to water in the Pecos, whose route we were following. One or more of us trailed well behind or on the hills to right or left, scouting for the enemy.

The earth was incredibly dry and was covered over vast areas with a white, saline substance left from the alkali in the area. Wherever there had been water standing, the ground was white, as if from snow.

Pa fell back and rode beside me. "We're out-numbered, Dan," he said. "They'll come with fifty or sixty men."

We saw not a living thing. Here and there were dead cattle, dried to mere bones and hide, untorn by wolves, which showed us that not even those animals would try to exist in such a place. By night-fall there was no grass to be found, so we brought the wagons together on a low knoll, with the cattle behind it.

There was a forest of prickly pear, which cattle will eat, and which is moist enough so they need little water. Half a dozen of us went out and singed the spines from bunches of pear with torches, and it was a pretty sight to see the torches moving over the darkening plain. But the cattle fed.

With daybreak, the wind rose and the sky was filled with dust, and clouds of dust billowed along the ground, filling the air and driving against the face with stinging force. The sun became a ball of red, then was obscured, and the cattle moved out with the wind behind them, herded along the course of the Pecos, but far enough off to avoid its twistings and turnings.

By nightfall the dust storm had died down, but the air was unnaturally cold. Under the lee of a knoll the wagons drew up and a fire was built.

Zebony rode in and stepped down from his horse.

Ma Foley and Mrs. Stark were working over a meal. There was little food left, but a few of the faltering cattle had been killed, and some of the beef was prepared. The flour was almost all gone, and no molasses was left.

Zeno Yearly came up and joined us. There was a stubble of beard on his lean jaws, and his big sad eyes surveyed us with melancholy. "Reminded me of a time up on the Canadian when I was headed for Colorado. We ran into a dust storm so thick we could look up betwixt us and the sun and see the prairie dogs diggin' their holes."

Squatting by the fire, I stared into the flames, and I was doing some thinking. Pa was relying on me, with Tap gone, and I hadn't much hope of doing much. The herd was all we had, and the herd was in bad shape. We had a fight facing us whenever Felipe Soto and his Comancheros caught up with us, and we were short-handed.

We had lost several hundred head and could not afford to lose more. And from what Conchita and Miguel said, we were heading into a country where we might find more trouble than we wanted.

We were almost out of grub, and there was no use hunting. Whatever game there had been around here had drifted out, and all we could do was keep driving ahead.

Our horses had come out of it better than most, for many a herd crossing the Horsehead had wound up with most of the hands walking, their horses either dead or stolen by Indians. About all a man could do was go on; but I had found that many a problem is settled if a man just keeps a-going.

It wasn't in me to sell Felipe Soto short. He was a tough man, and he would come back. They did not want any talk of Comancheros or of the Palo Duro Canyon to get around . . . there already was opposition enough from the New Mexicans themselves.

"We'll push on the herd," I told Zebony. "We should reach the Delaware soon."

It was amazing how the water and the short rest had perked up the cattle. There had been little grass, but the prickly pear had done wonders for them, and they moved out willingly enough. It was as if they, too, believed the worst of the trip was past. Knowing something of the country that lay before us, I was not so sure.

We closed up the herd and kept the wagons close on the flank. Zeno Yearly and Freeman Squires fell back to bring up the rear and do the scouting. Pa led off, and part of the time was far out ahead of us, scouting for ambush or tracks. The rest of us kept the herd closed up and we moved ahead at a steady gait.

Toyah Creek, when we reached it, was only a sandy wash, so we went through and pushed on. As we traveled, we gathered the wood we found where wagons had broken down and been abandoned, for there was nothing along the trail for fuel but buffalo chips and occasional mesquite, most of which had to be dug out of the ground to find anything worth burning.

The coolness disappeared and again it became incredibly hot. The heat rising from the herd itself, close-packed as it was, was almost unbearable.

Conchita rode over to join me.

"We have talked, Miguel and I," she said. "You protected us, or we should have been killed."

"It was little enough."

"We did not expect it. Miguel . . . he did not expect to be helped, because he is a Mexican."

"Might make a difference to some folks, not to us. When we first came into this country—I mean when Pa first came—he would never have made out but for help from Mexican neighbors."

"We have talked of you, and there is a place we know—it is a very good place. There is danger from Indians, but there is danger everywhere from them."

"Where is this place?"

"We will show you. It lies upon a route used by the *padres* long ago. By traders also. But there is water, there is good grass, and I think you can settle there without trouble."

"Where will you go?"

"To my home. To Miguel's mother and his wife."

"He did not mention a wife. I thought maybe . . . Miguel and you . . ."

"No, señor. He is married. We are grown up in the same house, but we are friends only. He has been a very good brother to me, señor."

"Like Tap and me," I said. "We got along pretty good."

All through the day we rode together, talking of this thing and that. The cattle moved steadily. By nightfall we had twelve miles behind us.

There was a chance the dust storm might have wiped out miles of our tracks, and that might help a little. But in the arid lands men are tied to water, and they must go where water is, and so their trails can be found even if lost.

Ira Tilton was out on the north flank of the drive as we neared the last stop we would make along the

Pecos. From that point we would cut loose and drive across country toward Delaware Creek.

Toward sundown he shot an antelope and brought it into camp. It was mighty little meat for such a crowd of folks, but we were glad to get it.

We were of no mind to kill any of our breeding stock which we needed to start over again, and the steers we needed to sell to the Army or somebody to get money for flour and necessaries to tide us over the first year. We were poor folks, when it came to that, with nothing but our cattle and our bodily strength for capital.

That night when the firelight danced on the weathered faces of the cowhands, we sat close around the fire and we sang the songs we knew, and told stories, and yarned. There was a weariness on us, but we were leaving the Pecos, and no cowhand ever liked the Pecos for long.

Firelight made the wagon shadows flicker. Ma Foley came and sat with us, and the firelight lit the gold of Conchita's hair to flame, to a red-gold flame that caught the light as she moved her head.

Rose Sandy came to the fire, too, sitting close to Tom, and very quiet. But I do not think there was censure among us for what she had done, for nobody knew better than we that the flesh was weak.

Pa was there, listening or talking quietly, his fine-cut features looking younger than he was.

"We will find a place," he said, "and we will settle. We will make of the Kaybar a brand we can be proud of."

There was hope in all of us, but fear too. Standing up at last, I looked at Conchita and she rose too, and we walked back from the fire together.

Miguel stood by his wagon, and when we passed him, he said, "*Vaya con Dios.*"

Freeman Squires shook me out of a sleep and I sat up and groped for my hat. It was still . . . the stars were gone and there were clouds and a feeling of dampness in the air. Stamping into my boots, I picked up my gun and slung the belt around me, then tucked the other behind my belt.

Then I reached for the Patterson, and as I did so there was a piercing yell far out on the plains, and then a whole chorus of wild Comanche yells and the pound of hoofs.

The cattle came up with a single lunge and broke into a wild stampede. I saw Free Squires riding like mad to cut them off, saw his horse stumble and go down and the wave of charging, wild-eyed cattle charge over him.

And then I was on one knee and shooting.

A Comanche jumped his horse into camp and my first shot took him from the saddle. I saw Pa roll out of bed and fire a shotgun from a sitting position.

In an instant the night was laced with a red pattern of gunfire, streaks of flame stabbing the darkness in the roar of shooting.

Zebony Lambert ran from the shelter of a wagon, blazing away with a six-shooter. I saw an Indian try to ride him down and Zeb grabbed the Indian and swung up behind him and they went careering off into the night, fighting on the horse's back.

A big man leaped past me on a gray horse—it was the blond man who had been with Webb Holt when he was killed.

A horse struck me with his shoulder and knocked

me rolling, a bullet spat dirt into my mouth as it struck in front of me.

Again I started to get up and I saw Pa firing from his knee. There was blood on his face, but he was shooting as calmly as if in a shooting gallery. Ben Cole was down, all sprawled out on the ground, and I saw Jim Poor rise suddenly from the ground and run to a new position, with bullets all around him.

Suddenly I saw Bud Caldwell charge into camp, swing broadside, and throw down on Pa. I flipped a six-shooter and shot him through the chest. The bullet hit him dead center and he was knocked back in the saddle and the horse cut into a run. Turning on my heel I fired again from the hip and Bud Caldwell fell on his face in the dirt and turned slowly over.

And as it had started, it ended, suddenly and in stillness.

The wagontop on one of the wagons was in flames, so I grabbed a bucket of water and sloshed it over the flames, and then jumped up and ripped the canvas from the frame and hurled it to the ground. A bullet clipped the wagon near me and I dropped again and lay still on the ground.

Our herd was gone. Freeman Squires was surely dead, and it looked like Ben Cole was, too.

Nothing moved. Lying still in the darkness, I fed shells into my six-shooter and tried to locate the Patterson.

Somewhere out in the darkness I heard a low moan, and then there was silence. The smell of dust was in my nostrils, an ache in my bones; the gun butt felt good against my palm. Behind me I could hear the faint rustle of water among the thin reeds along the bank, but nothing else moved.

They were out there yet, I knew that, and to move was to die.

What had happened to Conchita? To Ma Foley? Where was Pa?

In the distance, thunder rumbled . . . the night was vastly empty, and vastly still. A cool wind blew a quick, sharp gust through the camp, scattering some of the fire, rolling a cup along the ground.

With infinite care, I got a hand flat on the ground and eased myself up and back, away from the fire-light. After a moment of waiting I repeated the move.

Thunder rolled . . . there was a jagged streak of of lightning, and then the rain came. It came with a rush, great sheets of rain flung hard against the dusty soil, dampening it, soaking it all in one smashing onslaught.

When the lightning flared again, I saw my father lying with his eyes wide to the sky, and then the lightning was gone, and there was only the rumble of thunder and the rush of rain falling.

CHAPTER FIVE

In a stumbling run I left the place where I lay and ran to my father's side.

He was dead. He had been shot twice through the body and had bled terribly.

Taking the rifle that lay beside him, I leaped up and ran to the nearest wagon and took shelter beneath it. If any of the others lived, I did not know, but my father was dead, our cattle gone, our hopes destroyed, and within me, suddenly and for the first time, I knew hatred.

Under the wagon, in partial shelter, I tried to think ahead. What would Soto and his men do? All my instincts told me to get away, as far away as possible before the morning came, for unless I was much mistaken, they would come to loot the wagons.

How many others were dead? And did any lie out there now, too grievously wounded to escape? If so, I must find them. Knowing the Comanche, I could leave no man who had worked with us to fall helpless into their hands.

Carefully, I wiped my guns dry. The Patterson still lay out there somewhere, but I had my father's breech-loading Sharps. The shotgun he had also had must still be lying out there.

The storm did not abate. The rain poured down and the Pecos was rising. It was a cloudburst, or something close to it, and the more I considered it the more I began to believe that my enemies might have fled for shelter, if they knew of any. Or perhaps they had gone off after our cattle, for without doubt they would take the herd.

Suddenly, in the wagon above me, there was a faint stir of movement. Then thunder rumbled in the distance, and lightning flashed, and on the edge of the river bank, not twenty yards off, stood two bedraggled figures. I knew them at once.

Tim Foley and his wife!

They lived, at least. And who was in the wagon? One of us, I was sure . . . yet could I be sure? Perhaps it was some Comanche who had started to loot the wagon.

Carefully, I eased out from under the wagon. The rain struck me like a blow, the force of the driven rain lashing viciously at my face. It would be completely dark within the wagon, and I would be framed against the lightning, but I must know. The Foleys were coming, and they must not walk into a trap.

One foot I put on a horizontal spoke of the wheel, and, holding to the edge of the wagon with my left hand, I swung myself suddenly up and into the wagon.

There was a startled gasp.

"Conchita?"

"*Dan!* Oh, Dan! You're *alive!*"

"More or less. Are you all right?"

"Of course, but this man is hurt. He has been shot."

Risking a shot myself, I struck a light. It was Zeno Yearly, and there was a graze along his skull and a crease along the top of his shoulder. Evidently the bullet had struck him when he was lying down in the wagon, and grazing the side of his skull, it had burned his shoulder. He had bled freely, but nothing more.

The rain continued without letup, and through the roar of the rain on the canvas wagon cover we heard the splash of footsteps, and then Ma Foley and Tim climbed into the wagon.

Zeno sat up, holding his head and staring around him.

"It's safe, I think, to light a candle," I said. "They have gone or they would have shot when I struck the match."

When a candle was lighted I rummaged in the wagon for ammunition.

"Here," Tim Foley said, holding out the Patterson, "I found it back there."

Taking the gun, I passed the Sharps over to him, and began cleaning the Patterson, wiping the rain and mud from it, and removing the charges.

"Are we all that's left?" Ma Foley asked plaintively. "Are they all gone?"

"Pa's dead, and I saw Squires go down ahead of the stampede. I saw Ben Cole fall."

"Jim Poor got down under the bank. I think he was unhurt then, if the river didn't get him."

Huddled together, we waited for the morning, and the rain continued to fall. At least, there would be water. We must find and kill a steer, if we could find a stray. And somehow we must get to the Rio Grande, or to the Copper Mines.

For we had been left without food. What had not been destroyed in the brief fire in the other wagon was undoubtedly damaged by the rain, although I hoped the damage would be slight. And there had been little enough, in any event.

Our remuda was gone, the horses stolen or scattered, and the chances of catching any of them was slight indeed. The trek that now lay before us would in many ways be one of the worst that anyone could imagine, and we had women along.

The responsibility was mine. These were our people, men who worked for us, and my father was dead. In such a case, even with the herd gone, I could not, dared not surrender leadership. Now, more than ever, we needed a strong hand to guide us out of this desert and to some place where we might get food and horses to ride.

Fear sat deep within me, for I had encountered nothing like this before, and I feared failure, and failure now meant death . . . at least, for the weakest among us.

All the night long, the rain fell. The Pecos was running bank-full, and so would be the arroyos leading to it. Our way west was barred now by one more obstacle, but, once the sun came out, the arroyos would not run for long, and their sandy basins, long dry, would drink up the water left behind. Only in the *tinajas*, the natural rock cisterns, would there be water.

The sun rose behind a blanket of lowering gray cloud, and the rain settled down to a steady downpour, with little lightning, and thunder whimpering among the canyons of the far-off Guadalupes.

Stiffly, I got to my feet and slid to the ground. Donning my slicker, I looked carefully around.

The earth was dark with rain, the ground where the camp stood was churned into mud, and wherever I looked the sky was heavy with rain clouds that lay low above the gray hills. The Pecos rushed by—dark, swirling waters that seemed to have lost their reddish tinge. Crossing the camp, I picked up Pa's body and carried it to shelter under the wagon, then began to look around.

On the edge of camp I found Bud Caldwell . . . he was dead. Another man, unknown to me, but obviously a Comanchero, lay dead near the river bank.

Ignoring their bodies, I gathered the body of Ben Cole in my arms and carried him to where Pa lay.

We desperately needed horses, but there were none in sight. There was a dead horse and a saddle lying not too far away and, walking to them, I took the saddle from the horse, tugging the girth from beneath it. The horse lay upon soft mud, and the girth came out without too much trouble. Then I removed the bridle and carried them to the wagon.

Tim Foley got down from the wagon. "Tim," I said, "you and Mrs. Foley can help. Go through both wagons and sort out all the food you can find that's still good. Also, collect all the canteens, bedding, and whatever there is in the way of ammunition and weapons."

He nodded, looking around grimly. "They ruined us, Dan. They ruined us."

"Don't you believe it. We're going to make it through to the Copper Mines, and then we'll see.

If you find Pa's papers, account books and the like, you put them aside for me."

Zeno Yearly got down from the wagon also. He looked wan and sick, but he glanced at me with a droll smile. "We got us a long walk, Dan. You much on walking?"

Together we hunted around. There was no sign of Jim Poor, but he might have been drowned or swept away by the river.

The one thing none of us was talking about was the kids. Tim's two boys and Stark's children. Nobody had seen a sign of them since the attack, yet I had seen them bedded down and asleep when I was awakened to go out for my night guard.

Zeno and me walked slowly up along the bank of the river. Whatever tracks there had been were washed out. It was unbelievable that they could all have survived, but the fact that we saw no bodies gave us hope.

Zeno and I spread out, and suddenly he gave a call. He was standing looking down at or into something. When I got over there, I saw that he was standing on the edge of some limestone sinks.

The earth had caved in or sunk in several places that were thirty feet or more in diameter. Looking across the hole where Zeno stood, we could see the dark opening of a cave.

Zeno called out and, surprisingly, there was an answering call. Out of a cave under the very edge where we stood came Milo Dodge.

"Heard you talkin'," he said. "You all right?"

"You seen the youngsters?"

"They're here with me, all dry and safe. Emma Stark is here, too."

Slowly, they climbed out of the cave and showed

themselves. Milo climbed up to where we were.

"Frank Kelsey's dead. He lived through the night, died about daybreak. He caught two damned bad ones, low down and mean . . . right through the belly."

"Pa's dead," I said, "and Ben Cole."

"Emma Stark got the youngsters out when the first attack hit, and I'd seen this place, so I hustled them over here. I got in a couple of good shots, and missed one that I wished had hit."

"What do you mean?" He had a look in his eyes that puzzled me.

"Ira Tilton," Dodge said. "He was with them. When they came riding in he was alongside Bud Caldwell. I took a shot at him."

"Remember the fight Tap had with Webb Holt? If Ira was with them, that explains how those other men showed up so unexpectedly. He must have warned them."

"I'll make it my business," Milo said coldly. "I want that man."

"You'll have to get to him before I do," Zeno said. "I never liked him."

Slowly we gathered together, and it was a pitiful bunch we made.

Tim Foley, Milo Dodge, Zeno Yearly, and me . . . three women, five children. Foley's boys were fourteen and ten . . . Emma Stark's youngsters were a girl thirteen, and two boys, one nine, one a baby.

"First off," I said, "we'd better move into that cave, Milo. The women and youngsters can hide there while we hunt horses. I can't believe they were all driven off, and I think we should have a look around. Some of those horses may come back to camp."

We stripped the wagons of what was left that we could use, and took only the simplest of gear. We moved our beds and cooking utensils down there, and what little food was left, and we moved our ammunition too.

Zeno and I started out in one direction, each of us with a rope. Milo and Tim started out the other way. Unluckily the storm had left no tracks, but we had agreed not to go far, to keep a wary eye out for Comanches, and if we found nothing within a few miles, to return.

Zeno and me climbed a long, muddy slope to the top of the rounded-off ridge. The country was scattered with soapweed, prickly pear, and mesquite. Far off, we saw something that might be a horse, or maybe a steer—at that distance, we couldn't make it out.

"There's another!" Zeno picked it out with his finger. "Let's go!"

We started off, walking in the direction of the animal we had seen, and when we had gone scarcely half a mile we could make it out to be a steer. It was Old Brindle, our lead steer.

"You ever ride a steer, Dan?"

"When I was a youngster—sure. I don't think anybody could ride Old Brindle, though."

"Maybe," Zeno looked at him with speculative eyes. "Toward the end there, he was getting mighty friendly. Acted as though he and us were handling that herd together. Let's go get him."

Well, we walked along toward him, and pretty soon he sighted us. We saw his big head come up —his horns were eight feet from tip to tip—and then he walked out toward us, dipping his horns a little as if ready for battle. A man on the ground is usually fair game for any steer, although they will rarely attack a man on horseback.

He came toward us and I spoke to him, and he watched us, his eyes big and round, his head up. Turning away, I started toward that other animal. "Come on, boy!" I said. "You're with us."

And you know something? That big old steer fell in behind us like a big dog, and he walked right along, stopping when we stopped, moving when we moved.

"He might stand for a pack," I said, "and if he did, it would take a load off us."

"We can try."

And then we had a real break.

Rounding the clump of mesquite that lay between us and the other animal we had seen, we saw it. Standing there in a sort of hollow was that line-back dun of mine, and with him were two other horses from the remuda. One was a bay pony, the other a paint.

I called out to the dun, and he shied off, but I shook out a loop. He ducked and trotted around, but when the loop dropped over his head he stood still, and I think he was glad to be caught. Horses and dogs thrive better in the vicinity of men, and they know it. Moreover, they are sociable animals, and like nothing better than to be around men and to be talked to.

Rigging a hackamore from some piggin strings, I mounted up, and soon had caught the paint. Zeno was packing the bridle I'd found on Bud Caldwell's dead horse—if it was his—and he was soon riding the second horse. The third one was more shy, but he seemed to want to stay with the other horses, and when we started back toward camp he followed along and pretty soon Zeno dabbed a loop on him.

Foley and Dodge returned empty-handed. They had seen fresh tracks, however, made since the rain, of both cattle and horses.

We camped that night in the cave, and made a sparing supper of the remnants of some salt pork and beans.

"This cave goes away back," Foley commented. "Looks like the whole country's undermined with it. I used to live in a limestone country in Kentucky, and believe me, caves like this can run for miles."

At daybreak we loaded what gear we had and moved out. The youngsters and the women were to take turns riding, and surprisingly enough, Old Brindle seemed pleased with his pack. That cantankerous old mossyhorn was full of surprises, but he had gotten used to folks, and he liked being around them. Not that Conchita and the youngsters hadn't helped by feeding him chunks of biscuit or corn pone touched with molasses.

We made a sorry outfit, but we started off. The bodies of Pa and the others were buried in a row, and what little we could find of Freeman Squires.

There was no sign of Zebony Lambert, of Jim Poor or the Sandys.

The last I'd seen of Zeb he had jumped on a horse behind a Comanche and gone riding away into the night, fighting with him. Maybe he was a prisoner, and maybe he got off scot-free. Anyway, we had found no other bodies, though in hunting horses we had looked around a good bit.

We kept going, and by nightfall came up to a place in the bend of Delaware Creek. There had

been a big encampment here at some time in the
past, and there was a lot of wood lying about,
and one busted-down wagon from which two
wheels had been taken.

The grass was the best we had seen in weeks,
and there were a couple of clumps of mesquite of
fair size.

About sundown Zeno killed an antelope, and we
had antelope steaks for supper. It was the first
good meal we had since leaving the Pecos.

We took turns standing guard, for we figured
we weren't finished with the Comancheros, and
wanted to be ready for them. It was nigh on to
midnight when I heard a horse coming. He was
coming right along, but when he got somewhere out
there in the darkness, he stopped.

My dun whinnied, and he answered, and came
closer. It was Conchita's big horse.

Shaking her awake, I explained, and she got up
quickly and went to the edge of the firelight, calling him. He came right up to her and started to
nuzzle her hand as if looking for corn or sugar or
something. He was wearing a saddle and bridle
of Spanish style, with a high cantle and too much
tree for my taste. There was a good rifle in the
scabbard, and the saddle-bags were evidently
packed full.

Conchita opened the saddle-bags. There were
a couple of small packets of ammunition and a
buckskin sack containing some gold pieces.

She handed this to me. "We can use that," she
said.

Nothing had been said about Miguel, but I could
see by the stillness of her face and a tightness
around her eyes that she was trying to maintain her

composure. His body had not been found, and nobody could recall seeing him after the first burst of fighting.

Obviously, the big horse had been captured along with the rest of the stock, but he had thrown his rider at some later time and returned to us.

"No man had ridden him," Conchita explained. "He would have watched for his chance to throw any rider but myself, or perhaps some other woman."

We moved westward, and the clouds withdrew and the sun came out. Heat returned to the plains . . . the grass grew sparser again, there was little fuel. We men walked . . . and we saw no Indians.

On the third day we killed an ox we found on the desert. Obviously left behind by some wagon train passing through, perhaps long before, he had fattened on mesquite beans. We killed and butchered the ox, and that night we dined on good beef and cut much of the remainder into strips to smoke over the fire.

In the distance we could see the tower of Guadalupe Mountain shouldering against the sky.

Surprisingly, we made better time than with the herd and wagons. On the first day after finding Conchita's horse we put sixteen miles behind us, but we made dry camp that night.

Morning came and we were moving out before dawn, with Zeno and myself off in the lead. The women and youngsters on the horses came in between, and Tim Foley brought up the rear with Milo Dodge.

The desert shimmered with heat waves, and on the open plain weird dust-devils danced. A chaparral cock appeared from out of nowhere and ran along beside us. Everywhere we passed what had been pools from the rain, now dried up, the earth cracked and turning to dust. Our canteens were nearly empty, and there was no food left but the strips of dried, smoked beef.

The soil was hard and gravelly; there were frequent limestone outcroppings, and low hills. Westward was the beckoning finger of Guadalupe Mountain. Toward dusk we made camp in a little valley where the grazing was good. There were a few trees here, and three springs, one of them smelling strongly of sulphur and a soda spring, but the third was pure, cold water.

Foley helped his wife from the saddle, and for a moment they stood together, her arms clinging to his. Her naturally florid features were burned even redder by the sun and wind, but she was pale beneath the color, and he led her carefully to a place under a tree, where she sat down.

The children scattered to gather wood and cow chips for a fire, and Zeno led the horses into the shelter of the trees.

Tim Foley walked over to where I stood talking to Zeno Yearly. "My old woman's about had it, Dan. She's done up. If she don't get some food and proper rest soon, we won't have her with us long."

"You're looking kind of long in the tooth yourself, Tim," I said, "but you're right. Seems like we'd better get some meat before we pull out of here."

"This is Apache country," Milo Dodge said, "so keep an eye out."

It was finally settled that I would go alone, and the other three would remain behind to keep a sharp lookout. Foley's boy was provided with a rifle, for he was fourteen and coming on to manhood, and they settled down to guard the women folks and the horses.

Wearing my two pistols, with the Patterson fully loaded, I walked out. Twice I saw rattlers, but I left them alone.

The evening was still. The desert was gathering shadows in the low places, and the distant mountains were taking on the soft mauve and purple of evening. Somewhere out on the desert a quail called . . . and after a minute, there was an answer. These were the blue quail, which rarely fly, but run swiftly along the ground. They were small, scarcely larger than a pigeon.

Twice I paused, and with piggin strings, the short strips of rawhide carried by a cowhand for tying the legs of a calf, I rigged several snares where I had seen rabbit tracks.

But I found no game. Toward dusk I did get a shot at a quail, and killed it. Returning home, I had only the quail to show. At daybreak I checked my traps and found I'd caught a large jackass rabbit. What meat there was on him was divided among the women and children.

So we started on at the break of dawn. The Guadalupe Peak loomed higher than ever, and the long range that stretched out to the north from behind it seemed dark and ominous. Tim Foley, who was the oldest of us all, fell down twice that day. Each time he got up slowly, carefully, and came on.

We camped that night after making only a few miles, in a small grove of live oak and pines, with the mountain looming over us.

Tim Foley dropped to the ground, exhausted,

and it was Milo and Zeno who stripped the saddles from the horses and helped the women down. Taking my Patterson, I walked out at once.

To tell you the truth, I was scared. We men had gone a whole day without food, and during the past four or five days had been on mighty short rations. Tim was older than we were, and had lived a life in the saddle, but it was still a good long trek to the Copper Mines for all of us.

Nobody had much to keep them going, and if I did not scare up food of some kind we were not going much further.

Several times I saw deer droppings, but all were old, and I saw no deer, nor any recent tracks. Because this was Apache country, I did not wish to shoot unless I was sure of a kill.

It was very still. Sweat trickled down my chest under my shirt. The sky overhead was very blue, and the clouds had gone. For some reason my nerves were suddenly on edge, yet I had heard nothing, seen nothing. Carefully, I edged forward.

Far overhead a lone buzzard circled lazily against the blue. The vague trail I followed now had carried me over a thousand feet above the tiny valley where our camp lay concealed. Drying my hands on my shirt, I started forward again. Suddenly, on the edge of a cliff some fifty yards away, I saw a bighorn sheep.

He was a big fellow, and he was watching something below him. His big horns curved around and forward, and he had the color of a deer, or close to it, and the same sort of hair. It was the first bighorn I had seen.

Carefully, leaning my shoulder against the cliff, I lifted the Patterson and took a careful sight on a point just back of his neck. I was trying for a spine shot, hoping to stop him where he was. Shot through the heart, he might disappear into the rocks and be lost. Deer will often run half a mile after a heart shot and the bighorn might do even more, and this was a rugged country.

But even as I laid the sights on the point where I wished the bullet to strike, the poise and attention of the sheep worried me. Lowering the rifle, I eased forward a step further, and looked down into the rugged country below.

The first thing I saw was a cow . . . it was a white-faced longhorn cow, and then behind it came another and another, and they were our cows. And then a man stepped from the brush. It was Jim Poor!

Holding still, I watched them slowly come from a draw onto the open mountainside, at least thirty head of cattle, some cows, some young stuff, and a few old steers, and behind them walked two men, and a woman who rode their one horse.

Catching myself just as I started to call out, I looked again at the bighorn. He had drawn back and turned away from me, and he was ready to get out of there, and fast. Lifting the Patterson, I caught my sight again, and squeezed off the shot.

The bighorn leaped straight up and landed with his legs spread out. He started to go forward and I steadied the rifle for another shot. Just as I was about to fire, his knees buckled and he fell forward on one shoulder and lay still.

Glancing into the basin below, I saw no one. Only the cattle, standing now with their heads up, staring, nostrils distended. Grinning, I lowered my rifle and, knowing how a voice can carry in that still air, I called out.

"You boys scared of something? A body'd think you all stepped on a hot rock!"

"Dan? Dan Killoe?" That was Zeb's voice.

"If it ain't," I yelled back, "then Pa fed me for a long time for nothing!"

They came out in the open then, and I saw that the woman on the horse was Rose Sandy, and the men were Zeb Lambert, Jim Poor, and Miguel. And then another came from the brush, and it was Tom Sandy!

I let out a whoop and started to go down the mountain, then remembered that sheep.

"Jim! Come on up here! I've killed me a bighorn!"

He clambered up the slope. "You're a better butcher than I am, Jim, so skin him out and I'll talk to those boys and then come on up and help you pack it in."

The horse on which Rose was riding was the one Zebony had taken from that Indian he rode off behind. He had been well outside the circle of the fighting before his battle with the Comanche ended, and by the time he started back the rain was pouring down and the fighting was about over.

The country was covered with Comanches and Comancheros, so he had found a place where a notch cut into the river bank and concealed himself there with the horse. He had put in a wet and miserable night, but at daybreak he saw some cattle to the south and started around to gather them, and then he met Rose and Tom Sandy.

Miguel was with them, and in bad shape. He had been captured by the Indians, had killed his captors and escaped, but had been wounded again. These, though, were merely flesh wounds, and he had recovered quickly in the succeeding days.

Banding together, they had rounded up what strays they could find and started off to the northwest, heading toward a limestone sink Miguel knew of. There they had found water and some friendly Lipans, who traded some corn and seeds they had gathered for a steer.

Twenty miles west they had come upon Jim Poor. He was standing beside a horse with a broken leg . . . he had ducked to the shelter of the river bank, but caught a horse whose owner had been shot, and when the shooting died down, believing everyone in the camp was dead, he had started west alone.

Nine days later we reached El Paso, a small town of one-story adobe houses, most of it lying on the Mexican side of the river. On the north side of the river there were several groups of settlements, the largest being Coon's Rancho and Magoffinsville, the two being about a mile and a half apart. There was a third settlement, about a mile from Magoffinsville, around another ranch.

Zebony came to me after we had found shelter and had our small herd, once more led by Old Brindle, gathered in a pasture near the town.

"Dan, what are we going to do?"

"What we started to do," I said. "At least, I am. I'm going on, and I'm going to find us an outfit, and I'm going to use what cattle we have to start a ranch."

"And then?"

"Why, then I'm going hunting. I'm going hunting for a man with a spider scar, a man named Felipe Soto."

Pausing for a second, I considered the situation. Around me I had a lot of good folks, and they had come west trusting to work for my father and myself, and it was up to me to see they made out. Yet there was scarcely more than fifty dollars among the lot of us, and cattle that we dearly needed. And to go on, we must have horses, gear, and supplies of all kinds.

Ahead of us lay miles of Apache country, and where we would settle would probably be Apache country too. Being a slow man to anger, the rage against Soto and his Comancheros had been building up in me, and I feared it.

There was in me a quality I had never trusted. A quiet sort of man, and scarcely twenty-three, I liked to work hard and enjoyed the pleasure of company, yet deep within me there was a kind of fury that scared me. Often I'd had to fight it down, and I did not want the name of being a dangerous man—that is for very young boys to want, or older men who have never grown up. Yet it was in me, though few of those about me knew it.

Pa knew—he had been with me that time in San Antonio; and Zebony knew, for he had been with me in Laredo.

And now I could feel it mounting. Pa was dead, cut down in the prime of life, and there were the others, good men all. They were men who rode for the brand, who gave their lives because of their loyalty and sense of rightness.

Within me I could feel the dull fury growing, something I had felt before. It would mount and mount until I no longer thought clearly, but thought only of what must be done. When those furies were on me there was no fear in me, nor was there reason, or anything but the driving urge to seek out my enemies.

My senses became super-sharp, my heart seemed to slow its beat, my breath seemed slower, I walked with careful step and looked with different eyes. At such times I would become utterly ruthless, completely relentless. And I did not like it.

It was the main reason that I rarely wore a handgun. Several times the only thing that had saved me was the fact that I carried no gun and could not do what I wished. Twice in my life I had felt these terrible furies come over me, and each time it left me shaken, and swearing it must not happen again.

Now there were other things to consider. We must find horses, a wagon, and the necessary supplies for the rest of our trip. Our herd was pitifully small, but it could grow. We had two young bulls and about twenty head of cows, mostly young stuff. The rest were steers, and a source of immediate profit, even if their present value might be small.

Some of the people at Magoffinsville preferred to call their town Franklin. Others were already calling the town on the American side El Paso del Norte, but most still referred to the three towns by their separate names. At Magoffinsville I tied the line-back dun at the rail in front of James Wiley Magoffin's place and went in. Zebony Lambert and Zeno Yearling were with me.

Magoffin was a Kentuckian who had come to the area thirteen or fourteen years earlier and had built a home. Then he erected stores and warehouses around a square and went into business.

When I walked through that door, I knew there was little that was respectable in my appearance. My razor had been among the things lost in the attack, and I had not shaved in days. My hat was a beat-up black, flat-crowned, flat-brimmed item with a bullet hole through the crown. I wore a worn, fringed buckskin shirt and shotgun chaps, also fringed. My boots were Spanish style, but worn and down at heel. The two men with me looked little better.

"Mr. Magoffin," I said, "the Comancheros took my herd. We're the Kaybar brand, moving west from the Cowhouse to new range northwest of here, and we're broke. We came into town with only our women and children riding, and the rest of us afoot."

He looked at me thoughtfully. "What do you want?"

"A dozen horses, one wagon, supplies for seventeen people for two weeks."

His eyes were steady on me, then he glanced at Zebony and Zeno Yearly.

"Women, you say?"

"Yes, sir. The wives of two of my men, the widow of one, and there's five children, and a single girl. She's from New Mexico."

"Mind if I ask her name?"

"Conchita McCrae."

He glanced over my shoulder toward the door, and I felt the hackles rise slowly on the back of my neck. Turning slowly, I saw Felipe Soto standing there, three of his men behind him.

My fist balled and I swung.

He had expected anything but that. Words . . . perhaps followed by gunplay, but the Texan or New Mexican rarely resorted to his fists. It was not, in those days, considered a gentleman's way of settling disputes, while a gun was.

My blow caught him flush on the jaw. Being six feet two inches tall, I was only a little shorter than he was, but half my life I'd been working swinging an axe, or wrestling steers or broncs, and I was work-hardened and tough. He did not stagger, he simply dropped.

Before the others could move, Zebony covered them with a pistol and backed them up.

Reaching down, I grabbed Soto by the shirt front and lifted him bodily to his feet, slamming him back against the counter. He struck at me, and I slipped inside of the blow and smashed a wicked blow to his belly and then swung to his chin.

He fought back, wildly, desperately, and he was a huge man and strong, but there was no give in me that day, only a cold burning fury that made me ignore his blows. He knocked me down . . . twice, I think. Getting up, I spread my legs wide and began to swing, and I was catching him often. I drove him back, knocked him through the doors into the street, and went after him. He got up and I smashed a wild swing to his face, then stabbed a wicked left to the mouth and swung on his chin with both fists.

He was hitting me, but I felt none of it. All I wanted was to hit him again. A blow smashed his nose, another split a lip through to the teeth. Blood was pouring from a cut eye, but I could not stop. Backing him against the hitch-rail I swung on his face, chopping it to a bloody mess.

And no one stopped me. Zeno had a six-shooter out now, too, and they kept them off.

Soto went down and tried to stay down, but I would not let him. I propped him up and hammered on him with both fists until his face was just raw meat. He fell down, and grabbed at the muddy earth as if to cling to it with all his might.

He was thoroughly beaten, and Magoffin stepped forward and caught my arm. "Enough!" he said. "You'll kill the man!"

My hands were swollen and bloody. Staggering, I stepped back, shaking Magoffin's hand from my shoulder.

Soto lay in the mud, his huge body shaking with retching sobs.

"Tell him," I said to the Soto men, "that if I see him again—anywhere at all—I'll kill him.

"And tell him, too," I added, "that I want my herd, three thousand head of cattle, most of it breeding stock, delivered to me at Bosque Redondo within thirty days.

"That will include sixty head of saddle stock, also driven off. They will be delivered to me or I shall hunt him down and beat him to death!"

With that, I turned and staggered against the door post, then walked back into the store. Magoffin, after a glance at Soto, followed me inside. Zebony and Zeno stood watching the Soto men pick up their battered leader and half drag, half carry him away.

"That was Felipe Soto?" Magoffin asked me curiously. "I have heard of him."

"That was him," I replied. My breath was still coming in gasps and my heart was pounding. "I should have killed him."

"What you did was worse. You destroyed him." He hesitated. "Now tell me again. What was it you needed?"

"You must remember," I said, "I have only fifty dollars in money."

"Keep it—your credit is good with me. You have something else—you have what is needed to make good in this country."

Conchita turned pale when she saw me, and well she might, for in the excitement of the fight I had scarcely felt the blows I received, and they had been a good many. One eye was swollen almost shut, and there was a deep cut on the other cheek-bone. My lip was puffed up, one ear was swollen, and my hands had swollen to twice their normal size from the fearful pounding I had given him.

"Oh, your poor face!" she gasped. Then at once she was all efficiency. "You come here. I'll fix that, and your hands too!"

She poured hot water into a basin with some salts, and while she bathed my face ever so gently, my swollen hands soaked in the hot water.

It seemed strange, having a woman fuss over me that way, and it was the first time it had happened since one time as a youngster when Tap's mother had taken care of me after I'd been bucked from a bad horse.

That started me thinking of Tap, and wondering what had become of him, and of Karen.

The Foleys never talked of her around the camp, and what they said among themselves I had no idea. She had taken on more than she was equipped to handle when she followed after Tap, and it worried me.

Everybody was feeling better around camp because Zebony and Zeno had told them about the deal I had made with Magoffin. Not that it was so unusual in those times, for a man's word was his bond, and no amount of signatures on paper would mean a thing if his word was not good. Thousands of head of cattle were bought or sold on a man's word, often with no count made when the money was paid over. Because of that, a man would stand for no nonsense where his word was concerned. A man might be a thief, a card cheat, and a murderer, and still live in the West; but if his word was no good or he was a coward, he could neither live there or do business with anyone there.

"You reckon that Soto will return your cattle?" Tim Foley asked skeptically.

"If he doesn't, I'll go get them. I have told him where he stands, and I shall not fail to carry out my promise."

"What if he takes to that canyon?"

"Then I shall follow him there."

We had a camp outside of Magoffinsville. It was a pretty place, with arching trees over the camp and a stream running near, and the Rio Grande not far off. It was a beautiful valley with mountains to the north and west, and there seemed to be grapes growing everywhere, the first I'd ever seen cultivated.

We sat around the fire until late, singing the old songs and talking, spinning yarns we had heard, and planning for the future. And Conchita sat close beside me, and I began to feel as I never had before. It was a different feeling because for the first time I knew I wanted a girl . . . wanted her for always, and I had no words to speak what I thought.

Soon we would be on the trail again, moving north and west into the new lands. Somewhere up there was Tap Henry, and I would be seeing him again . . . what would be our relationship, now that Pa was dead?

Tap had respected Pa . . . I did not think he had such respect for me. He was too accustomed to thinking of me as a youngster, yet whatever we planned, Tap could have a share in it if he would do his part to make our plans work out.

I got up and walked out to where the horses were, and stood there alone in the night, looking at the stars and thinking.

Magoffin would supply us with what we needed, but the debt was mine to pay. We had few cattle to start with, and such a small herd would make a living for nobody. Whatever happened, I had to have the herd they had stolen, or the same number of cattle from elsewhere.

If Felipe Soto did not bring the cattle to me, I was going after them, even to Palo Duro Canyon itself.

Conchita came up to where I stood. "Are you worried, Dan?"

"They came with me," I gestured back toward the people at the fire; "they trusted my father and me. I must not fail them."

"You won't."

"It will be hard."

"I know it will, Dan, but if you will let me, I want to help."

CHAPTER SIX

We came up the valley of the Mimbres River in the summer of fifty-eight, a handful of men with a handful of cattle and one wagon loaded down with supplies.

We put Cooke's Spring behind us and trailed up the Mimbres with the Black Range to the east, and on the west the wilderness of the Mogollons. We rode with our rifles across our saddle-bows, riding through the heart of Apache country, and we came at last to our Promised Land.

The Plains of St. Augustine, a vast inland sea of grass, surrounded by mountains, made the finest range we had ever seen, with nothing in sight but a few scattered herds of antelope or wild horses.

Our camp was made in the lee of a cliff close by a spring, with a bat cave in the rocks above us. We turned our cattle upon the long grass, and set to work to build a pole corral to hold our saddle stock.

Cutting poles in the mountains, we came upon both bear sign and deer sign. Zeno Yearly stopped in his cutting of poles. "It is a fair land, Dan, but

135

I've heard tell this is an Indian trail, so we'd best get set for trouble."

"We're building a fort when we have the corral, but first we must protect our saddle stock."

The fort was not so much to look at, not at first. We made a V of our wagons, pointing it toward the open valley, and we made a pile of the poles for the corral along one side, and threw up a mound of earth on the other side, with the cliff behind us. Though it was not much of a fort, it was a position that could be defended.

Three days later we had our Texas house built, with the Foleys occupying one side and the Stark family the other. We had also put up most of a bunkhouse, and had our cattle fattening on the long grass. We had scouted the country around, killed a couple of deer and a mountain lion we caught stalking a heifer from our herd.

We were settling in, making a home of the place, but it was time I made a move.

News was beginning to filter through to us. There was trouble down in the Mimbres Valley—a shooting or two, and the name we heard was that of Tolan Banks, the man Tap Henry had mentioned.

And then one day they came riding up the valley, Banks and Tap, and a third man with them. It was the blond man who had ridden with Caldwell.

Tap was riding a grudge, I could see that. He rode up and looked around. "What the hell is the idea? I thought you were going to settle down in the Mimbres with us?"

"Before we talk about anything else," I said, "you tell that man"—I indicated the blond man—"to start riding out of here. If he comes around again, I'll kill him."

"He's a friend of mine," Tap replied. "Forget him."

"Like hell I will. He was one of those who ran off our cattle. He was in the attack on us when Pa was killed."

Tap's face tightened. "I heard about that. I couldn't believe it."

Zebony was standing by the corral, and Milo Dodge was in the door of the Texas with Jim Poor.

"You tell that man to leave, Tap."

His face stiffened. "By God, kid, you don't tell me what to do. I'll—"

My eyes held them all, but mostly the blond man. "You," I said, "start riding. And keep riding. When I see you again, I start shooting."

The man touched his tongue to his lips. "You think you—"

I shot him out of his saddle.

A moment there had been silence, and then I was holding a gun with a slow twist of smoke rising from the muzzle, and the blond man was on the ground.

Whatever Tolan Banks might have done he did not do, for Zebony was holding a rifle in his hands, and so was Milo.

"Tap," I said, "you pick that man up and ride out of here. You're welcome any time, but when you come, don't come with a murdering renegade like him."

My bullet had gone a little high, and the man was shot through the shoulder, but from the look of it, he was badly hurt.

Tap Henry sat very still on his horse, and there was a strange look in his eyes. It was as if he was seeing me for the first time.

"I'll come back, Dan. I'll come back looking for you. Nobody talks to me like this."

"You're my brother, Tap, by raising if not by blood. I want no trouble with you, but when you start traipsing around with men who have attacked us, it is time to ask where your loyalty lies."

"You'll be seeing me too," Banks said.

My eyes swung to him. "I was wondering when you were going to put your ante into this game," I said, "and I'm ready any time you are."

He sat his horse, smiling at me. "Not now . . . not right now. You've too many guns against me."

"Ride out of here then."

Banks turned his horse and Tap got down to help the wounded man into the saddle. Jim Poor came down to help him.

"You come back when you want, Tap. But come alone or with Karen, and come friendly."

"Where is Karen?" Tim Foley demanded.

"She's in Socorro," Tap said sullenly. "She's all right."

Foley held a shotgun. "Are you two married?"

Tap glanced at him bleakly. "You're damned right," he said. "What do you think I am?"

"Take care of her," Foley said. "I'm no gunfighter, but this shotgun doesn't care who it shoots."

Tap rode away, leading the renegade, who was swearing in a high, plaintive voice.

There I stood, in the sun of a bright day, watching them ride off down the valley. There went Tap, who had been my hero as a youngster, and there went the last of whatever family I had, and I watched him go and was lonely.

Ours was a hard land, and it took hard men to

ride it and live it, and the rules had to be laid down so all could read, and the lines drawn.

Tap Henry was different. It seemed to me Tap was rootless, and being rootless he had never quite decided where he stood, on the side of the angels or against them. Well, today should force him to a decision. He knew where I stood.

If that blond man had been trying to sneak a gun on me, I was not sure . . . nor did I much care. He had been there when my father was killed, and was as guilty as if he himself had fired the shot—and he might have.

One thing I had learned. It saves a lot of argument and trouble, and perhaps mistakes leading to greater violence, if folks know exactly where you stand. We came to a raw and lonely land, a land without law, without courts, and with no help in time of danger. There were men who wished the land to remain lawless, for there were always those who were unable to abide by the rules of society; and there were others who wanted schools, churches, and market days, who wanted homes, warm and friendly. Now I had taken my stand . . . I had drawn a line that no man could mistake.

After they had gone, nobody had any comment to make. The work picked up where it had ceased, and went on as it always must; for birth, death, and the day-to-day matters of living never cease. There are meals to be prepared, cattle to be cared for, meat to be butchered, fences to be built, wood to be cut. For while man cannot live by bread alone, he must have the bread before other things can become real. Civilization is born of leisure, and leisure can come only after the crop has been harvested.

In our hearts we knew that, for lonely men are considering men, given to thought to fill the empty hours of the lives they live.

Yet now the time had come to ride eastward, to be sure that we recovered our herd. I doubted if it had yet been sold, and while my warning to Soto might cause him to deliver the herd, I doubted that it would. Even if he wanted it so—which I doubted —there were others involved.

"Tim," I said, "I'm riding after the herd. I'm leaving you in charge. Jim Poor and Tom Sandy will stay with you—and Miguel."

"I go with you, Dan." Miguel looked up from the *riata* he had been mending. "It is better so. Soto, he has many friends, and we are a people who protect our own. If you go among them, a stranger, all will be against you, even if they lift no hand.

"If I go with you to tell what Soto has done, and that you are good people, your enemies will be only the Comancheros." He smiled. "And I think they are enough for trouble."

There was no arguing with him, for I knew what he said to be the truth. The Spanish-Americans of Texas and New Mexico were clannish, as they had a right to be, and I would be a stranger among them, and a *gringo*. They would know nothing of the facts of my case—whether I was a true man or false. In such a case they would either ignore me or actively work against me.

And then Conchita declared herself. She, too, was coming. She had much to do. She must go to Socorro. There were things to buy . . . In the end, she won the argument, and she came with us.

Zebony, Zeno Yearly, Milo Dodge, Miguel, and

myself made up the group. It was a small enough party for what we had to do.

Socorro was a sleepy village on the Rio Grande, built on the site of a pueblo. A mission had been established there as early as 1628, but during the Pueblo revolt the people had fled south and established a village of the same name on the Rio Grande, returning in 1817 to reestablish the village. All this Conchita told me as we rode toward the village from the west.

Though we were a small number, we were veterans at the sort of trouble that lay before us. Growing up on the frontier in Texas is never easy, and Zebony had killed his first Kiowa when he was thirteen. He had spent a week dodging Comanches even before that, and had seen his family killed.

Zeno Yearly had come west from Kentucky and Tennessee, where he had lived at various places along the Natchez Trace and in the mountains. Most of his life he had lived by hunting. Milo Dodge had been a Texas Ranger with Walker, and had served as a boy in the army during the War with Mexico.

We rode into Socorro, a tight, tough little band. And there we would buy supplies and start east, for we had far to go to reach the land of the Comanchero.

It was cool in the little *cantina* where we went to drink and to listen. Conchita was in the store, and her brother had disappeared somewhere among the flat-roofed adobe houses.

We four went into the *cantina* and ordered the wine of the country, for they were raising grapes and making wine at Socorro, as at El Paso and elsewhere. There were old apple trees here, too, planted long ago by the friars, or so it was said.

Zebony put his hat on the table and combed out his long brown hair, hair fine as a woman's and as beautiful. Yearly watched him, touching his long mustache from time to time.

There was a stillness within us, a waiting. Each knew what lay beyond this place. For out there was a wild and lonely land where the Apaches roamed, and beyond that, where we were going, the Comanche—great horsemen and great fighters, and we were few, going into a harsh land where many enemies awaited us. But this was what we had to do, and not one of us would draw back.

The wine was good, and after a while the owner brought us each a huge bowl of *frijoles*, a stack of *tortillas*, and some eggs scrambled with peppers and onions.

Miguel came in, standing inside the door until his eyes became accustomed to the dimmer light, and then he crossed to our table and sat down. Leaning toward us, his eyes very bright, he said, "It is well that we came here, for my friends tell me something very interesting."

We looked at him, and waited. Miguel took out his *cigarito* and put it between his lips.

"Soto is not at Palo Duro . . . he is on the Tularosa."

"That's east of here, ain't it?" Zeno asked.

"It is a place—a very small place which I think will get no larger because of the Apache—a place called Las Placitas. It is near Fort Stanton, where there are soldiers."

He lighted his *cigarito*. "It is tell to me that Soto brings his cattle there to sell to the soldiers."

"I didn't know there was a fort over there," Dodge said. "Stanton, you say? There was a Captain Stanton killed there a few years back."

"*Si*, it is name for him. The fort was built . . . 1855, I think. So these people come to the Rio Bonito and they begin a settlement, but I think the Apache will run them out."

"Soto is there?"

"*Si* . . . with many men. And a large herd of cattle and some horses."

"Why, then," I said, looking around the table, "that is where we will go."

We walked out on the boardwalk and stood there together, four men looking up and down the street, and knowing that trouble might come to us at any time.

And then I saw Karen.

Or rather, Milo Dodge saw her. "Dan . . . look."

She was coming toward us, and I thought she looked older, older by years, and she looked thinner, too. As always, she was neat, and when she saw us she almost stopped; then, chin up, she came on.

"Karen . . . Mrs. Henry," I said, "it is good to see you again."

"How do you do?" We might have been strangers. She spoke and started to pass on. "Your folks are still with us. Tap knows where we are, and they would like to see you."

She had gone past us a step when she stopped and turned slowly around. "I do not think you like my husband," she said.

"Whenever you folks feel like coming home," I said, "there's a place for you. Pa left no will, and though he sent Tap away, that makes no difference.

If Tap wants to come back, it will be share and share alike."

"Thank you."

She started away, then stopped again. Maybe it was something in our manner, maybe it was just the way we were armed, for each one of us was carrying a rifle, and each had two or more pistols.

"Where . . . what are you doing?"

"We're going after our cattle, Karen," I said. "Felipe Soto has them over at Las Placitas."

"But . . . there's so many of them! You won't have a chance! Why, there must be twenty men with him—or even twice that many."

"Yes, ma'am, we know that, but they're our cattle."

That was how we felt about it. They were our cattle, so we must go after them, and thieves must not be permitted to escape the consequences of their deeds. We had a land to build; we had peace to bring to the land, and for a few years now we would have to bring it with a gun. To the violent, violence is the only argument they understand. Justice they understand, but only when it is administered from strength.

Before the sun was over the eastern mountains we were miles upon our way. We crossed some desert, we crossed the lava flows, and we came up through the live oak and the pines to the mountains and the Rio Bonito. We followed it along toward the cluster of adobes and shacks along the stream.

There were scarcely half a dozen, and a few tents, a few tipis. We spread out as we came into the town, and beyond the town we could see the herd. There were some men on horseback where the cattle were, and some of them wore plumed helmets and blue uniforms. That would be the cavalry.

We rode our horses down there, and we saw men come into the street behind us and look after us. A couple of them started to follow.

"One thing," I said, "this here's my fight. If anybody comes in that ain't asked, you boys do what you've a mind to . . . but I will do the talking and if it is man to man, I'll do the shooting."

They understood that, but I wanted it on the line so they could read the brand of my action.

Felipe Soto was there, and when I saw who was with him I felt something turn cold inside of me. Tolan Banks was there, and Tap Henry.

There were eight or nine of them, and four or five Army men inspecting that beef.

Walking my horse up to them, I saw Banks speak suddenly, and Soto turned sharply around.

I did not take my eyes from Banks and Soto. "Captain," I said, "these are stolen cattle, stolen from me. The brands have been altered, but skin any beef here and you will find a K Bar brand before it was changed."

"I am buying beef," the Captain replied coolly, "not fighting over it, or sitting as a court in judgment of ownership." He turned his horse. "When you have decided whose beef it is, I shall be in Las Placitas."

He turned his horse and, followed by his brother officers and a couple of sergeants, he started away.

My eyes sought them out, man by man. On each man I directed my attention, and on each I let my eyes rest for a minute. I wanted each man to believe that he was marked.

"Well, Soto, you did not deliver the beef. I have come for it."

"Dan—!" It was Tap. "Dan, for God's sake!"

"Tap," I said, "you'd better decide where you stand before the shooting starts. Riding the fence can give a man a mighty sore crotch, and you've been on it long enough."

"Now, wait!"

"To hell with that, Henry!" Tolan Banks yelled suddenly. "You're with us or against us! Stand aside and let me kill that Killoe whelp!"

What I did, they did not expect. For years Tap and me had practiced shooting on the run, shooting while riding at a dead run, like the mountain men did, and I slapped spurs to that line-back dun and he jumped right into the middle of them.

They outnumbered us, so as I jumped into them I jumped shooting.

It looked like a damned fool trick, but it was not. They had been sitting there as we came up and no doubt everyone of them had picked a target. They had us cold and we had them the same way, and in about a split second a lot of men were going to die.

Starting off with a cold hand that way, a man can shoot accurately, and I would be losing men. So I jumped my horse into their group, which forced them all to move, and each had to swing to get on his target again.

My Patterson was across my saddle, and as I jumped I shot. My bullet missed Soto and knocked a man behind him sidewise in the saddle, and then I was in among them. One more shot left the Patterson before it was knocked from my grip, but I had already come out with a draw with my left hand from my belt.

Soto swung on me and his gun blasted almost in my face. Knocking his gun up, I shot and saw him jump back in the saddle like he'd been struck with a whip. He shot at me again but I had gone past him and he turned fast, but his big horse was no match for that dun, who could turn on a quarter and give you twenty cents change. The dun wheeled and we both shot and my bullet hit him right below the nose.

He swung around and fell back out of the saddle, kicking his foot loose from the stirrup at the last minute. He started up, gun in hand, blood flowing from his face in a stream. But I went in on a dead run, holding my six-shooter low and blasting it into him. I saw the dust jump from his shirt twice as I went into him, and then he went down under the dun's hoofs and I wheeled around in time to see Tap Henry facing Tolan Banks.

"I'm with them, Tolan! That's my brother!"

"To hell with you!" Banks' pistol swung down in a dead aim on Tap's chest and Tap triggered his gun charging, as I had.

Banks left his saddle and hit the ground and rolled over, all flattened out. He made one heave as if he was trying to get up, and then he lay still.

The gray dust lifted and slowly swirled and settled, and the riderless horses trotted off and stood with their stirrups dangling and their heads up, and men lay on the ground.

Yearly was down, and Zeb was gripping a bloody arm, his face gray.

Four of them were down, and I knew my jump

into them had given us the break we needed, for my boys had been sitting still taking dead aim.

The Army came riding up. One of the men rode right to Zebony. "Here! Let me see that arm! I'm a surgeon!"

We rode around, looking at the men on the ground. Felipe Soto was dead, and of the others only one man was alive.

Among the dead was Ira Tilton. I had never even seen him in the brief encounter, nor did I know whose bullet had put him down, but he had died an ugly death.

By the look of it the slug had been one of large caliber and it must have hit the pommel of the saddle or something, because the wound looked like a ricochet. It had ripped across the belly, and he had died hard, a death I would wish for no man.

I turned to the officer as he rode up. "Captain, that man was Felipe Soto." I indicated the sprawled body of the big Comanchero. "He has been selling rifles to the Indians for years. His own people will tell you of it."

"I am buying cattle," the Captain replied, "and personal feuds are not a part of my business. However, I do know of Soto, but did not realize that was who it was."

He glanced at me. "My name is Hyde. It is a pleasure to know you, sir. That was a nice bit of action."

Zebony picked up my Patterson from the ground and handed it to me. "You'd better see the Doc. You're bleeding."

"I'm all right. I just—" Glancing down, I saw there was blood on the skirt of my saddle, and my left leg was sopping with it.

"You!" the surgeon said. "Get down here!"

It was Tap who caught me when I started to get down and almost fell. He steadied me with an arm to a place under a tree, and he pulled my shirt off.

A bullet had gone through my side right above my hipbone, but the doctor merely glanced at it. "You've lost a lot of blood, but it's only a flesh wound."

Hearing a pound of hoofs, I looked around in time to see Conchita throw herself from her horse and come to me. The doctor looked at her, then at me. "If she can't make you well," he said dryly, "nothing can."

Zeno was going to be all right. He had caught two slugs, and he was in bad shape, but he was going to pull through. Tap Henry told me that some time later, for about the time that Conchita arrived everything faded out. I had started to speak, and then everything blurred. The next thing I knew it was hours later and I was in bed at the Fort.

"Are the cattle all right?"

"Sold 'em," Tap said, "all but a couple of hundred head of breeding stock."

"Looks like I'll be here for a while," I said, "so you'd better take the boys and start for home with that herd."

"Dan." Tap hesitated, as embarrassed as I'd ever seen him. "I've been a fool. I'm . . . well, I never intended for the herd to go to Bosque Redondo. Banks and me wanted to use it to grab land on the Mimbres."

"I guessed it was something like that."

He looked at me for several minutes. "Dan, I'm going to let Karen ride back with the boys. I'll wait here until you can ride, and we'll go home together."

"Sure," I said, "that's the way Pa always wanted it."

ABOUT THE AUTHOR

LOUIS L'AMOUR, born Louis Dearborn L'Amour, is of French-Irish descent. Although Mr. L'Amour claims his writing began as a "spur-of-the-moment thing," prompted by friends who relished his verbal tales of the West, he comes by his talent honestly. A frontiersman by heritage (his grandfather was scalped by the Sioux), and a universal man by experience, Louis L'Amour lives the life of his fictional heroes. Since leaving his native Jamestown, North Dakota, at the age of fifteen, he's been a longshoreman, lumberjack, elephant handler, hay shocker, flume builder, fruit picker, and an officer on tank destroyers during World War II. And he's written four hundred short stories and over fifty books (including a volume of poetry).

Mr. L'Amour has lectured widely, traveled the West thoroughly, studied archaeology, compiled biographies of over one thousand Western gunfighters, and read prodigiously (his library holds more than two thousand volumes). And he's watched thirty-one of his westerns as movies. He's circled the world on a freighter, mined in the West, sailed a dhow on the Red Sea, been shipwrecked in the West Indies, stranded in the Mojave Desert. He's won fifty-one of fifty-nine fights as a professional boxer and pinch-hit for Dorothy Kilgallen when she was on vacation from her column. Since 1816, thirty-three members of his family have been writers. And, he says, "I could sit in the middle of Sunset Boulevard and write with my typewriter on my knees; temperamental I am not."

Mr. L'Amour is re-creating an 1865 Western town, christened Shalako, where the borders of Utah, Arizona, New Mexico, and Colorado meet. Historically authentic from whistle to well, it will be a live, operating town, as well as a movie location and tourist attraction.

Mr. L'Amour now lives in Los Angeles with his wife Kathy, who helps with the enormous amount of research he does for his books. Soon, Mr. L'Amour hopes, the children (Beau and Angelique) will be helping too.

BANTAM'S #1
ALL-TIME BESTSELLING AUTHOR
AMERICA'S FAVORITE WESTERN WRITER

☐	12879	THE KEY-LOCK MAN	$1.75
☐	12925	RADIGAN	$1.75
☐	12631	WAR PARTY	$1.75
☐	12986	KIOWA TRAIL	$1.75
☐	12732	THE BURNING HILLS	$1.75
☐	12064	SHALAKO	$1.75
☐	12670	KILRONE	$1.75
☐	11119	THE RIDER OF LOST CREEK	$1.50
☐	12424	CALLAGHEN	$1.75
☐	12063	THE QUICK AND THE DEAD	$1.75
☐	12729	OVER ON THE DRY SIDE	$1.75
☐	13057	DOWN THE LONG HILLS	$1.75
☐	12721	TO THE FAR BLUE MOUNTAINS	$1.75
☐	10491	WESTWARD THE TIDE	$1.50
☐	12043	KID RODELO	$1.75
☐	12887	BROKEN GUN	$1.75
☐	13151	WHERE THE LONG GRASS BLOWS	$1.75
☐	12519	HOW THE WEST WAS WON	$1.75

**Buy them at your local bookstore or use this
handy coupon for ordering:**